NATURAL BLONDE

ALSO BY LIZ SMITH

The Mother Book

LIZ SMITH
NATURAL
BLONDE

a Memoir

HYPERION

New York

Original book design by Richard Oriolo

MASS MARKET ISBN 0-7868-9012-6

FIRST MASS MARKET EDITION

10 9 8 7 6 5 4 3 2 1

This book is dedicated to my heroes . . .
My late brother James,
My baby brother Bobby,
My cousin Bryson Sherrill,
My loyal and faithful Edward Beeman.
And to
The true natural blond
My godson
Spencer Graham McFadden Hoge.

ACKNOWLEDGMENTS

I OWE SLOAN SMITH AND ELIZABETH MCCALL my chief thank you, for they made me. They also made a lot of sacrifices for the wayward children they seldom understood. But they gave us mostly unconditional love—the greatest gift. I am deeply indebted to the "heroes" listed in my dedication. My brother, Bobby, has been incomparable. My brother James said, "Go for it. To hell with what people think of it." (He did add that he felt it would be "too much trouble." I only wish he had lived to see the troubling result.) I want to salute my lifelong supportive Texas friends—the late Bobbie Morris Simms, Jean Wingo Thurmond, Nancie and Hal Wingo, Nita Mae "Tootie" Boyd Brooks Lewallen, Nancy Foley Prothro, Louise Lewis Barnhart and Sidney Simms.

   I am especially grateful to Cynthia McFadden, who frequently sent me back to rewrite and put up with much complaining. She remained, as always, infuriatingly right and ethical to the max. I was lucky to have a literary agent, Joni Evans of William Morris, who is herself a better editor than most. Talk about tender loving care. Then there is my real editor, Maureen O'Brien, who talked me into doing this book over tea in the lobby of the Beverly Wilshire Hotel where she assured me it would be "fun, painless, fabulous." What a liar—what a woman! She has a fake front page in her Hyperion office that reads: "LIZ SMITH WALKS ON WATER." Who could resist such a person?

In my office are my all-important "family" of many years. They are Diane Audrey Judge, Mary Jo McDonough, Denis Ferrara and Rachel Clark. And our longtime friend Saint Clair Pugh was with us before his retirement. These people really made this book possible. Each was magnificent in adversity. I am also grateful to Barbara Kaster, Carole Duncan, and Carmen Greenlee of Brunswick, Maine, for painful research.

I was heartened all along by great pros such as Michael Korda of Simon & Schuster, Jason Epstein of Random House, Helen Gurley Brown of Hearst, Marie Brenner and Dominick Dunne of *Vanity Fair*. I was cheered on and helped by Iris Love, Joan Ganz Cooney, Pete Peterson, Judy Miller, Alex Kuczynski, Louise and Henry Grunwald, Peggy Noonan, Lee Bailey, Elaine Stritch, Jimmy Mitchell, Harry Haun, Barbara Walters, Joe Armstrong, Bob Benton, Suzanne Goodson, Harvey Schmidt, Elizabeth Taylor Peabody, Dan Sokol, Renata Adler, William Goldman, Peter Rogers, George Trescher, Arnold Scaasi, Parker Ladd, Herb Schlosser, Michael Black, Billy Norwich, Barbara Goldsmith, Tom Jones, Susan Isaacs, David Blasband, Joel Schumacher, Holland Taylor, and the former governor of Texas, Ann Richards.

I had some really good advice from John Guare and Mike Nichols and I took it. Many more contributed, cautioned and tried to keep me from error. All mistakes are my own.

CONTENTS

INTRODUCTION

Now about this book — at first I was totally bald for a number of years. Then, I grew up a brunette.

What pushed me over the edge was when I started appearing live on television and my longtime friend Vincent Roppatte of Saks Fifth Avenue convinced me some mild "streaks" would look good on camera. Every time I went to Vincent I was more of a natural blonde. I wisecracked that in TV one didn't grow older, just blonder. But when I went home to Texas, my brothers went crazy for me. They just adored my new look. I had spent my childhood trying to get their attention and approval. Now I had it because of chemicals.

So I think "natural blonde" perfectly describes my condition, and my inner and outer selves, too. None of us is exactly what we may seem. Becoming a natural blonde has also helped me not to grow old.

Now I suppose I will have to defend myself for some of what follows in this book. I could have cleaned up my illicit past even more than I have, because after all, every memoir belongs solely to the memoirist. As it is, I realize I have stretched and made myself the hero of my own life and times.

But I can't think of any other way I could bear to have written it.

America and Liz entered the twenty-first century in a schizophrenic manner. With one hand in the past, some of us still "wrote with a feather." With the other hand, we now tap the keyboard and use the mouse of technologies almost too advanced to imagine. We are afflicted at every turn with a permissive, oversexualized, materialistic culture that seems out of control. We could hope to put the brakes on a bit, but it seems more important to perhaps become semi-civilized, more cultured, better educated, benignly tolerant, fully forgiving and free in spirit.

Yet we carry around a lot of old Anglo-Saxon Puritanism and leftover Victorianism that most people want to clutch to their hearts for *other* people to live by. This ongoing hypocrisy is ingrained in us and operates even when we follow our most basic human instincts.

And after seventy-odd years, I begin to share a theory with Gore Vidal, whose mind and genius I so much admire. According to his biographer Fred Kaplan, Gore believes that Federico Fellini's famous film *La Dolce Vita*, which exploited Anglo-Saxon Puritanism, pretended that "this was decadence when it was only life as it is lived."

I hate to brag, but some years ago the Reverend Jerry Falwell named Bill Moyers and Liz Smith as the two people raised in a Southern religious background who had fallen the furthest and disappointed him the most.

Well, Reverend, I'm sorry. But it wasn't sinful decadence; it was only life as it is lived.

PROLOGUE

IS IT POSSIBLE THAT GOSSIP can be good for you? Yes. It's been very good for me. I've made an enormous amount of money and had a lot of fun from gossip. It beats being a hardworking news reporter by a country mile.

But that's not the larger question you're asking, is it? Well, surprise, surprise! Many academics have asked this same question. There have been papers written, theses explored, studies made. The findings are that gossip is cathartic. It is useful. It serves a number of purposes. Gossip relaxes you, establishes you and makes you feel better; indeed, one such scholarly paper posits that it makes you live longer. Gossip is an enormous way of exchanging information, and thereby of exchanging power. There *is* power in telling something you know or think you know.

Gail Collins of *The New York Times* writes this in her book, *Scorpion Tongues*: "Gossip empowers both the tale carrier and the recipient—gossip answers a wide range of human needs—it bonds both teller and listener together with a sense of sharing something slightly forbidden."

The Northwestern University sociology professor Gary

Fine says, "Gossip is a bit like Greek tragedy, an emotional release valve that allows us to express a whole range of human feelings—envy, anger, compassion—and to find solace in other people's woes."

People crave news. Houses in early New England were built close to the road so that passersby might give the latest: "Hey, didja hear? They shot Lincoln two months ago in Washington!" And a little gossip makes it even more so. "And I hear Mrs. Lincoln forced him to go to the theater that night!" People are now used to news that also entertains.

Walter Winchell said that all gossip is history. Oscar Wilde added my personal favorite—to wit: "But scandal is gossip made tedious by morality." Still, if gossip becomes history (and it certainly does—just consider the 1,000 days of John F. Kennedy) then gossip has its own importance as a historical reservoir.

Gossip is based on a common impulse: *Let me tell you a story*. This makes it a basis for studies of history, biography, autobiography, memoirs, *romans à clef*, novels, diaries and letters. Everything is grist for history's mill, even—or perhaps, especially—gossip.

The Phoenicians invented the alphabet on which Western language is based.* And the Greeks adapted it further. The very first evidence we have of the earliest things written in Greek are two incisions on Mt. Hymettus. They date back to the eighth century before Christ. Scholars seldom cite them because they are dirty gossip. The first says, "So and so is a cocksucker." The second reads, "So and so is a pederast." So the more things change, the more things stay the same.

Among the first gossips of history was Homer. At first Homer, or whoever he was, repeated his tales aloud, memorizing them, getting others to memorize them and thus, by repetition, turning them into literary legend. Finally, someone began writing these stories down. *The Iliad* and *The*

---

* Recent findings, however, insist that it was the Syrians of Palestine (the Canaanites) who deserve this distinction.

Odyssey became the bedrock literature of Western civilization, never equaled until Shakespeare. And what are these tales full of? Why, gossip, of course. Gossip and propaganda caused the Trojan War. Add sex, envy, jealousy, illicit romance, intrigue, plots, counterplots and ambition—the stuff of life.

Today Erica Jong says, "Gossip is the opiate of the oppressed." And it does seem that everybody wants to know—in the words of the lyricist Alan Jay Lerner—"What the king is doing tonight?" They then take delight in the king's conquests, his travails, his hangover, his embittered marriage, and his extramarital dalliance—whatever. They sometimes find out that the rich, famous and gifted are just as miserable as they are. Thus, gossip gives comfort. Joan Rivers notes, "It's nice to know, when everything is going wrong in your household, that Elizabeth Taylor has problems, too!"

In *The Moralities of Everyday Life*, psychologists John Sabini of the University of Pennsylvania and Maury Silver state: "Gossip brings ethics home by introducing abstract morality to the mundane. Gossip then may also be a means of social control in that it allows individuals to express, articulate and commit themselves to a moral position in the act of talking about somebody else. Thus, it is a way that we come to know what our own evaluations really are. It is a training ground, both for self-clarification and public moral action."

These guys Sabini and Silver really love gossip. They say it is "common…a cross-cultural universal…a curious pleasure…it highlights the idleness of talk…people gossip to advance their interest…gossip also makes people more interesting…gossip freshens the news…sharing a secret has charm…socially, one has an obligation to talk, and gossip is a pleasant, easy, universally accepted way to fulfill the obligation…gossip means taking a stance…dramatizing ourselves, our attitudes, our values, our tastes, our temptations, our inclination, our will…gossip helps one get to know people…gossip lets people get things off their chests, get their outrage supported…allows them to be the hero of a moral drama with a minimum of inconvenience...gossip is a means we have to externalize, dramatize and embody our moral perceptions...it helps us at times to establish precedents for reasonable solutions."

If you always say merely, "Hello. You're looking well. Isn't this lovely weather?"—then you are a social bore. If you say, "Let me tell you a story you're not going to believe," you'll be unforgettable. Gossip makes you interesting and boosts your self-esteem at having information to relate.

Because of the happenings of the last several decades, we have all become more cynical and less innocent. Is this bad? Isn't knowledge power? And we became that way chiefly from gossip. Do we really still want the kind of press that operated "a gentleman's agreement" with the Congress and White House and told us little white lies about the people we were to elect? Isn't it better to know the truth? Shouldn't we examine the feet of clay of our peerless leaders? Wasn't it better when Betty Ford ended speculation about her substance abuse and publicly declared it, thereby becoming a role model?

Here's a yellowed scrap of paper from a defunct publication called *L.A. Style*. The unknown author commented perspicaciously, "Gossip is good. It is that most rare of guilty pleasures—completely democratic and fully participatory. It helps us sort things out."

I have a little theory of my own. I think gossip is one of the great luxuries of a democracy. It is the tawdry jewel in the crown of free speech and free expression. You don't read gossip columns in dictatorships. Gossip is for leisure, for fun, for entertainment, for relaxation. Should the day come when we are enduring big, black headlines about war, famine, terrorism and natural disaster—then that kind of news will drive gossip underground and out of sight.

Then we won't have gossip to kick around any longer. And just like Richard Nixon said, when he reminded us that we wouldn't have him to kick around any longer, we'll all be sorry.

Captain John Smith

Didn't belong to the B'nai B'rith,

He was a full-blooded Briton,

The Same as Boadicea and Bulwer-Lytton,

But his problem and theirs were not quite the same,

Because they didn't have to go around assuring everybody that

that was their real name . . .

—OGDEN NASH

PART

ONE

a Memoir

FROZEN

JUSTICE IN

TEXAS

A T AGE FIVE OR SIX, I learned you couldn't trust the ice. Not that I'd ever seen much ice in Fort Worth, a city with an occasional blue norther, but generally warm and pleasant weather. Still, I realized that the ice above Alaska to the North Pole could open up and swallow you. I saw it happen right up there on the movie screen to the actress Lenore Ulrich.

The movie was *Frozen Justice* and it must have been late 1928 or early 1929 because I was with Dott. She was our maid and the Depression hadn't struck us yet, so she was still with us.

Dott and I were sitting in the colored balcony although she had tried in vain to get me to sit downstairs in the "white" section. Black maids with white children were allowed to exempt themselves from the segregation rules back in the late twenties. Otherwise, segregation was a rigid reality.

I still tried always to drink from the fountain labeled "colored." This wasn't my sense of justice so much as my insistence on showing off and being "different." Usually some indignant white adult would yank me away as if I were on the edge of a precipice.

Down deep in my bones, just as the flickering movie

screen influenced me, so the all-pervading black-and-white question haunted my childhood. I was totally fascinated from early childhood with what the great jazz musician Mezz Mezzrow termed "The Race," in his famous book *Really the Blues*. When I read it later, at age sixteen, I felt validated. Black people were my secret passion. I wanted to sit separated with them at the movies. I was enthralled with how they looked, their talk, their humor, their food, their music, their laughter and the terrible way most of them had to live without seeming even to notice it.

The writer James Fox has noted this throwback to the Old South where people lived closely with their servants "treating them like subordinate relatives...", living closely enough to "inherit the religious customs and diurnal superstitions of The Race...to adopt their particular humor and sense of the ridiculous."

I was, of course, only a white princess in a paternalistic racist society, but I didn't know that. Black people were extra good to little white children. They seemed, actually, to like and really care for us. After all, we had not yet grown up to be monsters and masters.

Dott would always sigh and take me up to the balcony. "Your daddy wouldn't like this," she'd say. Dott herself wasn't black. She was coffee-colored and later, when I began to see Lena Horne on the screen, I would get Lena and Dott all mixed up in my head because my own fabulous "mammy" was such a lovely slim creature, very like Lena.

There were only three places I felt at home as a child: 1919 Hemphill where I'd been born, the Travis Avenue Baptist Church where I went every Sunday and the Tivoli Theater, which was a passion. It was a little neighborhood "picture show" and I have always assumed it must have been a backward Fort Worth theater owner who wrote the movie distributor, saying, "Don't send us no more of them movies where the hero writes with a feather!"

Frozen Justice is the first movie I remember. And so I encountered my first star. Lenore Ulrich was a Broadway actress who never quite translated to the silver screen. At the time, I only knew that she was an incredible creature up there in the light, suffering torments because she was torn between the bright lights of Nome and her Eskimo heritage. Lenore Ulrich looked about as much like an Inuit half-breed as I did. But she struggled womanfully through the snow in this, her first talkie, cracking her whip over the dogsled and getting up on the bar in Nome to drink and "carry on," as they'd say in Texas. Then she'd realize what degradation there was in "civilization" (downtown Nome) and she'd crack her whip and sled back to the ice floes where Momma was chewing blubber in the igloo and her step-Papa was out trying to spear a polar bear for dinner. Half-white Lenore was never satisfied anywhere. (There was a moral in this movie somewhere; there always used to be morals in movies. Now there are usually just explosions and car and plane crashes, and digital greed is rewarded.)

In the end, rushing between Nome and the ice floes of home, Lenore fell into a crack in the ice, the ice then moved and she and her dogs were crushed to death. I felt terrible about the dogs and howled all the way home, with Dott saying, "Shh. Shh. It's only a movie!" When we came in with me blubbering, my mother, Elizabeth, wasn't one to question her own wisdom in sending a five-year-old off to see whatever was playing. She was unconcerned that I might have experienced something tragic and unsuitable for a child. She just rocked me in her lap and described meadows full of flowers and little rabbits playing until I calmed down.

Good Christian WASP women of her day didn't have psychological qualms about child rearing. They had never heard of Freud, PMS, "having it all" or being "liberated." They knew that someday God and Jesus would sort it all out for us if only we all had the faith of a grain of mustard seed. (I heard so much about the grain that I have never become a big mustard fan.) Baptist teaching had a lot of good things just like the Boy Scouts law of being trustworthy, loyal, helpful, friendly, courteous, kind, obedient, cheerful, thrifty, brave, clean and reverent. And I have tried to live by those verities to some extent, but a lot of religion just bounced off of me.

Even by late 1920s Jazz Age standards, it was lax of my mother to offer me up to the early cinematic baby-sitter just to get me out of her hair. But she wasn't much concerned with details of child rearing. She was Southern Baptist to the core, except when the core interfered with minor pleasures, which she did not consider a "sin." Movies were one of these (thank heaven!). Card playing was another, and ballroom dancing was her romantic passion. (She and Daddy were forever twirling around together, showing us just how it was done.) *Honi soit qui mal y pense* might have been her motto had she wished to defend herself. But she didn't know it meant "Evil is to him that thinks evil," even though she had gone to college in Mississippi. She had enough innate class to find some of the narrow-minded hard-shell Baptist doctrines uncouth. She deplored the foot washers and snake handlers who spoke in tongues. "They are just showing off," she'd say.

Fanaticism was not for her. She didn't like it in a fundamentalist Baptist way, just as she disapproved of the pomp and panoply in the Catholic Church. And I believe she liked to irritate her mother-in-law, a woman who was determined to make everyone's life hell on earth. My "Big Mama," Martha Tipton Smith, didn't think that men and women should even go swimming together. This was too narrow-minded for my mother.

My father, Sloan, was too busy to worry about what messages we were getting at the movies. He could be an exacting personal taskmaster, but he had a sweet bent, and heartfelt cultural aspirations. (His fondest memory of his own youth was when he had gone to New Orleans to hear Amelita Galli-Curci as Gilda in Verdi's *Rigoletto*.)

Unlike my mother, he hated organized religion and thought most preachers were phonies and hypocrites. In spite of these dichotomies, I leaned more toward being a creature of the silver screen than of the Baptist church. *Frozen Justice* marked me for life. I could never forget it. And as I began to grow up (I won't say mature, for I never did), I found myself like Lenore Ulrich in the movie. I was forever to be pulled between my Southwestern roots (that absolutely wholesome and corny upbringing) and the bright light aspects of big city life (the glam-

our and glitter of show business). I can't blame Hollywood or
Lenore or whoever wrote *Frozen Justice*. Most humans display
divergent dual characteristics and most of us are torn between
here and there, and this and that.

The Tivoli became and remained the epicenter of my
early life. My parents exerted no censorship or interest in what
we saw there. We children were simply allowed to go off every
Saturday, when the program changed. There were no X or R ratings. (The Hays Office exercised certain cautions after 1934. For
instance, couples were never shown in double beds. I thought
twin beds were absolutely quaint; personally, I had never seen
one except in the movies.)

As time went by, the Depression caused us to lose Dott,
although she remained in our lives until she died in her
nineties—a successful Fort Worth restaurant owner.

After Dott, Bobby and I were allowed to go by ourselves
to the movies. (James, five years older than me, was already living in another world.) We went to the Tivoli each clutching a
precious dime and were treated to a cartoon, a serial, a trave-
logue, coming attractions, the March of Time, a newsreel, the
feature. It went on and on and it was marvelous. We never
missed a program change and sometimes we'd stay all day
watching the whole shebang over and over again.

Our only other outing, aside from visiting relatives, was
to go to *Sundayschoolandchurch*, always spoken as one word.
And never to miss it unless we were at death's door.

So we hated Sundays, but Saturday was a very big deal.
We'd get on our bikes and coast gleefully downhill to the Tivoli.
The coming back uphill was tough, but it was a life lesson. You
get something; you give something up. Sometimes we'd have
fifteen cents, enough for the movie and a five-cent Rockefeller
hamburger. Or we'd take peanut butter and jelly in a paper bag.
I really don't recall any popcorn concessions in those early
movie houses.

My mother never asked what we were about to see. She
just trusted that those people in Hollywood wouldn't be releas-
ing anything that wasn't okay. Sometimes we'd get the erotic

John Gilbert nuzzling Garbo and a bunch of grapes...or Nick
and Nora Charles, of the *Thin Man* movies, and their dog
Asta...or Jimmy Cagney blazing away at the mob or being a
part of it...or the Marx Brothers and their mayhem (my Uncle
Willie was once removed forcibly from a theater in Dallas because he laughed so loud at Chico, Groucho, Harpo and Zeppo
that he disturbed people)...or sometimes we'd find ourselves
left with something really "cultural," like the documentaries of
Robert Flaherty, *Man of Aran* or *Nanook of the North*.

   Though disappointed at the thought of a Saturday without
a big Clark Gable–type star, I realized I rather liked *Nanook of
the North*. It reminded me of *Frozen Justice* and later, the only
screenplay I ever attempted was about an overnight Ice Age,
with an advancing North American glacier covering miles in
days rather than years. This screenplay caused producer David
Brown to warn me that movies about snow and ice are "never
successful." I tried to argue that Howard Hughes had seen *Ice
Station Zebra* repeatedly. But David wasn't convinced. When
my cowriter Patty Goldstein and I pitched our idea to another
producer, Jennings Lang, he growled: "You gals should write
about something you know, something like what makes those
Cosmopolitan girls tick?" We were so distracted by the fact that
we knew Jennings Lang had once been shot in the balls by Walter Wanger, the irate husband of actress Joan Bennett, we could
hardly pay any attention to his advice, or keep our eyes off his
fly. When he said, "What do you two know about an Ice Age?"
we both burst out laughing and assured him we knew zilch, zero,
nothing. We left his office clutching our reject, titled *Freeze*. We
were practically in hysterics. But Patty and I still think our movie
idea was "high concept." (Man in Miami wakes to find his swimming pool has frozen solid overnight!) Anyway, nothing can pry
me away from the impact made at age five by *Frozen Justice*.

I KNOW THIS DOESN'T MAKE me unique. Every American of my generation seems to have been marked by the movies.

I simply realize that I wasn't interested in life on this planet until I became aware of the flickering screen, about age five. Soon, however, I replaced Lenore Ulrich with two other big personalities, Tom Mix, the king of the cowboys, with his hatchet face and big white hat, and his horse, Tony. I fell madly for both Tom and Tony and remained in this unnatural state until, later, I found Fred and Ginger, dancing "The Carioca" on a black glass floor in *Flying Down to Rio*. I have seldom recovered entirely from any of my movie crushes. And so stars have claimed my life and dominated my fantasies. I almost always and invariably dream of famous stars.

I used to leave movie theaters feeling I was the essence of Bette Davis or Carole Lombard or whoever. I could remain in this state for several hours until something distracted me and I returned to being myself. My mother spent an entire summer going mad while I marched up and down in our driveway shooting off my cap pistols and yelling over and over, "I'm Tom Mix! I'm Tom Mix!" (I still keep his photo up in my office and nobody ever does me the favor of recognizing him anymore.) Mother would jerk me into the house exasperated. "Stop this silliness. You are Mary Elizabeth Smith. Get out of those dirty coveralls, take a bath and put on a little dress before Daddy comes home!"

I would crash down to reality and do as I was told. It would linger in my mind that I "might" be Tom Mix even as Dott was buttoning me up into some crinoline or pinafore. But I didn't go on with it. I was a horrible little coward and I did want to please Mother and Daddy—up to a point.

WHEN I READ THE LIFE of Salvador Dali, I was flabbergasted to learn that his memory went back to the womb. I can't recall a single thing about babyhood except what I was told by others. *Frozen Justice* was actually my second memory. My first is of being spanked for taking a toy train away from Bobby. I must have been about five. I can see him—his bright white hair, his merry blue eyes, his amazingly beautiful baby eyebrows—teetering around the room in a blue romper. Someone picked me up and paddled me. Mother? Daddy? Dott? My aunt Mary Eula, for whom I had been named Mary?

I quickly got over it because I adored him and must have known, down in my heart, that he would become the companion of my youth. He was to be my real life shining star, but this is the very first I even recall of his existence.

So why was my brain in neutral for the first five years of my life? I don't even remember Bobby's arrival in 1927. It is daunting to learn that others recall being in the womb, remember their cradles, their parents' faces, the life around them. It took Bobby, a toy train, a spanking and *Frozen Justice* to wake this sleeping beauty.

DADDY/SLOAN

I REMEMBER A SCRATCHY SENSE of alarm and yet, safety. Being lifted into a male aura, feeling his close-shaved face (he used a dangerous straight razor, "stropping" it on a worn leather strap that hung in the bathroom). He smelled mostly of tobacco and seldom had his hands free from opening Lucky Strikes, striking matches, puffing, putting out cigarettes—sometimes rolling his own if the mood struck him.

He was fastidiously clean, but hated soap and thought it was bad "to lather up your skin." He loved manicures, tubs, being fussed over. "Come and tweeze this hair out of my ear. It's twanging and driving me crazy!" He was masculine but dandified, affecting bow ties, Borsolino hats, fine-tooled boots, two-tone shoes in summer and straw hats with boater ribbons. He hated the hair on his body and clipped under his arms with scissors. When the safety razor became popular, he never stopped praising it. Now he could shave under his arms. I never knew any other man to do this until I saw Jeffrey Hunter in *King of Kings*. His Jesus was clean under the arms.

My brothers convinced me that Sloan was crazy on this point and I realized early on that he was eccentric and no yardstick for what to expect of males in general. Yet he was testosterone-fueled. Woe to anyone who mistook his bantam size and courtly good manners, his generosity, and his fine cotton shirts and well-tailored suits for sissification. From his Irish mother he had inherited a molten center that could boil up and explode with volcanic force. He and his sister, Hassie, were so much alike that for them to even be in the same room meant an evitable fight. The Smith family reunions were testy affairs that broke apart and left factions not speaking for months.

Yet he had a deep abiding respect for women and courtly ideas about females. There were only two kinds, he'd say— ladies, and the other kind. Yet he actually adored the entire female sex and often said that one good woman was worth hundreds of useless males. He frequently opined, "After I met your mother, I never looked at another woman." Well, he looked, observed and remarked on how women dressed, acted and behaved. But even my brothers felt he was the most faithful of husbands. When I would later ask how long he and Mother had been married, he'd laugh. "Honey, I don't remember a time when I wasn't married to your mother."

One had to admire his gentlemanly ways, which were simply the veneer that covered up his benighted and pinched background. He had been born into a family of eight children in one of the nongarden spots of rural West Texas—Putnam, near Cisco. He had never had a toy as a child unless he made one out of a corncob. A great Christmas was one where he received an orange. He had gone to work at age eight as a Western Union messenger on horseback. He had quit school at the fourth grade and was totally self-educated, wrote in beautiful Spencerian handwriting and could do long division in his head. He demanded and deserved the respect he received.

He had been given a girl's name after a cherished aunt and had fought over being Sloan since childhood. He was as proud of his name as Lancelot with a maiden's scarf on his lance. He never tolerated a slur and usually refused to answer to any nickname, but he called my mother "Sweetie" and she called him that back. Still, he would chide others like my grand-mother McCall for referring to her as "Baby." He detested small talk. "Canned conversation!" he'd remark.

He was big on behavioral advice—"Be a man!" he'd say to my terrorized brothers as he rehung the razor strop after some butt-popping punishment. These spankings, for all of us—even me—were rare, but memorable, given his incendiary nature. He was an autocrat very like the man in *My Philadelphia Father*.

If he didn't want to discuss something, a firm "Let's don't talk about that" was final. We learned early on not to sass him, or ask too many questions, not to complain about slights offered us elsewhere (he might spring to our defense). And, we never questioned his judgment—out loud.

Like all natural athletes, he was careless of his talents. He could run at a ten-foot fence, vaulting over it with one hand. He almost never drank and was an early health nut, ordering grains from Battle Creek, Michigan, urging us to eat prunes and beets and telling us that "too much ketchup thins the blood."

I constantly fell off, was bucked off, or raked off the horses he set me on. But I never saw a horse he couldn't ride. He loved all horseflesh; especially high-strung temperamental gaited ponies.

During the Depression he infuriated Mother by keeping a polo pony in the backyard and an expensive English saddle on the stairway in the living room. "Like a decoration!" Mother would complain. "We can't afford livestock!"

I loved everything about the West—cowboys, Indians, fringe and flash. He would say I had no taste. "Tacky!" he'd erupt. And he never sat in a Western saddle that he didn't make fun of—especially the horn. "For tenderfeet to hang onto," he'd chide. He tolerated my worship of "cowboys" although he said they were low-class and not heroes like Tom Mix. He loved an-imals and from his travels was always bringing home raccoons, armadillos, terrapins, rabbits and wounded birds. But when we begged for a dog, or cat, he was contemptuous. He disliked do-mesticated pets. Their habits offended him. Dogs and cats were "dirty." His irrational likes and dislikes, his good and bad judgments, his prejudices and passions remain a kind of crown of thorns, even to this day.

He was beyond impulsive and impatient and when I find myself snarling because someone is too slow, I am always forcibly ashamed to find him still here inside me. He had a teasing side that could be hard on children. He would go get in the car and begin racing the motor in the driveway: "All you chillun who want to go with me, come—now!" Where was he going? We would hang uncertain on the running board. "No, take it on faith. Go or come. Gamble." Mother would come to the front door. (I see her with a broom or a mop. She loved housekeeping, hated cooking.) "Sweetie, don't tease and torment them. Tell them where you are going." He would ignore her. We'd be torn as he put the Oldsmobile or the Model T or the V-8 into gear and slowly the car would move backward toward Hemphill Street.

If we went, sometimes we'd end up ceaselessly waiting in the car while he went to a mysterious house, parked us and did his "cotton business." But if we failed to go, the others came back burbling about delicious treats, or a trip to the zoo, or a boat ride. We learned to take our chances.

When he was home from his long auto trips buying cotton all over Texas, Oklahoma and Arkansas, life was so exciting we could hardly stand it. He would make plans to repaint the house all by himself and pay us a nickel an hour to help. One year, he covered the roof all by himself in asbestos shingles. "This house will never go up in flames," he would promise, daring the gods. (It never did and is still standing in Fort Worth's somewhat deteriorated South Side. Sloan's shingles are still intact.)

After a long absence, he'd come home and throw down his suitcases into which he'd tossed pennies and coins for us to count and divide. He'd bring us parrots, hats, serapes, spurs and baskets of tomatoes, oranges, grapefruit, which he'd send us out to sell. He wanted to teach us the joy of entrepreneurism. We were thrilled, exhilarated, terrified, and all three of us hated going door-to-door. But he was implacable. Woe to one who came back laden with unsold produce. "I take all the risk and you chillun can keep all the profits. But you are too lily-livered to sell anything." Remembering the slammed doors and irritated rejections, it's no wonder I grew up almost unable to say "no" to anybody.

James and Bobby seemed able somehow to resist his horsey ambitions for them. But I know he must have tried and failed because I recall sitting paralyzed in many a saddle too big for me while he adjusted the stirrups, fiddled with the bridle and made mysterious talk about "choke reins." Cigarette smoke whirled around us as he stood muttering—"And you—you are the only one—you are my best boy!"

ONCE, WHEN I WAS ABOUT six, a pony ran away with me in Forest Park where they had horses for hire. I was wearing my flannel shirt, my "leopard" chaps and my real cowboy boots given to me by my aunt Eula's beau, Frank Dye. Daddy was riding ahead when the pony realized he was in charge. He had already tried to reach back and bite me. Daddy had laughed. "Just show him who's the boss." The pony turned en route and took off for the feedlot. I held on for dear life with Daddy coming pell-mell behind me. He knew the pony would dig in its front legs to stop. Margaret Mitchell wasn't to write this Bonnie Blue Butler scene until 1936, but Sloan could just see me thrown over the pony's head with a broken neck. Blind with tears, I dug my sloped boots deep into the stirrups, heels down. I managed to stay on. Sloan dismounted in midair and struck the pony in the side of the head with his fist before dragging me into his arms.

The story of my triumph became embellished. I preened, but not too much. I was still a coward and knew it. I had failed to show my mount who was boss. My boy cousins and James looked on with veiled eyes as Daddy bragged about me. "My best boy!" he'd whisper, holding me between his legs, scattering ashes over everything.

Hello, Dr. Freud!

MY LIFE

WITH THE

JAPANESE

I WAS BORN WITH A Japanese battle-ax hanging over my head. All of my early life, Daddy was working at buying cotton for The Japan Cotton Company. The difficult part was that the company was headquartered in Dallas while we lived in Fort Worth, thirty miles away.

Today, Fort Worth and Dallas are like the same big metropolis. But back then, traveling thirty miles wasn't easy. Every time we went to Dallas, I seem to remember, we'd have a flat tire. There was lots of sitting on the side of the road, waiting to be "fixed" or towed. But then I also remember when people had broken arms from having had the hand crank that started the Model T turn backwards on them. I even remember desperate souls in cars with flats and no spares—they would resort to "riding on the rims." When you saw someone tooling along lopsided, with sparks glittering up from the bare iron rim, you felt truly sorry for them. They were poor and had no spare. (Judging who was "poor" and who was "really poor" during the Depression became an art—an art practiced fearfully by those of us on our own way down.)

Daddy was a little irritable about having to go thirty

miles to work in Dallas, though that was when he was lucky. Often he would be away for months, "buying," traveling all over Texas, or looking for cotton in nearby states. Several early summers before the stock market crash of 1929, when we three children were really young, we'd gone to live with Daddy in the Rio Grande Valley while he was buying. It was here I was told that "the only good Mexican is a dead Mexican" and other Texas shibboleths. "Mexicans don't know a damn thing about how to cure leather!" "Mexicans always say 'mañana' but mañana never comes." And my mother couldn't get over a maid we had who was paying to get her dead husband out of purgatory and into heaven. When my mother remonstrated, the maid said simply, "But Miz Smith. I must go on paying because he is almost out. Only his left heel is still in purgatory!" (Naturally, Southern Baptists who believed in the same kinds of mysterious Christian things—only different—could never cope with the "ignorance" they ran into in the Rio Grande Valley.)

Even as a child I found this rampant racism unfair. The Mexicans of Brownsville were exotic to us. And I have to laugh when people say, "You're from Texas—of course you speak Spanish." Of course, I don't. In those days no self-respecting Texan wanted their children to speak Spanish. We were as protected from the possibility as little WASPs in Manhattan at the Brearley School were protected from learning Yiddish.

But, back to the Japanese—they were another strange race to us "superior" white Texans. Originally, The Japan Cotton Company was to be located in Fort Worth. That's why we were living there. The Japanese had established themselves in the Panther City with a battle-ax as their trademark. It was on everything—their pencils, their order forms, their stationery and their cotton bales. But when the very polite, erudite and brilliantly educated Japanese tycoons went to apply for membership in the Fort Worth Country Club, they were turned down flat. "Let those monkeys out on our green links?" "No!" said the Fort Worth Establishment.

The Japanese hierarchy—Mr. Yammamoto, Mr. Toroguchi, Mr. Surabachi—went promptly to the Dallas Country Club, where they were admitted with a quick finesse that belied even those times. Dallas was more metropolitan, more cosmopolitan, more "big city," and as my father said, "More about money!" He would never have used the phrase "Money talks and bullshit walks," but that was what he meant. The Japanese promptly moved headquarters to Dallas, leaving their Fort Worth employees high and dry.

Sloan, in a characteristic burst of impetuosity, had already bought two houses in Fort Worth. He had one of those big pre-1929–type salaries and thought he could pull it off. He bought 1919 Hemphill for us (it was more upscale) and 1811 Jennings, just three blocks and social light-years away, for his parents. Now he was stuck in Fort Worth with three children, two parents, two mortgages.

The Japanese seemed to like my father; for one thing, he was as small as they were. He was dapper and dressed as well as they did. He had the courtly manners of the true roughneck. He knew when it was moot to behave. And...he knew cotton like nobody's business. He could stand in any cotton field and finger the bolls between his calloused index and third finger and tell you exactly what grade the field would produce—anywhere from a fine quality shirt to a rough and rugged tent ducking.

Sloan admired and respected the brains of his bosses, as well he might. They were all Princeton, Yale and Harvard graduates. And he never stopped shaking his head over their educations and manners.

These Japanese men came from a feudal society that had little regard for females. But they doted on little girls U.S.A. style. (It was already happening—the era of America's love affair with Shirley Temple.) The men of The Japan Cotton Company paid no attention to my brothers, but would sit with me when visiting and attend my every move. They brought me beautiful fragile geisha dolls with sable hair under glass bell jars, brilliantly painted lithographs of tigers and butterflies and diminutive silk kimonos, explaining that in Japan, these were treasures. They would tie my obi and make me parade around for them, clapping their tiny hands with delight. It was a big feather in Sloan's cap that he had little Mary E. to show off to his bosses. It made him marvel and wonder. "In their own country, why, I'm told they sell little girls or throw them away like dirty tissue paper. They even drown them. I wonder what it is about Mary Elizabeth they like so much?"

I don't know the answer even now, except it represented a rare moment in my early life when I was the center of attention. I had to really straighten up and fly right with Daddy's bosses. I had to wear organdy dresses and black Roman sandals to receive them.

The Japanese of this company were very busy men in those days. They were buying cotton, yes, and other American goodies, such as scrap iron by the ton. The world would know soon enough what the Japanese battle-ax meant.

After the stock market crash and as the Depression set in, Sloan continued to work for them. Only now, they had him "on commission." We children soon learned that "on commission" was not a good thing. Daddy had to work harder, travel farther and take chances on what he bought, pay his own expenses, pare down, make do. He would roam the hotter-than-hell, 100°-plus wilds of West Texas looking for good deals on cotton, traveling now in a V-8 with a washtub and a 100-pound block of ice melting in the backseat to make his own mobile refrigerator. In those days it was the only form of "air-conditioning."

HEMPHILL STREET

A S THE GREAT DEPRESSION BIT down, suddenly a dollar became a lot of money. At ages seven and twelve, James and I ended up each being given a dollar to buy our Christmas gifts because actually, even ten cents bought a lot then.

I had mapped out my list for ten gifts when James came to me with a stunning proposal. We had often gazed at the sapphire blue bottle of Evening in Paris toilet water in the drugstore. We wondered what sort of rich person could afford it. James said he wanted to buy the dollar bottle for Mother at Christmas.

This was an amazing unJameslike thing, so extravagant. Later, I realized it was also romantic and sentimental, but I'm not sure I understood those terms at the time. I argued, "But then you won't be able to give anything to anyone else!" James said, "MES,* if you go halfers, we can give her the cologne together and still each have fifty cents for others."

I saw the beauty of it, but it ruined my crappy little plans. I said no. He asked again. Then looked at me pityingly, as if I were a worm, and walked away, never to bring it up again.

*A nickname based on my initials.

I bought a nail file for Daddy, a cheap lipstick for Mother, a doily for Dott, tweezers for Aunt Eula, and a toy for baby Bobby, key chains for my cousins, as well as one new lime-colored Crayola for Louise Lewis, next door.

Christmas arrived. Mother drew out an awkwardly wrapped gift from under the tree and opened it. There, glittering, was the Evening in Paris. James didn't have any gifts for anyone else. He'd shot his bolt for Mother. She was overwhelmed. She cried. Daddy and Aunt Eula were enthusiastic and congratulatory. "Aw, Mama!" said James as he was hugged. I was furious and ashamed. I always called her Mother, but James even had his special "Mama" and nobody else could use it. No wonder I feared he was her favorite.

My conscience hurt over this for years. Long after I was grown I tried to tell James how sorry I was. He said he barely remembered it, using his favorite expression: "Well, good night, MES, what does it matter now? Forget it." As I stood at a lectern in Austin, in December of 1998, to give my tribute at James's unexpected funeral—he had been killed instantly when a utility truck ran into the side of his car—the vision of Evening in Paris flashed before me. I launched into my tribute saying that at the healthy age of seventy-nine, it had taken a truck to erase the considerable genes of a man who had lived through WWII and never been sick. Standing there, I thought it might be cathartic to tell the Christmas story, but it didn't seem like the time to exorcise my demons.

And anyway, I was still too ashamed that I'd been too selfish or small-minded to share in one of my big brother's beaux gestes. I wanted to get through praising James without busting out crying and feeling again like a kid who had been disloyal.

When I left the lectern I was still seven years old. But James was more alive and more heroic for me than ever.

MY YOUNG LIFE ON HEMPHILL Street was inextricably tied up with our next-door neighbors—the Lewis family on our

left. The Oberwetters on our right had older children who were
James's contemporaries. But Louise Lewis was to be my best
chum, cradle through high school. The myth was that she and I,
born three months apart, were carried around on pillows together to be shown off as babies.

Louise and I had been flower girls during the wedding of
one of her aunts. We looked adorable, but evidently I was a flop
at throwing petals. Louise lofted hers like butterflies. She always
said, "But Mary Elizabeth just threw wads of hers, like they
were bombs." I rather liked this description; evidently I enjoyed
failing at being a girl.

Louise could not only toss petals, she had childhood mystery. She and her younger brother, Buddy, were being raised by
their aunt Vellene and her grandparents. The Lewises were well
off. They owned a vast furniture store on the North Side near the
stockyards. Louise was a saucy, flirtatious, mischievous little
(and big) girl, an imaginative playmate. She and Buddy were
happy kids in spite of their somewhat "orphaned" situation.

The Lewis house was two stories, a big porch, a porte
cochère, numerous garages out back and a fantastic triangular
sand pile under a big tree. Here we spent most of our time. The
Lewis house was full of books, paintings and music. Vellene
treated children as if they were intelligent, perceptive beings, to
be reasoned with. She imbued us with dollops of culture and answered our questions. She encouraged my interest in history and
as I grew older lent me books. I was amazed, for outside of my
grandma McCall, she was the only person I knew who read for
pleasure.

And the Lewis family offered an early brush with movie
glamour. Louise's uncle Bill, who lived alone upstairs, was an
artist. He created the huge cutouts of movie stars used to deco-
rate the big film palaces downtown. Bill drew the stars to scale—
Garbo, Gable, Dietrich, Lombard, Crawford and Shearer. Then
he'd make a graph and blow the face up to four feet tall on a
heavy beaverboard. He'd then paint the faces and they'd be
posted all over the lobbies and outside the building, clearly seen
from the street.

As feature films changed, Bill brought home the discards, which Louise and I collected in the garages out back. We played among them, never knowing quite what to do with these huge relics, but reluctant to let them go. We thought they were works of art. Inevitably, they were ruined by time, handling and the weather. We were sure Bill personally knew the stars he was drawing, but he'd just laugh. "Naw! I never see 'em!" Had these items survived, I know they would be priceless to film fans.

So the movies surrounded me even at home.

THE LEWIS FAMILY ALSO GAVE me my first brush with scandal though heaven knows they didn't mean to. Louise's father had been killed on a lookout point, which was a kind of "lovers' lane." He was with a woman not his wife. A robber ordered the couple out of their parked car and Mr. Lewis put his hand in his pocket. The assailant shot him, leaving the hysterical woman behind. (I never knew what the deal was with Louise's mother. She sometimes came to visit her children but that was seldom.)

My mother was so afraid we might offend the Lewises by even knowing of this unhappy business that we were inculcated from our first moments of understanding never to bring the matter up. Mother lectured us repeatedly: "Old Mr. and Mrs. Lewis and Vellene and Bill have had enough tragedy. They don't need you reminding them. I don't know how much Louise and Buddy know, so you are not to be the ones to tell them anything. Or even act as if you know about it."

My scandal-mongering technique was being stifled in its cradle. This was poor training for my future career. The talk about this "situation" went on often in our house—questions as to what "really" happened? It was gossip, family gossip, a staple of Southern life—and for all I knew—life everywhere. When Daddy brought home a detective crime magazine describing the unsolved murder in a graphic, lurid manner, we were allowed to see it, but never was it to be mentioned next door.

I don't think I ever slipped up on this though I was very close to Louise and often wanted to ask about her feelings. But she had the true dignity of the wounded. She never mentioned it either. No wonder the Lewis family lives vividly in my memory. They were my first introduction to gossip and scandal. And then, Uncle Bill kept us feeling "inside" at the movies with his gorgeous cutouts of the stars.

BOOKS WERE A BIG ATTRACTION to me at the Lewis house. But I had grown up in my own house full of books. I loved them and used to pull them out of the shelves and just "handle" them; leaf through looking at the typefaces. I couldn't read them as they were all in German. Mother had simply bought a lot of nice-looking volumes when she'd bought the bookcases. She only cared that they looked great.

From the time I can remember I was frustrated—until I learned how to read. When the Sunday papers arrived, if Daddy was home he'd read the "funnies" to me. Then I would go get my partner in crime—Louise—and we would "read" everything out loud—*The Katzenjammer Kids*…"Major Hoople" (*Our Boarding House*)…*Krazy Kat*…"Maggie and Jiggs" (*Bringing Up Father*). Louise was a great little actress and she was better at pretending she could read than I was. Other kids in the neighborhood would cry because we could "read" and they couldn't.

If Daddy hadn't read to us first, we'd look at the comic strips and make things up. Louise was really good at this. But whatever talent we had, we came by naturally. Sloan liked to read the entire newspaper to us. "Oh, here's something interesting. The police are looking for three kids who are wanted for various crimes in the South Side. Mary E. and Bobby Smith and Louise Lewis are the culprits and an arrest is imminent." We would rise up in alarm and beg to see the offending article. Daddy would laugh and turn the page. "Here are the cotton futures…"

As I learned to read, among the German tomes I found

one in English—*Mechanics of the Boiler Room*. I actually studied it, although it made no sense and I'd look again at the German books thinking perhaps they'd reveal themselves. No wonder I grew up with so much empathy for those who can't read. I already had tried to push the literacy envelope.

The day I discovered that one could go to the public library and "take out" books was one of the happiest of my life. I went on the streetcar and forced myself to enter the foreboding building. In the entrance hall they had placed the skeletal head and tusks of a mammoth. One had to pass this formidable, frightening display and also go past a mannequin of a Chinese rickshaw man. The rickshaw was authentic, life-sized, and the mannequin very scary. I had already seen enough of Ming the Merciless in the *Flash Gordon* serials to know I was afraid of most things Oriental. I'd grit my teeth, clutch my library card, dash past these guardians and heave a sigh of relief as I began plucking books off the shelves. I selected at random. I read at random. No one ever suggested I might be reading above my understanding or that certain books were not suitable. They let me carry off whatever I wanted. It was a far cry from *Mechanics of the Boiler Room*. And I wasn't so scared leaving, because I had a clutch of adventures and unknown thrills in my arms. I would start reading on the streetcar as it clanged along Hemphill—called the longest street in the world. Sometimes I rode past my stop.

I became such a fanatic that Mother hid books from me and ordered me out to play. The only birthday party I recall is one where I was given a sequel to *The Wizard of Oz*. I opened it, left the party and climbed a tree to read my new book. I knew I wouldn't have to return it to the library. Mother came and confiscated the book and sent me back to the party. At my great age, I still feel guilty when I read for pleasure. To me, books are sensual, passionate, forbidden fruit.

When the Germans marched into Poland in 1939, we still had the German books on our shelves. I said, rather officiously to Mother: "You would have bought the works of the criminals who invaded Austria, Czechoslovakia and now Poland." She sighed, "Well, honey, I was just trying to make the living room look as if intelligent, cultured people lived here."

SLOAN HAD NOT BEEN PLAYING the market before 1929, but we were as marked by the crash as if we'd been in it to the hilt. The Depression began to hit hard. Herbert Hoover became two dirty words. The initials FDR rang a touch of optimism and I recall that we drove around the morning his National Recovery Act went into effect to see the blue eagle signs in every business window. (The Supreme Court declared the NRA "unconstitutional." But we had begun to believe in Roosevelt because we had to believe in something.)

Daddy now faltered in his mortgage payments and eventually the house Bobby and I were born in on Hemphill Street went back to the bank. We moved into the less "social" neighborhood of Jennings, crowding into a not-so-nice older Victorian house with Granddaddy Smith and Big Mama. It was a terrible comedown, especially for my mother. She was determined that Bobby and I would not be transferred to the less social Jennings school district. She paid extra for us to continue to attend the *comme il faut* E.M. Daggett in the school district where we had started kindergarten.

In the early thirties, Daddy received an engraved parchment from The Japan Cotton Company. It was an elaborate justification for Japan's having marched into and taken over Manchuria in 1931, turning it into something called Manchukuo and installing over it their puppet, the last Emperor of China. One sentence stuck in my memory. It read, in effect, "Japan feels it is its duty to bring peace to China. What neighbor, if his neighbor's house were afire, would refuse to fight that fire? China is ablaze with Communism. Japan must fight the fire of Communism, no matter what the world community thinks." This was the first I'd heard of Communism.

Soon after, we saw the rape of Nanking in the newsreels, The Japan Cotton Company closed its Dallas doors. Its officers went back to Japan "to prepare for Pearl Harbor," Sloan would later say. At the time most Americans didn't know there was a place called Pearl Harbor, or that it stood between us and the Japanese Navy and Air Corps. That was a few years away. At the time we were still concerned with coping with the New Deal, vanquishing the Depression and learning how to be poor and needy, while pretending to still be as middle class as we'd been before.

During World War II, I often thought of my early Japanese admirers. I wondered how they were faring. If I had kept their elegant little Japanese gifts, I'm sure today they would be rare and valuable. But time and tide had their way with my "playthings" and they vanished, in the same way nineteenth-century Japanese culture vanished in the rubble of war.

BEFORE THE DEPRESSION, PEOPLE LIKE me qualified for what Harry Evans calls "The Turmoil of Normalcy 1920–1929" in his book *The American Century*. Women had only had the vote for three years when I was born February 2, 1923. I like to think of this time as The Booth Tarkington Era. Dogs still slept in dusty town streets without getting run over. Little boys, like Penrod and Sam, fished with a string and a bent pin. The combustion engine was just beginning to pollute the atmosphere, replacing the smell of horse manure. Sinclair Lewis had created the fictional all-American nothing—George Babbitt. Mark Twain was still considered a children's storyteller rather than a radical great of American literature. Norman Rockwell was becoming the nation's own idealized portrait painter.

Children ran away from home daily with a bandana on the end of a stick but everyone knew they'd be home by suppertime. We were seen but not much heard. My generation was afraid to misbehave. We were punished instead of being "understood." And a bad conscience was worse than any switching.

Early on I'd had a severe lesson in morality. I loved the Stripling's department store downtown because it had a fabulous toy department. Plastic hadn't been invented; toys were beautiful wooden, tin or steel works of art. Mother always left me there when she went shopping and one day I discovered a hook-and-ladder fire truck in red and yellow. The driver was a little man of heavy lead or steel with hands outstretched to the wheel. He had a plug in his bottom to fit him into a hole. I wanted the truck; I took the driver.

When Mother saw me playing with this at home, she pointed out that the driver was now useless. "How can the truck go to a fire if the driver is missing?" Then she lectured me quietly about stealing. The next day we went on the streetcar to Stripling's. I had to give the driver back to the manager. I said I was sorry and the manager had me personally replace the man in the seat.

Mother took my hand and we went home. She never mentioned the incident again and I never stole anything else in my life. (It would have been good, but boring, if I had obeyed all the other commandments the way I obeyed that one.)

It's a cliché to say people never locked their doors in those days, but when we moved out of the house I was born in, we were unable to give the buyers a key. So life then was mostly unadulterated pleasure for kids. We were fed breakfast and if there was no school, we were turned loose. We canvassed the neighborhood, we checked on maids, cooks and yardmen, we tested toys in other people's houses, we tried out porch swings and we collected hard green chinaberries for our slingshots. We never went home for lunch that I recall, living on peanut butter, apples and other fruit from neighbors' trees. As the afternoon grew shaded, we picked fresh flowers for the dinner table. You had to be careful with the thorns on roses and could only take them if Mother said it was "time." And when you picked nasturtiums and violets, you had to work your fingers all the way down to the earth. Woe to the person who brought short-stemmed flowers for the vase. This represented an aesthetic failure.

One morning from our tree house I saw a man being dragged out of a cellar. Bobby and I ran to the spot. The man was black and sooty, ashy and stained. The firemen told us he'd been standing in water in a basement and had touched a hot wire. Electricity had burned him black. We looked our fill at this dead man. Nobody shooed us away. That night at dinner we had a lot to say about the "lectrocuted" man and we decided to wear red hats, yellow coats and rubber boots and fight fires. This ambition warred with our admiration for the garbagemen who came down the back alley with their big dray horses. We'd inhale the effluvia and hang on the fence as they emptied the big drums we'd filled. We also waited for the iceman. He smelled particularly revolting personally. A card in the window said we needed twenty-five, fifty or seventy-five pounds. So the iceman stopped his horse in the street, chipped out a block of ice, returned his ice pick to its scabbard, hefted the ice on his leather-clad back. A bike tire attached to the bottom of his "cuirass" warded off drips. When he trudged to the house we'd then raid the wagon for ice chips among the wooden splinters.

James wanted to be a garbage man. Bobby wanted to work on trains like our uncle Ed, who always came home dead tired and said to our auntie: "Iris, fix me a T-bone!" In my dreams I was in the movies. I was Tom Mix—and later, I was Ginger—and Fred.

The electrocuted man wasn't our only dash of reality. Our beloved Dott had married a huge man named Raford but because Daddy didn't approve, he wasn't allowed to live with Dott in her little house out back. (And you thought slavery ended with the Civil War?) Raford came home weekends to take Dott away. When he did that, he'd hold my hand and walk me under the corner streetlight where we'd "stomp bugs" until time for him to go. I worshiped Raford. His big feet made crackly sounds on the bugs. But Sloan said his nickname was "Ice-Pick Red" because he'd killed a man in a fight.

One day Daddy collected James and me and ordered us into the car. "Raford has died in a knife fight and we are going to see him," he said. Mother protested. We were too young for such a viewing. Sloan just herded us out and drove us to the Negro funeral home. There on a slab lay a totally naked Raford, silent as a stone, a white sheet pulled up to his waist. We stood there, amazed and enthralled. Daddy turned and we followed him out.

In the car he said, "Let that be a lesson to you. Sorry people like Raford die from fighting. Now you be nice to Dott. She is very upset and I am paying for this no-good funeral." Then he added, "But if you do get in a fight, be sure you win. And don't fight fair. Just pick up a rock or a pair of pliers or anything you can lay hands on and knock the person's brains out." James looked at me behind Daddy's back and slowly shook his head. My role models were certainly at odds with one another.

The only real tragedy of our childhood was the realization that Sloan, Jr.—Mother and Daddy's first child—had died when he was a year old, from meningitis. His beautiful picture over our parents' bed haunted us. He was mystery and myth, never "to be" for us, but among us constantly. "If Sloan, Jr., was here, you wouldn't dare push me."

When Mother sat us down to look at the famous art reproductions in a book she'd bought to give us "culture," we'd always beg instead for "stories." How she met Daddy in the little town of Ennis when he peeped at her under a window shade from the room he rented next door; how they went dancing through the courtship and were called Mutt and Jeff, because she was tall, he was short. And how Sloan, Jr., became ill on a train trip and couldn't be saved, not even by Mother's two doctor brothers.

We knew Baby Sloan had learned to say, "Mama... Daddy...cracker...light." He was more real to us than the blond Christ child by Raphael hanging over Daddy's desk. And there were other big stories we loved—the Leopold and Loeb thrill-killing of someone Mother referred to as "little Bobby Franks in Chicago." We wanted also every word about the sinking of the *Titanic*. And we always wanted a recital of Baby Sloan's death. All of these tales reduced us to tears.

My mother was sweet and never tired of repeating these sagas for our undying, morbid curiosity.

LOWER EDUCATION

IF THERE'S ANYTHING I WOULDN'T want to live over again it's school. I was so shy that when walking I'd cross the street if I saw I was going to have to pass someone on the sidewalk. Then I'd get into the rat's maze of politics, personality and popularity that constituted school life and I'd start acting up, acting out and showing off to try to make myself acceptable to the "A" group from kindergarten on.

The only things I liked were the drama and speech classes. I played all kinds of small roles in little plays. Bobby always says, "You were the crowd noise." But finally I was unexpectedly tapped for the lead in a fairy tale where I began as a caterpillar that turned into a butterfly.

My mother was thrilled at my sudden recognition and began frantic work on my costumes. She felt this experience might change me into a really sweet little girl—the one she longed to have. I was good at memorizing and stepping out when the spell was upon me. I still am. But mostly I recall the humiliation of the early spotlight, being sewn into my caterpillar suit and carried in the janitor's arms onto the darkened stage to be plopped down like a sack of potatoes, waiting to speak my lines when the curtain went up. I had to lie at a very unnatural angle and stretch up my head to speak. We caterpillars are like that.

And even I didn't think, with my Ella Cinders straight haircut and bangs, that I made a very beautiful butterfly. (Periodically, my poor mother would make me get a permanent but the result was even worse. How could I know, at eight or so, that the question I came to call "What Have You Done to Your Hair?" would haunt me into maturity? It's what everybody "at home" says when you go back for a visit!)

So I didn't enjoy "starring" when I felt I didn't deserve it. I liked it better when I had some small part supporting a little blonde princess who lived in the best part of town. Her stardom and popularity I could understand.

What I remember of the E. M. Daggett School was trying to fit in socially. I hated phys. ed. and was no good at sports. If I joined my school pals in a Saturday outing downtown where we'd have lunch and go to the movies, I felt out of place. "What's wrong with you?" one friend asked. "You are so much fun at school, but here you don't say anything." I was insecure, worried about my clothes and whether I had enough change to pay my way. This was a defining social moment for me. I realized I was not "performing" up to expected snuff. So I learned early to mend my ways, to pretend I was something that I was not. That is to say—socially secure.

Instead of school, I was much more interested in Walter Winchell, who I listened to every Sunday night as he played his rat-a-tat-tat Morse code and said, "Good evening, Mr. and Mrs. North America and all the ships at sea, let's go to press." About this time I made up and wrote a newspaper of my own on an old Underwood of Sloan's. Winchell and the Lux Radio Theater and the little theater off Times Square where Mr. First Nighter was always hurrying to his seat on the aisle had captured my imagination. There was no gainsaying the lure of New York. It was a place I envisioned from listening to the radio and going to the movies. And, I must have been about ten when I'd go to play softball at the spacious house of Suzanne Stinnet. She lived in a big two-story white manse in the "good" part of Fort Worth. And she was exotic because her parents were…divorced! Suzanne's friends loved to go there; the refreshments were super. We had real ice cream, not that dead giveaway dessert of the Depression—Jell-O.

Suzanne was sweet, great looking, wore beautiful clothes and I admired her so much that years later I named a Burmese cat after her. But back at the age of softball, I was definitely already living "on the wrong side of the tracks." I had started kindergarten with Suzanne and many others while living on the right side. So I was still accepted. And anyway, I think they liked me. I only came unglued when they did things like start private clubs where one needed a twenty-five-cent initiation fee that I didn't have. I'd say, "I can't. I haven't got it." And someone would just say, "Okay, *you* can get in for nothing."

This did not help my self-esteem. And I hated softball. One day, I left the game and wandered into Suzanne's house. I decided to examine the exotic Mrs. Stinnet's bedroom. This was daring, wrong and unbelievably crazy of me.

Next to her bed were stacked many magazines and I immediately sat down to go through them. Suddenly, Mrs. Stinnet came into the room. She was wearing a peach negligee. I knew what it was from watching movies. Certainly, she was not in the ubiquitous "housedress" of my mother's world.

"Oh, hello, Mary Elizabeth. How are you?" she asked. I jumped up and apologized for crashing. She waved a languid hand. "No, no, you are welcome here. What are you looking at? Oh, *The New Yorker*—yes, I like it, too. Keep on reading. Come any time you like, come up here and help yourself. I wish Suzanne liked to read." She drifted away.

It was incredible that I, of all sissies, didn't die of fright. But I was too enthralled by *The New Yorker* to react normally. And ever after that, I did as Mrs. Stinnet suggested. I went to the game. Then, I'd go upstairs and look at *The New Yorker*. I can't say I read it, but I absorbed it. And when I first encountered a Peter Arno cartoon, it reminded me of Mrs. Stinnet. It showed a woman, a typical Brenda Frazier brunette, sitting nude before a vanity. She was mumbling, "Oh, my God! I forgot the men's favors!"

This had a deep effect on me. I puzzled over the meaning for months. But I loved Suzanne forever for having the "right" kind of unusual mother who wanted to introduce me to the glories of *The New Yorker*. And the glossy sophisticated magazine that Harold Ross said was "not for the little old lady from Dubuque" gave a little Texas girl an itch that she didn't then know how to scratch.

WHEN WE MOVED TO 1811 Jennings with our Depression-era tails between our legs, only my granddaddy Jerome Bonaparte Smith, who loved everybody, was thrilled to see us. He was a true Smith, an ironsmith, and this was his real name. This smith made three cast-iron skillets for my mother that she prized. I still have one of them.

Our Jerome "Bony" claimed to be descended directly from Napoleon's brother, Jerome, who'd been sent to rule Louisiana before "The Purchase." Granddaddy's own widowed mother hadn't been able to speak English. She spoke a bastard Cajun-French and had traveled her children from Louisiana to Texas in an oxcart to escape the demoralizing life of New Orleans. Once when the young Bony went back in search of his roots, he found an uncle who was a riverboat gambler. Granddaddy tried to board but his uncle pulled a pistol. "Don't come up here or I'll shoot you. Go back to Texas. This is no life for you."

I thought Granddaddy had his nickname because he was tall and bony, a regular Jack Spratt to Big Mama's fat self. But in the Depression when the masses began to name their offspring "Franklin D. Roosevelt Jones," I realized how Jerome Bonaparte Smith had probably gotten his name. Still, I liked the thought of adding a bit of Corsican to my Scottish-Irish roots.

We settled into a crowded, less upscale life. Big Mama kept chickens and when dinnertime came, we kids tried not to miss her rush into the backyard to snatch up a young fryer and boldly wring its neck. The chickens would cluck with terror and we would, too. Big Mama would turn her prey like a whirligig until the heavy body flew away and the chicken rose, staggering and headless, taking steps, spurting blood. When it collapsed, she'd contemptuously throw away the head in her hand.

My mother fled to the living room. She couldn't endure such indignities though she'd been raised in Mississippi and had seen many killings for food. Big Mama would plunge the headless chicken in boiling water, then sit down and snatch off its wet feathers. The smell was not good, but the fried chicken later was divine. And we'd had the excitement of our fear of Big Mama, of sudden death in the arena, plus a delicious sizzle to look forward to.

Big Mama didn't approve of what she called "the picture show," but she did tell me one of my first film star stories. Hollywood was celebrating an actress named Adrienne Ames, a Joan Crawford type, but less successful.

I was lying on the floor looking at a movie magazine when Big Mama stepped over me with clothespins in her mouth and a basket of wash. "I made a dress for her once; there, she's the one.

"And God has punished me ever since."

I couldn't believe it. I sat up, asking, "How?" Big Mama sat down. "When your daddy first bought this house for us, we moved in and I rented out a room in the back. This one in the magazine takes the room and says her husband is on the road. We never saw him. One day she asked would I make her a dress for two dollars? That was a lot of money, so I took her material and she gave me a pattern she'd made herself. I started on it, but couldn't finish. It had no sleeves. She said, 'I don't want sleeves.' I told her no one could go on the street in a dress without sleeves. She said, 'I can.' I said such a dress was against my religion, so she upped the price to three dollars. Then she went all over the neighborhood, showing off her arms. She also smoked cigarettes, on the street. She kept saying she was going to Hollywood, and I guess she did."

Big Mama hung her massive bulldog head. "And it was my fault, God forgive me." That evening I was given a rare quarter and sent to the Liversey Grocery Store for a pound of round steak. I rushed off down the alley, happy that I wouldn't have to say "Charge it" while Mark Liversey looked at me askance. We always owed him so much money.

I was basking in the glow that Adrienne Ames, a woman dating Bruce Cabot in Hollywood, had slept in the back room at 1811 Jennings. Someday I'd meet her and say I was Martha Tipton Smith's grandchild, not a fact I usually wanted to advertise.

Adrienne Ames had her minor heyday long before I could get to California. She died, virtually forgotten, of lung cancer in the forties.

My darling granddad Bony also died of cancer not too long after we moved in with him. Big Mama moved around to visit her daughters, making each one miserable in turn. Because of the Depression, we were visited by waves of relatives out of Mississippi and West Texas. They came to find work. For a while my maternal grandma, Sally Ball McCall, was with us. She was just the opposite of Big Mama, a former schoolteacher who kept a step ahead of our homework and never raised her voice. Even my father was on his best behavior around Sally Ball, for, as he said, "I know a lady when I see one."

She'd married a Mississippi doctor thirty-three years her senior and when he died, after giving her four daughters, she found only $100,000 in bills due him in his desk. She had finally moved to Texas with my mother to keep house for her adult stepsons who had moved west. We loved having her with us because she read to us. I remember her reciting graphic childbirth scenes from Pearl Buck's *The Good Earth*. "Isn't that a bit advanced for the children?" my mother asked. Grandma would say, "Well, they have to learn sometime."

It tickles me now that Grandma Sally Ball McCall always bragged a bit that she was descended directly from George Washington's mother, Mary Ball. And, she had the family tree to prove it.

Okay, so I'm descended from the Father of Our Country

on one side and from that vile Corsican on the other. Take it or leave it.

Sometimes we went to Mississippi so Mother could visit her relatives in Potts Camp and Holly Springs. Mother didn't really want to have anything to do with her home state. It depressed her. She hated its "ignorance, its poverty and the awful way they treated their Nigras." Those were her exact words.

But we children loved the novelty of our aunt Lela and our uncle William's little worn-out Mississippi farm and the way they lived in an old frame house set in the red clay, up on two-by-fours, so that chickens pecked around below the floorboards. We liked to help with the milking and turning the milk into butter in a big wooden churn held between the knees. It was fun snatching eggs from under sitting hens and I recall tagging alongside my uncle as he went down a row with an old iron plowshare behind a mule.

At the height of the Depression, I asked, "Why are we all so poor?" William flicked the reins on the mule's bony back. "Well, honey, it's because the banks have all the money." At night when the coal oil lamps were lit and there was no "picture show," no radio, no electricity and even taking a bath was a hardship, I didn't like Mississippi so much myself.

Whenever I'd urge mother to let us have a picnic, or suggest eating outdoors, or by candlelight, she'd put her foot down. "My whole life was like that, a picnic you call it, until I met your father in Texas. Give me electricity, flushing toilets and grocery stores for food every time!"

She had managed as the child of a doctor, in spite of her "country" upbringing, to go to college. She had an inborn cultured and ladylike behavior, believing that the best-mannered person in the room was the one who never made others uncomfortable. I could never pay her a greater compliment than that.

She showed us wonderful sepia photographs of herself in her navy blue Mississippi State College for Women uniform. But if I asked what she'd studied or learned, she'd say, "I don't remember. I wanted to get out and go keep house for my older brothers in Texas."

Once I tried to engage her in a literary conversation: "Mother, you were born in Oxford, did you know that was the home of America's greatest fiction writer?" She answered absently, intent on threading a needle, "Who would that be, honey?"

"William Faulkner! Mother, he wrote *Intruder in the Dust* and many other famous books." She mused, "Faulkner, Faulkner. No, I don't think we knew any Faulkners."

It was the perfect Southern belle answer. I was surprised she didn't ask me what his grandmother's maiden name had been.

ZING! COLE PORTER WAS HAVING his way with me as I entered puberty. Around age thirteen I was busy learning every lyric of "Night and Day" from the Fred and Ginger film *The Gay Divorcee*. I also tried to learn every nuance of their dances and love scenes. Soon I had much of it down letter perfect. I had banished any specter of the Great Depression, which swirled around every life in the 1930s. I was able to forget that the Smiths had come down in the world. And I thought suddenly that I knew all about love and romance, thanks to the movies. As I rehearsed for my future career in show business, I was alternately Fred, then Ginger, then both. Sometimes I played one of the sidekicks—Eric Blore or Erik Rhodes or Edward Everett Horton or Alice Brady. I rather missed the delicate Franklin Pangborn, who usually played a fairy at a hotel desk or something similar. He wasn't in *The Gay Divorcee*. By then, I was totally in love with the entire cast. I was in love with the movies in general—and with love.

I knew that real romance was when Fred raised his eyebrow and began to sing in his imperfectly perfect voice, where he lifted himself along, up and over notes that dared to be mastered. Ginger was more routinely talented. She could sing, dance and wisecrack. With her blond pageboy, she was a goddess, but less divine to me than Fred, who had risen above his baldness, his slight build and his lack of conventional good looks. I loved him also because he was a better-dressed, sweeter and spright-lier version of my own dad.

I had the Jennings backyard all to myself and I danced around the sturdy bright zinnias planted in Big Mama's flowerbeds. I was already a flower connoisseur and I personally found zinnias rather tacky: too hearty, too tough and too easy to grow. Give me nasturtiums, phlox, daisies, roses and larkspur every time.

I heard the front doorbell ring from the backyard and, never wanting to miss anything, I tapped up the driveway toward the front. It was my aunt Helen ringing the doorbell. This almost never happened. No one ever went into the front hall or the living room, unless escaping from the rest of the family. Aunt Helen was older than my mother, slight, refined, soft-spoken, self-effacing, shy and reserved. Not a very interesting woman, but sweet. She lived in San Antonio where she was married to my favorite adult male relative, my uncle Jack Cheslyn.

Helen and Jack had no children. My brothers had told me that he had three testicles, which I understood made him "special" and was no more than I expected from such a colorful guy. Bandy-legged and tough, he was a natural roughneck, but a real artist who made his living as a sign painter. Once a coworker fell off a scaffold. Jack caught him, breaking both elbows. He was a riot in his double cast, asking us to light his cigarettes and put them in and out of his mouth as he blew smoke rings. Jack was the kind of guy I recognized when I went to the movies and saw Jimmy Cagney or George Raft or Humphrey Bogart. My mother had often mused as to what in the world Helen ever saw in Jack? They were so opposite in every way. We would just look at our mother amazed. We adored Uncle Jack and his rough and ready ways, his great good humor, profanity and talent. He was always so good to us. Once when a bee stung me, he took apart his cig-arette in the car on the road, wet the tobacco with spit and pressed it onto my sting. "There ya go, MES. You'll soon be good as new."

He also told us funny stories, bought us candy right before mealtime, let us play with his paints and drew us wonderful creatures. But my mother never "understood" Jack and my father basically didn't approve of him. "He was in the navy," said my father, knowingly. "It left its mark on him in vulgar ways." Well, now my parents' misgivings about Jack had come home to roost. Now Jack had slipped from the heavens. He had fallen in love with a sixteen-year-old girl in the complex where he and Auntie lived. He had told Helen that although he loved her and always would, he needed to be with this teenager or die.

She took the bus to Fort Worth. She stood forlorn at our front door, which nobody ever used. She had two suitcases beside her. When mother answered the bell, I went into the side door of the house and was right behind her, tapping and swaying. I heard Auntie say to my mother: "Well, Baby, I've come to ask you and Sloan to take me in. Jack doesn't want me anymore!"

My mother was going *tch-tch* and there was a lot of mysterious whispering then and grown-up talk and I was sent back outdoors. James and Bobby and I sat in stunned silence through dinner while Daddy rumbled that Jack was "no good" and Mother kept shushing him because "Helen doesn't want to hear that, Sweetie!" And none of us said a word. We were just heartbroken to think our darling Uncle Jack was out of our humdrum lives. (Auntie was, too.)

The next day I was out in the driveway singing and Mother came storming out after me. She was very annoyed. She whipped me around, interrupting one of my best performances. "I want you to hush up, right now, with this 'Night and Day' stuff—this 'you are the one' thing. Can't you realize that your aunt Helen is broken-hearted and all you do is sing that soppy, 'yearning, churning, burning' nonsense? And what do you even know about such things? I want this to stop immediately. No more love songs around this house!!"

I was shocked, but I got the message. Heartbreak, which I had seen on the silver screen, wasn't so funny in real life. And it had moved in to live with us. I began to listen to the whispers around me. I didn't blame Uncle Jack for being bored with Auntie, but I couldn't bear it that he'd made her so unhappy. I saw at once that she was a woman with no other options. As usual, too,

I was torn between being good about Auntie's plight and sharing the thrill of imagining Uncle Jack with the sixteen-year-old. However, I did train myself never again to sing within earshot of the house. This ban lasted for three months. We got used to Auntie living with us; she was very helpful to Mother. My father had only the greatest respect for her. He finally quit blasting Uncle Jack when he saw how unhappy he made her. He even stopped talking about Jack's tattoos, which to him were anathema.

The end of this story is glorious. Jack and Helen reconciled and lived happily ever after until death did them part many years later. These two opposites had attracted and they refound their destiny when they got back together again.

One day, Jack, too, appeared suddenly at our front door with his hat in his hand. My father was huffy with him, really morally superior. But Jack paid no mind to my father. He just said to my mother, "Elizabeth, I am here to see Helen and to take her home with me if she will forgive me and let me." Helen flew her little birdlike body into his brawny arms. We all quietly withdrew. I knew enough not to even hum.

Later, we would hear the details. Uncle Jack told Aunt Helen, "Honey, I made the biggest mistake of my life. I spent three months with that dizzy girl, but finally, I just couldn't stand to hear her put 'The Dipsy Doodle' on the Victrola one more time. She played it until it really was 'driving me wild.' It was that stupid. I suddenly knew I was in the wrong place with the wrong human being. I missed you so much. I am so glad you took me back."

When my mother told this to my father, he dropped his sniffy attitude about Jack. He literally howled with laughter and whenever anyone wanted a happy reaction in our house, they'd just sing a few bars of "The Dipsy Doodle."

So this was my first brush with true love, passion, jealousy and drama. I never sang "Night and Day" again without feeling a little self-conscious and without hearing the strains of "The Dipsy Doodle" over Cole Porter's passionate words and music.

Years later, when Skitch Henderson and I were trying to

pick a song for me to do onstage at a Carnegie Hall benefit with his New York Pops Orchestra, he said, "I guess 'Night and Day' might be a little too demanding for you musically."

I said, "Yes, I can't hit the notes. But I could do a mean 'Dipsy Doodle.'"

Skitch looked at me as if I were crazy. I didn't explain, but just tipped my metaphorical hat to those two lovers—Helen and Jack—and selected an undemanding version of "That's the story of . . . that's the glory of love!"

IN 1936 THE OLD WORLD was spinning into more and more trouble. In my last year at Daggett Junior High, Franklin D. Roosevelt had just banished Alf Landon for a second term. At home Daddy held up the *Literary Digest* with its cover "Is Our Face Red?" The magazine had predicted a Landon victory based on the truism "As Maine goes so goes the nation." But it turned out only that "As Maine went, so went Vermont." FDR had a landslide. The magazine went out of business and I got the message; it is dangerous to be wrong in print. Still, Sloan's insistence that I follow current events caused me to become the editor of *The Daggerette* student newspaper before I left junior high.

Haile Selassie was dramatic telling the League of Nations that Italy had seized his Ethiopia. He said, "It is us today, it will be you tomorrow." A Civil War began in Spain and we believed Franco was the bad guy. (Who knew that someday much later he would become a name to conjure with on *Saturday Night Live*.)

In Germany, an ominous Gestapo took over the police and began keeping dossiers on every person in the Reich. Stalin started his purges, killing millions, but nobody seemed to know that. And in the U.S. we were treated to sit-down strikes with the cops carrying strikers out in sitting positions. This was funny. An exciting magazine called *Life* came into being from Mr. Henry Luce, who had invented *Time*.

But the all-important event of the year for me was *Gone*

with the Wind. Margaret Mitchell had changed the name of her heroine from Pansy to Scarlett, and *GWTW* was the rage. I was one of the lucky first to get my hands on a copy and I read its 1,037 pages over and over. I couldn't get enough of it. I was much more interested in whether Clark Gable would play Rhett Butler than in where T.C.U.'s Slingin' Sammy Baugh would go as a pro football star. (He had made thirty-eight passes for touchdowns in three seasons and Texans had gone mad for him.) But I was no Texas chauvinist. I had a larger worldview. I said, "Give me Rhett!"

THAT

OLD-TIME

RELIGION

NEXT TO THE MOVIES, AS I've said, church was a big part of my growing up. Yet it bored me senseless and drove me crazy. Dread settled over our house every Sunday as Mother began herding us to do our duty. If Daddy was home, he stayed in bed, snoozing, reading and ignoring her injunctions that he be a role model. We didn't want to go if he didn't go so she used this against him.

But he was unmoved. He'd been working his ass off since age eight when, as a Western Union messenger, a horse had kicked him and dislodged a kidney. He'd picked cotton and driven millions of miles for the Japanese. He would work sundown to sunup when on the road buying. So now he was home for a moment. He wanted to relax. We were with Sloan.

My mother was a moral force for doing the right thing. We'd hear them fighting. She'd say, "You should set a good example."

He'd go sarcastic. "Are those angel wings you are sprouting? No, you take them to listen to that big hypocrite pastor."

I don't know why my mother never "got it." She wasn't

going to reform a man who had his own philosophies. "I worship God in my own way," he'd say.

We still wound up with the full blast of that old-time religion aimed at us. Bobby reminded me after we were grown, how Mother would make us "stay for church" after Sunday school, even when we were too young to know what was going on. To keep us quiet, she'd ply us with soda crackers from her purse.

Bobby mused: "Those crackers. They always tasted like her face powder. (Pause.) I guess that's why vodka tastes so good *now!*"

A FEW INTERESTING THINGS HAPPENED at Travis Avenue. Our musical conductor was a man with only one arm. This made him a figure of great interest to us. B. B. McKinney became well-known in a minor way, because he borrowed a number of Hawaiian classics and put Christian lyrics to them. "Aloha Oh!" became "He Lives on High," with the same hip-swaying insinuation of the islands. And our church was great for visiting evangelists. My favorite was billed as "Hyman Appelman, The Converted Jew."

I didn't understand exactly what a Jew was. The Old Testament was sometimes interesting, but then would bog down in "begats." The Jews, I knew, were the children of Abraham, lived in what Mother referred to as "The Holy Land" and somehow Jesus, later on, was one of them, but it wasn't always clear. (I noticed early on that most Christians of my childhood didn't dwell on Jesus being Jewish, thinking perhaps the fact would go away.)

The Reverend Appelman was exciting—and sexy, like all good evangelists. He told us he'd caroused and lived it up in his youth. (Isn't that always the way?) And then one night in a Kansas City hotel room, he had picked up the Gideon Bible and started reading The New Testament. Jesus came to him just as He had come to Saul on the road to Damascus.

The Rev. A. would act everything out. Very dramatic! Jesus to Saul, lying in the dust, blinded: "Saul, Saul—why persecutith thou me?" I never forgot that and have often been tempted to use the question to adversarial lovers, teachers, friends, bosses, agents, press agents, movie stars and publications as varied as *Spy* and *The New York Observer*.

Hyman Appleman had turned from sinner to saved Christian in one red-hot moment. His life ever after had been a fight to "save" others. He lived as a personal outcast. His family had turned his picture to the wall.

This emotional part of the Baptist religion I adored. I liked seeing people step down into the water of the baptistery, just above the pulpit, and I liked going back after to watch Brother C. E. Matthews hanging his dripping wet, all-white baptistery suit, with its attached white rubber waders, up on a hook. Some poor soul had been sanctified. I also loved to see folks rushing down the aisle to "be saved" while we all softly sang, "Just as I am without one plea, but that thy blood was shed for me. And that thou bidst me come to thee, Oh, Lamb of God, I come. I come."

In time, I went down the aisle several times myself. I liked the attention. I had myself baptized twice. My mother didn't know this or she'd have killed me.

Travis Avenue did bring into my life one terrific influence. Katharine Presley, R.N., was a redheaded, bosomy and dynamic nurse. I fell under her spell in my adolescence when she was already a grown woman. "Nursie" as we called her, was a bit man crazy and she'd had many adventures. She educated me with her experiences both professional and personal. She never talked down to me and I admired her as a dedicated caretaker doing all the good a nurse can do. She was also funny as hell. Sexy, too. I wanted to be like her and when she told of past adventures as the nurse at Hardin-Simmons University in Abilene, Texas, she aroused in me a deep desire to go to college in West Texas.

My mother wanted me to go to Baylor or the U. of Texas. Sloan didn't weigh in on this; there must have been a big crap game somewhere. I became dead set on H-S U. Nursie had said, "Lizard, they have the greatest football players, wonderful guys. And they have the Hardin-Simmons 'Cowboy Band,' whose motto is 'Thirteen Times around the Goddamn World!' "

I was shocked. I asked, "But isn't it a Baptist school?" Nursie shrugged. "Yes, but that's the motto the football guys gave the band. And it stuck." I decided I'd go west when I graduated from high school. It must have been the word "cowboy" that got me.

WAS IT JUST ME, OR was it the State of Texas? I need to ask: Does anybody ever learn anything in high school? I didn't. Well, maybe I did learn a lot about one thing, but it was never on the curriculum. The entire four-year experience from 1937 to 1940 was an exercise in a subject I thought I already had a handle on— the study of boys—boys to the right of me, boys to the left of me, etc. I had a good grounding from being sandwiched between James and Bobby and having male cousins. But all I can remember about going to the sainted Robert Lee Paschal High were lessons from or about the opposite sex. If you think you've heard the name Paschal before, you are probably right. This high school has become famous in the works of Texas wordsmith Dan Jenkins. He has written over and over about Paschal in the days "when men were men and women were glad of it." He and his *Sports Illustrated* partner Bud Shrake were memorable students there, football was their game, and Dan emerged to become a best-selling author of what I like to call "The Chicken Fried Steak Football Cookbooks." These are novels variously titled *Semi-Tough*; *Dead Solid Perfect*; *Baja, Oklahoma*; and Dan's latest, *Rude Behavior*.

When James was in high school and I was looking up to him, Paschal had been called Central High and it entered the halls, not of ivy, but of notoriety, because its principal would gather his students in assembly and read aloud to them from the Joel Chandler Harris stories of *Uncle Remus*. This tome of black legend had been written around 1880. Br'er Rabbit, Tar Baby and the other characters were quite popular in the politically incorrect thirties. Segregated white adolescents of Central High, including my older brother, loved these readings. They were considered hilarious as the principal, Robert Lee Paschal, performed them with exaggerated Negro accents. He was amazed when the *Uncle Remus* stories were banned as racist. But instead of his being pilloried, Texans turned around and put his name on the school.

At Pascal, I had one incandescent teacher, Mary Sweet, so inspirational that hers wasn't teaching per se. She made my heart catch fire for the theater. I amassed scrapbooks of Kit Cornell, Helen Hayes, John Barrymore, the Lunts, etc. Under her direction I acted in several plays. I was a pinstriped villain, "Mrs. Pencil," in one of these. (As you'll see from my book jacket, I've been addicted to pinstripes ever since—and, I suppose, to villainy.)

I was happiest when Miss Sweet pushed us to ask our parents for scarce money to attend the rare legit plays that came to the Majestic Theater downtown. Long before I had the sense to evaluate what I was seeing, I sat enthralled at a viciously profane *Tobacco Road* and fell madly for Alfred Lunt and Lynn Fontanne when they arrived on a double bill of *Amphytryon 38* and *Idiot's Delight*. I saw Eugenie Leontovich in *Tovarich,* so when the movie came out, with Claudette Colbert and Charles Boyer, I was ahead of the game. Now and then we attended the last gasps of vaudeville as it made its way into burlesque. Or enjoyed the great "Hi-de-hi-de-ho!" of Cab Calloway onstage, dressed in all white tie and tails, even though a white hierarchy wouldn't let him sleep in Fort Worth's hotels.

Just as with the movies, my parents never asked why I wanted a few dollars to go see a stage play. There was a joke going around about a nice old Baptist lady who saw *Tobacco Road* without knowing it concerned Southern white trash. At intermission, she was stirring around looking under her seat. She sighed. "Oh, shit, I just dropped my goddamned program!" This

tale titillated us beyond belief and we used it as an excuse to repeat "shit" and "goddamn," words we were never allowed to say.

Whatever I was really learning was from Daddy and the
white heat of current events. He was always quizzing me on
the news. But it didn't dawn on me how bad things were in the
world until the day in 1940 when the Germans marched into
Paris. My French teacher was awash in tears. Sitting under her
pictures of the Eiffel Tower, the Champs Elysée, the Louvre, we
imagined these hung with swastikas. We wept with her.

Here was another unsung teacher, a cultured French-
woman. What was she doing in Texas? Later she wrote in my
yearbook, "I shall never forget my little monkey of French
class." And she wrote it in French. What was even better—I
could read it, "petit singe," indeed.

As the world hurtled toward disaster, Winchell was writing feverish columns and I was studying him. His pillar was
awash in anti-Nazi propaganda. Later I'd learn that none other
than the president, FDR, was leaking info to him to encourage
U.S. entrance into the European war. High school matters
seemed less and less relevant.

BUT "BOYS" WERE STILL SERIOUS business. I am reminded here of a story told me by the Broadway star, Elaine
Stritch. She was dating the actor Jack Cassidy. Her parents, Mildred and George Stritch, came to New York from Birmingham,
Michigan, to meet him. They were Old Guard Roman Catholics
and Mr. Stritch worked for the B. F. Goodrich tire company. (He
always referred to it as the G. D. B. F. Goodrich tire company.)
Jack Cassidy had charm, humor and talent galore. But after the
four of them dined at "21," things didn't work out well. When
the Stritches returned to the St. Regis, George began to pace,
wearing out the carpet.

Finally, Mildred asked, "What's the matter with you,
George?"

He sputtered: "Mildred! Did you see that guy Elaine is going with? Did you notice? Why that SOB was wearing suede shoes!"

This may not seem so funny these days, but was a perfect comment on the stringencies with which parents still behaved and judged their children's significant others during the forties and fifties. I recognized instantly that to Mr. Stritch, suede shoes on a man were tantamount to "makeup" or "wearing jewelry," a question of character. I could just see my own father reacting in the same narrow-minded manner.

All through high school, my boyfriends were a source of great horror to my persnickety dad. The only men in my life he ever approved of were himself and my beloved first husband, George Edward Beeman. (Sloan died having never forgiven me for getting a divorce from Ed.)

On the edge of puberty, I found I wasn't a big success as a girl. My tomboyish side through my teens kept getting me in trouble with the "I enjoy being a girl" establishment. I didn't care about girly clothes, makeup or jewelry. I never bothered with how I looked. For my first formal dance in 1939, Mother made me a perfectly hideous yellow-flowered evening dress. My date, some poor sap from a good family who I had known since kindergarten, had not picked out a girl for the dance. Left with leavings, he asked me. That night he stood at the front door and handed me a tightly packed corsage of rosebuds. "They're Talismans—my mother said to tell you," he stammered. I examined them, thinking of the Sir Walter Scott novel where the teacher had made me go back, reread and explain what a "talisman" was.

Bumbling in his unaccustomed tuxedo, my date pinned the corsage to my shoulder. I thought how silly, soon the roses would be crushed. None of this kind of "dating" made any sense to me. I would have preferred staying home to read Mary Shelley's *Frankenstein*—with all the lights in the house turned on and Bobby to stand guard outside the bathroom door if I had to go. (I was always sure The Creature was going to get me.) I'd even have preferred staying home and playing some childish game with Bobby, who at least never bored me and could always provide realistic sound effects of bombs, guns, airplanes and his specialty, Donald Duck.

But peer pressure was great. Fort Worth had its own strict rules for the social realities. One of the rigors of the system was teenage dating, with all its attendant self-consciousness, mortification and worries about "being popular." We were pubescent and, of course, interested in the opposite sex, but I honestly did not know a single girl who had "gone all the way." And I was careful not to go there either. Sex was experimental, not conclusive.

My mother thought the way to enlighten me about the facts of life was to busily discuss various topics while she offhandedly performed household chores. Her favorites were menstruation, "rubbers," the rigors of childbirth, which she enjoyed describing in excruciating terms, the unforgivable males who became aroused while dancing. And then, there was her bugaboo—menopause, always hovering and much to be dreaded. (I swore when my time came I'd never let the word pass my lips.) It was all queasy-making and I wanted only to escape these little lectures. Such talks never seemed to give me any information I really needed and they ended by scaring me to death.

I had quite a lot of "street smarts" in any case. After all, I had two brothers—one an untouchable god and the other my serious slave. I had mostly male cousins. There was always a lot of informal sex talk in which these randy creatures seemed not to notice they had a girl (me) with them. I had seen many an erection, handled a few of them, and been enlightened beyond my need to know by the neighborhood smart alec, Mabel Soule, who knew all about getting your period. Or "being unwell," as some called it.

I had been "molested," I suppose, by one of my handsome rarely seen East Texas cousins, who was six years older to my nine or ten. But I had rather enjoyed it. I know one is supposed to go to court over such things, or spend years on the couch, but he gave me a certain yen for his kind of self-assured, dynamic good-looking guy. I don't believe these occasional explorations hurt either one of us though I'm not advocating it.

In Texas in those days, people thought nothing of popping children into bed with siblings, cousins, aunts, uncles and grandparents. You can learn a lot sleeping with adults—how they fart, scratch, snore, masturbate, pretend to be asleep when they are not, how they arrange to let you feel them up without noticing.

I used to tell a joke about how a virgin in the South is a girl who can run faster than her brothers. My poor siblings asked me not to tell this one anymore, as, they said, "We never laid a glove on you." It was true: They were my knight protectors. But I did spend a lot of years sleeping next to Bobby when he was a kid and having the duty of waking him periodically to hold the potty under him. He usually slept through this coached peeing, but my interest was pragmatic. I didn't want to wake up in wet icy sheets. I was never tempted to take advantage of him. He was my responsibility—my baby.

Getting one's period was an unusual issue in our house and one of the rare off-limits things to be openly talked about, so long as Daddy wasn't around. From nine on, my little girlfriends had been getting their periods. But not Mary Elizabeth. Nothing happened. Finally at thirteen, I found it so embarrassing as my pals took "off the floor" days from Phys. Ed., that I faked it and took one, too. James and Bobby were forever asking, "Didja get it?" I was mighty embarrassed by my delayed maturity.

Age sixteen—finally, I got it. I was delighted and went dancing around the neighborhood looking for Bobby. "I got it! I got it!" He was thrilled for me. "What's it like? Does it hurt? Are you wearing a Kotex? Now you can have a baby. Can I see it?" Of course I slapped him and he laughed. When poor James came home from having dished up Taylor's ice cream all day for a Depression-era pittance, Bobby told him. James looked at me shyly at dinner and I felt a new respect from him. This was refreshing because I knew perfectly well that he had always thought I was an idiot. Now, I was a grown-up idiot.

After they invented Tampax, I used to make Bobby go in and buy it for me. He'd squirm and try to beg off, but I was unrelenting. "It's good for you to do nice things for women," I'd say. I guess this made an impression; later, he would marry four women five times and I have always more or less taken credit for the fact that he likes the species so much.

Now that I was a woman, my parents paid more mind to what I was doing and Sloan was appalled at my poor taste in boyfriends. There was that rascal Randall Jones. He had a Marine Corps tattoo on his upper bicep. This, for Sloan, was the kiss of death. Even a man mowing a lawn without a shirt on was enough to send him into a conniption fit. "Who wants to see that man's titties? Lower-class trash!" Or he'd snort, "Tattoos are for jailbirds." He'd give these opinions with all the conviction of those who have just barely escaped themselves from the lower classes.

I went with Randall for a while. Then one day he cancelled a date because he had been arrested for forging a check. Soon he went to jail. So Sloan had been right after all, about tattoos. I felt I owed Randall a loving and interesting correspondence. The local postmaster took it on himself to inform my father that his daughter was "receiving mail from a state prison." There was plenty of thunder over that, but I stuck by my guns. I thought of myself as a heroine in a Jimmy Cagney movie. When Randall got out, he said prison had ruined him. As he was young and gorgeous I don't doubt it. But I didn't know what he was talking about. I thought the whole thing was so romantic.

Then, there was C.A. East, whom I met as a junior at Paschal High. "Hi, I'm Chips East," he said, curling his beautiful rosebud lips. Blond and Tab Hunter-ish, he came limping into an English class at the beginning of a semester, wearing a leg brace. "Oh, this—hmmm, an oil rig fell on me, sweetheart." He was older than the rest of us and decided to finish high school while recuperating. Chips—a real movie star nickname. He amused me with his charming wiles—"Can you help me with this grammar here? Can you help me write this essay? Could I look over your notes?" I could. I did. He was a grown-up, head and shoulders above the callow boys all around me. I loved his stories of dalliances with movie goddesses (made up, I suppose) and his days in Hollywood. I was still just a kid in bobby sox and hardly his type, but something about me appealed to him. We had a Prince-Stoops-to-Ella-Cinders-in-the-Ashes kind of relationship and it went on for a long time.

I suffered while he nonchalantly discussed other girlfriends with me. When we were necking, I obeyed his injunctions. "Don't look at me! Don't look at me! Let's not get emotionally involved." I knew somehow he was lonely, loved to talk and show off, needed my admiration. So I was always there for him.

He had been places and done things and seen things so there was nothing I wouldn't do just to hear his stories. But Daddy couldn't stand him. "Too slick!" "Too old for you." "What does he want with you?" "Why do you fall for these phonies?"

Sloan would be out watering the front yard with a garden hose when Chips would drive up and honk. I'd burst out the door and run for whatever convertible he had commandeered. "Gentlemen do not honk for ladies. Gentlemen come up to the door. Ladies stay inside." Chips and I would escape and I'd breathe a sigh of relief because I knew Sloan was perfectly capable of turning the hose on both of us.

Then there was Dave, introduced to me by Chips. When Chips learned I'd taken up with Dave while he was dating some beauty queen in Dallas, he flew into a jealous rage from which our friendship never recovered. Daddy thought Dave was even worse than Chips. "A total faker," he pronounced, after inspecting a sales notebook my new beau had carelessly left in our living room. "This deadbeat hasn't made a sale in over a month!" I forget now what Dave was selling, but I was enthralled by his sophistication. He had been to New York. I loved his Countess Mara ties, and the fact that he took me to buy pajamas and as we left the store he handed me the top while he kept the bottom. I had just seen this happen in the 1938 Claudette Colbert–Gary Cooper movie *Bluebeard's Eighth Wife,* and it made me feel like a million bucks.

I should add that all these guys I dated were fabulous dancers, as males had to be in the forties. In those swinging days of Benny Goodman, Harry James, Artie Shaw, Jimmie Lunceford, this was important. And I was a good dancer, too, thanks to the patience of James and his three best pals—Rector Generalski, Greene Simpson and John Hart. They taught me so well that even though I was just a skinny, gawky kid, there was at least one thing about me boys really liked. I could "cut a rug."

My first real boyfriend had been a bantamweight named Jack Tobin. His sister, Mary, was one of my pals. Jack became enthralled with me and this was so unusual that it went to my head. I began to lord it over him. If he liked me so much then I must be something special. I preened and swanned around. My father hadn't noticed Jack one way or another, until he saw he was wearing a cross on a chain. Jewelry? On a male person? Roman Catholic at that! Well, neither of our families was happy about our dating, but we persevered. Jack was my most wholesome boy-girl experience, something right out of the Andy Hardy movies. We were all pairing up like teenage crazies as if for the rest of our little bourgeois lives.

And, indeed, my best gal pals—Louise Lewis and Betty Jo Boucher—went on to marry their high school sweethearts. So guess who didn't? Right! Jack Tobin got tired of my pushing him around and found another girl. I suffered for several weeks like Judy Garland on a bad day.

While it lasted, this teenage pregraduation glamour was quite something. We went speedboat riding on Lake Worth. We danced under the twirling silver ball at the Lake Worth Casino. We went to every movie, including ones downtown at the big theater that resembled the Temple of Karnak. We studied together and rode the miniature train at the Forest Park Zoo.

We were innocent and absurd. We petted in V-8 sedans with ample backseats and wondered how far the couple in front was going to go, because after all, no girl dared go further with her date than the other girl on the double date.

And I had some terrific and hilarious adventures in dating with two of my favorite cousins, Bryson Sherrill, Jr., whom I had grown up with, and Charles Smith, who I came to know in high school. We were about the same age. I remember having a "date" with Charles when he came to visit from West Texas. I was aware that in spite of some entertaining kissing, this could not go anywhere. As for Bryson, Jr. (he was actually called "Bubba"), I can still hear his laugh. He was the original "hot pilot" of the forties, saying to his date as he trickily shifted the floor stick shift with his knees, "Well, honey, whaddaya want to do—first?"

I thought he was the cutest, the funniest guy in the world and he has played through my dreams in an erotic fashion all my life. He could never realize how much I admired, and, yes, desired him. But, of course, some things were out of bounds. Still, all these lovely young men gave me a boundless enthusiasm for a phallic vision of love, romance and sex.

Soon, these Galahads would disappear for the duration, some of them permanently. In 1939, the Nazis marched into Poland and World War II began. In that same year, James, Bryson, Jr., Rector, Greene and John entered the Air Corps together (later named the Air Force) to avoid the Selective Service draft. They hoped to become officers and gentlemen.

Only James and Bryson, Jr., would return. The other three would die in combat. Then, in 1940, I graduated from Paschal High into a world thoroughly at war. The U.S. wasn't in it yet, but FDR was giving us plenty of incentive to join the Brits. This world was now my oyster, but I had never liked oysters, and once I got one in my mouth, never knew what to do with it. And so I approached college and the dilemma of what to be when I grew up, all choked up.

PART
TWO

a Memoir

PART

TWO

THE COWBOY COLLEGE

I HAVE ALREADY NOTED THAT the unofficial slogan of the Cowboy Band of Hardin-Simmons University was "Thirteen Times around the Goddamned World!" Some were scandalized by this sacrilege, but H-SU attracted many who yearned to—in the words of Shakespeare—kick against the pricks. That is, rub life the wrong way, back up to the hairbrush.

Just because my pal Katharine "Nursie" Presley was funny and told great tales of her life there was no reason for me to pick up and go. This was a devout Southern Baptist place. I was jumping from the frying pan of Travis Avenue to the fire of a nonsecular college. Chapel was compulsory six days a week. We had an early curfew. There was no swearing, smoking, drinking, card playing, dancing. You could not get in a car without written permission. Also, Abilene was a "dry" Texas town. No liquor, wine or beer was sold unless it was bootleg.

Was I out of my mind?

Aside from the band, H-SU's big claim to fame was its winning football team, which boasted "Bulldog" Turner as a center. Many players went on to pro ball. Both the team and the band were wild and wooly entities whose subliminal raunchiness operated under a kind of holier-than-thou exterior. Lip service rendered to religion was all a "game" and almost everybody knew it, except the pious people running the place. There were a number of religious students, studying for the ministry, but these people were shunned for the most part.

That's just the way it was. So, naturally, H-SU was the perfect place to cut chapel, sneak out after curfew, learn to smoke, drink, play cards, dance—and, yes, get in the cars of strangers. (The latter rule couldn't be enforced since the only way to get from campus to downtown was to hitchhike.)

I don't remember a single course I took or a single teacher at H-SU. I didn't learn a thing except how to make a few lifelong friends and kick up my heels. I made an inspiring and longtime relationship with the redheaded and smart-as-a-whip Bobbie Morris Simms, who I met there when she was only a precocious fifteen or sixteen, and in Nita Mae Boyd Brooks Lewallen, my assigned roomie. And I'll always miss the other real cowgirl I met there—Carolyn Evans Bauer, from a fine West Texas ranching family. She died young, taking her gift for music and poetry with her.

I kept busy for my year and a half in Abilene. I had seldom been out of Fort Worth for the first eighteen years of my life so I worked on developing all kinds of forbidden social skills. I met my first husband there. In time, I left H-SU under a cloud, having amassed forty-nine of the fifty demerits needed for expulsion.

But while pretending I was a freshman student, I had a ball. My roommate, Nita Mae, was a secular beauty whose mother had died too young. Her doting dad, rancher Jack Boyd of Sweetwater, worshipped her. She'd been called Tootie all her life and it had stuck. Usually I called her Tootie Mae, and she called me Lizzie Mae. We went away to her ranch on weekends and rode horses and fell off into cactus beds and made Jack buy us big steak dinners. We were always hungry. We went to rodeos and rattlesnake roundups and Tootie pressed her beautiful Nudie of Hollywood cowboy clothes on me. Jack pressed us into real roundups where old cowhands snipped off the gonads of young calves to keep them from turning into bulls. These select parts were thrown in the "prairie oyster" pail for frying. The bawling little calves had been turned into instant steers, and were ministered to by Tootie and Liz. We would "run the dope bucket," meaning we painted their wounds with black sticky medicine on paintbrushes and sterilized their branding wounds.

Tootie always said, laughing through tears, "Dammit, Liz, you paint my boots more than you paint the calves! Watch what you're doing." At one point she convinced me to gallop at dusk on a frisky quarter horse. I was scared to death. He ran under a telephone pole and the guy-wire to the ground struck me just across the neck, whirling me off so hard I didn't breathe for a minute. Assuring herself that I wasn't quadriplegic, Tootie howled with glee at the grit in my teeth. I decided my career as a cowboy was over; I swore never to get on a horse again.

I did finally take my very first drink—Seagram's and 7UP. I was such a failure at smoking and drinking that I never really much tried the first. I temporarily gave up the second after my first hangover. (I wouldn't take another drink until I had fallen in with a show biz crowd in New York.)

Tootie was easygoing. She let me cover the walls of our dorm room with photos of movie stars. A true girl of the golden west, she thought I was nuts to be so movie mad. She could take 'em or leave 'em. We had a defining moment about the importance of our roots when Tootie fell in love with the University's one sophisticated guy—a gifted saxophone player and jazz aficionado.

"This is terrible," her daddy moaned to me. "I can't leave my Bar Nothing Ranch to her if she marries this sax man. What am I going to do?"

He needn't have worried. Tootie would soon fall in love with the World's Champion Cowboy—Louis Brooks—and Jack Boyd's dynasty was assured. Today, the late Louis and Tootie herself are respected honorees in The Cowboy Hall of Fame.

And I have one of Louis's winning calf-roping belt buckles, which he gave me personally. I had finally touched the fringe of cowboy greatness.

I KNEW HARDIN-SIMMONS WAS WASTING my time and vice versa, but one day, I put my mind to studying. I had seen George Edward Beeman, the tall, dark and handsome right tackle of the football team, and I had been told he was a loner and no girl could get to first base with him. I decided I'd go for a touchdown, to mix a metaphor. I made him my course study.

First I went to the registrar's office and found out what classes he was taking. Then I discovered the buildings those classes were in. When one of my classes let out I'd run like hell just to be near his next exit. I'd breeze by and say, "Hi!" and keep moving. Finally, he saw me so often he began to look for me. And pretty soon—we were an item.

A GANG OF US USED our thumbs to go downtown one Sunday to catch Clark Gable and Lana Turner in the romantic comedy, *Honky Tonk*. On the corner where we always stood to catch a ride back to college, we were too many for the first car that stopped. As the driver sped away, leaving a few of us, he yelled back out the window, "The Japs just bombed Pearl Harbor!!"

"What's Pearl Harbor?" we asked, to no avail. Back in the dorm, we found it on the atlas. Radio reports were terrible, wounding our national pride. Hundreds were dead, ships sunk, Hickam Field all shot up. The next morning, four of us girls met our boyfriends after breakfast. Nobody went to class that day. We were eight, piled into an old V-8 sedan, girls on laps, to hear President Roosevelt announce, "A date which will live in infamy." Japanese envoys had been in Washington on a peace mission. But a state of war now existed between the United States and the Empire of Japan.

The moment the speech ended, we females found ourselves unceremoniously dumped. The guys, including my own peaceable and sweet George Edward, gunned off downtown to enlist. By noon, they belonged to the U.S. Army Air Corps. In days, the majority of male students and teachers were gone from Abilene.

Women became instantly dispensable. Nobody asked what we thought or wanted. There was a war "on," and we were the last item on the agenda. Our guys were gone; we wouldn't hear from them for many days.

Now this Baptist enclave of higher learning seemed more backwater than ever. Soon I had earned more demerits for being caught climbing out a window after curfew and rushing off to the local Polish nightclub where signs read: NO BOOZE. NO SLACKS. NO JITTERBUG PLEASE. With fifty demerits you were expelled, so I simply expelled myself, deciding to join the U.S. at war. It wasn't patriotism, just sheer unadulterated boredom.

WAR AND

MARRIAGE

FREE FROM THE RIGIDITIES OF a religious college
and with a year and a half of "freedom" from family under
my belt, I went from Abilene to Fort Worth. Elizabeth and
Sloan—as I now often called them in a fit of modernity—had
moved down to Gonzales, Texas, where Daddy was buying cotton for a war-engaged cotton mill in this little town of 5000 people. I didn't want to be a small-town girl. With "a war on," I
wanted to be part of it. I decided to pretend I was an adult.

In Fort Worth, Consolidated Vultee was desperate for
workers, even women. They were building badly needed B-24
airplanes that would eventually bomb the oil fields of Ploesti
and help bring Mussolini and Hitler to their knees.

Women? On the assembly line? America was undergo-
ing a sea change in its workforce, one that would change life forever after the war. I was dying to play Rosie the Riveter and
took a tour through the giant plant. Gleaming silver bombers
were being put together amid clang and clamor. I signed up and
found a place to stay with old friends, June Shepherd and her
mother, Lila. They also worked at C-V and they were two single
man crazy, fun-loving women.

Then I was told that working on the actual production line required a hair net. Women with long hair had problems with whirling machinery. I felt I looked an idiot in a hair net—everybody does. My vanity was enormous. So I ended up serving the war effort in a secretarial job instead. C-V didn't care; they were just as needy for typists to do eighty words per minute and I was one of those. I thought the whole thing was an adventure.

And it was. At night, in wartime America, people danced. We had no nylon stockings, so we experimented with leg makeup. Perspiration made it run down into your shoes. One of my 4-F dates wisecracked that the only thing worse than lipstick on his collar was leg makeup on the back of his white suit.

Dating and dancing as if the world might really be coming to an end, I still wrote faithfully to Ed Beeman. He was now a full-fledged bombardier in B-17s out of England. Between missions he wrote me ardent love letters, asking me to marry him "when—if I get back." The *if* got to me. I immediately responded, "Yes—when you get back." That could be light-years, I thought, as I carried Ed's V-mail letter that read: "Honey, the last time I saw Paris, the sky was full of flak!" I thought this was so cute.

TIME MARCHED ON. ALL OF a sudden, my betrothed had flown his twenty-five missions. All of my friends were marrying right and left. Most of them seemed happy. So I suppose I thought that the marriage vow itself had some magic property for happiness. My unexamined life would stumble on to the altar. No guy who had flown twenty-five missions over embattled Europe deserved what Ed Beeman was about to get—me for a wife. But, at the time, I thought I was just peachy keen.

I quit my war job and went to Gonzales to offer my parents another challenge—a twenty-one-year-old's wedding. I picked out silver, china and had bridal showers—all the usual. I moved as if in a dream, or in a movie from which I might wake up and find myself recast. Ed was a handsome war hero with

combat ribbons on his chest and new captain's bars. He invited
Bobby to be his best man and the proud young kid stood up with
him. Sloan seemed thrilled to give me away. Mother preened
herself with new social status in the somewhat closed Gonzales
society. Some part of me kept saying, "When this Baptist ceremony is all over I can just go back to normal, to being me."
Whatever that was! Of course, it's not as if nothing good and exciting didn't happen. We went to Santa Monica on our honeymoon. The Air Corps put us in a gorgeous ocean-front hotel,
debriefed their captain, and we saw Hollywood. At night we hit
the clubs. Trying to get into Slapsie Maxie's on the strip or to
see Sophie Tucker, I got quite a kick when we were stopped at
the door. "Captain, you can't bring a kid in here."

Ed said, "This is my wife."

I had to send for my birth certificate to prove I was
twenty-one. And then when we went to Grauman's Chinese
Theater, my feet in high heels fit perfectly into Tom Mix's boot
steps in the concrete.

We ended up in Alamogordo, New Mexico. Now my
captain was busy from dawn to dusk training green B-29 flight
crews. He gave them the vast benefit of his many missions flying over Germany in a B-17. They were going to bomb Japan in
the coming invasion.

My life consisted of reading *The Joy of Cooking* every
afternoon before we went out to dinner. Both of us were desperate for diversion from one another. I had quickly "done" Alamogordo—the bowling alley was the only big attraction. I went
shopping for privileged goods at the PX, flirted with handsome
grounded officers who couldn't fly for one reason or another,
then I'd meet Ed at the officer's club for dinner and too many
drinks. Numbed by my own uselessness, I took a job for the Air
Corps in something called Air Inspection. I typed lists all day.
Life was pretty humdrum, although the Office of Strategic Service* had men prowling the local bars looking for people who
talked too much or could be blackmailed. New Mexico, it

*It later became the C.I.A.

seemed, was awash in important secrets. Now and then we went to El Paso for fun, or up to the mountains of Ruidoso. Our favorite spot was one of the most unusual national parks in the U.S. The White Sands of Alamogordo were open to the public then, day and night. We'd bury bottles of beer and wine in the ice-cold hills of white gypsum sand that had been blowing off the mountains for eons. It had formed a white "necklace" in the desert, and under a full moon this was a thrilling and romantic place. For me it was a mindless time. My new husband wanted to forget the horrible things he'd experienced in the Eighth Air Force—the men killed on his missions, his own tortured moments hunched over the bombsight with Germany beneath him. He wouldn't discuss anything substantive about his time abroad. He deflected my curiosity with tales of London in the Blitz or how much he'd admired the singer Vera Lynn, or harking back to our idiotic college days. We had arguments over his having adopted the European use of knife and fork. He never mentioned Japan, but I knew he was dreading the coming invasion.

My life was my new freedom from family as a grown-up wife to a war hero who had earned his Air Medal. There was the glamour of crushed Air Corps caps in a pile, and men who wore battered flight jackets and elegant gabardine pants called "pinks." They were men who moaned in their sleep and smoked nervously. They swore and drank Scotch and said "fuck." They were all about mindless "fun" and I was all about getting some more gas coupons and keeping up with the latest in swing music, plus playing Myrna Loy, without much success. I thought if I didn't look shocked or dismayed when they set up fourteen stingers on the Ruidoso bar and threatened to drink them all at once, I could get away with playing the perfect wife.

In the predawn of July 16, 1945, a shattering blast literally knocked us out of bed in the little frame house we shared with an officer named Moskowitz and his gorgeous blonde Copacabana showgirl wife. We all ran outside in nightclothes but couldn't see a thing. Later, a formal statement avowed that an ammunition dump had exploded. The blast had shattered windows eighty-nine miles away in El Paso.

Three weeks later, on August 6th, when the U.S. dropped the atom bomb on Hiroshima, we realized we had been present—asleep, in fact—at The Creation. The first atomic bomb had blown us out of bed when it exploded in the Los Alamos desert, up above Alamogordo. The Manhattan Project, which none of us even knew existed, had reached fruition. It was no wonder there were undercover men in the bars.

No wonder Ed had often come home from training missions saying, "You know, Babe, there's something out there in that goddamn desert they won't let us fly over. What could it be in that goddamn desert?"

I reacted to his irritating profanity. Prissily, I asked, "Why do you refer to it as that goddamn desert?"

He'd laugh. "Because that's all it is!"

So now we knew the desert was the site of the first Atomic Bomb—capital letters. This bomb had worked and President Truman ordered one of the only other two dropped on Hiroshima. Three days later, August 9th, we dropped our last one on Nagasaki. The Japanese didn't know that was all we had: They surrendered. But in that moment of epic tragedy, we thought only that it was good news. It meant no invasion of Japan.

When we read of the seared Japanese civilians, we didn't even flinch. We still remembered the Bataan death march. The casualty lists of Saipan and Guadalcanal were fresh in our minds, though we hadn't heard then of the writer John Hersey, or of radiation sickness, or of mutual deterrence. We didn't know we were living through a modern apocalypse. It was the end of innocence, however, and there was no turning back. The genie was out of the bottle. We still lifted many glasses in celebration that week.

Years later I went back to Alamogordo to visit the one friend I'd made there, Margaret Burch. She was a New Mexican who extolled the virtues of being a "Yankee." She'd say, "Go North, Tex. That's where it's at." Looking around Alamogordo in the sixties, I couldn't believe how much enjoyment I'd actually had in this unassuming place. I was surprised to find the residents had posted on the outskirts of town a large sign reading: ALAMOGORDO—HOME OF THE ATOM BOMB.

By then I had learned that this was a dubious distinction. I was already living through what the anthropologist Margaret Mead came to call "the REAL generation gap." This consisted of those born before and those born after the Bomb. It came to be my own demarcation line. It was the first time I realized that maybe I had better grow up.

ALAMOGORDO WENT GIDDY WITH DELIGHT over the Japanese surrender. The big B-29s would now probably never be put to use. Los Alamos didn't have to worry anymore that they'd only made three atom bombs and used them all up. Ed wasn't going to have to risk his life again. This comforted me to the point where I could let myself think about what *I* wanted. The marriage had lasted over a year: long enough for me to know it wasn't working for me. I was bored. I wanted a divorce. I'd tried to discuss this but my darling would just tousle my hair, or hug me and say something profoundly hopeless like, "Oh, Babe. Don't talk like that."

We had invited some former college classmates to come party with us in Ruidoso. One dizzy, sweet girl named Billie Edwards decided she and Ed would each take a chaw of tobacco. We were driving to Ruidoso and we knew they were just showing off. We forced them out of the car. So they sat on the back fenders. It was a dumb move for adults. The driver forgot about them, made a sudden turn and the next thing we knew, Billie and Ed were sprawled in the winding road behind us. We rushed back to them. Both were holding their heads, moaning. Because they had swallowed the tobacco, both were sick and vomiting.

At the hospital, Billie had a fractured skull and Ed a serious concussion. I went to see him every day and finally the doctor assured me he'd be fine. So, I sat down by his bed, took his hand and told him I was leaving him. I planned to go to Gonzales, I said. I didn't know what I'd do, but I'd be in touch. I promised him he would be happy with a better woman than I was. He cried. I cried. The war was over and so were we.

I left Alamogordo—where I seemed to be desperately wanted—for Texas, where absolutely nobody would even want to see me. Scared to death and terribly ashamed for what I had wrought and was leaving behind, I got on a bus and went home.

HIGHER

AND HIGHER

EDUCATION

NOW I WAS A FISH out of water indeed. I had gone where—when there is no place else to go—they have to take you in. Mother and Daddy did, of course. But I could no longer pretend to be a wife. I had no career, no skills beyond stenographic ones, no aspirations even.

I found I didn't mind being in Gonzales. It had an old-fashioned rather Southern air. It was an okay place to escape to, a nifty hideout from reality. I was fascinated as well with its important history.*

My parents had loved Ed Beeman. They were not glad to see me in these circumstances. They couldn't believe I didn't want to "work at" my marriage and "fix it." Disappointed was an

---

*Gonzales was called "The Lexington of Texas." Here the early Texicans, as J. Frank Dobie named them, stood their ground, refusing to give in when the ruling Mexican Army demanded their cannon. Gonzales made a flag that read COME AND TAKE IT! And finally, near the Santa Anna Ford on the nearby Guadalupe River, the first shot of the Revolution of 1836 was fired. Later, a majority of men from Gonzales marched sixty-five miles on foot to defend the Alamo in San Antonio. They died there to a man.

understatement. I was twenty-two, but very much still a dependent child who had never grown up.

The idea of divorce intruded on their new sense of well-being. Sloan and the wealthy Ainsworth family, who dominated Gonzales and owned the local cotton mill, were manufacturing a heavy ducking called "osenberg"—for army tents, gunnery sacks and rough usage. Sloan bought cotton with the mill's money. If cotton prices went up, Sloan and the Ainsworths sold what he'd bought and took the profit. If prices fell, they consigned the lot to be made into whatever the army ordered. I called this "speculating" with Uncle Sam's money. But no one thought he was more patriotic than my darling little daddy. He didn't see a conflict. The business of America is business, was a motto he'd lived by long before Calvin Coolidge thought it up.

Although I had no moral ground to stand on, throughout the war I had liked to rag my feisty father. "Isn't that speculating?" I'd ask.

He'd just stare at me. "I see you're still here eating at this speculator's table." I'd fall silent. No moral ground.

And maybe it was this fling that inflated Sloan's urge to gamble. He took more chances and was always looking for "a big score." He bet wildly on horses and could be heard dissecting his selections as if it were a science. "Never discount Calumet!" he'd opine over the *Daily Racing Form.* "That Elizabeth Arden is a smart woman. She knows what she's doing when it comes to horses," he'd say of the cosmetic queen whose own champion had bitten off one of her fingertips.

Sloan was now often off at the Maceo gambling casinos of Galveston where he'd inevitably lose at roulette and blackjack. But he often came home loaded down with poker or crap winnings. Money would be gushing out of his hand-tooled Lucchese boots where he'd stuffed it for safekeeping.

I then discovered my mother looking teary with her hands full of mail. "You know I just don't think it's right for the *Baptist Standard* and the *Daily Racing Form* to come in the same mailbox." But she didn't complain too much either—no moral ground. She was also at the speculator's table and now had her own little agenda of social climbing, devout church-going and good works to validate her prestige. (She did well. Single-handedly she raised money to save and restore the Gonzales Public Library. Yet I don't think she ever read any book except the Bible.)

The Nazis had surrendered back in May. Now that the Japanese had quit, many felt discombobulated and at loose ends.

I sat around listlessly until Sloan said, a bit sarcastically, "Maybe you'd like to get serious, Mrs. Beeman. H-SU doesn't seem to have left a mark on you. Why not start over at the University of Texas? It's close to home." Then he extended his cotton-calloused hand with $1,500 cash. "I won this on a horse named Soapstix. It'd pay your first semester's tuition."

I leapt at the offer. But I couldn't sit around until fall so I went to the Warm Springs Polio Hospital in nearby Ottine and began typing medical records. The facility had the same natural hot sulphur springs as Warm Springs, Georgia, and was full of patients felled by a recent outbreak of poliomyelitis.

Some were only affected minimally; others were in iron lungs. Some became quadriplegics and paraplegics. Dr. Jonas Salk hadn't then discovered his vaccine and the disease was frightening in its relentless winnowing process.

I would handle the forms, sent by doctors all over Texas, on the patient's arrival. They'd read: "Right arm: Unaffected; Left arm: Unaffected; Right leg: 95% affected, etc." I'd begin to cramp and tense as I typed. I wanted every patient to be okay. But in time I came to rejoice that paraplegics weren't quadriplegics.

The hospital's nurses were a cadre of the most warm-hearted, caring, considerate and fun-loving young souls I'd ever met. After each shift, they'd break into pairs and parties and go off in great spirits to pub-crawl through the honky-tonks in Cuero, Luling, Shiner and Seguin. They especially liked the Ranch House, the only "nightclub" in Gonzales, with its Spanish moss hanging from great pecan trees over an alfresco slate dance floor. These nurses never took anything seriously except their work and even that they conducted without sentiment.

I suffered over "my patients." I'd force myself to visit every day until they recovered or went home to live disabled lives. The nurses laughed at me: "Tex, you've got to develop a philosophy. It doesn't help for you to suffer for the patients. Empathy is wasted. Don't feel their pain or try to imagine it. Just be there for them, talk straight to them. Act normal with them; that's what they want."

Act normal; talk straight. Later, I would realize that this cadre of nurses, who had come en masse from Louisiana and were the happiest campers I'd ever seen, were about ninety percent gay. I had never even heard the word *gay,* except in its joyous dictionary sense, and when they used the word, I thought they were referring to their genial dispositions. Not one of them tried to enlighten me.

In September, I was happy to leave my depressing job and go back to college. I signed up for a journalism degree because the U of T actually had such a thing. Remembering my idol, Walter Winchell, and the newspapers I'd created as a kid, it seemed as good an idea as any.

I didn't know one single person in Austin or at the university. I was green and starting fresh. The U of T had a few dormitories, but most people were assigned to rooming houses with a housemother and dorm rules. I moved into one only blocks from the main drag, a street that fronts onto the path leading to the administration building—and the now notorious tower.*

I instantly loved the look of the campus, which had a traditional forty acres, though actually oil money had made the university rich and it was much bigger than that. (I couldn't know then that the expression "40 Acres" would be the making of me at this center of learning.)

Every night I said a little prayer of thanks for Soapstix and for Sloan—because they had given me such a marvelous chance to finally amount to something.

---

*Later, in 1966, Charles Whitman would kill twelve people and wound thirty-three others using a rifle atop this tower. It has only recently been reopened to the public.

.   .   .

AT FIRST THE BEAUTIFUL CAMPUS with its live oak
trees was oddly quiet and deserted. I might go a week without
talking to anyone. I was still married; I was older and not feeling
like making new friends. I was past being "collegiate" and didn't
suffer the girls in my "house" gladly. They all seemed so giddy
and immature. And it was strange for the U.S. not to be at war.

But, what a relief: I had forgotten what my brother James
even looked like; he'd been in Greenland as a weather observer
for so long. Soon he'd be coming back. Sometimes I'd take a
bus to Gonzales for the weekend. Now Mother and Daddy
seemed reconciled to me and would even listen to my new intel-
lectualizing and theorizing and how I was learning this or that.
They didn't care for my radical ideas—maybe former v-p Henry
Wallace would make a good president! ("Why, he's a Commie
red!" said Sloan.) I thought Negroes should be allowed to go to
the university; how could they get a "separate but equal" education elsewhere in Texas? ("Hogwash!" said Daddy.) Nevertheless,
the Smiths seemed proud to have a child "in the university."

At first there were almost no males on campus. Only
geezers and prodigies exemplified by the song Bette Davis had
sung in a 1943 movie *Thank Your Lucky Stars*: The lyrics said,
"They're Either Too Young or Too Old."

But then, veterans started appearing—men who had lain
in foxholes and advanced in tanks and gone down in submarines
and landed in flaming airplanes and been bored to death in the
infantry. They were all coming on the new G.I. Bill. Uncle Sam
was offering the chance for a free college education and scores
took him up on it.

At first they arrived wearing old civilian clothes mixed
with government issue. Soon they became a flood. Classes
swelled to eighty people in a course with guys sitting out on
steps, listening to a teacher they couldn't see. We grew to
20,000 and Austin took on a shine of excitement. These were
grown men and I enjoyed every minute of their arrival.

Eventually, my divorce was granted for $50 by a jaundiced judge who eyed my complaint of "incompatibility" and drawled, "Mare Lisbeth, do you swear this is the truth, the whole truth and nothing but the truth?" I crossed my fingers behind my back and said, "I do, Your Honor." He banged down his gavel. "Granted!"

I was no longer Liz Beeman and he let me take back my maiden name. It was very freeing to be an anonymous Smith again.

I examined my new classmates who had looked death in the face, eaten C rations and written V-mail as they waited for the lights to go on again all over the world. And I wondered what trouble I could get into next. Believe me, it wasn't at all what I expected.

COMING BACK TO LIFE AFTER my freshman year, I decided to be aggressive. I went to the office of the college humor magazine, *The Texas Ranger*. There was a wild man there who had on an orange jumpsuit, open to the waist. He seemed in charge. I tried to avoid examining his expansive chest hair and said I wanted to write for *The Ranger*. "I'm John Bryson," he barked. "I'm the editor. What do you want to write?" I told him the Warner Bros. movie star Zachary Scott had been a U of T alum and a story on him would be interesting. "You're on!" yelled the wild man.

I came to enjoy Bryson in spite of his fixation on dirty jokes. He was one of those ugly guys with true sex appeal, the mind of an anarchist, the heart of a child. But he didn't stick around. He was too talented. A story of his on college cheating caught the eye of *Life* editors and soon he was off to work for Henry Luce.*

My Zach Scott story over my first byline in *The Ranger* signaled a new life for me. I looked down my nose at the sorority-frat crowd and the football crazies, but began to love

Bryson became in time a great photographer; perhaps you recall his photo of Ernest Hemingway kicking a can.

my classes and the idea of learning. I divided loyalties between the Journalism School and the Drama Department. I met another *Ranger* editor, Bill Yates, who would go on to glory when he replaced Mort Walker, the creator of the cartoon *Beetle Bailey*. And finally I met *The Ranger*'s Floyd Wade: a good-looking, suave and sophisticated guy with a girlfriend named Scotty Robinson. Even on into my New York life, these two people would have a deep effect on me.

To all who entered their orbit, they were like Scott and Zelda Fitzgerald, disturbing and vitalizing. Scotty was a Southern belle from Missouri. She arrived scattering cigarette ashes and putting an "o" on the end of everything. "Liz-O," she named me. And Floyd pronounced that I had the best byline name he'd ever heard. "It's a natural!" Scotty and Floyd were glamorous for their time. They had their lives planned. He'd become another Henry Luce; she'd become a famous artist.

They would be rich, famous, married with kids. But for now they were just experts in the nonchalant drinking and living it up of college life. They were also better read than most. I adored them. Floyd decided I should be his associate editor, but the entire university student body elected the editors of *The Ranger*. So Floyd dreamed up a campaign to get me the job. The campus was overrun with signs: FOR A GOOD TIME, CALL LIZ SMITH. LIZ! SHE'S A PEACHY DANCER! This didn't get me elected, but got me known. The guy who was elected defaulted and I inherited the job anyway.

The university had a fine journalism reputation and under the popular Professor DeWitt C. Reddick set out to teach us, on the job, how to be reporters, researchers, feature writers, columnists, photographers, editors. (Media studies in the form of TV and radio were yet to be born.) We put out an excellent newspaper, *The Daily Texan*. (Some said it was the best daily in all of conservative Texas.) Dr. Reddick liked me and somehow I ended up writing a column called "40 Acres." The editors gave me my head. They never censored me. I formed a headstrong taste for trivia, rumor, jokes, smart sayings, gossip and anything else I considered to be "news." It was a heady experience.

Outside of studying *Hamlet* with one of the last of the great Shakespearean authorities, B. Iden Payne, I had no business at all with the Drama Department. But I made friends there that I have today. Many are household names. There's Pat Hingle, who you see in many movies. He was Commissioner Gordon of the recent *Batman* films. There is the one and only Rip Torn. There is actress Barbara Barrie, who went on to be nominated for two Oscars as best supporting actress. Despite her talent, she'd still be unknown today but for playing Brooke Shields's grandma in TV's *Suddenly Susan*. Our really budding Hollywood star was a divine blonde cookie, Jayne Mansfield. And there was Kathryn Grant. She acted, emoted and met Bing Crosby and wed him. There was a tall, handsome hunk, Fess Parker, who became TV's Davy Crockett, and is now a major California wine maker. But my close pals were Tommy Jones and Harvey Schmidt. Tom was a wicked wit from Coleman, Texas. He and Harvey went on to compose and collaborate on what became the longest-running musical in world theater history—*The Fantasticks*—and another, *I Do! I Do!* for Mary Martin and Robert Preston. And from Journalism came cartoonists Rowland Wilson, Bill Yates, and Robert Benton, who went on to become a major screenwriter and movie director.

(Benton says today that I was "the first movie star type" he'd ever met. So why, when he won the Oscar for *Kramer vs. Kramer,* didn't he thank me instead of his wife, Sallie?) Journalism also brought forth Ronnie Dugger, who created the liberal gadfly mag *The Texas Observer* and then Cactus Pryor, still a major player in Austin as a local radio TV voice.

Was there something in the water at the University of Texas in the late nineteen forties?

MY DIVORCE HAD MORE OR less revived me and I became again the social creature I normally am. I began to feel I "belonged" and was a part of it all. Then—bang, something incredible happened. I fell in love. My actress friend Holland Taylor says that falling in love is like being hit by a truck. Well, that was me. I was flat. The only problem was ... the object of my affection was a woman.

The details are ordinary. I believed down deep inside that such an amazing thing had never happened before to anyone and so did she. Neither of us stopped to feel guilty, just a bit confused. Neither had the sense—culturally, historically, psychologically or even through examining history and literature—to discover what this phenomenon was or where we could possibly hope to go with it. Still, we were definitely living in the Bible Belt. Religion was king in the late forties, even at a secular state school, so we had enough "smarts" to keep it to ourselves. We had no confidantes.

To make matters more complicated, this fellow student was engaged to an army officer still overseas. Part of the time we were fixated on one another. Another part of the time, she was planning her wedding, wondering if she'd recognize Mr. Right when he got back.

The usual things happened that always happen in a highly charged, incipiently tragic, dangerous emotional relationship trying to defy convention. We were often apart and we wrote love letters. Our smartly suspicious parents all but simultaneously twigged that their offspring had become deranged. They decided to read our mail. And that was all she wrote, as my friend Dan Rather would say.

The first thing we knew, both families were in active alert to separate us. She suddenly left school and went home. She was so shattered by her loss of face with her fine, upstanding, beloved good Christian family that she instantly capitulated to all their wishes and demands. They told her she had no choice, having been influenced by an unscrupulous "older person who had been divorced." We must never see each other again. Both of us must ask God's forgiveness. This may have been proper, but I was in the full rebellion of true love. (Or maybe just in love by myself?)

After a few abortive tries, she refused to speak with me or even to say good-bye. In time I saw that as a good pragmatic move. But now my mother—in desperate conferences with the loved one's parents—came to Austin to "bring me home to Gonzales for the end of term." Bobby was now a precocious, horny, impossibly handsome teenager—catnip to girls and aching to run away and join the Merchant Marine (which he eventually did). Mother had Bobby with her and I wondered why? Didn't she have enough problems with me? She sent him off on an errand and gave me an old-fashioned Baptist Sunday-go-to-meeting-come-to-Jesus talking to. I had committed a sin, a blasphemy against nature. I tried to stand my ground, to be loyal to my feelings. I thought if I could make her see how strong and pure my feelings were, she'd understand. But the more she wept and prayed, the more I saw how useless it was—hopeless. "You have broken your father's heart," she kept saying. I didn't need help getting to Gonzales, but realized that she wisely wanted her showdown with me away from my volatile father. She had probably said to him, "Let me handle it."

Finally, driving to Gonzales past fields of ubiquitous blue-bonnets, I sat in the backseat with Bobby. He took my hand and squeezed it. Then whispered, "*Illegitimati non carborundum!*"*

This was the only time I cried a little bit.

I have never told Bobby what his support meant to me so I'll just say here it meant everything. He was in my corner; I knew I could go on. My father just looked at me as I came in the front door and then left the room. For three months that summer he never spoke to me, not even at meals. It was during this awful time that Bobby suddenly, unexpectedly began showing up for every occasion to stand between me and reality. He'd be full of brass and chatter, jokes about the Aggies and the local gentry. He was a diplomat on a mission. He even talked of cars and football, those two inevitable Texas topics he knew I disdained.

---

* *"Don't let the bastards wear you down."*

"Have you ever been over to Shiner to try their beer? You know down here they call it 'China.' They say, 'Let's go get some of that good China beer.'" Trying to act relaxed, I asked if the beer had a man on horseback with the horse rearing up? Bobby would wisecrack, "No, that's another beer—the only beer with a picture of the factory right there on the bottle."

Mother would caution, "Bobby..."

He'd tell us all the local gossip—how the man who owned the funeral parlor had a mistress in the beauty salon. She complained he was stingy and he said, "Listen! There are Mexicans living on a cracker a day would like to have what you have." Or he'd talk of rich locals, the Michaelsons, who owned the café and bus stop. "Their son, Ikey, died and they told his siblings he was now an angel in heaven. One day there was a rare snowstorm and one of the kids, who'd never seen snow, but had seen Gonzales's many chicken-plucking factories, ran out screaming, 'Look, look, up in heaven they're picking little Ikey.'"

Daddy couldn't resist Bobby and he'd start laughing in spite of himself. But he never looked at me or talked to me. My mother had already done her thing. Now she became saintly in her loving care for me. I was amazed at this exercise of true Christian charity, but I knew it was sincere. The ordeal was over for her. She had spoken her piece. Now, like Jesus, she would forgive seven times seventy. If I would, in the words of the future, "don't ask, don't tell," she'd be fine. She hated the sin but loved me, the sinner. I appreciated her; I had to. In many respects she was the kindest and wisest of women.

She would glance at Sloan in pain and consternation that he seemed so implacable. I knew their private moments discussing me must have been hell. I was sorry. But by now I was determined to go on being their child. I wanted to graduate. I wanted and needed their financial support. I worked part-time that summer typing abstracts for real estate. I studied. I suffered. I had given up on love—or vice versa. Sometimes I thought of the gay nurses at Warm Springs, but no—it hadn't been like that for me. There was nothing "gay" about it. Idealistically, I had experienced the full-blown romantic heartbreak star-crossed lovers megillah. I had what Christopher Morley called "The Mortal Pang" in his book *Kitty Foyle*.*

On the day I was gratefully going back to Austin for the new semester, Sloan silently came toward me, handing me a set of new car keys. There was a maroon Plymouth sitting in the drive. Cars are so important in Texas that the symbolism of this staggered me. He spoke to me for the first time in three months. "Mary Elizabeth, I thought you could use this for your final year at the university. Good luck. Be careful. The horses have been lucky lately."

I looked at the keys, at him, and said, "Thanks. This is wonderful—Daddy." I drove away, however, without kissing him good-bye. Somehow I didn't feel a twinge of conscience even though he was supporting—oversupporting—me. I felt cold, as if part of me was frozen. The next time we met, we acted as if nothing had ever happened between us. We were now all grown up, polite and minding our own business. Soon we became pointedly affectionate again. We always had been in our family and now wasn't the time to undo that. The punishing parent-child thing had died of overkill.

Yet after this, I don't believe I ever said an unfettered, open, frank or totally honest word to either of my parents again. I told them what they wanted to hear. I was careful with their feelings, their prejudices, their beliefs and value systems. I had to admire them although I couldn't share all of their beliefs. I didn't care to rock their boat. I realized how generous they both were, how shaped they were by their own standards and morals and background. And in a way, like most generations separated by years, we could never fully come to terms. I had broken their

A daring work for its time, the thirties, where a male writer gets into the head of a gutsy and determined young Irish girl who falls for a member of the Main Line uppercrust. It tells how she recovers, goes to New York, makes her own fame and fortune. This novel became a mantra for me after age sixteen.

hearts and they had broken mine. We were very reserved and careful ever after.

I loved having the Plymouth until one day, many months later, Sloan suddenly appeared in Austin saying, "Honey, I need your car. I'm a little overextended. I'm sorry." I said, "It's okay, Daddy, come easy, go easy." (This was his joke about poor guys picking cotton all week, being paid, shooting craps and losing on the first throw, lifting their empty hands to say, "Come easy, go easy.")

He laughed and drove away in what had been "my car." I learned later he had taken Mother's car, too, and one he had given to Bobby. The bookies must have been hot on his trail.

ONE PIECE OF U OF T lore I loved concerned the inscription chiseled over the Administration Building. It bore the words of Jesus: "Ye shall know the truth and the truth shall make you free." It was said that the Board of Regents had wanted this taken off to be replaced by a statement from Nietzsche: "Discipline is the foundation of the state." Fortunately, Nietzsche, beloved by Hitler, wasn't too popular after World War II.

I became involved in what my father referred to as "radical" campus activities. But now my hitherto useless enthusiasm for "The Race" amounted to something. In 1946, a postman named Heman Marion Sweatt decided he wanted to come to the U of T. The problem—Mr. Sweatt was black. He was told to get a separate but equal education elsewhere. He protested that he couldn't. A lot of students, including me, protested too. We raised all kinds of hell. Mr. Sweatt finally won his case using the University's great rare books collection as an example of the quality he could only find in Austin. (The University was awash in beautiful tomes and classics. It had bought two rare Gutenberg Bibles from Russia early in the thirties, outbidding the Library of Congress. Magnanimously, then, the University gave one to the USA.) In September 1950, after I had left school, Mr.

Sweatt broke the race barrier and entered the Law School. When I go back and find a statue to Dr. Martin Luther King on today's campus, I think of Heman Sweatt, who paved the way for the end of segregation in Texas, long before the Civil Rights Act of 1964. And I am proud of my small part in that.

ON MY LAST CHRISTMAS AT the university, the Smiths gathered in Lamesa, Texas, where Sloan had business. Only James was missing; he had returned from the war, married and was beginning his own family in South Texas.

Lamesa means *the table* in Spanish, and the land in West Texas was as flat as a tabletop. We took two cars—Mother and Daddy in one, Bobby and me in another—to drive over to Midland to visit the Simms family. Bobby was at the wheel; I was in the front right "death seat" reading *Time* magazine. "Do we have to go so fast?" I asked just before he pulled off onto the shoulder to avoid a car that had stopped in front of us. Whammo! We had smashed into a vehicle on the shoulder that had run out of gas. A deathly still silence followed and then I heard water running. It was me, bleeding on the seat. Bobby had sagged onto the steering wheel, his knees having cut perfect slits through his pants. I could hardly see and since Bobby didn't answer, I thought maybe he was dead. I struggled out of the car. Our parents had heard the sound of the crash behind them and turned back. They loaded Bobby into the front seat, seemingly unconscious, and I got in the back with Mother holding a handkerchief to my forehead. "Don't," I said, "it hurts too much." I was covered with slivers of shattered windshield.

As I walked into the emergency room of the Lamesa hospital, I got a look at myself: Hamburger for face. They took me to the emergency room. Bobby wasn't dead; but he did have a concussion. The doctor who examined us said, "I was afraid of this on Christmas eve. It's a good thing I have saved lots of plastic surgery thread and needles for you." He began sewing me up without anesthetic because they assumed I was in shock. At midpoint, he stopped his team and made them all rescrub and re-glove. In the end I had 110 stitches in my face, a broken jaw and would lose ten teeth. But as there were no seat belts in those days, I was extremely lucky. "We thought you might die," said the doctor, explaining why I couldn't have anesthetic. I laughed. I wasn't about to die.

For three days I resembled "The Mummy," but when they uncovered me, the doctor sat there, saying, "Beautiful! Beautiful!" Actually I looked like a basketball with appropriate stitching. But the massive doses of the new drug penicillin made my face heal almost overnight.

Bobby was very unhappy, saying that he had "hurt" me. But I said, "Don't be an idiot. We must lead charmed lives." Now I had to go home to Gonzales with no front teeth and so began my long anterior life in dental chairs the world over. I missed taking my final exams, but eventually made this up and left the U of T with a BJ degree and more than enough credits for a Masters. But I never wrote the thesis; my thesis was to be life as it is lived.

THROUGH THIS LITTLE TRIBULATION, MY glamorous classmate, Scotty Robinson, had been stuck at home in St. Louis waiting and calling me. She wanted to go to New York to join Floyd Wade, who was already there, but her mother insisted she have a "chaperone." And I was it. Finally, I took the only money I had, $50, after buying a one-way train ticket and, scars and all, set out for New York. By then, Scotty had already escaped her mother's bonds and gone on ahead of me to join Floyd.

My enormous love affair with New York City was on the verge and I had some dazzling new front teeth to start out with, plus a great exaltation at leaving Texas and just being alive.

PART

THREE

a Memoir

WHICH WAY'S

TOWN?????

SOME OF MY FRIENDS HAVE suggested the above should be the title of this memoir. But Texans hate to emphasize how "hicky" they really are.

A very tired Liz arrived in Penn Station about 11:30 one night in September of 1949. I'd been sitting up on a train for three days. I had two suitcases and there was no one there to meet me, although, of course Floyd and Scotty had "promised." By then I should have known that a few martinis tended to make them forgetful.

I struggled to a telephone booth and called their hotel, which was in some lower depth of Manhattan's East Twenties. A strange man promptly tried to get into the booth with me. "This is starting out just great," I grumbled, holding my luggage and fending off this masher.

Okay, no answer at the hotel room. I hobbled off for a taxi and traveled through dark and dismal narrow streets to the address. As I arrived, so did Floyd and Scotty, flushed and jubilant. We fell on one another and after much talk, went to bed in a single room; they in one bed, me in the other.

The next morning, the story goes, I rushed to the window, looked out into gray nothingness at the building across the narrow street and asked, "Which way's town?"

I don't know that I did this. It has become legend. But I do recall I was disappointed at the bleakness, wondering where the bright lights might be? Floyd had a car because he was working in Teaneck, New Jersey, so the second night he drove us right into the heart of Times Square where the Camel cigarette guy was blowing smoke rings and every lightbulb in the world was burning. I remembered G.K. Chesterton's quote: "What a garden of delights this place would be if only one could not read!" I had found—town. It was thatta way, in Times Square.

Floyd then drove us to a small Greenwich Village restaurant where we were taken up by a handsome man who was more interested in Floyd than in me or Scotty. When she and I went to the ladies' room, she fixed me with her enormous evocative eyes and said smartly, "Liz-O, I think the guy buying us drinks is just as queer as a five-dollar bill." This was a typical Scottyism.

I said, "A five-dollar bill is not queer. Do you mean a two-dollar bill?"

She nodded. Then she burst out laughing. "Isn't New York wonderful?"

It was. Indeed it was.

As days passed, we looked for jobs by day and by night sampled the jazz world's Birdland and Marie's Crisis (a landmark hotspot downtown) and anyplace else where we could afford to nurse a drink all evening. New York grew more and more enthralling. I had envisioned hanging out with the Algonquin Roundtable crowd, but of course, they were no longer extant for the most part. As time went by I would encounter the still living Dorothy Parker, the real George S. Kaufman, the theater legend George Jean Nathan, but many of my literary idols were dead. One man I had wanted to know was Franklin P. Adams, who had written "The Conning Tower," a column I would try to emulate. But I realized New York has one Golden Age after another and different heroes for different times.

For the first three months, I couldn't quite believe where

I was. This was the Emerald City of Oz. It was all too thrilling, different and unknown. The horrid, dark little flat on West 81st Street that Scotty and I began sharing with a girl we'd selected out of the want ads couldn't contain me. I had spent much of my life supine—reading. But now I couldn't concentrate to read anything. I'd try, and the dim roar that was Manhattan outside on Central Park West would interfere. Soon, I'd find myself running down the stone steps, pausing to listen to the thunder of the subway entrance, wondering what to do, where to go, how to seize the nettle that was The City?

Soon I got a job typing at the National Orchestral Association because I needed a paycheck. And I spent my spare time job hunting in the upper echelons of journalism, where I felt I belonged—the offices of *The New York Times, The New Yorker, Newsweek, Time* or the eight or nine newspapers flourishing then. But my college degree didn't stagger anybody and never once did I have a "proper" job interrogation. Young women wanting to work in publishing in 1949–1950 needed to be debutantes who had gone to Vassar, Smith and Bryn Mawr.

Broke and ever worried as I was, New York was still the most wonderful place in the world to be. Every Saturday, my Texas pals—Floyd, Scotty, Joan Walker, Weldon Sheffield, John Keffer—and I would gather for lunch at À La Fourchette— "at the fork"—oh, I thought that was so chic. I loved to try to say it correctly in French. One could get a fabulous entire meal for $1.50. This was on what has become Restaurant Row—West 46th Street. We saw everything in the theater, buying standing room, if we couldn't afford a seat. There was much to do that didn't cost us. Just walking the Village was a thrill. "And on that corner in that frame house lived Edna St. Vincent Millay. Didja know that?"

But what about my "career"?—as they say in the cartoon where World War III is declared. One day I saw an item about the actor Zachary Scott and his wife, Ruth, entertaining in their Central Park West apartment. I hadn't even known that Zachary Scott lived in Manhattan. Naively, I stepped into a phone booth and asked information for his number. I know you hardly believe I got it, but soon I was speaking to the star himself. "You may not remember me, Mr. Scott, but this is Liz Smith who interviewed you for *The Texas Ranger*. We met at your delightful mother's house in Austin."

He was charm and consideration itself. "Zach, call me Zach." Of course he remembered me. I was such a good writer. Where was I? What was I doing? I needed a magazine job? "Well," said this beautiful savior of the silver screen, "tomorrow morning at eleven you call this friend of mine who is the editor of *Modern Screen*. I will have talked to him and I'm sure he'll help you. His name is Chuck Saxon."

At the time I didn't know—and neither did Mr. Saxon—that he would eventually leave the movie mag biz and become a major cartoonist for *The New Yorker*. His Helen Hokinson–type Connecticut ladies became classics. But for now, all Saxon said was, "Yes, I'll see you. Bring your work."

After reading my article on Zach, Saxon looked at me. "You have a very virile writing style. I think we can find a place for you here as an associate editor." We were in the old Delacorte Building at 25 Fifth Avenue near The Marble Collegiate Church. (My mother was so pleased. She envisioned me taking time off from fluffing up a little copy about Jane Powell and then running across to Norman Vincent Peale for spiritual counseling.)

So began a number of years as an editor, caption and headline writer, proofreader and general factotum. But first, after my interview with Saxon, I had to go back to the apartment and look up the word "virile" in the dictionary.

Modern Screen was silly. This was the last gasp of the old movie magazine era with *M.S.* and *Photoplay* at their peak. The articles were always love letters to the stars, or rueful urgings as to how they might better care for themselves. Each issue carried a poll slip where readers were asked to say who they wanted to read about next. Unfortunately, they would usually fill in the names of actors in the current issue. So every month we were doomed to rehash Tony Curtis, Piper Laurie, Tab Hunter, Shelley Winters, Debbie Reynolds, Liz Taylor, etc. It was public relations garbage at its best.

I would go in to Saxon. "Look, there is this young guy we should write about named Montgomery Clift. He is going to be big." Saxon would answer, "Nope. He is not on our voting list. Maybe later." I don't think I ever sold a single story idea to my boss. But he liked my work well enough to beg me to move to Hollywood and be our West Coast editor. I was too much in love with New York to even consider it.

I was making $65 a week, but could actually say out loud I was a magazine editor (of sorts). A Broadway producer named Harry Rigby gave me the nickname Miss Modern Screen and would often take me to famous nightclubs and restaurants. I, who had grown up in the cotton business, thought I was in high cotton indeed.

Meanwhile, Scotty and Floyd decided to get married, so I lost my roommate. I couldn't afford to live alone. I convinced my brother Bobby to come to Manhattan and try his hand at modeling and broadcasting. He had a magnificent voice, had made a good reputation in Texas radio and TV and would win many news awards. I felt my life would be perfect if I had my Bobby around. And as he often did exactly what I wanted, pretty soon he arrived.

Bobby was better looking than any movie star and much brighter and funnier than most. He had never met a woman he didn't like and the Merchant Marine had taught him how much fun a guy with the constitution of an ox could have. These factors presaged his ultimate downfall, although at the time I simply marveled at him. Or felt green with envy. He had such stamina and was so great looking. He had eyebrows and eyelashes I would have killed for.

While making desirable job rounds, he worked at night as a waiter in a restaurant on Christopher Street called Verney's. He made out like a bandit because the clientele was largely gay men who didn't believe he wouldn't whip off his apron and go home with them. But Bobby was devoutly heterosexual. He liked his tips, he didn't mind gay guys, he liked the cook slipping him a secret steak and he loved waiting on an occasional star—such as Greta Garbo. But he'd only go home with someone female.

In what had once been a magnificent town house drawing room on West 69th Street, baby brother and I lived in one big room. We had two double beds, a dining table, a couple of chairs and chests, a Pullman kitchen, a sink and a bathtub—in the room. No toilet. That item was down the hall. This was endlessly awful for me. But Bobby didn't seem to mind. When I caught him peeing in the sink, I realized why he wasn't inconvenienced.

Those days began my evolution as an enabler to Bobby. He drank. He had been drinking since his stint in the Merchant Marine and then in the Air Force after the war. He was young and healthy, feeling his oats. But when we went out on little weekend sprees, I would end up comatose the next day with a hangover. He would spring out of bed and ask, "Baby, what's the matter?" He didn't understand the term hangover. I just couldn't take the aftermath and he never experienced such a thing until years down the road when it was too late.

In the fifties, we thought we were the luckiest people on earth. Usually we were so broke we creaked when we walked. I remember strolling with Bobby in Times Square where we licked our lips over advertised five-dollar steak dinners. Sometimes subway fare for the next day would be counted out, put aside and then we'd go spend every red cent left in the Automat, adding crackers and ketchup to make a big meal.

Bobby recalls our stepping off a curb at 47th and Broadway against the light and leaping back on again. A cab driver yelled, "Why doncha go back to the country, you hicks?" Bobby turned to me and asked, "But how did he know?"

When I couldn't bear our poverty any longer, I took on some extra jobs. After a day at *Modern Screen,* I'd go at 6:00 P.M. to Blue Cross and type until 9:00 P.M. On weekends, Bobby and I both became proofreaders at *Newsweek,* thanks to our friend Joan Walker. She was the weekly's newly named and very unsaluted editor in charge of—something bizarre, which we seldom saw—television. Three jobs made for an exhausting life, but it was compelling. And by now, from all three, I was making about $200 a week.

At *Newsweek* we had nothing to do creatively. We seldom saw any real writers or editors. But we were "very important" to the process of accuracy and "closing the magazine." We worked under Robert Austerlitz—a maverick intellectual who always wore a black knit tie because "I am in mourning for the world."

I enjoyed the tiny bits of access, stimulation and news I got out of proofing *Newsweek* every week. Once, in the hall late at night, I even saw the editor-in-chief, Osborn Elliott. Someday, this man, who in time became a legend at the Columbia Graduate School of Journalism, would be my friend. But was I a mind reader then?

A computer generation can't imagine the proofreading process, which was all too human, "hands on" and detailed. You would sit down as a "pitcher" (reader) with a "catcher" (listener). The person reading enunciated every single syllable, spelling anything that even looked moderately difficult and using an arcane made-up language to indicate capitals, question marks, periods and commas. An exclamation point was called, for instance, "a screamer." A question mark, a "query." The word "up" preceded every capital.

Here is a sentence: "Today the Vatican announced that Pope Pius XII would read from Revelations in the Basilica of St. Peter. His Holiness has invited 1000 orphans to listen, asking, 'Is it not good for them to hear?'"

To be absolutely sure everything was correct, the pitcher would say out loud to the catcher: "Quote UP Today the UP Vatican announced that UP Pope UP Pius UP X UP One UP One would read from UP Revelations in the UP Basilica of UP St. S T stop UP Peter stop. UP His UP Holiness has invited 1 zero zero zero orphans to listen, com, asking single quote UP Is it not good for them to hear query single double quote."

The catcher would put a pencil mark over every word to indicate that it was okay and whole editions of *Newsweek* went through this process. After a few months, I began to read everything the *Newsweek* way, so that the Best & Co. department store became to me "UP Best Jigger UP Co. stop."

The best part of this job was the fun Bobby and I had in

our exposure to the cynical intellectual charms of Mr. Austerlitz. He taught us a lot. When we finished working, we'd all stroll down onto 42nd Street and over to the New York Times Building where we'd enter on 43rd Street and go up to the cafeteria. We had no business doing this, but nobody ever stopped us. And it cost only pennies to eat there.

Years later, living through one of the worst eras of NYC crime, I saw the movie *My Favorite Year* with Peter O'Toole. As the film opened, there was a shot of the Rockefeller Center NBC corridor and the elevators. "This must be in the fifties," I said out loud. My companion asked why I said that. "Because there are no security guards on the elevators."

MEANWHILE, BACK AT *MODERN SCREEN*, my first live movie stars were to be Shirley Schrift and Issur Danielovitch Demsky. Well, those had been their original names. I just assumed I'd be meeting and running into film stars by the dozens working for *Modern Screen*. Of course this wasn't the case.

Not counting Zachary Scott, I did finally meet my first early live stars. The boss of bosses, Albert Delacorte, Sr., had summoned all employees to a huge storage room full of our magazines. Here he planned to pass out our Christmas bonus checks. We were stunned and delighted when a handsome blond athletic god in a glen plaid suit jumped up on a stack of boxes and began calling our names. There, from his personal hand, the hand of Issur Danielovitch, we gasped as we took our checks. He was now the young Kirk Douglas of *Champion* fame. (*Paths of Glory, The Bad and the Beautiful* and *Spartacus* were yet to come.)

Years later, I became friendly with Anne and Kirk Douglas and some of their famous sons. I told Kirk that he was my very "first." He insisted he remembered the occasion, *and me.* Kirk is not only a marvelous actor, good writer and indomitable spirit, but he is a marvelous purveyor of bullshit!

Modern Screen offered me one more live movie star. I

was sent on an assignment with Shelley Winters. She was already a star at 20th Century-Fox (the place used to have a hyphen in its name before Rupert Murdoch cleaned it up). I was to follow Shelley around New York as she went shopping, and record her every deathless utterance. Shelley was thought of as sultry and she could actually act. She was yet to do *A Place in the Sun* with Elizabeth Taylor and Montgomery Clift. This was long before her roly-poly *Poseidon Adventure* days.

I met Shelley at her hotel. She was wearing a wide, fifties "Dior" skirt with starchy petticoats, high heels, white gloves and a little hat. We were limousined up to 57th Street, with her grousing all the way. She didn't behave in a very "starry" or glamorous manner for my taste. I thought she was a real "kvetch"—a word I hadn't even learned yet.

At Lillian Nassau's elegant shop of fancy flowers, vases, artifacts and other froufrou decorator items, Shelley fingered every object. "How much?" she'd whine. "Would you like to give it to me as a gift?" The salespeople would just flutter and not answer. Then she'd say, "Can I get it wholesale?"

Having grown up with a profligate and extravagant father, I was shocked. You mean that movie stars can be mean-spirited, greedy and grasping, I asked myself? Never had I been so disillusioned. I felt I'd never be able to watch Shelley with an open mind again. I left her after several hours of this continuing show in other shops where she would fulminate and say, "Well, *Modern Screen* could pay for this, couldn't they?" I wanted to give the renamed Shirley Schrift short shrift!

I don't remember what I ended up writing about this "fabulous Hollywood star," but I returned to my editing chores disillusioned. Saxon guffawed when I complained. I was barely making enough to live on, but I'd never have thought of asking for a freebie. That would, of course, come later.

BECAUSE I HAD ATTENDED THE U OF T, I managed to meet the peerless leader of Texans in New York—the already mentioned Joan Sandefer Walker. Joan was our most sophisticated friend. Her mother had been a *Vogue* editor. Her Texas father, Stanley Walker, had been the most famous managing editor in the newspaper biz, at the helm of the *Herald Tribune* in its heyday. Joan had been born in a New York hospital, a fact she never let the others of us forget. We had all been born at home. "You are so low," she'd tell us. We felt she must be right; after all, she had a job at *Newsweek*.

She lived in a neat little walk-up on Madison Avenue in the Thirties and there she made an art of talk and dinner. She served me the very first artichoke I'd ever seen and taught me how to eat it. We Texans would go, sop up her food and gather NYC "lore" under Joan's tutelage. She knew important people because of Mummy and Daddy. And it was always a privilege, upon leaving, to walk down the four flights carrying her garbage. You could still deposit garbage right into baskets on the streets back in the fifties.

It was Joan who tried to get me a "real"—not just a proofreading job— at *Newsweek*. But her tenure there was iffy. No one believed TV had any future. So Joan had no clout. More impressive was the man she would marry, *Newsweek*'s drama critic Tom Wenning.

Through Joan and Tom, I was introduced to a handsome blond man who resembled one of those Nazi storm troopers in the movies. Joan said, "Liz, this is Walter Osborne, one of *Newsweek*'s best writers. Didn't you go to school with his wife, Anne, at that horrid Hardin-Simmons?"

Ever since my failed marriage and my ill-fated love affair with the "wrong" sex, I had kept myself above sexual, romantic feelings. I was determined never to let anything like that happen again. It had taken me almost two years to recover.

But I perked up. My heterosexual self evidently still existed. I was happy to discover this. Walter Osborne was a "dish," over six feet, funny and fabulous. We did the usual small talk. Anne and Walter and their several kids, with one-on-the-way, lived in Chestertown, Maryland. He commuted to New York when it was necessary; and it always was. He was sure Anne would love to see me. Why didn't I come down for a weekend and bring a friend?

My pal, Weldon, and I went and had a very good time. It was great to see Anne again. She was as bright and sardonic as ever, a typical pre–Women's Liberation restively brilliant woman who was now trapped in *über* motherhood. And then there was that electric current between Walter and me. Mr. Osborne was not only a good writer, he was a natural-born teacher and storyteller in the grand tradition. He loved to brag and never stopped telling me about his grandfather, Herman Melville. Anne and I would listen and rag him about it. *Wonderful Town* had opened on Broadway in 1953 and we'd repeat the line, "I was reading *Moby-Dick* the other day—it's, er, about this whale!"

Walter began to call me in New York. He started educating me. He took me to see *Richard II* and recited most of it into my ear during the play. He took me to Bleeck's, the famous artists' and writers' restaurant close by the old Metropolitan Opera House. There he pointed out a rather feeble, overdressed gent who was Lucius Beebe, a man who stepped right out of Café Society and into my *New Yorker*/Peter Arno/Walter Mitty dreams. Walter showed me how to play "The Match Game" and how to make a martini. ("Just roll the vermouth around in the glass and then pour it out before adding the gin.") I was both shaken and stirred by all I was seeing and learning. Walter took me to good restaurants and taught me how to order. And he made me want to read all the things he'd read of which I had never heard. And to see the plays, the operas and the ballets.

The inevitable happened. I didn't quite fall in love with him; I was too gun-shy and he was too married. And I did have enough sense to hit the nail on the head. One day he was carrying on about how adorable I was—how fresh—how lively. I popped off, "Oh, Walter, I just remind you of Anne when she isn't pregnant."

"You know," he said reflectively, "it's true."

My conscience had already been hurting me about Anne and those kids. Or maybe it was just that by then, I already had

everything the Walter Osborne Ph.D. course had to offer. I
tugged myself back down to earth and stopped seeing him.

EARLY ON IN THE FIFTIES, Bobby gave up on New York.
He decided to go back to Texas where he knew the ropes better.
And anyway, there was all that vodka to drink and all those
women he hadn't married yet. (He ended up with three children
and five wives, plus cancer of the larynx. These days he is a retired solid citizen who no longer drinks and tries to convince all
and sundry not to smoke.) We have remained close over the
years, but I still miss him. He was my best roommate.

TOP AND

BOTTOM

BANANAS

WHEN I WASN'T WORKING THREE jobs, I'd get to-gether with my Texas pals and hit the nightlife of the city. There was too much to do and it was wonderful. One evening I went to a party being given by a Houston ballet philanthropist in a big East Side town house.

"There's Kaye Ballard," someone said as a slim brunette descended the stairs.* I gazed but didn't recognize her. "She is just back from London where she starred in *Touch and Go*. A great musical comedy performer."

Kaye came over and introduced herself. We joked and chatted. She was full of show biz sass and I admired her emerald eyes. "I just love Texans!" she said, which made me wonder if she'd ever really known any. As she turned to go, she said, "Call me. Let's be friends," and handed me a card.

In the early fifties, Kaye was sexy and slim. She was a major name on the supper-club circuit. She would score big off- and on Broadway in the musical The Golden Apple. *She'd land on the cover of* Life. *Later, she would develop some heft and become the personification of the Italian housewife that she played on TV in* The Mothers-in-Law.

Later I looked at the card. It read "Kaye Ballard ORgasm 3-6668." She was making a joke about her Oregon telephone exchange in Greenwich Village. We became lifelong friends and this chance meeting affected the next chapter of my life—maybe all of it, if one believes in fate.

Soon I left *Modern Screen* to work for a music publisher named Pete Kameron. He had become Kaye's manager, almost as a hobby, for he was already managing The Weavers singing group and they had a big hit in "Good Night, Irene."

Again, I was exposed to a world I'd never even imagined—record promotion, disc jockeys, the concept of "payola," songs "with a bullet" in Billboard, plus all the rigors of nightclub booking, standup comics, club owners, "special" material. But I lapped it up at Pete's knee and he took a friendly interest in my show biz education. "You'd be a natural, Liz, but you're not Jewish!" he'd say. Then he'd light another joint and laugh. "Let's talk about sex and I'll tell you what women really like!" (I had been rather shocked when I realized that the charming Mr. K. was a rabid exponent of "free love," even in the early fifties.) But I enjoyed the relaxed, informal atmosphere of packing records, delivering and listening. I realized, however, that I wasn't getting anywhere.

Kaye and Pete then begged me to go out with the national touring company of *Top Banana* in 1953 to look after Kaye. She had the second lead to Phil Silvers in this musical hit. Chicago was our chief stop and theater life was heady in the Windy City in those days. A fearsome drama critic named Claudia Cassidy reigned supreme. But if you or your show was a hit with Claudia, you were home free. Chicago would lick your boots and open all doors. Gypsies and stars alike loved Chicago.

Top Banana's road company was first-rate and except for its star, the irascible Phil Silvers, its rather marvelous and insecure cast was made up of lovable performers—many of them famous from the days of burlesque. Veterans like Joey Faye (you may remember he played a grape in the famous Fruit Of The Loom TV ads), Herbie Faye, Danny Scholl and the later-to-be-recognized in legit, Jack Albertson, were in the cast.

Theater people were supportive of each other on the road. Casts visited back and forth and got together in clumps after the curtain. The *Top Banana* gang met the ethereal Audrey Hepburn who was playing with her husband, Mel Ferrer, in *Ondine,* where Audrey appeared onstage decked out in seaweed and fishing nets. At parties Audrey never said much; Mel did all the talking. Henry Fonda, Kurt Kazner and Leora Dana were in town in *Point of No Return,* and Elaine Stritch, then only twenty-seven years old, was slaying them as the Ambassador from Luxembourg in *Call Me Madam,* co-starring with Kent Smith. I would meet the Oscar winner, Van Heflin, whom I had adored in the Lana Turner movie *Johnny Eager.* He informed me he did not drink water. Why? "Fish fuck in it." A kid named Bobby Short was playing the piano at the original Black Orchid. His sophisticated repertoire wasn't so unusual then. A lot of people still loved songs that had literate lyrics. When Bobby discovered I was the only white person he'd ever met who could do "the camel walk" dance step, we became friends for life.

On Saturday nights, after two shows that day, everybody would go to see what was the last gasp of Chicago's burlesque. The *Top Banana* cast, so versed in this dying art, had a particularly good time. They knew all the jokes, all the setups, all the sight gags, and all the strippers still left in the business.

It was here that I saw the legendary Lili St. Cyr. She was a rare burlesque queen, who came out and then left dressed to the nines. In between, she'd slowly divest herself of every stitch, standing behind her maid. Then she'd take a bubble bath on stage. That done, she toweled down in a provocative manner and departed, fully clothed. (No thrown gloves or pasties for Lili.) She was billed as "The Anatomic Bomb" and had already defended herself in court, saying she tried in her act for something "refined and elegant, with a bit of classic Russian ballet thrown in for good measure." Lili had been born in 1918 and when she died she'd been married five times. She defended what she did for a living: "If one has morals, they can't be taken away by me or anyone else." I felt these were words to live by.

Top Banana's male actors were mostly lovely guys. But

Mr. Silvers was Frank Sinatra without the charm, the talent or the sex appeal. He knew Sinatra and had a severe case of Sinatra-wannabe-itis. Silvers was dour, sarcastic, threatening, and he desired, above all, to be "intellectual"—like Sinatra, who could actually read.

Imitating a Milton Berle–type burlesque comic who is catapulted to stardom by early TV exposure, he should have been on his knees to the funny creators of *Top Banana* (H. S. Kraft and Johnny Mercer) and to the critics who adored him. Instead, nothing was enough. He seemed to hate the masses and looked down on his own chorus kids. He behaved toward the latter in a dictatorial high-handed manner. He wasn't much better to his leading lady, a veteran of burlesque herself, Kaye Ballard.

Although she brought to this musical her own life talent earned since age sixteen, when she had left Cleveland and joined the Spike Jones Band as a flute player and a comedienne, Kaye couldn't catch a break from Silvers. He only liked routinely beautiful women and Miss Ballard was her own work of art. He fought with her constantly and simply refused to let her join the Old Boys' Club he had set up with the men in the cast. Since Kaye worshiped these comic veterans, this worked a hardship on her.

I was on the road with Kaye to keep an eye out for Pete, to stop her from throwing away her money or making impetuous show biz deals that couldn't be consummated, to soothe her relations with the musical's producers and maybe to get her a little extra press.

But column mentions for her in *The Hollywood Reporter* or the Irv Kupcinet column in Chicago's *Sun Times,* or back in New York for Dorothy Kilgallen, drove Phil Silvers crazy. He soon developed a serious hate for me. Once, playing word games with the actors' wives in a big hotel suite, Silvers joined us. I answered a question about Mozart. Silvers snarled, "No, that's wrong, stupid!" My answer turned out to be correct and this made him more furious. He leapt from his chair yelling, "Out, out, get out." The collective wives were aghast. This volatile star always made them nervous, but he was their meal ticket and they wanted to adore him.

I left, not wanting to put them in a difficult position. Now Silvers took more out on Kaye, upstaging her, stepping on her lines and insulting her backstage. This made for a very unhappy show. I called Pete to say that I had outlived my usefulness to Kaye and should return to New York. But a fight developed between the producers, the star and the featured players—against the chorus. Equity got into the middle of it and Pete had me stay on, begging Kaye to stay quiet and keep out of it.

But she had become desperately infatuated with the lead dancer, a fellow Italian. He was hotheaded and feisty and Kaye, with her loyal Calabrian upbringing, turned him into "family." Although she had second billing to Silvers, Kaye antagonized the producers by standing with the chorus in the Equity quarrel. I guess I should have applauded her defense of the underdogs but I had been hired to keep her out of trouble, to defuse her emotional and unguarded approach to life and her career. She was famous for crashing and burning, for having antagonized the important likes of Jerome Robbins, Abe Burrows, Jule Styne and others.

I remonstrated with Kaye that she was "a star" and should consider what was best for her career. And anyway, I added that I thought the dancer was just "using" her, and was an opportunist.

Now I had hurt Kaye's feelings, saying that this guy she was crazy about was only using her. So instead of dumping him, she dumped me. The show departed for its next stop. And I was left in Chicago without a good-bye from Kaye. I realized I shouldn't have interfered in her private life so I didn't really blame her.

Elaine Stritch and I had become friends in Chicago and she had her own problems. She was romancing her leading man, Kent Smith. He was divorced and not a Catholic, and the needed annulment for remarriage didn't seem to be in the cards. Elaine begged me to continue touring with her, run her affairs, do her

PR and listen to her tales of woe. But I was thoroughly sick of legit shit. I was tired of temperamental crazy actors who had more talent than common sense.

Kaye's manager wired me money and I quit "the road." By the time she returned to New York, Kaye and I had "made up" and she regretted deserting me. Elaine and I also became fast friends. I value both women and I have learned much about comedy, human nature and true emotion from these gifted performers. I think, however, we wouldn't still be friends if I had hung in there as either one's second banana.

I REVELED IN NEW YORK, couldn't get enough of its surprises. One night I dropped into a fashionable bar in Greenwich Village and sat down next to a girl on a bar stool, alone, drinking a martini. She caught my eye because she was wearing a dark green suede trench coat. At the time, this was very offbeat and chic. She began to drop theater names. I began to drop theater anecdotes. How else were we going to find anything out?

Selma Lynch turned out to be one of those "nice Jewish girls" as the saying goes. She had an Irish name simply because, in the past, an Irishman handling Ellis Island immigrants had given up on Grandpa's Polish name. He scribbled a new one, announcing, "From now on, my friend, your name is Lynch— like me."

We struck up a friendship and she introduced me to her boss, Gus Schirmer, Jr. Gus was plump and delightful. And soon after, he invited me to come be his "gofer" in summer stock. "Why can't Selma do it?" I asked.

"She has to stay in Manhattan and run the office," said Gus, who was not only an actor's agent, but doubled as a producer/director. He was the scion of the famed music company bearing his name. So that summer, I learned a lot about how the theater works. I also met numbers of people who had either already reached the pinnacle or were on their way. Some of these were: Carol Channing, the wide-eyed star of *Gentlemen Prefer*

Blondes, which was the first musical I had ever seen. (I paid $2.50 to sit in the last row of the Ziegfeld balcony and I could have sworn the star was playing every word right to the top where Flo Ziegfeld was said to have a peephole from his office to the stage. Billy Rose had used the peephole as well when he bought the Ziegfeld.)

Then there was Shirley Jones, the beautiful ingénue of *Oklahoma!,* discovered by Gus and off to Hollywood. I met Jimmy Kirkwood of the Kirkwood & Goodman comedy night-club team. They prefigured Rowan and Martin and the Smothers Brothers, doing the same sort of vis-à-vis comedy that later took off on TV. Lee Goodman would come on stage all dignified and suddenly Jimmy would bounce on, stand in front of Lee and say, clapping his hands, "Let's all tell about the first time!" Later, this zany guy would win the Pulitzer Prize for writing *A Chorus Line.*

Then there was Alice Pearce, the comedienne's comedienne. She always played maids and though supremely uncomely, was married to a handsome man who wrote "I've Got the World on a String." Every New Year's Eve since I've thought of Alice and her husband John, in bed drinking champagne and eating caviar. This introduced me to a new concept of celebrating.

And there was Gus's great friend, Tallulah Bankhead, in all her debilitated glory. By the time I met Miss Bankhead, it had been a long time since *The Little Foxes.* But she was still the heady, throaty voice from radio's "The Big Show" and she had produced a jillion show biz anecdotes.

We were in Connecticut doing "stock" when Gus sent me to buy beer for a cast party. I skipped off. I was still wearing bobby sox. At the liquor store, they refused to sell me alcohol. I protested that I was a divorced woman, long past twenty-one. "Nah!" said the owner, looking me over. I ran back to the theater happily empty-handed, glad I didn't look my age.

This was the summer that acquainted me with "the rose in the toilet" syndrome. Actors in tiny theaters were forever being told not to flush when the play was on, as it could be heard all through the audience. Gus solved the problem. He would stand one long-stemmed rose in the backstage commode just before the curtain went up.

In Provincetown, I recall sitting on a beach with a clever lyricist named Marshall Barer. Lots of good-looking male actors were lolling nearby. Marshall stood up, shook off the sand and announced loudly: "You will now see one homosexual writer hit the ocean."

I sat there in shock. Neither marriage, divorce, two brothers, World War II, work in a bomber plant, a university education, an ill-fated same-gender love affair, nor several adulterous and diverting years in Manhattan had prepared me to hear such a candid remark. The world was still light-years from sexual, let alone gay liberation.

Some years later, Tallulah Bankhead had made one of her serious efforts by appearing as Blanche Dubois in Tennessee Williams's *A Streetcar Named Desire.* I went twice to the City Center to see this *tour de force*. On the first occasion, the audience was full of gay fans who went completely overboard, greeting Tallulah's every utterance with raucous responses that turned the evening into a campy farce. I was told she was quite upset by this. But on the other occasion, I was blown away by her stage presence and feeling.

One night Gus invited me to go to New Jersey's Papermill Playhouse. His friend Tallulah was starring with the aforementioned Jimmy Kirkwood in a little summer stock revue called *Hello, Darlings!* Tallulah wore a Yankee baseball uniform on stage and did a number of amusing turns and said "Hello, darlings!" quite a lot. After the show, we went to a nearby cottage where she was staying.

The living room was full of theater types. Tallulah was playing hostess in an old worn pair of gray flannel slacks that made her look as if she'd been hit in the ass with a shovel. She greeted everyone as "Hello, darling!" and circulated, observing herself in every mirror she passed. This couldn't have been pleasant, for by now the great lady's face was quite a ruin and her long straggly hair, a glamour trademark, did not help. Looking in the mirror, Tallulah would slowly lift and curl the ends of her pageboy as she talked. It was a gesture out of silent films, very Mae West. But soon, she and Gus repaired to the bedroom where they lay on the bed talking.

Kirkwood decided they were just taking the necessary Demerol to get them through the night. Emerging, Tallulah showed us to the door, displaying special affection for Gus. I was about to step out the door when a great quiet fell and I suddenly found myself addressing the star, which I certainly had not intended. "Miss Bankhead," I said into the momentary silence, "I just want to tell you that until I saw you play Blanche in *Streetcar*, I had never understood a thing about that woman or her character or that play. You made it all come clear to me."

Tallulah looked at me, then at Gus, who seemed amused that I had spoken, and she roared: "Quiet! Quiet! I want all of you smart-asses to hear what this adorable child has just said to me—go on, darling, repeat yourself." I stammered and stuttered, wishing the floor would open up, but finally I reblurted my compliment.

"Gus—Gus, darling—who is this young woman?" asked Tallulah. Not waiting for a reply, she took my hands in hers and said, "You may call me Tallulah!"

I said, "Thank you, Miss Bankhead," and that more or less ended our episode. Gus died laughing. "You are so unbelievably naive and refreshing," he said as we drove back to New York.

Years later, I met Tallulah again, but of course she didn't remember me. We were at a Come As You Wish to Be party, made up by the press agent Betty Lee Hunt at The Living Room nightspot. Tallulah entered wearing a sash that read "Miss Bette Davis." I came, naturally, as Tom Mix. A bunch of us went dancing after at El Morocco and I recall her admiring a small hand mirror I had with the El Morocco zebra stripe motif on the back. Although I knew I'd never be able to find another of these "collector's items"—for "Elmo's" was on its last legs as a nightclub—I gave away my prize to Tallulah, who accepted with childish joy. It was the least I could do for a true legend.

Gus had so many famous friends, it was magic to go to

his apartment, for he had clipped sections from every great movie musical that he had rented, splicing them all together. (This was in the era of film reels; video had not been invented.) We'd sit at dinner and watch Fred Astaire, Ginger Rogers, Judy Garland, Lena Horne, Tony Martin, Mitzi Gaynor, Cyd Charisse, Donald O'Connor, Gene Kelly, Ann Miller and the rest do their stuff! (And I'd think about the next person who was watching a rented movie musical that had no musical moments!)

Gus also had marvelous stories. Not the least of these was of how his father had "kept" Gloria Swanson, but had never gathered up the nerve to try to sleep with the famous star of the "silents" and of *Sunset Boulevard*. Swanson would order old Mr. Schirmer, Sr., into a closet when her master, Ambassador Joseph P. Kennedy, came calling, and leave him there for hours—frightened and alone among the perfume of her furs and gowns.

In the early fifties, Gus introduced me to weekend life in the Hamptons of Long Island. I can see him now sitting on the beach squeezing lemon juice on his hair for bleach. I would go away with him to a little saltbox house in Watermill, where his favorite pastimes were cooking exhausting, impossible meals, schlepping to beaches with coolers and umbrellas and shopping in Southampton, where he hoped always to observe the social set at leisure.

Gus was hopelessly smitten with the likes of Babe Paley, C-Z Guest, Cordelia Biddle Robertson, the young Dina Merrill, the young Gloria Vanderbilt, the McDonnell sisters, whose father and one of whose number, Anne, had invented the light switch, and who married Henry Ford II. Gus loved the rotogravure and society pages of the local papers. They showed in a glamorous sepia tone the rich and social playing polo, racing cars, golfing at the Maidstone, going to services at the Church on the Dunes. Or they'd be lunching at the Southampton Beach Club. Gus paid no mind to East Hampton; it was too *nouveau*. But Southampton was still social, still exclusive, and still quite "restricted."

He would interrupt my reading to show me pictures of

his favorites. "Look, Noodle, doesn't Mrs. Winston Guest look divine here in this camel's hair coat thrown over her shoulders? You know she was painted nude and her Diego Rivera portrait hung over a bar in Mexico and in her own home there is a portrait of her husband, Winston, in his mother's arms, painted by John Singer Sargent. Here she is on her way to Tony Duke's Boys Harbor party."

I would look and fall back into my book. I was trying to read myself to death since I burned quickly on the beach, cared nothing for food, couldn't cook, didn't drink at the time and the idea of "The Hamptons" and/or "going away for the weekend" simply escaped me in those days. Everybody in New York seemed to be addicted to his weekends out of town, but I couldn't yet understand why anyone would ever want to leave the confines of Manhattan. It had taken me so long to get there!

At this point, all of my efforts went toward learning about New York life. I was the stagestruck out-of-towner with a whole history to learn, plus all the multicultural ethnicity of New York to rivet my attention. On weekends with Gus, I buried myself in books.

Gus tolerated his "Chocolate Noodle," a nickname lost in the recesses of the past. He would take me to Saks to buy me clothes that would make me look more like his beloved society ladies. I didn't care one whit about his idols and I didn't understand his yearning for their world.

In retrospect, I seem like a selfish and narrow-minded provincial little prig. Little did I know that only a few years hence, I'd be completely involved, as an observer and reporter, in this same social milieu. In spite of my studied indifference, Gus's background stuff would prove invaluable to me and I would often wish I had paid more attention to his fantasy life as a socialite observer.

Decades later, working for the New York *Daily News*, when I rang the bell on Christmas Eve at the Winston Guest estate in Oyster Bay and the fabled C-Z herself answered the door, I breathed a prayer of love and good wishes to my old friend Gus. Here was Mrs. Guest, now my friend. She'd recently been on the cover of *Time* as the last of her kind. She was accompanied to her front door by at least twenty dogs—each a different variety from purebreds to mutts—each wearing a bright red Christmas ribbon. This charming and unexpected scene seemed right off of a magazine cover. Soon, I asked Mrs. Guest to show me the Sargent painting of the infant Winston. She was delighted and surprised that I knew about it.

It was at this party by the way, that I felt a tiny sting of triumph. I began my social coverage career in 1955 at the bottom of the heap. Aileen Mehle, the society columnist known as Suzy, was the queen of all she surveyed. She decreed to New York hostesses that she would not come to parties where I was invited. This aced me out pretty well. C-Z Guest was the first to ignore Suzy's exclusivity dicta. She invited us both to her Christmas Eves and let the chips fall where they would. Suzy stayed on her side of the room; I stayed on mine. No shots were fired. But I was through the breach in the lines, thanks to Mrs. Guest.

Only recently Mrs. Guest and I were talking about this and she said, "Did you know that Aileen didn't want me to invite you to Winston's funeral? But you came and you sat next to Roy Cohn like a very good sport. Nobody else wanted to sit by him. When Aileen objected, I just said to her, 'For heaven's sake, Aileen—Winston *loved* Liz!'"

Gus must have been twirling with delight in heaven.

HOORAY FOR

HOLLYWOOD

BUT LET ME LOOK BACK a second to before I gave up my movie magazine career.

No self-respecting fan mag editor could live forever reporting to work on lower Fifth Avenue without eventually making an actual trek to Hollywood. My honeymoon foray in 1945 counted as tourist stuff. But when I went back as a *Modern Screen* VIP, it was a different ball game and I was even on a minor expense account.

Arriving around Christmastime, I dialed a woman named Lynn Bowers, who was a kind of underground legend in La-La Land. Lynn was a "somebody's somebody"—a ghostwriter for the powerful columnist Louella Parsons. Louella and her aide, Dorothy Manners, often called on Lynn to pinch-hit for them. Ms. Bowers was also a halfhearted press agent and freelancer who knew many stars and did them favors. Her connection to the film world ranked high in my limited firmament. I was only slightly put off when I met Ms. Bowers in person and found her to resemble a Boston bull terrier. But she was dogged, tenacious, hardworking, generous and loyal to her pals.

Almost immediately, she took me to a small party at

Louella's. Miss Parsons was charming and vague. She waved a hand at her living room, filled wall-to-wall with richly wrapped gifts. "My loot!" she laughed. Lynn whispered to me, "She ain't kidding. And the stars, producers and flacks know their name will be mud if they don't do right by Louella at the Yuletide. It's the same over at Hedda Hopper's." We had to move to a library for drinks because Louella's gifts were overflowing. It was here that a fine figured old dragon gave my black suit the once-over. "I guess you're the girl from New York," said this lady, who happened to be Ida Koverman, the important aide to MGM's Louis B. Mayer. "I guess you're one of those who thinks New York is the only place to live!"

I shrugged and answered, "Well, I wouldn't want to visit there!"

Miss Koverman gasped. Evidently nobody ever answered her back in jest, or without first kissing her ass. Just as Louella's word was law *tout* Hollywood, Miss Koverman had the power of life and death on the MGM lot. But I wasn't trying to "go" Hollywood and I didn't want anything from MGM. Still, Lynn snatched me away from Koverman as if I had stirred up a rattlesnake.

In spite of my transgression, Lynn kept hauling me around, impressing me. Because of *Modern Screen*, people were very nice. "Want to meet Rock Hudson?" asked Lynn. "He's a real doll. Do you know Marilyn Maxwell—she and Rock go out together. Oh, I know what. Why don't you go with me to Joan Crawford's house on Christmas Day." At that she indicated her fireplace mantel. It was a sea of invites and cards. Sure enough, Crawford had invited Lynn for "after lunch on Christmas Day." In a large bold hand was written, "and bring a friend."

This was the first time I'd ever seen mantel cards. Sly advertisements as to who you knew, who invited you, who remembered you at Christmas. I yearned to have lived back in the days of Edith Wharton and Henry James when people left calling cards with the corners turned down at Mrs. Astor's. But growing up in Fort Worth, I hadn't ever seen anything like that, nor cards displayed on the mantel to signify how popular and desirable you were.

Actually, I had only one famous name to really drop—Zachary Scott. Well, I thought, where better to drop the actor's name than at Joan Crawford's? Hadn't they costarred in one of her greatest films, *Mildred Pierce*? I jumped up and down metaphorically and accepted. I knew I'd have at least one sentence to say to Joan. Lynn eyed my fanzine enthusiasm as if I were nuts, but she remained taken with me. "You've got something, kid," she'd say in her best Bogart manner. "That ridiculous Texas thing of yours. Enthusiasm and naiveté mixed with a certain sophistication." I decided the "sophistication" was just my new black suit. In those days, nobody wore black in Hollywood, so I stood out.

Lynn went out of the room and returned, tossing something into my lap. It was a clear plastic purse with a gold chain, studded on the outside with colorful plastic circles in red, green, blue and yellow. Even I knew this was supremely tacky. "After all I've done for Crawford, all the space I have given her in Louella's column, all the errands and favors, this is what that big freckled bimbo has given me for Christmas. For Christ's sake! You couldn't even carry a Tampax in this thing; everybody would see it. You'd look like a junk bag if you put in lipstick, keys and money. Crawford has the world's worst taste. But she's a star and can get away with anything. Just wait until you see her collection of fuck-me shoes!"

Fuck-me shoes? I wasn't that far yet from the Baptist encampments of my youth where we got demerits for saying "gosh!" and "darn!" (Everybody knew these were just euphemisms for taking the Lord's name in vain, or saying the dreaded "damn.") I asked Lynn what such shoes were, though I thought I knew. Lynn laughed. "You know, ankle straps with lots of toe showing. You know, showgirl shoes."

Realizing that Joan Crawford had bad taste and wasn't always generous didn't deter me from a spasm of incredible hero worship. After all, I had followed her career from the days of early movies. And one of the funniest performances on earth to me had always been the young Crawford with Clark Gable and Fred Astaire in *Dancing Lady*. In this movie, Joan is all eyes and mouth. She dances with her hair, shaking her curls more than she shakes her feet. She can't seem to tap dance worth a lick. I often wondered what the youthful Astaire, already a legend on the Broadway and West End stages, had thought of his nondancing leading lady in his very first movie?

Such musings aside, the idea of going into the actual presence of Joan Crawford was daunting. She was still a big star.

It came to pass that we made our way to Miss Crawford's marvelous house on December 25th, a warm, mild California afternoon. I forget the exact location but these days when I drive through the famous "flats" of Beverly Hills, with the big mansions crammed up one against another under tall palm trees, I see lots of houses that could have been Joan's. It was very near the place where the Menendez brothers later murdered Mommy and Daddy.

Miss Crawford's entrance hall opened onto a magnificent room with a huge white Christmas tree at the end and many brilliantly wrapped presents. Crawford came to the door in person. And she was drawing all the limelight of the afternoon to herself, greeting Lynn effusively, very much lady of the manor in a white satin dressing gown and (I glanced down) white mules with pom-poms. (Not fuck-me shoes exactly, maybe just "tickle me a little" types.) I didn't know why the star was in a dressing gown in the afternoon, but what did I know? Where I had come from, anything resembling bedclothes was called a "kimono" or "bathrobe." These were usually like the ragged wrappers worn in the movies by ladies of the evening who were being dragged into night court to explain themselves. (I recalled the rough answer Crawford gave in one such old black-and-white film when she was asked by the judge to describe her profession. "Social worker!" she had snarled through her slash of dark lipstick.) Well, never mention "rope" in the house of a man who has been hanged, so I knew not to bring up this movie. Whatever roles Crawford played on film, here she was the perfect lady. And, in person, she and her white satin gown were the stuff that dreams are made on. She looked deep into my eyes, still holding my hand as Lynn rambled on. "I told you, Joan, this is the girl from *Modern Screen*, Zach Scott got her the job there. They say she's a natural. She's from Texas, Joan, like you. She can dance the Charleston, too, just like you. You're gonna love each other!"

Well, I already loved Joan Crawford. And I had, since seeing her as a child in the Tivoli Theater. But now I was practically fainting from too much attention. Crawford fixed me with the same gaze she'd given Clark Gable in *Strange Cargo*. (I was reminded of Ring Lardner's classic line, "She gave me a look you could have poured on a waffle!") She was absolutely riveting—sincere big eyes, a superpower smile. She drew me close to her silky bouncing bosom and in a cumulus of perfume, we walked arm in arm until we came to another room with another more normal-looking green fir tree, smaller, just as pretty, with all its gifts still pristinely wrapped.

Here, I met her godchild from Houston, the young actress Gale Storm, Gale's parents and men in tweedy jackets wearing I.D. bracelets, which my father would have considered "disgusting." And there was one rather weird, flamboyant Oscar Wilde–type named Arthur Blake. (I learned later he was one of the foremost female impressionists in the world of supper clubs. His pre-eminent nightclub character was Louella Parsons, saying, "My first exclusive. Marion Davies never looked lovelier than last night at the opening of blah, blah, blah.") And there were the four matchless children right out of a fairytale—dressed to the nines, the three girls in frilly shiny dresses and the little boy in a miniature gray flannel suit with a necktie knotted at his collar. They all had beautiful manners and looked supremely uncomfortable. Christina, Christopher, Cindy and Cathy. They were, of course, Miss Crawford's adopted children.

We made the smallest of talk while Crawford personally fixed our drinks with her own hand as if a servant might taint the proceedings or perhaps poison us. I'll never forget the glasses. They were heavy crystal with big gold grommets cemented or blown into the sides and clanking gold chains so that one could hang the drink around the neck like a horse's feedbag. With each sip, the chain would fall against your mouth and give you the creeps. As I settled back, trying to keep the chain off of my fillings, Crawford announced that we would now watch while the children opened their presents. I was surprised. It was already three in the afternoon and these poor kids hadn't opened a single present yet!

I thought of the old Smith ménage on Christmas past, those early mornings when three wildcats woke and without getting out of their pajamas tore into Mother and Daddy's bedroom screaming, "Christmas gift!" trying to be first to yell it to everyone else. Then we'd descend on the living room and create shredded mountains of tissue paper, ribbon and dead cardboard boxes while yelling, "Look at this!" or "Oh, I didn't want *that*!" or "Why did you get a football and I didn't?" Soon we'd rush outdoors still in our "jammies," to try the new bike, the new kite, the banished drum, while our parents watched us and drank coffee. We were allowed to misbehave terribly on Christmas morning because we had always behaved so well on Christmas Eve with its lighted tree, its carols and my mother's reading from the Gospel according to St. Luke. On Christmas Eve we exchanged presents with our parents and each other and Daddy gave us silver dollars, when he could afford it. But when it was Christmas Day—Santa time—they let us go crazy. So we never ever asked if there was a Santa Claus because we *knew* there *was* one. And when we finally, gradually no longer believed, we had other youngsters to carry along with the myth, and in any case, Mother and Daddy always came through for us.

The Crawford children, however, seemed all but paralyzed, as if dipped in paraffin. After much motherly stage-managing, one of them would tentatively select a gift and open it as if it were a bomb. The moment it was unwrapped, the wrappings were first neatly folded away, the ribbons wound onto a ball, and Joan would make the child march around the room to display the gift to each adult. "Oh, isn't that divine? Why, it's from Betty Grable and Harry James's little girl Victoria. How lovely!" Joan acted out each child's enthusiasm. Joan would then order the child to sit down and write the description in a little record book. "You will begin your thank-you notes this very night!" she said firmly. The children smiled wanly. I shuddered. And I wasn't surprised to hear that Christopher had run away from home and been brought back forcibly.

I glanced at my fellow guests. I had read that Crawford was one of the screen's sexiest stars, that she didn't miss much. Douglas Fairbanks, Jr., Franchot Tone, Greg Bautzer, Clark Gable and scores of others had loved her madly. Some had even married her. I had imagined there'd be at least one strong, dominating male presence in a Noel Coward smoking jacket, lighting a pipe, lifting an intimate eyebrow in the star's direction, looking bemused and tolerant. Married or single, she was said to be red-hot. But on this day, there was no evidence that she had any private life beyond her marionettelike children, plus an odd lot of fey fellows and some run-of-the-mill acquaintances. I should have known, I thought. She must have been rather desperate to invite Lynn Bowers and a total stranger to her house for Christmas.

At one point, I asked, "What about the gifts under your big white tree? When will you open those?" She sighed like Atlas with the world on her shoulders. "Oh, I don't know. I can't really imagine when I'll have time. This day is just for the children."

The children would, I figured, be opening until the first day of spring at the rate they were going. Later I'd be told how merciless Joan could be with her youngsters. She'd wake one from a deep sleep to take them down and point to a hand towel hanging slightly askew in a bathroom. "How could you leave this mess?" she'd berate the little offender. Later, when Joan Crawford as mother became an open book after Christina wrote *Mommie Dearest,* I figured that waiting until 3:00 P.M. to open your Christmas gifts and then having to show them to a group of idiotic adults and make a record would be enough to put any kid over the edge. Christina became infamously well-known after her revealing book and people mostly said, "How sharper than a serpent's tooth!" Christopher remained adversarial to his mother all his life and refused to speak of her after he grew up.

Christina Crawford wrote her book too early to catch the current child abuse awareness wave. Many fans then were horrified that I sided with this daughter who had written the controversial "no wire coat hangers!" memoir after her mother was dead. But I believed Christina and her tales about a perfectionist who was a demanding parent. Still, I continued to regard Joan as one of the great movie stars of all time. She had tried to perfect herself out of her poor white trash background. She believed in the grandeur she created on the silver screen. And she treated her children as personal property because she was a control freak.

Indeed she was larger than life. Glamorous, cagey, smart, ambitious, ruthless, tough, always acting, pretending to be sick in bed the night she feared they wouldn't give her the Oscar. (They did!) Years passed. Joan moved to NYC where she posed for Blackglama mink as a part of the "What Becomes a Legend Most?" advertisements. She would often go to "21" with the ad exec Peter Rogers, who had developed a magnificent crush on her. He was tall, handsome and funny and she always needed that kind of escort.

"As we would get out of the limousine," Rogers remembers, "Joan would throw her mink ahead of her out of the car onto the sidewalk. Then she'd pick it up with just one finger, talking to me the whole time, never looking at it. And she'd drag it behind her into '21,' all the way to the table. Sometimes, she'd whisper to me, 'Let's show them how a legend enters!'" At her table, she would order 100-proof vodka, plus a water glass also filled with more 100 proof.

My friend Peter never tires of telling one of his favorite Crawford tales. He was in Barbados visiting another great star, Claudette Colbert. He knew it made Crawford jealous for him to visit Claudette, so one day he telephoned Joan after shopping in Bridgetown. "Hi, darling, I was just thinking of you because I ran across some beautiful silk fabric from India here in Barbados and I wondered how much you'd need to make a dress."

"Oh, how wonderful of you," said the enthusiastic star. "And, Peter, don't forget. Get me four yards for the dress, then two yards for the gloves and bag, and three yards for the shoes and the hat!"

Her sense of humor was mordant and wicked and her sense of camp as a screen icon with an image to maintain was even more so, for like all great satirists and enhancers of reality, she half believed her own legend. The glamour, the gowns, the gossip, the glitter, the furs, the never letting down, the haughty exterior, the largess to fans, the homage to the press—all of it counted.

I knew Crawford could be funny. I later heard that she had hired a gay New Yorker, Adele Strassfield, as a secretary in Hollywood. This was back in the sixties when people were not so tolerant of sexual deviation and Adele decided she'd work for the demanding star but keep her girlfriend in the background.

Adele toiled over Crawford's massive fan correspondence and conducted other business in a little white cottage behind the main house. The star would drop in often to see how Adele was doing and to affix her dashing signature to letters and photos. She liked Adele and was amused by her flattering sycophancy. One day Adele had gone to the main house for something. She heard the cottage phone ringing and made a dash to get back. But just as she reached the door, Crawford was exiting with an odd look on her face. The star held open the screen door elaborately for Adele and then moved outside. Adele turned to look after her. "Adele—someone named Muriel just called." Adele gulped and said, "Yes, Miss Crawford." Crawford let the screen door slam in Adele's face as she moved away, adding; "She said, 'Bring home two lamb chops!'" At that, the star walked across the lawn singing loudly and with feeling, "Life is just a bowl of cherries. Don't take it serious; it's too mysterious!"

After having won an Oscar for *Mildred Pierce* and having been one of the biggest of Warners and MGM stars, Joan Crawford wore out her welcome in Hollywood. But she survived. She remained "a star" no matter how shabbily she was treated and what she had to stoop to do. Realizing her film career was kaput, she married Alfred Steele, the head of Pepsi-Cola and then embarked enthusiastically on a new role, playing the model corporate wife and spokeswoman for Pepsi to the hilt. She became a PR demon for this American soft drink and treated it as if it were as important as brain surgery.

It is an oft-told tale how she and Alfred posed together for an ad in the Caribbean as part of the "Come to Jamaica: It's no place like home!" campaign. The photos were ready to go into the ads showing Joan and Alfred with a donkey when Mr. Steele died suddenly of a heart attack. Alan Kahler, who was the ad man, telephoned Joan a few days after the funeral to express his sympathy. He told her, "And the photos were so good. We will, of course, send you a set for your private use."

Joan asked, "Private use? What do you mean? Aren't you still using them in the coming ads?" Alan paused. "Well, Joan, we really can't, what with Alfred being—er, dead."

Joan snapped, "Oh, for heaven's sake. Can't you just air-brush him out?"

After my Christmas with Crawford, we continued a kind of nodding acquaintance through the years until she finally retired to her all-white, vinyl-decorated apartment in New York and, like the spartan Christian Scientist she was, died virtually alone without making even a murmur about the cancer that killed her.

Through the years before, however, she never forgot me. After all, I was— *ta-da!*—an important thing to her: a member of the press. At one point, *Cosmopolitan* asked me to write a roundup piece on what the stars liked to eat for dessert. (Those were the good old days when the press still asked *what* stars ate, not *who* they ate!)

I left a call for Joan, asking the question, and promptly forgot about it. I was being routinely awakened early every morning by someone I was mad about who was naturally attached to someone else and never free to talk until the Someone Else left for work. (Ah, youth!)

So, when the phone rang at 7:00 A.M. I picked it up sleepily and said, feigning irritation, "How dare you disturb me—an all-American beauty, at my rest? Who the hell do you think you are?" There was a long and penetrating silence and then came the equally icy words: "This is Joan Crawford calling. Obviously, I got you at a bad time." Big hang-up!

I raced around for ten minutes locating Crawford's number and dialed her back with a breathless apology. "I am so terribly sorry, Miss Crawford. I was kidding with a friend. I thought you were someone else. Really, you are so nice to call me back in answer to such a silly question."

Remote quiet. Then Crawford answered in tones that were a cross between Eleanora Duse and Mrs. Patrick Campbell. At the same time she dripped a bit of venom. "Why, Liz, dear, I didn't find the question silly at all. Frankly, my idea of a perfect dessert is to suck on a great big dill pickle!"

I never had a chance to see or talk to Joan Crawford again. But I made her dill pickle the star of my "Question & Answer." Many people asked if I had just made it up. But nobody needed to make anything up when dealing with Crawford. She was her own auteur, her own legend, her own icon, her own nebula—a woman who hauled herself up by her bootstraps and created her glittering star self from scratch.

LENA MARY

CALHOUN

IN THE EARLY- AND MID-FIFTIES, much to the benefit of my then lackluster social life, I had the luck to fall in with some young ladies working in the theater. I came to know them through Shirley Herz, who had come to New York from Philadelphia and was struggling to become a legitimate theater press agent. This meant serving a tortured apprenticeship, joining a tough union and clawing one's way up.

Shirley's best friends called her "Sam Spade" because she was the master detective. She knew everything that was going on. Through her I met other ambitious young people who wanted a life near—if not exactly upon—the wicked stage. There was Betty Lee Hunt, one of the most brilliant, imaginative and hardworking of all theater flacks. Betty Lee had a real claim to fame. In time, as something called off-Broadway began to happen, she was one of the pioneers shining a bright light on innovative stages. As I recall, an irate and irascible producer once paid her salary in buckets of small change.

In lean times, I would go and make a bit of money by writing for Betty Lee's office, creating items that went out to various columnists in New York's newspapers. Betty Lee taught me and another beginner, Diane Judge—who, today, manages my office—lessons we never forgot: "Whenever you send a 'free' item to a columnist—you know, real news, something hot or juicy—just be sure you put one of our clients' names into it somewhere."

Diane and I protested that this wasn't quite kosher. But Betty Lee would wave off our objections. "Okay, okay—so you didn't see the client there, but I'm telling you now the client was there, so write it the way I want it."

Oddly enough, Walter Winchell and Dorothy Kilgallen were easy columns to "break" if you had a scrap of real news. And I learned how to do the same item over in each of their journalistic styles. But the one I wanted to "break" was Leonard Lyons in the *New York Post*. He was fixated on VIP names and had certain pets like Moss Hart, Marlene Dietrich, Ernest Hemingway and Somerset Maugham, who intrigued him. But I had little luck with Mr. Lyons. I once sent him a great item about Sophie Tucker mulling a musical role as a nun. As her slogan was "The Last of the Red Hot Mamas!" I used the tag line "There goes the last of the red-hot mama superiors!" I didn't see how this could miss, but it did.

Frustrated, I sat down and dreamed up an item about how one of our clients, producer Gus Schirmer, was planning to make a musical from Edith Sitwell's very intellectual book *English Eccentrics*. This was completely far-fetched. No one could possibly have entertained such an absurd idea. But this was the one item Lyons printed. My conscience hurt ever after.

Then there was the well-connected Ruth Mitchell. She had been a Broadway dancer who decided to try her hand as a stage manager. She was following in the tradition of the legendary Elaine Scott Steinbeck, but it was really hard for women to get such jobs. Ruthie went on to become a director/coproducer with the famous Harold Prince.

I also met the diminutive, endearing Florence Klotz. She was struggling to become a costume designer under the heavy hand of the genius Irene Sharaff. Florence was so petite that the director Burt Shevelove once wisecracked, "Flossie looks like something you stand on a very low coffee table." Flossie always acted as if she didn't care "if school kept" or what became of her. She feigned absolutely no ambition. I suppose this—and her talent for making stuffed cabbage—is why she eventually won five Tony Awards!

By the time I landed in this cadre, they were mostly "on their way up." They had already worked variously for such grand people as Leland Hayward, Richard Rodgers, Oscar Hammerstein, Josh Logan, George Abbott, etc. They had buckets of theater lore.

I loved hanging out with them. Ruthie's Sunday brunches featured rising stars and established names above the title. So, unaccustomed as I was to bagels, lox, whitefish and cream cheese, I'd find myself sitting down noshing on largess from one of her Broadway beaus. Flossie would tell stories about the temperament of Madam Sharaff. Diane would bring us up to date on the doings at the Metropolitan Opera, which was too rich for our blood, but she was an SRO expert. Shirley had the best buzz on what chorus girl had been in what star's dressing room. Betty Lee was all over the place. And I loved every minute of it. Having met these mavens of grease paint, I soon met all their important pals. And one such was the incomparable Lena Horne.

Lena was wed then to the fine musician/conductor Lennie Hayton and this famous couple had shaken the stardust of Hollywood from their heels and come to live in Manhattan where they felt less *Sturm und Drang*.

I would go to the big Upper West Side apartment of Lena and Lennie with my new legit friends. There, we always ran into Duke Ellington's gifted arranger, Billy Strayhorn, who was known to the cognoscenti as "Swee'pea." Here, I also met Saint Clair Pugh, an old friend of Lena's and the direct link to Lena's close pal from their MGM days Ava Gardner. (Ava and Saint had grown up together in Smithfield, North Carolina.) Saint was a daunting presence, wearing a bow tie, professorially dangling his Phi Beta Kappa and smoking a pipe. (In my later column years, he would work with me for two decades.) Lena thrived on this inside show biz crowd. She'd segue around the room making wisecracks. Or tell how her pal Ava won the role of Julie in the movie of *Show Boat*. The part clearly should have been Lena's and Ava always said so. Lena loved it that Max Factor had to invent "Light Egyptian" makeup for Ava. Or, Lennie and Lena and Saint would reminisce about the years when they'd first met in Paris in the early fifties. This was all too exciting for words. Lena would use Saint and me to practice and perfect her "Southernisms." She had a perfect Deep South accent when she wanted to have one. (Saint and I didn't seem to have any choice.)

Lena had been born in Brooklyn to upper-class black professionals. But she'd spent summers in Georgia when she'd been very young and her favorite joke on herself was to add fuel to the rumors that she was descended from the white senator John C. Calhoun, who had reigned in South Carolina before the Civil War.

She would laugh sardonically about this. We would sit around and eat soul food and talk about drinking "White Lightning." Lena would produce a fruit jar of the clear liquid but I don't think anyone really drank it. It was just the "outlaw" idea of it. These were nights of soulful talk—about music, musicians, jazz, Lady Day, the Cotton Club, the Deep South, racial prejudice, race records* and the horrid things that had happened in Hollywood.

Lena and Lennie's interracial marriage was ahead of its time. It had shaken Hollywood to the roots. Both had suffered. And although Lena did make two marvelous movies with all-black casts, *Cabin in the Sky*, and *Stormy Weather*, Hollywood never really knew what to do with her. MGM could only pose her next to a fake tree in a white satin gown and make her sing something sultry about love and sex, so long as nobody white

---

Offbeat and underground early black recordings of rhythm, blues and jazz. Many race records were vulgar and obscene. They had enormous vitality. "When yo' house catch a' fire, ain' nobody 'round/Throw your jelly out the window, let it ooze on down/ Oh, sweet Mama, Daddy's got them Deep Ellum blues."

came near her. The shot would be cut from the picture in the South.

The lure and lore of being nobody in such gatherings was bittersweet, but I learned a lot. I tried hard to hold up my end of things and when Lena and Lennie invited me to a party they were giving for Noel Coward, I did my part and brought Rock Hudson as a "date." I had finally met Rock through his Hollywood press agent and I guess he was being accommodating to "Miss *Modern Screen*."

Lena began calling me "Mary Elizabeth" and would often sign her notes to me "Mary Lena Calhoun." Years rolled by and in the early sixties I turned up in San Francisco to find my pal Lena opening at the Fairmont Hotel. Onstage there was a different woman. To a large and elegant audience of blacks and whites, Lena introduced some unusual "noncommercial" songs. One was Billie Holliday's famous "Strange Fruit," about a Southern lynching. And at a big party given for her after, I realized I was the only white person there. The good-looking crowd celebrating Lena represented the cream of black San Francisco. That night I knew what it was like to feel in the minority, and out of the mix. Lena would provide my amateur Ph.D. to my study of "The Race."

But I didn't realize what demons were now pursuing Lena. The Civil Rights movement was in full swing. Lena went down South to visit the Civil Rights leader Medgar Evers. Hours later, he was assassinated. This changed Lena. I believe she blamed herself for not having been "black enough" in a white world. She and Duke Ellington had for years been the darlings of sophisticated Caucasians who couldn't really open their hearts to the rest of their people.

Thus, for a number of years Lena avoided many of her white friends. But in time, this really good woman, this incredible font of talent found the spirit of forgiveness to overlook how shallow we all had been as her devoted admirers. We had extolled Lena for her great sex appeal, her divine gifts and her gorgeous glamour. We hadn't dealt with her as a black woman; we didn't want to, perhaps. We were simply thrilled to know such an international star, one who transcended her race. But Lena wanted us to love her *for* her down-home self, *and* for her race *and* to behave better toward her brothers and sisters instead of treating her always as "special."

And when she opened on Broadway in her 1981 hit show, *The Lady and Her Music,* I went as sheer audience and wrote as a critic, not as a friend. I said with heartfelt sincerity that "few things in life are perfection...but Lena Horne onstage at the Nederlander Theater has reached it...Her gestures are spare and telling, as in a Japanese Noh play; her movements—lithe, sinuous, youthful, exuberant and sometimes funny. Her flawless Southern dialect is as precise as the greatest Oxford English, as deliberately chosen as a glittering French phrase. A performance of fire and dynamite..."

I was very pleased to be asked by PBS to speak about Lena in its recent "American Masters" documentary. And in 1999 I spoke onstage at Lincoln Center in a four-generation all-star salute to "Lena...the Legacy." There I praised one of the greatest stars of our time, and made Lena laugh when I said, in a backward compliment: "Thank goodness for the white honky in Lena's woodpile," implying that the ancient Senator Calhoun seemed to have improved Lena's already incomparable genes.

RADIO DAYS

AND TV, TOO

WHEN A PAL SAYS, "PLEASE take over my very good job because I intend to travel with the international *Porgy and Bess* company," your ears perk up. That's what happened with the beautiful Polish girl-about-New York, Rose Tobias. She had been part of a killer triumvirate of ambitious Manhattan beauties, including Shirley Potash (later wed to *Time*'s Dick Clurman) and Ruth Cosgrove (later wed to Milton Berle). These three tried to insinuate their way to the top by dating VIM (Very Important Men) and in the fifties, I must say, that was often the only way for a woman to get to the top.

Rosie was like one of the Gabors, her good looks and high cheekbones have lasted to this day. Whenever she called me I'd listen carefully, because there was much to be learned from an authentic New York Jewish girl by the likes of me. She'd burble, "Well, last night I slept with Phil Silvers."

I'd ask wonderingly, "Why?"

She'd snort. "Because—because he's Phil Silvers, silly."

Rosie had a job as a guest-getter for a CBS radio show called *Mike & Buff's Mailbag*. Her boss was a young comer named Mike Wallace and the "Buff" of the *Mailbag* was Buff

Cobb, the granddaughter of the famous Southern storyteller-comedian Irving S. Cobb. Mike and Buff were married and they were hot. In 1953, I was back from touring with *Top Banana,* and living in a one-room walkup over the Peacock Espresso coffee shop on West 4th Street just off Sixth Avenue. Rosie was offering me a career leg up. It was an exciting period in New York—the fifties, with the city bouncing back from World War II. In spite of a national atmosphere of ongoing poisonous Red-baiting politics, America seemed to be regaining its health.

As usual, I resisted. "I don't know how to get guests for a radio show." Rosie said, "Oh, sure you do. I'll tell you everything you need to know and give you all my contacts. This job is a cinch. It's fun and Mike and Buff are going places at CBS. And I have this chance to be the PR rep for *Porgy and Bess* as it tours Russia and the rest of the world. I don't want to miss it. But I promised Mike I'd find him an intelligent replacement and you are it! Don't you think it'll be great for me, overseas with all those fabulous men in that sexy company?"

How did I always manage to run into these oversexed, ambitious and deliciously driven egos? I don't know—just lucky, I guess. I understood Rosie's fascination and obsession with the handsome all-black cast of *Porgy and Bess.* I understood she wanted to travel on somebody else's dime around the world. I just couldn't see her leaving her cushy job. But once she had recommended me to Mike as her successor, she set me on an upward journey—it would be a long trip, but I have to give her a lot of credit.*

Mike Wallace had served in the Navy during the war and came to New York from Chicago, where he'd been an announcer and aspiring actor. He had jet-black hair and a craggy,

---

*Rose returned from her trip around the world and fell in love with a fine British actor named Maxwell Shaw. She has lived in England ever since and became a first-class casting director for films. My favorite Rosie story concerns her mother, who once requested that Rosie hand her "a Kleeneck!" Rosie said, "Mother, it's not Kleeneck; it's Kleenex." Her mother said wisely, "Well, I only wanted one!"

pockmarked face that made him look rugged and compelling. I loved him the instant we met. His wife, Buffy, was a girl just oozing Southern charm, full of giggles and easy laughter. I adored her lore about life in Hollywood, for she'd been married already to two celebrities who were notably hard-to-get guys, the actor William Eythe and the Hollywood lawyer legend Greg Bautzer. I figured she had to be some kind of very special woman. Mike thought so, too. She represented a kind of show biz "aristocracy," theater history and WASPy charm. It intrigued him. In any case, I was simply blown over by the combined glamour and sex appeal of Mike and Buff.

I went to work on East 53rd Street in the CBS offices with a will. I was determined to be the best guest-getter anybody had ever had and later Mike would say that I had been "nonpareil." "In one week Liz got us Lili St. Cyr, Faye Emerson and Eleanor Roosevelt."*

Each week we surveyed our incoming mail and selected the most interesting questions to discuss. We'd agree on a guest expert. For the lady in Iowa with kitchen problems, we'd invite the current Fannie Farmer to come talk. We asked Mrs. FDR, I recall, to discuss the problems mothers have with their in-laws. Was there a protocol for dealing with them? (Mrs. FDR had in-laws coming and going like revolving doors; all of her children seemed forever to be marrying and divorcing.) And once I recall I invited the Random House head, Bennett Cerf, to come and talk about how to get a book published. "What's in it for me?" he snapped. He was the only turndown I ever experienced. "Yeah, Mike and Buff are friends, but I don't need this crap."

Mike and Buff were wonderful together on the air: sweet and sour. Hot and cool. They knew how to argue. He could be

---

*Miss St. Cyr was the famous strip artist I'd seen in Chicago. Faye Emerson was an actress whose décolletage on TV caused controversy; she had also been wed to Elliott Roosevelt. Mrs. Roosevelt—well, she was Mrs. Roosevelt. But when I got her personally on the phone, she was down-to-earth and charming. If Mike and Buff wanted her on the air, then she'd be there.

volatile but she could always defang him. They made a perfect pairing—he was aggressive and smart, a born devil's advocate. She was a charmer, a lady, a Southern belle with tales to tell. In a pinch she'd quote her famous grandpa and she had a good sense of humor. The guest expert would enter in and the lighthearted nature of the show—with a pinch of Wallace vinegar and Cobb sugar—would froth over the top. *Mike & Buff's Mailbag* was a CBS hit. It seems quaint now, but in those innocent days when there were Commies under every bed and a horrible "police action" in Korea and a disgusting guy called Senator Joe McCarthy in the Senate, it was a nice relief and definitely a forerunner of many a talk show to come.

Our producer was the genial Lew Melamed, a man who had already seen and heard everything. And we had a crazy writer, who shall remain nameless except in my heart. He spent most of his time in the office smoking marijuana (or Mary Jane, as it was called then) and walking about twirling a wet washrag to take up the smoke.

The entire situation was so easygoing that it wasn't like work at all. Rosie had already pointed out that Mike and Buff were the new kids on the Manhattan social block and everybody invited them everywhere. So I had a certain measure of fame by association. I was very aware that they were a part of the Moss and Kitty Hart, Harry Kurnitz, Nedda and Josh Logan, Martin Gabel and Arlene Francis, Dorothy Kilgallen and Richard Kollmar crowd. I even got to meet some of these people and a great training ground for getting into the life of New York my little job turned out to be. Calling up famous people cold, saying I worked for Mike and Buff, inviting them to appear on CBS radio, was easy. And then on the day of the recording, I got to meet world-famous names. A few I connected with and continued to know through the years.

Mike was extra good to me. At one point he gave me a raise out of his own pocket when CBS refused to do so. He listened to my ambitions and my problems. He petted and cosseted me. I was still in deep dental recovery from my car accident in Texas and sometimes my ill-fitted temporary bridges came loose and I would drop my two front teeth. He found all this impossibly dear and just kept encouraging me. "Be yourself. You're great. You're going to make it big time in *New York*!" Despite the fearsome reputation he has today as the veteran killer on *60 Minutes*, he was the kindest and most sensitive person I had met in the Big City.

But the Wallaces had a teeny, tiny problem. They were madly in love with each other. Yet he was fearsomely insecure and jealous of his petite and fluffy little bride. He would come in with a storm cloud hovering over his handsome face and demand to know, "Where is she? Where's Buffy?" I'd say that she had gone to Saks to shop—or whatever. I never felt I had to lie for her; she really wasn't up to anything that I knew about. He would ask, "Did Adam Clayton Powell call here? Did he ask for Buffy?" And soon Buffy would sail in with her arms full of shopping and they'd have a contretemps over the sexy Harlem political leader, Mr. Powell, who she'd swear she hadn't seen.

The *Mailbag* and I sailed along for a year with great success and no problems except this one. Mike, who believed his wife was the sexiest, most alluring woman in the world, continued to demand some kind of fealty from her that she was already offering—or so I believed. One day the producer came to me. "Now, little girl," said Lew, "I want you to be prepared. It looks like our stars are going to separate and get a divorce. That'll be the end of this cushy job, so I won't blame you if you look around elsewhere."

I was heartbroken. And sure enough, they separated and we sort of filled in with shows in the can and waited around wondering if we would proceed. Melamed then phoned. "Be there at nine sharp tomorrow, honey, because they are getting back together and we are way behind schedule. We will be taping promos all morning. We're back in business."

I arrived giddy with relief and so did Buffy. She was wearing one of her girly-looking dresses, very bouffant, a pert little hat with a fetching veil, her blonde curls peeking out from under. She looked at me and winked. We were women, after all—conspirators against the crazy men in the world. I was so divinely happy that morning, one would think I had reconciled with somebody. All of a sudden, Mike came in. He looked impossibly sexy in his blue blazer and white shirt and rep tie. He was testosterone in motion. He ignored Lew and the writer and me and rushed right over to Buffy, crushing her in his arms. The three of us just stood there like mimes out of a job. Buffy recoiled a bit and adjusted her veil. Then Mike reached into his pocket and whipped out a Tiffany box and offered it to her. We could see from across the room the ring glinting inside.

Buffy squealed and put it on. They whispered together and the three of us looked away and tried to get into our own conversation to give them some room. We were pretending not to listen to them when there was an explosion like World War III in their corner of the room. Mike had suddenly started on Buffy with certain accusations. She had backed all the way up into the corner. And she just wasn't having any. She threw up her hands, threw down the jewelry box and said, "That's it! I've had it. This is the end. You are too much. I'm finished!" She ran out of the recording room and he ran out after her. We stood there like a clumsy cart that had lost its horses.

We had. *Mike & Buff's Mailbag* went off the air. The Wallaces did not reconcile. I was reassigned to work on a show for Kathy Godfrey and I felt lucky to still be getting a salary. Then months later, Mike telephoned to tell me he had met a wonderful girl named Lorraine and was getting married. I congratulated him and told him the truth—how much I missed him. "We'll get together," he said.

But we didn't—not for years. This time around, the fearsome Mike married a woman who was quite possessive and he didn't get out much anymore. I did go to see him perform on Broadway as the romantic lead in a play by Harry Kurnitz, *Reclining Figure,* about Lord Duveen. He was excellent, but an acting career was not for Mike. He went on to create *Nightbeat,* a hard-hitting, first-of-its-kind TV talk show where he never gave the interviewee a break. And the rest is history. CBS lured him back and he became one of the network's most valuable players. Today, in his early eighties, he is still a broadcast legend.

Mike and I did get together again. He followed my career with nice notes and occasional calls and after I became a full-fledged newspaper columnist, living and working in the very world he inhabited, we spent more time together socially. When he married the widow of his former TV partner Ted Yates, he earned the happiness he deserved—a ready-made, grown-up family of fabulous boys, his stepdaughter, grandchildren and the devotion of his current wife, Mary. I have been privileged to spend many Thanksgivings with the Wallace family. In 1999, Mike and I hosted together the Skitch Henderson eightieth birthday celebration at Carnegie Hall. When we saw the tape together, the two of us burst out laughing. "We should get these genes and sell them!" said Mike, for somehow the cameras had made us look impossibly attractive. It was a great moment for me to stand next to Mike Wallace as his costar.

He is still the greatest guy I ever worked for and in spite of his teasing, prickly manner, one of the sweetest human beings I have ever known.

BEING A PRODUCER FOR *THE KATHY GODFREY Show* wasn't half as much fun as working for Mike and Buff. Kathy had a little bit of her famous brother's much-vaunted charm and folksiness, but it was only a smidgeon compared to Old Red's. I supposed they'd given her a show of her own as a sop to their big radio guy Arthur Godfrey, who had CBS owner Bill Paley's ear.

The entire experience was so ho-hum that I can't even remember our premiere. So I was easy pickings the day an impossibly handsome "vest pocket" kind of perfect little man came in to see me. Even if he hadn't been good-looking, his tailor would have won the day for him. "My name is Norman Frank," he announced. "Word all over CBS Radio is that you are the best of all possible assistants. How would you like to leave CBS Radio and go with me to NBC-TV to produce segments for Dave Garroway's *Wide Wide World*?"

Needless to say, I left Mr. Paley's domain without a backward glance. I didn't bother to investigate Norman Frank. If I had, I'd have discovered that he had a reputation as the most ruthless, most efficient SOB ever to entertain an ambition. But—I found out anyway.

It may be trite, but like many another Tiny Mite, he was always busy making up for his lack of size. He was so glorious-looking he literally stopped people in their tracks. It was as if Robert Taylor had appeared in half-size. I used to enjoy walking slightly behind him to observe people's reactions as they passed.

He was a brilliant producer. He operated from the theory that like Caligula, "I don't care if they hate me so long as they fear me." I did fear him, but as he was no Mike Wallace, at first I had no emotional investment, so I thought if I couldn't do the job, I'd just pass on. I was surprised that although he could reduce strong men towering over him to jelly, he was always very nice to me. He never yelled or tormented me, though it was obvious when I disappointed him. He would fix me with an unyielding stare, which seemed to last an eternity. Then he would say quietly, "Well, what are we going to do about this? How do *you* intend to fix it?"

This challenge would set me off. So Norman Frank taught me the virtue of becoming a part of the solution instead of always being a part of the problem. I often cite this when asked to advise young people how to rise in the world. Like many underlings in an underpaid job, I had often been tempted to lower my standards, to "lay dead kittens" at the feet of my bosses. Then I'd say, "It can't be accomplished. It's no use. We can't do this one." (Inside, the underling gloats and says, "They make the big money. They have the credit and the power. Let *them* solve it!")

I stopped all that. Norman Frank and I were in an imperceptible race to impress one another with what we *could* do. I grew perceptibly as a helper, facilitator and hard worker. I made Mr. Frank's problems, the show's problems, my own. He and I came almost immediately to the notice of our NBC executive producer, a legend in his own time, named Barry Wood. Other segment producers, like the successful novelist, Gerald *The Last Angry Man* Greene, would ask to borrow me for difficult assignments. (I loved the big warmhearted and totally Jewish Mr. Greene. And to my delight, he loved me. He signed his book to me, "To Liz, the only Texan I've ever liked!")

Wide Wide World was a show ahead of its time. That is, it happened before they invented satellites to carry TV signals and before they invented videotape and mini-cameras. *Wide Wide World* was put on the air every Sunday morning with cameras as big and unwieldy as refrigerators. Flexibility in those days was not TV's long suit. And *Wide Wide World* was a live show—the forerunner, in a manner of speaking, of the kind of TV Roone Arledge later created for ABC and the *Wide World of Sports,* yet to come.

Every Sunday at 11:00 A.M., when most Americans were entering their church doors, our star, Dave Garroway, introduced actual, live, real happenings across the U.S.A. and in the Western Hemisphere, or from wherever we could get and transmit a TV signal by what was then called "line of sight." (For instance, you could bounce a TV signal off the Empire State Building to another tall building, radio tower or electric tower or from one mountaintop to the next peak that was "in sight.")

There has always been a lot of quibbling and posturing about truth in television. Or there was then. (Those were the glory days of Fred Friendly and Edward R. Murrow.) But I discovered that my *Wide Wide World* bosses didn't want to know too much about how much we TV slaves, who went into the field, had to fudge to bring off those "spontaneous" live events between 11:00 A.M. and 12:00 noon on the Sabbath.

It was also one of my jobs to research and suggest suitable happenings. Many times these events had to be rearranged and made to happen. If the Cuero Texas Turkey Trot took place each year on Thanksgiving Day, suddenly, miraculously, the Cuero turkey industry would be convinced to stage the Trot's parade on a Sunday at precisely 11:00 A.M. Anything to be on television! This might be to the consternation of the local churches, but business is business. What was good for NBC-TV was good for the folks who sold turkeys. Or the ones who did the Luling Watermelon Thump or a Pennsylvania Marching Band or Baton Twirlers of Oklahoma.

It was the line producer who had to get an event pulled together, organized, ready to step out and start on a hair trigger for the New York control room. We had to have suitable "locals" coached in clever or funny or trenchant things to say for give-and-take with Mr. Garroway, who remained safe in the studio at 30 Rockefeller Plaza. (Mr. Garroway never gave us line producers the time of day unless we screwed up. I met him but have no warm, cuddly memories. I was new to celebrity in those days and was less understanding and forgiving. I am sure Garroway also had a hard row to hoe. He simply was paid better than the rest of us.)

TWO INTERESTING THINGS HAPPENED TO me on *Wide Wide World.* First, Norman Frank sent me to Toronto to arrange a great skating event in a major Canadian indoor stadium. It seemed pretty routine until he said to me long-distance, ominously, "And I don't want to see any empty seats in that stadium when we pan the camera."

I hadn't really even thought about an audience. Now I kicked myself; I panicked. It was a big place. The event would have no audience because it was being staged expressly for us, although *Wide Wide World* would never want to admit that. I rushed off to the Toronto newspapers where I babbled on to editors and reporters about how I was this big deal producer for NBC-TV in New York and wanted to invite the people of Toronto to see our live show next Sunday, absolutely free.

We got massive press coverage and a huge audience and, very proud of myself, promptly at 12:00 noon, as the last blade left the ice, I rushed off to the airport to go back to New York in triumph.

I arrived to discover that the Canadian Broadcasting Company, with whom we had cooperated, was demanding that I be fired. Canadians all over had been furious to discover that they could not see this event, taking place in Toronto, on their own TV sets. "We were live shills for NBC!" raged the CBC brass.

"You have to go see the big boss," said Norman calmly on Monday morning. So I reported to Barry Wood's magnificent suite where I had never been before. I had made a Canadian network look bad, so I thought I was done for. Mr. Wood smiled at me: "The CBC wants your head. But personally, I'd like to give you a medal. Don't worry. You made plenty of big executives here and in Canada sit up and notice you, your effort and your ingenuity. And we learned a lesson. Don't throw line producers to the wolves in situations where the brass has obviously not thought something through to a conclusion and a consequence." No wonder Barry Wood was a legend.

The second adventure I had on *WWW* concerned a pickup from Concord, Massachusetts, where we went to celebrate the glorious April 1775 first shot of the Revolution. We had, of course, moved it to an approximate Sunday. I went down and toured the battlefield. We paced every step of the "rude bridge" at Concord. I met the great-great-grandchild of Ralph Waldo Emerson or whatever he was. This cute kid was eight or nine and he was our "coup" for this remote. The camera would come up on the battlefield and come toward what we inevitably referred to now as "the rude bridge that arched the flood," and he'd recite:

> *"Their flag to April's breeze unfurled,*
> *Here once the embattled farmers stood,*
> *And fired the shot heard round the world."*

We were convinced that this would be a killer segment.

Sunday was approaching. We were sanguine and calm there on the battlefield at dawn. Cranky camera, sound and light men made dirty jokes and wisecracks, they slurped coffee and ate doughnuts and I didn't have that "if anything can possibly go wrong it will" feeling. No, I had rehearsed our young hero to perfection. He had the poem down pat and now he was in my charge.

But he seemed nervous. He was nothing like he'd been during our rehearsals. There he was, eight or nine years of pre-pubescent quivering Jell-O. I said, "You've recited this poem all your life, haven't you?" He nodded. "You've now got the chance to give this to the world again, just as your famous an-cestor gave it in print. This will be a snap. Don't worry. You can do it and I'll buy you the best football you've ever seen after it is all over." (I wasn't supposed to bribe people, or so Standards and Practices said, but looking at this terrified kid I decided he was every bit as deserving as the turkey industry of Cuero and we always gave *them* a break.)

The kid liked the football idea. He nodded. He'd try to pull himself together. He would start to rehearse. But he'd flub. Finally he went to pieces and began wailing, "I can't do it." I began to believe him. I got on the phone to New York. I told the control room, "Look, I'm desperate here. This kid has been great in rehearsal, but I'm afraid I'll give him a heart attack if I keep trying to set him up." The clock was rolling toward 11:00 A.M.

"Keep trying!" yelled New York. "We're desperate here, too. What can we do? We have nothing there—no marching bands, no soldiers in uniform, no music to recreate the incident, no, nothing but that fucking rude bridge. Liz—we have no pic-ture! No picture!" (These are the worst two words in television. We were counting on the impact of this charming little boy doing this great classic poem!)

I screamed back, "Give it up! Give it up! Give the god-damned poem to Garroway to read. I need an ambulance for this little boy, not a camera crew on him."

There was silence from New York. Then I could hear the producer talking in the control room. He sounded calm. "Come in as we rehearsed. Pan slowly over the bridge and battlefield. Garroway will read the poem, but we are fucked."

The child was hurried away. The crew and I were just standing there, expecting nothing but doom. There was indeed no picture of anything but the green landscape of Concord, and

the silence of the Revolutionary dead, and their dead enemies—
the British. The cameraman was panning America's sacred first
battlefield, but his heart wasn't in it. The red light was on. Garroway slowly read the words of the poem as the camera moved.

    I guess less is more. We won critical raves for our elegy
to Concord, our visual poetry above the poetry of Emerson, our
simplistic but satisfying look back with a TV camera and no
hoopla. They wrote glowingly of Garroway's haunting voice
over the image of the empty battlefield and "the rude bridge that
arched the flood—."

I THINK WE WON AN Emmy. And, the kid never did get his
football.

THE COWARDLY

LION

SUMMER CAME AND NBC ASSIGNED me to a series of replacement shows with big stars, who would follow one another in monthly sequence: Perry Como, Polly Bergen and Tony Bennett would each fill in while *WWW* was on hiatus.

Stars! I was wary. I had already experienced the supreme indifference of Dave Garroway to the production staff. We simply hardly existed for him.

Summer replacements weren't much different. Stars are stars. If I had worshipped Perry Como, Polly Bergen and Tony Bennett all my life and thus expected them to connect with me, I was as naive as any fan. No matter how hard we worked, solving problems, booking, erasing technical woes, "gofering" for this and that, whatever, we remained invisible to the stars. We were like wallpaper. And most of us by now were too professional to let fan worship show. We'd have had our fingernails slowly removed before we'd have asked for an autograph, a posed photo or anything to prove we'd been there and done that.

Tony Bennett was the nicest of the lot and in the end, gifted each of us with a nice engraved silver geegaw from Tiffany. The others didn't bother. (Years later, after Tony and I became friends, he had absolutely no memory of ever doing this summer show for NBC. "I guess it came and went," he laughs.)

The guest stars for these little summer revues were all different. We had booked them through agents or press agents or—occasionally—directly. So they had some minor clue that we existed.

I had booked the genius Bert Lahr to do his famous "Woodman" stint. I adored this weird old guy. I had worshipped him as the Cowardly Lion of *The Wizard of Oz,* read all the history of him onstage with Ethel Merman in *DuBarry Was a Lady,* later sympathized with his short-lived Abe Burrows/Jule Styne revue, *Two on the Aisle,* where Broadway scuttlebutt had it that his costar, Dolores Gray, had pushed him around. Before the Como appearance, I had been amazed by his legit turn in the existential Samuel Beckett drama, *Waiting for Godot.*

Godot, where nothing much happens and two ragged tramps wait for it, had stunned the critics and mystified ordinary audiences. Were the tramps waiting for God? Was God simply "dog" backwards? Were they in hell? What the hell was it all about?

During our rehearsal in an actual theater where the Como show was to be put on TV, I was up alone, midorchestra, observing. Bert Lahr joined me. He sat down and whispered something friendly, like "How's it going, kid?" I murmured back, thinking how beneath him all this penny-ante TV was. *This* man had portrayed Frank Baum's cowardly lion and should have won an Oscar for it. Yet here he was on hold to rehearse a comic turn he knew backward and forward as we listened to Perry Como saunter through several love songs.

Many years later I would read, in *The New Yorker,* John Lahr's take on his famous father. And I realized that to his family, Lahr exhibited a singular sadness. To them he seemed lugubrious and distant. But this day in rehearsal he was warm and cozy. Perhaps the atmosphere of even pseudo–show biz— music, lights, a proscenium stage, exigencies of timing—made him feel more relaxed and at home.

The music stopped. There was interminable stage wait.

Now we could talk out loud. I decided to take the plunge and express my ignorance. I gulped. "Mr. Lahr, you were so wonderful in *Waiting for Godot*, but the play itself isn't easy. So what do you think the playwright Beckett meant by it? Can you articulate a theme?"

Lahr stared at me with his oyster eyes. He sighed. He shifted in his seat. Then he said, slowly and with the most august seriousness, "Well, you know, I have thought a lot about it. And I think, personally, it's about the Irish Rebellion."

Everyone to whom I have ever told this story says, "Oh, he must have just been putting you on; just pulling your leg."

I still don't think so. At any rate, that was the high point for me of that particular summer in the fabulous fifties.

THE GLORYFIER

HER CABLE ADDRESS READ "GLORYFIER" just as if she were the successor to such as Flo Ziegfeld or Billy Rose. (Today it would read Gloryfier.com.) And successor she was to these show business entrepreneurs, except she represented the underdog class—actors—and others hired by entrepreneurs.

Gloria Safier was one of the last of the best of the one-person agents on Broadway and in movies. Toward the end of her career, she graduated to being a literary agent, unearthing the work of Bob Benton and David Newman, of Tom Harris, whose first novel, *Black Sunday*, she arranged to have published, and discovering the popular Susan Isaacs. In her time she fought for many actors: Geraldine Fitzgerald, Mary Astor, Elaine Stritch, Constance Ford, Ann Sheridan, Arlene Francis, Diane Cilento, Louise Allbritton, Patsy Kelly, Ruby Keeler, Russell Nype, Leora Dana, Wally Cox and for designers Irene Sharaff and Peter Larkin, writers Irwin Shaw, Ellen Violett, Louise Fitzhugh and others.

An offshoot from the famous Selznick family on her mother's side, Gloria had served her apprenticeship, working as a $25-a-week press agent for Billy Rose. Then her cousin, the great ten-percenter Myron Selznick, imported her to Hollywood and taught her to fight the battles of talent against the system. But she didn't stay long on the West Coast; she was a born-in-Brooklyn native New Yorker and the theater was her first love.

In the fifties, people didn't go home after dinner in New York. They went to nightclubs and supper clubs: The Blue Angel, Ruban Bleu, Bon Soir, Village Vanguard, RSVP, Upstairs at the Downstairs, Bemelmans' Bar, Maisonette, The Harwyn Club or dancing at The Stork Club and El Morocco. One night I was sitting in the bar of the Blue Angel, waiting for the talented Bart Howard to go on the tiny postage-stamp stage to accompany Kaye Ballard. A woman in a red dress walked up to me. She seemed to be a handsome but not beautiful version of Ava Gardner. She pronounced: "I hear a lot of good things about you. I understand that you're okay. I'm Gloria Safier." She stuck out her hand.

I was later advised by people working The Blue Angel—Stan Herman, Portia Nelson, Jane Dulo—that I had been accorded a rare honor. And because of her client Elaine Stritch, Gloria and I became friends.

I had no idea how fateful it would be to become one of Gloria's gang. "The Gang of 9000," I used to call it. Her weekend open house was famous. People sometimes turned up for cocktails on Fridays and found themselves still there on Sunday evening when Gloria began to hustle everybody out. "Go home," she'd say. "It's a school night." It was hanging out at Gloria's that taught me to drink defensively. I found it very hard to keep up with everything while sober and though I was never a good drinker, I made a stab at it with some of the world's pros. This meant that I'd now and then find myself in Gloria's "recovery room," sleeping one off. The R.R. was a closet-sized space with only a single bed and barely room to get to it. There was nothing wrong with staying here, but invariably Gloria would shake you from a deep slobber to introduce you to someone special. "Hey, wake up. I want you to meet Alain Delon." The French heartthrob would be sitting there impassively on the side of the bed, waiting for you to come to your senses when you definitely did not look your best. I recall once passing through Gloria's own bedroom where a troubled brunette was snoring away, really sawing wood. Gloria nodded her head and said, "Vivien Leigh. She had one too many last night." Scarlett, my Scarlett snored? The things I learned under Gloria's tutelage. Ethel Merman, Ann Sheridan, Joan Blondell, Arthur Laurents, Ralph Meeker, Mary Astor, George S. Kaufman, Rex Harrison, Claudette Colbert, Greta Garbo, Gig Young and Frank Sinatra had all taken overflowing drinks from the hands of Gloria. (She didn't believe in stinting on the ice and left a trail of dribbles from the bar.)

Gloria could pick up the phone and find an instant job for anyone down on his luck. She would call Hubbell Robinson at CBS, call the Oscar Hammerstein office, call Leland Hayward, call Bob Kintner directly at NBC or call the movie man Sam Spiegel. Her tough brand of love mixed with mother hen concern was her own concoction. She was quick and impatient. When my father came to New York to see me, he fell madly for Gloria. She took him to the racetrack and they bet up a storm. "Gloria could have been my own child," Sloan said grandly, seeming to forget he already had one less suitable daughter. One day he said, "You know, I always worried about you. I feared these Yankees would take advantage of you in New York. But now that Gloria is your agent, I am going to stop worrying about you."

Gloria did indeed do a lot for me. She forced me to take jobs I was too backward to attempt. She goaded, needled and nagged the hell out of me—and out of legions of others whom she'd begin calling every morning at 7:30 A.M. to see what was going on.

It was from the window of Gloria's fourth-floor walkup at 110 East 55th Street in the late fifties that I often used to toss down the final and finished Cholly Knickerbocker column (I was the ghostwriter) to a cabdriver who would drive and deliver it by hand before 11:30 P.M. to the *Journal American* offices on 220 South Street. On the fifth floor above us, my friend and competitor Joseph X. Dever was also writing his society column to go to the *World-Telegram and Sun*. Sometimes when we got in trouble, Joe and I would confer and trade material. He'd give me one that was too hot for him, and vice versa. One night I carelessly tossed out my envelope and instead of falling to the street to the waiting cabbie, it landed on the air conditioner of the producer Jean Dalrymple and her husband, Army General Phillip Ginder, who lived on the third floor. I had to knock on their door, wake them and walk through their bedroom to retrieve Cholly's deathless prose. On the ground floor of Gloria's building was the Enrico Caruso beauty salon where I first met the seventeen-year-old Vincent Roppatte, the man who was later to transform me into a natural blonde.

Because Gloria couldn't bear any kind of injustice, there was never a dull moment at 110 East 55th Street. She was constantly calling the cops. The men of the Midtown North Precinct were her pals. They'd troop up the four flights, have a drink, say, "What's the trouble now, Miss Safier?" and we'd be off on some adventure. Once when a couple was having a fistfight on the street below, the cops didn't come soon enough. Gloria climbed up into the window and poured pitchers of iced water on their heads. I learned a lot about being brave from Gloria. Chiefly, that I wasn't.

At this juncture I was going with a TV director named Jimmy Elson, a denizen of Tulsa, Oklahoma. We were always at Gloria's. We didn't dare miss a thing, or miss the chance to hear the inside dish, or miss meeting another Safier VIP. Why, our own Gloria had been the inspiration that caused Freeman Gosden to name one of his characters Saphire on the *Amos & Andy* show.

Late one evening we were with Gloria and Saint Clair Pugh and they decided to go down and walk her poodle Rocky. While she was gone, Elson and I decided it would be hilarious if, when they returned, we'd be dancing nude in the living room. We stripped and began to tango. After a few minutes Elson said, "Let's stop a minute. I'm getting a hard-on." We sat down on the couch with pillows on our laps and started talking. Then we heard footsteps on the stairs. It was Gloria. We sprang into action and were indeed dancing in our altogether when in came our hostess, Mr. Pugh and a collection of friends they had run into on the street. The great thing was that all of them decided to just ignore our condition. Gloria just looked at us and said, "Let's have a drink."

Going out with Gloria was a treat. She knew every maître d' and headwaiter in New York. She was persona grata at Sardi's. And she would sweep you up in her excitement. "Come on, gotta see Peg Murray in *This or That*. I want to hit the Harold Pinter play and catch Maggie Phillips in *Fallen Angels*." I thought this meant a veritable week of free theater-going. But, no: Gloria went into one after the other. Enthralled at the opening of the drama *Homecoming*, I was besotted on the aisle, when suddenly Gloria sprang up, grabbed my arm and pulled me out. "Gotta rush, don't want to miss Peg's entrance down the street!"

I gasped. "But this is Pinter; we can't leave. It just started."

She'd nod. "I know, I know—there's too much to see." We'd catch Peg Murray's turn and then we were on to somewhere else to see a second act of a play that was, of course, quite meaningless. People would say to me, "Did you see the Pinter play?"

I'd say, "Sort of..."

Gloria also had a two-room shack in Quogue on the beach, which she called "The Mouse House." (A mouse had been found barbecued in the toaster.) This house went down in early Hampton history. It was this house she let Elson and me clean while she went grocery shopping in her Karmann Ghia Volkswagen. We knew she'd come back and we'd have to schlep hundreds of dollars' worth of groceries up over the sand dunes. But while cleaning we decided to burn some rush blinds left over from a previous summer. We were standing with our brooms in hand, dishing, when we realized we had set the house on fire. The sparks from the rushes had caught the dune grass, which had now burned up under the porch. Gloria returned to a very singed front porch, which now had charred ends. She said, "It's a good thing the house didn't burn or I'd be driving up and down Dune Road saying, 'Here! Get two hundred dollars' worth of groceries for only fifty bucks. I've got to get them out of this car so we can drive back to New York!' "

Gloria was obsessed with "class." This one had class; that one didn't. This one was "a sport." That one wasn't. Gloria lent her clients money, paid for abortions, set people up with dentists and constantly bailed out her friends. She once had a client, an actress from Australia, who fell gravely ill. Exhausting her own resources, Gloria went to the actress's friends to ask for help until her family could arrive from Down Under. No one would give Gloria a dime. She spent all of her personal savings on the woman's hospital bills, though she'd only met her the day she arrived from Australia. Fortunately, the girl's family finally came through. But Gloria had no way to know they would.

As I began to rise in the world, nobody was prouder of my success than Gloria. "I knew you could do it, Skeezix!"

Gloria remained my agent until, in 1985 at age sixty-five, she succumbed to stomach cancer. For years she'd smoked hundreds of cigarettes and drunk gallons of scotch. Then she stopped smoking and switched to vodka. But it was too late. During her illness, which she had almost never mentioned, she never complained.

In the days after she died, I realized how Gloria had defined parameters of my career, my friendships, my life in New York. What would I have become without her? Stumbling down Fifth Avenue in tears on the day of her memorial service, I found myself stopped on eight separate occasions by persons who associated me with her and offered their condolences. (New York is such a small town!) I went into St. Patrick's and, like any good Southern Baptist, lit a candle for my Jewish friend Gloria and tried to comfort myself.

They held her memorial in the Royale Theater and there wasn't room enough inside for all of her mourners. In my column that week I noted that her obituary said she had no children. I added these words: "Nonsense. She had hundreds of us."

WHEN IN ROME

THE SUMMER BEFORE NBC FIRED so many of us during the Eisenhower Recession in 1957, my divinely crazy actress pal Elaine Stritch called, all excited. Mega-producer David O. Selznick wanted her to fly to Rome and play a nurse in the remake of Ernest Hemingway's *A Farewell to Arms.* This was to star Mrs. Selznick, the actress Jennifer Jones, and the heartthrob Rock Hudson. Would I take a leave of absence and go with Elaine for a month because she was allowed to bring an all-expenses-paid secretary/companion?

Movie-mad as always and never having been to Europe, I said I would not only go, but be a great help to her as, after all, I knew Rock Hudson! I didn't bother to say how little I knew him. I'd taken Rock to the party Lena Horne had given because he wanted to meet the great Noel Coward. And he once had come to a party I had given down on Jane Street in the Village. Stupidly, I had forced him to go around the room while I introduced him to a large gang of friends. He had been gracious, which I mistook for being entertained and interested.

Now, completely forgetting that I was supposed to be climbing up the career ladder myself, I became Elaine's "person." But she had always offered me a very interesting time—in good days and bad. I had once painted her Sutton Place kitchen hot pink for her. I was unemployed at the time, but insisted on signing my name in the corner of this Pepto-Bismol masterpiece when I finished. Elaine just stepped back, looked and said, "Priceless!"

Elaine was on the verge of beginning rehearsals in a new Broadway musical to costar Don Ameche. Written by Jean and Walter Kerr, it was titled *Goldilocks*. She would just have time to go to Rome and make the movie, enacting a nurse who smuggles brandy via her ample brassiere into a World War I hospital. We departed and Elaine had the songs for her stage role to memorize. I memorized them overnight, which caused Elaine to say, "Liz, sing Irving Berlin. Sing Cole Porter. Torture anyone you like, but don't sing my songs from this show, because on opening night I will go out onstage and sing them myself in your Texas accent and that will be the end of my career." I forced myself away from *Goldilocks*.

This was a time when airplanes still had propellers and the flight from NYC to Rome took eighteen hours with a stopover in Shannon, Ireland. Elaine had her small black poodle with us—Jimmy La Femme. (He had been given this sissy name by Elaine's beau, the Actors Studio tough guy Ben Gazzara.) The three of us took off first class. We would take Jimmy to the lavatory and put paper down, begging him to do his thing. He would look up at whichever one of us was standing on the john to give him room, and hold out. He held out until we got to Rome. What a gent.

We were on our first European adventure—just like the 1940s authors Cornelia Otis Skinner and Emily Kimbrough, but I do think we had more fun. So we arrived in Rome in the best of spirits. Selznick had sent his secret weapon to the airport to soften up Elaine. Vittorio De Sica, in the *A Farewell to Arms* cast, was one of the most handsome and talented of all the handsome and talented Italian stars of the period. Elaine descended to the tarmac wearing a silver fox, looking every inch the movie star. I was behind her carrying the raincoats, the hand luggage and Jimmy. De Sica swept off his hat, bowed and kissed

Elaine's hand, murmuring greetings in Italian. When he got to me, I wasn't ready for a Continental hand kiss. As he took my hand, raising it to his lips, I firmly shook his, U.S. style, thereby jerking him off his elegant feet. The ugly Americans had definitely landed.

"Who the hell was that?" Elaine asked. I tried to explain Vittorio De Sica. "He's in the movie with you!" I hissed. I couldn't believe how ignorant Elaine was. But like all really big talents, she lived in a world of her own. As she said later, excusing herself, "Twelve years in convent school; I had not majored in Italian film stars!"

Now began a month of such outrageous hilarity that even today I can almost feel my ribs still sore from laughing. After the first five days we'd had so much hilarity and so many laughs that we had given up and would just say weakly, "Ha!" The moment we were settled in our large Residence Palace suite, a new hotel in the Parioli section of Rome, Elaine swept out on the balcony and began singing the famous song from *New Faces*: "You've never seen us before—We've never seen you before, but before this marvelous evening ends, New Faces and you will be good friends!" Italians appeared in the neighboring windows and at that, the valance fell down from the balcony on Elaine's foot. I can't remember going to the hospital, but do recall Jimmy Elson arriving to join us. And we gave room service hell.

On every corner of Rome there was a poster of Elaine with Charlton Heston and Anne Baxter from the movie she had made a year before titled *Three Violent People*. The Italians called it *I Violenti!* It made Miss Stritch extremely popular around Rome where folks seemed to assume she was indeed the hard-drinking, tough-talking madam she played in the Western.

Elaine's luggage had unfortunately failed to arrive with us, which meant she confiscated my own meager wardrobe and I was left with the dregs. This was the Nancy Walker role and I had to play it.

With Elson in tow we proceeded to "do" Rome. Every night we ate in the American restaurant George's. And every night, Elaine made new conquests. She was total blonde catnip to Roman males. One night a bedazzled waiter in a cocktail bar was trying to serve us and look down Elaine's considerable cleavage at the same time. Jimmy La Femme was standing by the cocktail table and the waiter mistakenly placed a cocktail napkin on Jimmy's black behind. On this same night we squeezed into an elevator that had signs in several languages purporting to advise the passenger PLEASE CLOSE DOOR ON LEAVING. Ours read "ON LOVING." We never forgot that one.

The movie was on the usual David O. Selznick "hold" as he wrote pages and pages of memos to everybody and quarreled with the first director, John Huston. We waited and Rome was a great place to wait. Rock Hudson took me to dinner at Apulia and told me "all" about his unhappy marriage to Phyllis Gates. I drank it all in, and went back to the hotel where I would doodle "Mrs. Rock Hudson" on the pad by my bed. I was sorely smitten. In her room across the way, Elaine was doing the same thing. After several weeks, Elson left us and returned to New York, saying we had broken his bank account with our drinking and carousing. But almost every day Elaine had a new admirer ringing our doorbell. She was, at the time, actually "engaged" to marry Ben Gazzara. But Ben had been wed before and the Catholic Church was not looking kindly on his and Elaine's coming union. In the meantime, Elaine—ga-ga over Rock, and never dreaming that I, too, was ga-ga over Rock, kept going out night after night with the leading man. When Ben arrived in Rome to see Elaine, he became so unhappy that he took me to the beach at Ostia one day to get my input. Naturally, I didn't have any. I had to be loyal to Elaine. So I just sat there like a lump with this really wonderful, sweet and sensitive guy who was always acting onstage as a gangster or drug addict. Finally I told him I didn't think Elaine was going to be able to marry him. She was too devout a Catholic. I remember that he wept like the great Method actor he was. And then, he recovered several months later and married the beautiful Janice Rule. He and I remained good friends over the years.

One night when Elaine and I were discussing Rock—as usual—I reminded her, and myself, that he was married. Elaine said, "Oh!" Then she had two martinis and said loudly, "Who cares?" Meanwhile, she had also taken up with an adorable Italian director named Andrea Volpe. He was married, too, but separated from the Australian actress Diane Cilento. Andrea became so frustrated by Elaine's kiss-and-run tactics that he asked *me* to go away for a weekend to Naples.

It was the beginning of my real love affair with Italy, because we saw Pompeii and ate buffalo mozzarella with the real buffalos standing in the field behind us. We sailed the Bay of Naples and dined on original Neapolitan pizza every night. Andrea taught me a lot about Italy and amused me greatly as he tried to deal with the Neapolitan dialect in his Roman way. When we returned to Rome I was pretty much over my crush on Rock and Andrea was pretty much over his crush on Elaine.

In the glory nights of that sustained time in Rome, producer Selznick and his personal star, Jennifer Jones, took us out one evening for an elegant dinner at the Hosteria dell Orso. I was seated next to a little man named Arthur Fellows, the longtime assistant troubleshooter for Selznick, a legend who had already scored with *Gone with the Wind* and now wanted to redo Hemingway's classic love story. Selznick was still at odds with the director John Huston and threatening to bring in a new hand at the helm. I was totally fascinated by being in the proximity of a gorgeous star like Jennifer Jones. I knew all about the tragedies of her life—how she couldn't keep her marriage to Robert Walker together; how he had died of an overdose of drink and prescription drugs; how Selznick had left his wife, Irene, the powerful daughter of MGM's Louis B. Mayer, to marry Jennifer. But talking to Miss Jones was torment. She was supershy and stuttered when she tried to speak.

Elaine was hanging on David's every word, sipping her martini like a civilized woman and pretending she was grownup. She was wearing the only decent thing I owned, a black linen suit. And I was desperately underdressed for one of the finest restaurants in Europe. But if I couldn't exactly make myself irresistible to David and Jennifer, I scored well with Mr. Fellows. He was the associate producer of *A Farewell to Arms,* and he was seriously smitten with my Southwestern charms, which I was hoping to discard, to cover up and recover from as I took on the sophisticated patina of Italy. I wanted to hear every pearl that dropped from Selznick's famous lips. Or anything Jennifer had to impart. Arthur wanted me to hear *his* words. Selznick was lecturing on things that were crucial to any entertainment junkie like me—for instance, why he felt he'd had to replace George Cukor with Victor Fleming on *GWTW*; why his version of *A Farewell to Arms,* in glorious Technicolor, with all the war stuff filmed in the snowy Italian Alps would erase forever the black-and-white version of Gary Cooper and Helen Hayes in the public's memory; why he might fire Huston and bring in director Charlie Vidor. I strained to listen, constantly removing Arthur's hand from my leg or lap under the tablecloth. We were in the presence of Hollywood lore at its zenith.

My blasé disregard of this driven Number Two man seemed to appeal to Fellows. He wasn't used to such independence. He usually had his way with all the ladies, who hoped he'd get them into a Selznick movie. My indifference sent him into some kind of benign ecstasy, and for the rest of my stay in Rome he pursued me. He would make me a star, get me a job as a director's assistant, as a screenwriter; he'd get me hired by Louella and Hedda, who were his best friends. He'd get me into the Screen Actors Guild; I could have a part in the current movie. I could have anything I wanted. What I wanted was for him to leave me alone.

Elaine was at her best in public situations like this night in the Hosteria dell Orso. The Stritch style was for her to actually *appear* to be the woman she resembled as she acted the hell out of any role. She had always looked quite mature, even in her late teens. She came from a fine upper-middle-class Michigan family, had real class, a full figure, gorgeous legs, a distinctive voice and curly blonde hair. She had pizzazz and personality up the kazoo. She told the best anecdotes in the world, loved to drink, dance and have fun. She put on quite a show for the Selznicks, proving that she was the sophisticated talent they thought she was. Inside, she was frightened to death, intolerably shy, and always needing a drink to get through the next moment. Her flirtatious manner with men got her into unending trouble. She wanted them to kiss and romance her, but not go too far, because she remembered only too well what the nuns had tried to teach her back in Birmingham and, after all, she was distantly related to Cardinal Stritch of Chicago.

Elaine and I now shared our burdens of avoiding the guys we had attracted. I had only Arthur Fellows; she had Roman legions beating on the door. She was good about Arthur. She'd head him off at the pass while I escaped the hotel down the service elevator. I fielded three or four of the many bees she attracted to honey and would make daily excuses while she primped for new conquests. Or made useless date after date with Rock. Those evenings went nowhere. I was careful never to act jealous of Elaine, indeed never to let myself be jealous! In fact, I was the perfect leading lady's foil and, anyway, I loved her very much as a friend.

Arthur Fellows was so dogged and aggressive and persistent that he interfered with my nonstop culture-vulture sightseeing. Elaine had a short attention span for "culture," but I was determined to see every single sight in Rome and try to understand what I was seeing. I wasn't surprised after I left Rome to hear that Selznick had fired Fellows in spite of all their years together. The movie was a disaster and heavily overspent. In this turmoil, Selznick slapped Fellows, who then broke David's glasses. The movie world secretly cheered for the downfall of both of these tyrants.

On my last day in Rome, for I had to go back to work at NBC, I was in front of the hotel with my luggage. A big limousine drove up, the window slid down, Rock's handsome face appeared. "You're leaving, Liz? Give me a good-bye kiss, girl!" I touched his perfect lips with mine. He grinned. He knew perfectly well his effect. The limo rolled off to Cine Citta. I had a long flight back to New York. My first trip abroad resonated with meaning, but I hadn't learned anything much beyond the guidebooks. Again, on the plane, I drifted, backslid, and let myself daydream of being Mrs. Rock Hudson.

By now, I'd read that the unexamined life is not worth living. But having a high old time and living for the moment was much more my style. In all this fun and games, did I actually examine any of this for the realities? I did not. I just relaxed and learned to love Rock Hudson from afar, the way most women did.

And this time I not only said a prayer of thanks for Sloan and Soapstix, but for friend Stritch, who had given me the experience of a lifetime in Rome.

ROCK HUDSON HAS BEEN MUCH criticized by new generations for his "hypocrisy" in not saying he was homosexual. He was a truck driver named Roy Fitzgerald who wanted to be a great actor. He became, instead, a super romantic leading man. And in his heyday, the fifties and sixties, in order to stay on top as a screen consort for the likes of Elizabeth Taylor and Doris Day, he had to live a personal lie, or have no career at all.

I went on knowing Rock after Rome and many years later, as a syndicated columnist, I was briefly involved in helping him ward off being blackmailed by a woman who swore she was going to the supermarket tabloids with her tales. She had been close to the actor and knew a lot. Rock told me about his problem, but in all the years I knew him rather well, he never confessed the nature of his problem. I didn't ask; he didn't tell. I hate blackmail. I simply promptly delivered to him a load of material I happened to have on this same woman. He showed it to her. She dropped her plans. It was a stalemate and I suppose, when all is said and done, it was just counter-blackmail. But I felt that we had thwarted a nasty injustice. If this was participating in a "cover-up," that's not how I thought about it. I respected Rock's reticence.

His critics might take a look at how ravaged this handsome, likeable star was from his fatal illness. He fought hard to preserve his privacy but was not only publicly humiliated, he lost his life in a horrible way. This was overpayment for the mere hypocrisy that in those unenlightened times was his attempt at self-preservation.

By 1983, I was using my column to propagandize, educate and fight against AIDS, then a strange new deadly disease. I think I was the first person in the popular press to write about AIDS. At the time that was a shocking thing to do. I was much criticized for bringing such a subject into what was supposed to be a frivolous entertainment column. Then, early on, at the urging of Dr. Mathilde Krim and Elizabeth Taylor, I joined the board of AmFAR and we have raised millions of dollars in this fight that still rages on, worldwide.

PEACOCK'S END

T HE YEARS AT NBC PUT me in contact with more celebrities than I needed to know. One I did need to know was Arlene Francis. Norman Frank and I moonlighted from *Wide Wide World* producing a morning outing of hers called *The Home Show*. Miss Francis was a delightful Armenian charmer who was the toast of New York—one of those all-time popular beloved souls. She was also a huge perennial favorite on *What's My Line?* where she played the "good cop" to columnist Dorothy Kilgallen's "bad cop" and both were seen every Sunday night on black-and-white TV.

My job on Arlene's show could be anything; for instance, flying all over town on a moment's notice trying to duplicate the medals of America's most decorated soldier, Audie Murphy. I had to locate everything from the Congressional Medal of Honor on down.

Arlene never forgot my efforts. She became my enduring supporter. She even put herself and her actor husband, Martin Gabel, on the line through the years trying to convince their pal—and my nemesis—Frank Sinatra to lay off of Liz. I enjoyed my friendship with the Gabels, who knew everybody and moved in only the best circles.

Arlene loved it that I, of all her acquaintances, knew about her short-lived movie career. At age sixteen she had played the girl in the arms of the ape, opposite Lon Chaney, in the original *Murders in the Rue Morgue*. And hanging with the Gabels, I got a life lesson from Martin, a short, sonorous, classical actor whose stature kept him from the very large roles for which he was so well suited.

One night I rushed to the theater from work, wearing a cable-knit sweater, a skirt and saddle shoes. Very collegiate. At intermission, Martin took me aside. "Why are you dressed like this?" I tried to explain. He said sternly, "Remember, the theater is a temple. You must pay proper homage to the gods of comedy and tragedy. Never let me see you like this again in the temple of Thespis."

I took his ridiculously formal words to heart and tried to be better dressed than was my wont. Now, when I sit next to people on opening nights and they are wearing dungarees and shorts, I flinch. It's a good thing the last of the theater gents has gone to his reward on Mt. Olympus.

In 1997, when Arlene was diagnosed with Alzheimer's disease and her son, Peter, was taking her to San Francisco to live near him, I had the privilege of reporting her departure from the city where she had reigned as a queen for years. Dressed smartly in a Chanel suit and looking marvelous, Arlene paused at the top of the airline stairway, glanced around, then turned to Peter and asked, "Is this black-tie?"

He said, "Yes," and she walked through the door.

WHEN A NETWORK GETS SOMETHING right, they will eventually screw it up. Now NBC dreamed up a replacement for the great franchise that had been Steve Allen's *Tonight Show*. They decided to roam across the U.S. showing what was really happening between 11:00 P.M. and midnight. It would be like

Wide Wide World five nights a week for night owls. They hired
the sports reporter Jack Lescoulie, the Hearst political columnist
Bob Considine and the breast-fixated gossip columnist Earl Wilson as their unlikely hosts.

Naturally, they wanted producers with fine credentials to
line-produce these spots every night. I said, when first approached, that this kind of feat was humanly, technically impossible. Then I remembered Norman Frank and the "never say
never, it can't be done" conversion I'd had. So maybe it could be
done if NBC was willing to throw a ton of money at the problem.

NBC then hired a wild man, who shall be nameless. He
told me in our first discussion that there would be nothing "fake"
about *Tonight! America After Dark*. All events would be authen-
tically happening, not "arranged." Nothing could be staged or
organized. I threw up my hands. I didn't want to do anything
"fake," but... What? We'd go to a nightclub in Kansas City and
"hope" for pictures? People would just be sitting around drinking, annoyed at the camera's intrusion. Something would have
to happen in this short time slot—happen on its own? How were
we to accomplish this without some planning, preparation and
"seeding"? I knew we had to "arrange" for events to occur that
would make plausible TV.

We had some good people. A guy named Stanley Flink
was our chief writer and a girl named Martha Weinman was our
brain trust. But because Martha was so beautifully put together,
she was always called "The Body" and I was called "The
Brain." (Later, "The Body" married a doctor named Lear and
went on to become an excellent writer for *The New York Times*.)
Stanley Flink spent his time taking notes on a disaster in
progress. He titled his novel *But Will They Get It in Des
Moines?* because this is what our intrepid producer asked us of
everything we suggested.

TAAD was just about the biggest bomb in history before
NBC pulled the plug and wisely replaced us with a new guy
named Jack Paar. I hated our show and begged to be given the
job nobody wanted, going out on the street "shaking hands"
with the cops. ("Shaking hands" is a euphemism for paying off

local police to look the other way during remotes, not to move our trucks, not to harass our crews and cameramen.) I'd step up to each policeman, shake hands and give him $20. When the big brass with gold braid on their hats and shoulders showed up, I shook hands holding $50 bills. I would be out on the mean streets with thousands in cash.

Regardless of such "efficiency," the show was doomed. Heads finally rolled, mine included. Nobody said anything about the glory days of *Wide Wide World,* or my five years of dedicated service. I was out of a job. And I would not return to NBC for twenty-one years. When I came back in 1978, I would be in front of the camera, not behind it.

PART

FOUR

a Memoir

IGOR/

CHOLLY/

GHIGHI

W HEN GLORIA SAFIER HEARD THAT my job at
NBC-TV had bitten the dust, this natural-born agent got
busy. She knew Don Maher, who was running Igor Cassini's
public relations firm Martial & Company. The latter operated in
tandem with Mr. Cassini's well-known syndicated society gossip column, which the Hearsts put out under a byline they
owned—Cholly Knickerbocker.*

Gloria barked at me. "Call this number. Go see Don
Maher. Cassini is looking for a column assistant." I murmured,
"But I don't know anything about these people in his column!"

Gloria was severe. "Never mind that. You can learn."

I had an interview with Maher, who told me sotto voce
not to let Cassini beat me down to a smaller salary than such and
such. And then I saw Cassini, who was suave charm itself. He
seemed distracted. It was obvious he wanted to get the interview

*Washington Irving used Deidrich Knickerbocker as the fictitious author
for his History of New York. Knickerbocker became a synonym for Manhattan's Dutch founders. As Cassini himself described Cholly, he "signified
any New Yorker, and in particular, a bon vivant."

over with. He had heard of my experience as a TV producer and knew I had a journalism degree. That seemed to be enough for him. "You're hired!" he said, emphatically. He then named an annual salary that was less than Maher had advised I accept, about $200 a week. And I, failing to do the arithmetic in my head, accepted. Mr. Cassini almost immediately said, "Call me Ghighi [pronounced Gig-eee]! It's been my nickname since I was a curly-headed little child. And if you use Igor, then people will get me mixed up with my brother, Oleg, who is a fashion designer. So I am Ghighi to my nearest and dearest and I hope you will become one of those." I was thoroughly charmed. What a guy! Dynamic, sexy, European, famous.

"I know all about your brother, Oleg," I said. "He was married to the beautiful Gene Tierney; he makes Hollywood costumes." Ghighi smiled. "Not anymore. Now he lives in New York and runs his fashion business. Oleg and I are very different and yet very much alike. We Russian-Italians come as a family unit, with our mother and father, and we are loyal."

I went away and read up on the two Cassinis. *Vogue*'s Diana Vreeland had characterized them as having "joie de vivre—a built-in sense of pleasure—beautiful manners—and the know-how to mix them with business."

I looked up some Cholly Knickerbocker columns and despaired. How could I contribute to a world of which I knew almost nothing? I saw that Cholly wasn't modest. The column often began: "Between you and me and the lamppost and 20,000,000 readers..." It was a column that Cassini had begun writing in September 1945, a time he said was "a heyday for gossip columnists that lasted through the early sixties."

Cassini had assured me I'd catch on to Cholly-style easily. "Anyway, you don't have to do anything at first. I want you as a backup to Ed Wilcox, who is my assistant. You'll be working here in this town house. We operate the column out of the basement. Up here"—he waved his hand to indicate luxurious paneling and carpeting—"we talk with Fiat, Pirelli and the rest of my public relations clients."

Did I say to my new employer, "Isn't that a conflict of interest—journalism and public relations under the same roof?" I did not. I was both too apprehensive and too glad to have a job!

SOON AFTER STARTING IN 1958, Don Maher introduced me to Jim Mitchell. "He's going to be John Perona's new public relations guy for El Morocco. You can teach him the ropes!"

Mitchell stood there in his dashing overcoat and a homburg hat. When he took it off, I swear he had his hair parted in the middle. He was so trim, so polite, but seemed so naive; I felt he'd never make it in the rarefied atmosphere of El Morocco.

By now I had been to this famous nightclub a few times—with Cassini. He'd introduce me around and say, "Get to know these people: the owner John Perona; the hatcheck girl, Eileen McKenna; the maître d', Angelo Zuccotti; the waiters. They are a fountain of knowledge." But it was difficult for me to go alone to El Morocco. I couldn't behave like Walter Winchell, Leonard Lyons and Earl Wilson. They were VIPs, known faces. As a woman of the time, I couldn't approach strangers at tables to ask questions, joke and swap secrets. And for me, escorts with proper clothes for El Morocco were not easy to come by.

Jimmy Mitchell was to change all of that for me. He would provide access to El Morocco for as long as it operated as a viable Café Society nightclub—that is, until the 1970s. And, as usual, I had been wrong in my precipitous judgment. Jimmy Mitchell turned out to be just right. He was good-looking in his slick black tuxedo, a well-bred, charming WASPy gent, open to learning any and everything, mannered to a fault, nonjudgmental, never controversial. He had also connected somehow emotionally with the old pro John Perona, walking in off the street to present himself, with his University of Miami education, as a promotional godsend.

Perona had opened his famous nightclub at 154 East 54th Street when Prohibition ended in December 1933. Once he formulated the blue-and-white "zebra" stripe decor with the white plastic palm trees, he announced an opening date. That night the elegant Angelo, who was always in white-tie and tails, stood at the door turning everyone away even though El Morocco was empty inside. People seeking to get in could hear the music but there was no way Angelo would let them enter. To say it created a "demand" is not enough. From that night on the doors were stormed. Jack Dempsey, a Perona pal, became a regular and every celebrity in the world came to El Morocco to be photographed by one of the bad boys of society, Jerome Zerbe. Kings and tycoons demanded the number-one booth. (It always seemed to be occupied by Lyndon Johnson, Aristotle Onassis or Clark Gable.)

Only the very elegant, social and extremely secure would request to be seated in Siberia on the far side of the dance floor. Otherwise, Siberia was a dumping ground for the *nouveau riche*. El Morocco had its hierarchies, its feuds, its regulars, and its history. Here, Humphrey Bogart battled a woman over a toy panda prize, the Duke and Duchess of Windsor posed in paper crowns, and the swordsmen of society measured their penis size against one another in the men's room upstairs—to general hilarity downstairs. (The winners were legion—Porfirio Rubirosa, Baby Pignatari, Milton Berle, Bruce Cabot, Forrest Tucker and New York's E. Haring "Red" Chandor.) One could hear the cackling and laughter when sitting in the Champagne Room upstairs for dinner.

Jimmy Mitchell had admitted up front to me that he didn't know anything about the world he was entering. "Don't worry," I said, vastly amused by him and feeling superior, "I'll help you." He called me every day for a while, telling me what had happened at El Morocco the night before. Soon we had a running section on El Morocco; the nightclub turned up constantly in the column. But the reason wasn't to give Mitchell a plus with Perona. It began as that perhaps, but soon it was apparent to me that "Elmo's" was just about the only "happening" place in town for the remnants of society. The Stork Club, for instance, was dying, done in by Sherman Billingsley's racism and Walter Winchell's stubbornness in backing his Oklahoma friend. That famous nightspot would close its doors in 1964. But El Morocco went on and on.

Café Society had come into being when the original Hearst-created Cholly Knickerbocker, an effete, snobby, sniffy dude named Maury Paul, noted that people were going out to eat on Thursdays—the cook's night out. He dubbed these people Café Society and it stuck. The world was changing then, back in the late twenties and early thirties, and rich people discovered they couldn't keep their names out of the newspapers, as they wished. (Social VIPs felt they mustn't be mentioned except for birth, marriage and death.) Now they were news. They had money. The masses looked up to them, down on them and were riveted by their comings, goings, doings, buying habits, marriages, divorces, affairs or whatever. (There was no rock 'n' roll society then, no TV society, no media society, but there were rich people—the so-called "upper crust"—to emulate, envy, make fun of and tear down to size.)

Soon Jimmy began to urge me to come to El Morocco and see for myself at night. The food was fabulous there—so it wasn't a hardship. Perona had recently moved the club to Second Avenue in the Fifties. I would show up with Mitchell and eat dinner, usually alone. Jimmy wore his "uniform," a simple tuxedo. He seldom sat down; "I'm on duty," he'd say. He would come to my table as the night wore on and tell me things that were going on. I'd jot it all down. He would introduce me around and tell me who was who in the gilded crowd. Night after night—sometimes I'd bring a friend so I could dance and blend in. God knows where I got the clothes. But Jimmy knew designers, so that helped, too.

We often left El Morocco absolutely potted to the gills. The food was rich, the champagne excellent. It's a wonder our livers held up. Under the delusion that we were the reincarnated Zelda and Scott Fitzgerald, one night Jimmy and I picked up an iron traffic stanchion and carried it up four flights of stairs, leaving it at the foot of the bed of our sleeping friend, Gloria Safier. It required several days and three handymen to get it back down to the street.

Pretty soon Jimmy Mitchell had lost his naive, innocent look. Now he knew everything that was going on. And he "owed" me for helping him, but soon I "owed" him. We enjoyed one another. We became a great team.

The column got better and better—more about the actual doings of the dregs of society, more inside stuff, more meaningful gossip, more of what happened last night in little old New York among what Cassini called "The Society of Achievement."

I credit whatever success I had working for Cassini to Jimmy Mitchell and he credits some of his success working for Perona to knowing me. We were two hands washing each other. When Mr. Perona died, Jimmy continued with the next management. He was much in demand for helping people get their children into good schools, for turning plain girls into Cinderella-type debutantes, for planning and overseeing parties. He became friends with the "right" people and took me on several glamorous jaunts overseas. We went to Monaco, or to Palm Beach or to Newport.*

I was speeding along writing about a world I'd hardly even dreamed existed. I thought for a minute there it was important. The perks were immense. The attention was gratifying. I ate in the best restaurants where no remonstrance could ever make an owner give me a check. I tipped lavishly, because Cassini had said, "That's all you can do!" At Christmas I was overwhelmed with lavish gifts. Sometimes when Igor went away to the South of France for months at a time, I was entirely on my own, writing the column by myself, completely in control. It was heady, unrealistic and actually ridiculous. But in the very beginning, it was terrifying.

When Cassini fired Ed Wilcox, he announced it to me suddenly and said, "I am going to Antibes for a month and while I'm gone I want you not to write the column as it usually appears, but do a special series called 'The Most Beautiful Women in International Society.' Here they are!" He handed me a list. I

---

*He is now writing his own book about El Morocco, Every Night Was New Year's Eve.

knew exactly one of these thirty famous women—Gloria Vanderbilt, who was an acting client of Gloria Safier's.

"How can I do this, Ghighi?" I gasped. "I don't know
these women or even how to find out about them." He waved his
hand and said, "Call our friend Gloria Schiff. She'll help you."
So for thirty days I interviewed the lovely Ms. Schiff, who
talked to me about her idols. C-Z Guest, Jacqueline de Ribes,
Peggy Bancroft, the Princess Hohenlohe, Babe Paley, Fiona
Thyssen, Princess Hercolani, Gloria Guinness, Marella Agnelli,
Gloria's own twin sister Consuelo Crespi, etc.

The effort was killing because the daily deadlines came
like bullets and were inexorable. Somehow the series came off.
The day it ended, I was in the dentist chair when a call came
from the man who ran the *New York Journal American*. Seymour Berkson was a distant authority figure to me, a frightening
presence, a boss of bosses. "Kid," he said, "just wanted to congratulate you on your series on beautiful women. I know
Cassini's name was on it, but everyone in town knows who did
it. Congratulations!" I certainly thought then that I was on my
way, that I would someday write the Cholly Knickerbocker column on my own, that I was destined for "social" greatness.

This was only the beginning of my five years as a ghost
to Cholly Knickerbocker, a job I would come to adore, enjoy
and eventually lose in quite a cataclysmic manner.

ONE DAY CASSINI SENT ME to see Harry Winston, the famous Fifth Avenue jeweler. "There's a story here," said my
boss. "Winston was the first man ever to lend precious stones for
stars to wear to the Oscars." (For several days I didn't twig to
the fact that Winston was one of Cassini's paid clients.)

Harry Winston *was* actually a good story. He was frank
and candid. "You know some of my success comes from how
cheap rich people really are. They love to borrow my jewels before buying them, to try them out." Harry had begun his career
at age twelve by finding an emerald in a pawnshop back in 1908.

He sold it for $800 and was on his way. By twenty-one he was a millionaire. In 1935 he became famous for buying the 725-carat Jonker Diamond and having it dangerously split into twelve separate stones. He also bought the Hope Diamond from the estate of Washington's Evalyn Walsh McLean. He later gave this "unlucky" diamond to the Smithsonian, mailing it to them in a registered plain brown wrapper.

I visited Harry in his office where he had a number of bits of tissue paper on his desk. In each was a diamond and Harry's eyes would shine as he untwisted each one to admire it. "It's alive, with color and light," he'd say with fervor.

I also saw Harry's rubber-lined room where craftsmen cut and polished stones and shaped platinum and gold into settings. Every few months the room was emptied and the rubber linings burned to recover all the filings of precious metal and diamond dust. "We find thousands of dollars in lost material," said Harry, with relish.

I never forgot Harry Winston's diamonds in tissue paper. He claimed that's when a diamond actually looked its best.

THE FIRST TIME I MET John F. Kennedy, he wasn't yet the president of the United States and he was wearing a gun. It was at a Wild West fund-raiser in the Plaza Hotel, a party dominated by Bobby Kennedy, who was running the whole thing, telling everybody what to do.

All the Kennedy sisters turned up and there was the impossibly attractive senator from Massachusetts, JFK himself, in a black string tie for his tuxedo, but with a Western gun belt around his middle. I don't recall seeing Jackie; it certainly wasn't her cup of tea. But the Kennedys as a family were gung ho for filling the campaign bucket.

Cassini had ordered me to cover the event. He and Oleg were present as guests, but Ghighi would wait for me to write up my version and then he'd add, subtract, edit and change it. He was actually very good at this. And if I seemed stuck for something to say, or if there was a day when we needed a strong lead for the column, I would go to him—if he was physically available—and throw myself on his mercy. He would grin. "Let me squeeze my brains!" And, indeed, he would—he could always come up with a story, an angle or an item. He was excellent as Cholly and better than anyone else could possibly have been. But he was tired of it, bored with it and he preferred to play golf, make money from his PR business and chase women while simply "editing" someone else's work under his byline.

The JFK party was vaguely interesting to me. I realized that the Kennedys might well ascend to the White House even though Ghighi told me they'd never make it. I followed them from afar, interested in them as celebrities, but a little mixed up. This was because one of the Cassinis was extremely involved with the Kennedys. (Oleg was backing JFK. He had aspirations, which would come to pass, to become Jackie's fashion advisor.) Igor went along for the ride because what Oleg wanted, he wanted for Oleg. But behind the scenes, he told me he was going to vote for Nixon.

The Kennedys then had much bigger fish to fry than the Cassinis. But I doubt they knew that one of the brothers was not in their corner and was actually a Republican. Perhaps they didn't care. To them, Igor was just Oleg's younger brother who would do as he was told. They knew him as a society columnist who had once dubbed Jackie "the debutante of the year." Ghighi was the guy who was married to the heiress Charlene Wrightsman and came to Palm Beach annually to visit his father-in-law, the very oil-rich Charlie Wrightsman. (Mr. Wrightsman was a tough old bird who was married to Jackie's good friend Jayne Wrightsman, a woman who had graduated from making excellent daiquiris to becoming an expert on fine French furniture. You can see some of Mrs. Wrightsman's collection and her largess in the Metropolitan Museum of Art.) The Kennedys knew Ghighi also as a celebrated and debonair "swordsman," a man about town and friend to their own randy father, Ambassador Joseph Kennedy. What's more, when it came to Cuba and the Dominican Republic, Igor was said to be the public relations advisor to two of the Caribbean's most powerful dictators, Batista and Trujillo. So if they needed anything from that corner of this hemisphere, they knew where to go to get it. All of this would bounce, rebounce and rebound to Igor Cassini's great misery only a few years later.

When Oleg was not around and I was alone with Igor, my boss was quite scathing about the Kennedys. He found them attractive, but that was all. He didn't think Jack, a Roman Catholic, stood a chance of attaining the White House. He was a "lightweight." Perhaps some of this rubbed off on me even though I was willing to let myself be charmed by a handsome young presidential candidate who said he was a Democrat—and sometimes even acted like one.

As we entered the sixties, I would go on to support JFK's candidacy, raise money for the cause, vote for him, and be shocked and mournful about his murder. Like many Texans, when it happened I felt ashamed and guilty. It would be years before I could make myself go to Dallas and drive the route into Dealey Plaza.

A TINY

LITTLE LADY

ONE FASCINATING THING ABOUT WORKING in New York journalism is the chance to observe the internecine warfare conducted at the monolithic *New York Times*. The impact reverberates throughout the Fourth Estate and laps at the edges of city business, finance, society, the arts, gossip. I took notice of this early on because I was befriended by the impressive columnist Charlotte Curtis—and to me, she *was The New York Times*.

Charlotte had grown up in Ohio, a place she never really left in her heart or head. She had begun on the women's pages and in style news, insisting that coverage of fashion, society, decor, etc., should be treated with the same emphasis on lively writing as politics and sports received.

Her *Times* mentor Sydney Gruson said she was "a conspirator of worldwide order. She was always trying to figure out ways of bending things to her will. I never thought she'd try to break things, just bend things." And her *Village Voice* pal David Schneiderman said she was "a tiny lady who went to all those chic, elegant dinner parties with a firecracker in her beaded purse...a troublemaker in the best sense."

Soon after I became a lowly society ghostwriter, Charlotte and I met at the pool of the Colony Hotel in Palm Beach. She was appropriately attired in a pink linen dress. I had on blue jeans because I'd never been to Palm Beach before and thought this was appropriate "informal" attire. (After all, that's what informal meant in Texas.) Charlotte laughed. "You are very brave not to care what Palm Beach thinks. Be sure you keep that quality. Don't ever become a part of 'them.'"

Of course, I *did* care what Palm Beach thought. I was young, callow and ambitious. But I cared more what Charlotte thought. She was the most generous journalist I'd ever meet. Not for her the petty one-ups of mean competition. She wanted to see newspapering improve on every front. Anything written well or honestly or with perception was in her interest.

We talked about the infamous Jerome Zipkin who was visiting The Colony from New York. He had excoriated the hotel owner, Joe Tankoos, saying the closets crushed the shoulders of his suits and there was no decent mirror. Plus, Mr. Zipkin required more space to lay out his massive collection of cufflinks, which went with him everywhere. Poor Mr. Tankoos rebuilt an entire suite to suit Zipkin, who then, sniffily, never returned to The Colony.

This sort of stuff went over big with our readers and Charlotte was a gold mine of gossip with no place to go. Since she knew everyone and everything that was going on, she had many brilliant asides. And she began to influence, advise, caution and shape my life more than anyone else in the business. She went on to spend her entire career improving me and convincing me that what I was doing was "social history," not to be taken lightly.

When Charlotte saw me standing in the cold with the rest of the observers at the Metropolitan Opera opening nights, she'd sidle up and whisper, "Now, that's Mrs. So and So, who is going with so and so and believe me, you can mention that she is with her daughter-in-law whom she detests. Write *that* and you'll be ahead of the others." She gave me tip after tip. I could not exhaust her goodwill. She would call me with ideas she knew the *Times* would never allow to be developed. She enjoyed having a secret protégé. But in her own world, she kept a dispassionate, fair-minded, disinterested "cool." She treated everybody exactly the same and had a mordant wit, a fine talent for expression and a deep sense of ethics. She was always for the underdog.

Charlotte herself had already jerked so-called Society out of shape and put it back together like some Marcel Proust covering the New York scene. She also would report the violent Democratic Convention in Chicago and become famous for writing up the Black Panthers preaching to the ermine-and-pearls crowd at Leonard Bernstein's. Tom Wolfe, who expanded on this for his book *Radical Chic,* noted "it wasn't anything she wrote that infuriated them. It was that she put down exactly what they said. That's always what seems cruelest of all, to hold a mirror to people that way."

I perceived via Charlotte that working for the *Times* was a bit like wearing a straitjacket. You were constantly exposed to stories you couldn't do. They might be too trivial, too tasteless or too unprovable by *Times* standards. This frustrated Charlotte. Through the Cholly years, and later with my own byline, I was the perfect receptacle for her overflow of information unfit for the *Times* to print. And this included the struggles within the *Times.*

Charlotte liked pointing out where the bodies might be buried, hinting that this or that would be a good story if only I'd look into it. And over the years she cautioned me again and again: "Don't become one of 'them'—the people you write about." She would whisper to me at parties where she felt I was having too much fun. "Don't forget Texas. Don't forget Ohio. That's where America really is. Not here." And she kept a certain smart independence even though she was very much "one of them"—in that she was invited everywhere, feared, adored, and appreciated by the very subjects she might skewer. She always kept her notepad handy to let people know she was working.

From knowing Charlotte I observed firsthand the rising tide of influence of the new *Times* managing editor, Abe Rosenthal. He and his team seemed to be in conflict with the "Old Guard"—editor Clifton Daniels, reporter Harrison Salisbury, and on their side, Charlotte—a diminutive success story of the kind that editors hate. ("We created her, now she thinks she's somebody special!") Through the years I came to personally like Abe Rosenthal, but I was always on the side of the Old Guard. I admired Mr. Daniels: so civilized, an urbane kind of Dean Acheson in newsprint. I worshipped the ground Mr. Salisbury walked on. He had won the Pulitzer and had written several great histories of our times including *The 900 Days: The Siege of Leningrad* and *New Emperors*. What a reporter! And I adored Charlotte because she wanted me to succeed when nobody else gave a damn.

Charlotte was in time promoted to be the Op Ed editor of the *Times* and thereby she escaped the new regime. They couldn't lay a glove on her, for the editorial pages do not report to anyone but the publisher. In this era, I went to talk to Charlotte for Andy Warhol's *Interview* magazine. She welcomed me to her domain at the top and tried to make me feel good about a personal career writing gossip. She reminded me that gossip is history and said it only depended on how one handled it. Then she told me the marvelous old Adolph Ochs story that "other newspapers publish gossip, but when the *Times* prints it, it's sociology!"

It was here in her elegant office that I urged her to pose for our photographer like Charlie Chaplin in *The Great Dictator,* where he is seen with the world globe balanced on his foot. "Charlotte, you are now handling editorial advice to the entire world. It will be a terrific picture!" Charlotte thought it over. "I think I should not. It's just too much fun for a *Times* editor to have." She was later pleased by the article, titled "Media: The Op Ed Page of *The New York Times* Meets the Gossip Column of the *Daily News*" and she was pleased with the more formal portrait taken of her by Cris Alexander. It had been retouched into a super-glamorous youthfulness and Charlotte found this utterly hilarious.

I said to her during our interview, "You have reached the top as one of the most influential women in journalism. Are you like Alexander with no more worlds to conquer?"

She said no. "I could leave the *Times* and do other things, write books, edit a magazine. But what I'd like to do is work in a garden, on a rich person's estate. I don't see the *Times* as the end of the line."

Soon Charlotte left the *Times* because of illness and the garden she entered was a Gethsemane of cancer. She went home to Ohio to her doctor husband and never uttered a single complaint. From time to time she would call to thank me for sending her my column every day and we'd catch up on all the gossip. She refused to discuss being sick. She died in 1987. I was the least of the distinguished throng that spoke at her memorial in Lincoln Center, an affair she had arranged in the last days of her life. I felt that my presence, which caused many *Times* people to wonder, was her last tweak at the Establishment.

I always like to think of Charlotte as improving some rich person's garden in the great hereafter of heaven, improving it as she improved so many others, and me. This is as good a hope for life after death as any other.

MARRY FREDDIE?

JIMMY MITCHELL INTRODUCED ME TO Freddie Lister. I was instantly attracted because I love to go to extremes. I'd already been married to a man who was 6' 4" and had played football. Now here was his opposite: Freddie, the Astaire-type, dapper and elegant. He was a travel agent from South Africa. I was intrigued. Freddie and I began to have lunches and dinners. He poured out his heart to me. He was terrified because he wasn't a U.S. citizen, ever fearful he'd be deported. I was touched and the longer I knew him, the more tender I felt. I actually worried about this little guy. We started dating.

One day Freddie fingered his silverware. "I'm afraid if I say this, you'll think I'm crazy, or that I just want to stay in the United States. But would you consider marrying me? I am really crazy about you and you're one of the few people I trust."

In my idiotic larky way, I laughed and exclaimed, "Marry Freddie?" It was a catchphrase for the leading lady Eliza Doolittle in *My Fair Lady*. But we began to wrestle with the question and we grew even closer. I decided maybe I'd like to marry again even though I certainly wasn't swept away.

One day I said, "Okay, I'll marry you but let's keep it

quiet in case it doesn't work out. You keep your apartment. I'll keep mine. But you can stay with me and I'll put the phone in your name."

Freddie and I soon took the train to Newark where we felt the marriage registration of Fred Lister and Mary E. Smith would not make any waves. I don't know what we thought a wave would do to us, but now we were locked in our giddy conspiracy. It was as if we were doing something incorrect. Maybe we were, but it felt like a minor sin. We got a license and on the day we went back to Newark to marry, we acted as if we hadn't a care or a thought for the future.

Freddie said, "Are you religious? Or should we just marry in a civil ceremony?" I was all dressed up and something atavistic and bridal came over me. "Let's just find a Baptist preacher," I said. Freddie was agreeable. We looked in the Newark phone book and a dignified voice answered our call. Freddie asked if the minister was free? He was and gave us an address.

We grabbed a cab, arriving at an ordinary-looking house and a handsome black man came to the door. He looked at us with real disapproval and said, "You are the couple who called. Are you sure you want *me* to marry you?" I looked at Freddie, wondering what he was thinking. But Freddie seemed unaware that the preacher was black. He nodded. We were now dancing with impatience to get on with it. My bouquet was shredding in the wind. The minister asked us in, examined our license and called his wife as a witness.

And so we embarked on a long, carefree and frivolous three-month honeymoon. Then we came back down to earth and resumed our careers in the blissful anonymity of Manhattan life. Freddie was in and out of my apartment. We spent weekends and took holidays together. But we kept our little secret. And a few years later, I went happily downtown with my groom and watched him take the oath and become a U.S. citizen.

For five years I was "Liz Lister," as Freddie liked to call me. I didn't meet anyone else who piqued my interest. Then one day, much later, I had an assignment from *Sports Illustrated* to go to Juárez and write about the Olympics coming in 1968. I talked to Freddie and said I wanted to get a divorce while in Mexico. I was restive.

Freddie's face fell. I asked, "What will change between us? We will always be loving friends. We'll see each other. But if I should die while married to you, it might complicate my will, surprise my family and embarrass us both. I have an urge to be free and you should go your way, too."

Freddie sighed and his lawyer made the arrangements. All I had to do was go to a certain address and take my passport. *Sports Illustrated* neither knew nor cared that I'd be getting a divorce on their time.

MY DIVORCE IN JUÁREZ WAS one of the last of those. Soon the U.S. would outlaw such quickie drive-in dissolutions. Why nobody has ever made a movie titled *Divorce Mexican-Style* I'll never know, for mine was hilarious.

In Juárez I went to the suggested address and found myself in a room with about thirty-five people. A beautiful señorita came and took our passports. Then a distinguished man in a double-breasted bespoke suit stepped in and said he was our attorney, Señor Somebody. We trooped downstairs, got in several large buses and went to a baroque courthouse. Here we stood together. Some people bonded, others were openly flirting, a few looked sad and some were openly weeping. I was detached and bemused. A man spoke to us in Spanish and this went on for quite a while. Then we were each required to say "Sí!" in a loud voice. If you didn't speak up, they asked you again. A gavel banged down, parchments were signed and each of us was given a document that weighed a pound and went on for pages in a language most of us couldn't read. I loved the big gold seal on my divorce paper; I still have it. By the time we left the bus, people were making dates and hilarity reigned, except for the sad few who hadn't wanted their Mexican divorces.

Juárez was a delightful madhouse of festivity and the

usual border town "raunch." That night I dined with a dashing *Sports Illustrated* correspondent in a place the name of which I have forgotten. But I will never forget the plank steak and the beautiful doe-eyed, well-dressed women who circulated through the dining room making small talk. The clientele was upscale.

When we left to go back to the impressive Paso Del Norte hotel, I commented: "What a great dinner. What a fabulous restaurant. What good-looking people!"

The correspondent dropped his cigarette in the gutter and exhaled. "Yes," he said. "It's the finest whorehouse in all of Mexico and everybody loves to eat there because they can shop for the best girls while dining."

So, what did I get out of my marriage to Freddie? Why, a wonderful, loyal, amusing friendship, some rather stupid playacting in the bedroom, and though I didn't know it at the time, the chance to become a millionaire. Oh, yes, and my only visit ever to a whorehouse. Madame Claude of Paris could have learned a lot from those ladies in Juárez.

THE CODA TO THE FREDDIE saga was that he and I went on as friends. We had abandoned attempts at physical intimacy. But we lunched and gossiped with gusto. He became my travel agent, of course. Years later, he cut in on me at a dance. As we swung toward the middle of the floor, he whispered, "I wish we were still married." I drew back, amazed.

"Why, Freddie, why?"

He laughed. "Oh, I don't know. I just enjoyed it. I have always loved you a lot—and respected you."

Years passed. Then one Christmas Eve, Freddie Lister disappeared. He was last seen boarding the Long Island Railroad to spend the holiday with friends. He never got off the train, according to his expectant hosts. He was never seen again. The police called on me. But I hadn't seen Freddie in weeks. I didn't know his Long Island friends. They were thoroughly investigated and their property was even searched for a missing body. The police asked me about Freddie and drugs. I had never known him to take drugs so I couldn't be helpful.

Before his disappearance, Freddie had become a very rich man. He and his business partner had a deal to leave each other everything. The partner had died and Freddie had inherited an unexpected $7 million from the business.

For seven years, the Lister family advertised "Have You Seen This Man?" Freddie's picture was forever staring out of the papers. Then, they inherited his fortune. I called his lawyer to ask, just maybe there might be something in it for me? The attorney was pointed. "Freddie never wanted a divorce. You did! I'm afraid you are out of luck. Every cent goes to his family in South Africa."

Well, come easy, go easy, as Sloan would have said.

HIGH AND

LOW SOCIETY

DOROTHY AND ALFRED STRELSIN WERE Manhattan superhosts in the sixties and seventies. This was because they had some money and knew enough to spread a little Wispride on a Ritz cracker. "Build it and they will come!" hadn't even been born as a slogan then. But people did come to eat and drink at the Strelsins.

The world of entertainment delighted Dorothy, for she had been a beautiful young thing in the first of the Leonard Sillman *New Faces* revues and she loved to laugh and kick up her heels. Mr. Strelsin was a tougher type of old bird. He was said to have variously made his fortune from selling munitions and everybody knew he had manufactured the Norden bombsight, which helped the U.S. win World War II. It always seemed to give Al a kick that I knew why bombardiers were issued .45 caliber handguns on bombing runs—so they could destroy the Norden bombsight in case their plane was forced down in enemy territory. (I was a gold mine of World War II minutiae.)

I loved to go to the Strelsins' Park Avenue apartment because all kinds of stars were there—big ones, arriving ones, departing ones, fallen ones. The song says, "There's no people like show people," and I guess Irving Berlin has always been right.

Ethel Merman was a big buddy to Dorothy Strelsin. But Ethel could be as mean as hell to most people, especially "civilians" (not in show biz). She liked me from the start and then, because I had written *The Mother Book* in 1978, she liked me even more. Everything about the thought of it set her blubbering. She assumed I was a really nice girl or I wouldn't have "written such a tribute to your mother!" The fact was the book wasn't a tribute to my mother. It was full of the lore of the very word "mother," from "mother fucker" on up. Some of it was downright negative about dear old Mom. But when I'd try to explain to Ethel, she never listened.

She'd have a few drinks and get all teary-eyed and start weeping over her own dear departed mother. The next thing we'd know, Ethel would haul herself up off the couch, start hitching down her underdrawers and announce to the room in general, "Well, I've gotta go to the little girls' room and empty my snake!"

Once I invited a PR friend, Harvey Mann, to come to the Strelsins because Ethel Merman was the love of his life and I felt they'd get a kick out of one another. When we arrived for the Sunday night *de rigueur* Chinese takeout, we found ourselves sitting at a big round table with cartons opened. (Just like the family in *The Godfather* before Sonny Corleone gets it in the tollbooth.) Ethel hadn't yet arrived. We were passing the egg rolls when she appeared in the door and made a big entrance, saying so that they could hear her all the way up in Harlem, "I see you've started without me, you shits!"

Harvey pointed his egg roll right at Ethel, carefully holding it in chopsticks like any trained Jewish person on Sunday night. He began to sing in tribute, "Have an egg roll, Mr. Goldstone!" His imitation of Merman was staggering. But Ethel was not amused. She began to scream: "How dare you? Just how dare you? Get out of here, you big fat faggot! You insane queen—get lost. How dare you sing my very own song from

Gypsy!" Harvey threw down his egg roll and rushed out of the apartment, sobbing.

None of us had spoken a word. Ethel then just slumped into his empty seat, picked up Harvey's chopsticks and said to me in a low sweet voice: "And, Liz, tell me, how is your dear sweet darling mother?"

Another night at the Strelsins', I found myself sitting on a kind of low loveseat, crammed between Al Strelsin and the exalted bandleader clarinetist Artie Shaw. They had me wedged between them, but I didn't mind. I had seen, heard and danced to Artie Shaw, before the War, in 1938, when his big band appeared at the Fort Worth Casino. I had long worshipped at the shrine of this man, who legendarily had married both Ava Gardner and Lana Turner: two of my idols. He had married these women in one brief, ten-year period of one lifetime. (Later, he had added the sexy novelist Kathleen Windsor, and segued to "Scarlett O'Hara's younger sister," actress Evelyn Keyes.) These women were just a few who melted when Artie put his lips to the reed and blew, or stared them down with his classic Latin lover look. He had true bedroom eyes, a dark, close-shaved beard and wore fabulous clothes.

But it was Artie Shaw's self-cultivated intellect, his preoccupation with psychotherapy and his obsession to improve himself and everyone around him that got me. And, of course, his much-vaunted musical talent that put him into the history books. (One of life's best experiences is listening to his early recordings of "Begin the Beguine" or "And the Angels Sing.")

There I was between Al and Artie. They were talking about celestial navigation or something technical. I didn't understand a word, but was dying to display my swing music knowledge to impress Artie, to let him know that *I* was the one at the party who really knew *who* he was and why. I managed occasionally to insert a word or ask a question. But mostly, these two men just talked over me as if I weren't there. (I knew that this was a *New Yorker* cartoon. I pictured myself a vapid, little woman wondering whether to order steak or shad roe, while "the men" discussed serious stuff. Men in tuxedos chatting while "she" lies on a chaise lounge. "We never told her about the Depression," says one cigar-smoker to another. Stuff like that.)

At one point I tried to leave. But Artie put his hand on my arm and pressed me back into the seat. Someone then called Mr. Strelsin away and Artie turned his burning focus on me. "Come on, girl. You're going home with me. I like you!" He was so authoritative. So commanding. No wonder Lana Turner had called him "my college education." I felt faint. I was sorely tempted. He was damned sexy. But then I thought about Ava and Lana and Kathleen and Evelyn. They hadn't been good enough for Artie Shaw so how could I possibly measure up to those goddesses?

I stuttered, stammered and escaped Artie's grasp. He probably shrugged. Another freshman had gotten away. In time, however, he and I became friends and in his later years, when someone stole his beloved clarinet out of a car in California, he called me to help him get it back. In time Artie Shaw lost his hair. And by then he had developed a stunning case of logorrhea or nonstop talk. To this day, I wish he'd make a musical comeback. But Artie has never felt he needed to come back.

And now I wish I had let him take me home. At the very least, I'd have been talked to death in a most interesting manner. And I might have learned something. And I could add myself to the pantheon that would read: Ava, Lana, Kathleen, Evelyn... and Liz.

"GO FUCK

YOURSELF!"

THE MOST INSTRUCTIVE THING THAT happened while working for Cholly Knickerbocker was a libel suit, one in which I had no part, beyond spectator.

I hadn't been there long and the dreaded Ed Wilcox was most definitely still in charge. He would set me to filing, checking or researching, anything to keep me from the actual process of column writing. But I was learning a lot every day if not exactly from the way he proceeded, for he was gross, profane, drunk half the time and no one to emulate.

He was also as far from the educated European background and social status of Igor Cassini as possible. He had a New York parochial vision. He had only disdain for the so-called International Set. He would rage around the office, then sit down and bang out something vicious against a restaurant owner who hadn't treated him right or someone he'd seen in his favorite haunt, P. J. Clark's, who had irritated him.

Hungover and bitter at being an assistant to someone he felt he could write rings around, he often just "took off" after his betters in general. Cassini tolerated him because they'd been in the Army together. He usually edited what Wilcox wrote and was always crossing out entire sections in disgust. This, I finally figured out, was why I had been hired. Cassini intended to replace Wilcox if I could ever learn the drill.

One day we were sitting in the basement rat's nest where we operated with our eyes just at sidewalk level. (We were like the girls from Ohio in *My Sister Eileen.*) Wilcox had written an item about the socialite Gregg Dodge of Palm Beach. Without naming her, his item went like this: "What wife of what wealthy Palm Beach car magnate was caught in flagrante delicto in her poolside cabana with an ex-FBI man? Screams, yells, the whole bit!"

I said, looking at it, "Maybe we should check with the Hearst lawyers?" He sneered, "Don't tell me how to write when *you* write like a woman with the curse. That's why it's a blind item, stupid. We don't name any names—what can they do? The source is Ted Howard, what more do you want?"

Ted Howard was one of the "gentlemen" column planters. He was courteous and exact. He was wintering in Palm Beach. If he sent the item, it was most likely absolutely one hundred percent true. I knew then that truth might be proof against a libel suit, but how do you establish "truth"? I was about to learn that this was an important question.

A few days passed and I heard Wilcox yelling over the phone. "Go fuck yourself!" he said, slamming down the receiver. I didn't think much about those fateful words because he turned in a fury. "Some jerk from Palm Beach calling to say we libeled him in the Gregg Dodge item. Says his name is Mr. Jones.* I told him I never heard of him and hung up."

Soon we heard from the lawyers for Mr. Jones. They offered this: We should retract our story, saying we did not mean to indicate that Mr. Jones was the man in the "Gregg Dodge item." (So much for blind!) But Ghighi, acting on Wilcox's certainty and Howard's responsible ways, refused to retract.

Pretty soon the Cholly Knickerbocker column was in

*Not his real name.

court defending itself from libeling someone in a blind item!
Now the Hearst lawyers, hardheaded, severe men, were on our
case. What could we prove, how could we prove it? It was embarrassing, for we couldn't prove anything. At first the attorneys
said they weren't too worried, because we hadn't mentioned any
names and we'd never heard of, or meant to libel, Mr. Jones.

Ghighi wanted me to go to court every day of the trial to
"observe, learn and see how things are done." And even the
Countess Cassini was there because her baby was being attacked. At one point the Hearst lawyers asked Cassini to call
Gregg Dodge and throw himself on her mercy. If she would
come to court and say the man in the item *was*, or *was not* Mr.
Jones—well, you can just imagine. Gregg had known Igor for
years. She even liked him. But he had taken a terrible shot at her,
blind or not. She told him quite emphatically that she wasn't
about to pull his chestnuts out of the fire.

She used words to this effect: "Ghighi, if you think I am
going to get on the witness stand and deny this blind item and
say either that I am the woman you referred to, or I am not—
what do you think my life would be worth with my husband,
Horace? And if you think I am going to even say whether or not
I know Mr. Jones, you must be crazy."

Mrs. Dodge was immune to Ghighi's pleas. He hadn't
written the item; he could only fume privately and blame
Wilcox. But if he placed too much blame in public, it made him
look foolish—as if he didn't have control of his own column.
Wilcox tried hard to look clean, washed and responsible on the
witness stand. But he was a Fourth Estate bum. It was obvious.

What it came down to, the Hearst lawyers told us—in no
uncertain terms—was that we must prove it *was* Mr. Jones with
Mrs. Dodge and smear the two of them as much as possible, or
we had to prove it was not Mr. Jones and we weren't even referring to him, but to some other man.

How could we do this? Then Mr. Jones served us with
his clincher. He said he had been running for sheriff of Dade
County. He lost the election by eighteen votes after the item ap-

peared. We had damaged his reputation and his job and earning
capacity. What's more, he offered exactly eighteen affidavits
from voters who said they had not voted for him because of the
item. Mr. Jones stated that he was definitely a friend to Mrs.
Dodge, though not "that" kind of friend, and so people associated him with her.

The Hearst lawyers were in a hopeless position. They attempted then to smear Mrs. Dodge and question her character in
court. She was young, blonde, beautiful and loved to kick up her
heels. She was married to a rich old man. But fortunately, to be
fair, smearing her didn't work either. The jury was on to Cholly
Knickerbocker!

And when Mr. Jones' lawyers pinned Wilcox down for
having shouted on the phone, been vulgar and abusive, and for
saying, "Go fuck yourself!" to their client—our fate was sealed.
The jury brought back a large judgment—for those days—of
$175,000 against the column for libeling Mr. Jones. They added
another $50,000 in punitive damages because Wilcox had been
so impolite, abusive and profane.

This was a humiliating and chastening experience for
everyone connected with Cholly Knickerbocker. And it was another black mark for Igor Cassini in the eyes of his employers
who already felt they were long-suffering where he was concerned. Perhaps he had been too long at the fair in their eyes (almost nineteen years). And perhaps they felt he wasn't paying
attention. They were also somewhat embarrassed by having a
columnist who was making a fortune doing PR and using his
own column as a client outlet. Probably the reason nobody
clamped down on him was because the newspaper's own managing editor, Seymour Berkson, had a wife, Eleanor Lambert,*
who was also in the PR business and making lots of hay out of
her Hearst newspaper connections.

*As I write this, Ms. Lambert, who invented "The Best Dressed List," is
still a successful mover and shaker in fashion-related and business public
relations and she is thriving in her nineties.

. . .

MY PERKS IN WORKING FOR Cholly grew immeasurably
and when Cassini moved our offices from East 61st Street to the
new Pepsi-Cola Building, I not only had a smashing office looking out onto Park Avenue at 59th Street, but was also given a
secretary. She was a beautiful, peachy-faced brunette fresh from
Great Britain—Caroline Jane Knott.

This kid was a delight. Smart, sweet and endearing. I
began to call her "Piggy" for some obscure reason. Everybody
was mad about her and I spent more time taking calls from her
impassioned young swains than she did taking calls for Cholly
business. One day Caroline came to work very excited. "Lizzie,
the most wonderful thing has happened. Mr. Cassini has invited
me to go to dinner with him in a party tonight at La Caravelle.
My date is to be an older man named Joseph Kennedy. He used
to be the ambassador to Great Britain!" I looked at this nineteen-
year-old and thought of her in the hands of that old goat, the former ambassador—the man who had warned FDR before World
War II that we'd better give in and let the Nazis have their way!

I said, "Wait here a minute, Piggy. I'll be right back." I
stormed in to Ghighi's office. "How dare you plan to pawn old
Joe Kennedy off on a lovely young girl like Caroline! Really,
Ghighi, this won't do. I won't let her go. Pimp for Joe Kennedy
among your own crowd!"

Ghighi raised an eyebrow, hitched up his pants and then,
seeing my point, shrugged and said, "Okay, I guess it wasn't a
very smart idea." (I *knew* it wasn't a very smart idea. I suppose
this is about the only moral victory I can claim ever to have exerted in the presence of Cholly/Igor/Ghighi's unending search
for money and pleasure. But I had seen Ambassador Kennedy
many times in La Caravelle, where he was a partial backer. The
management stood around red-faced and embarrassed as he
groped ladies in his booth or brought in rather unappetizing
prostitutes for dinner.)

I went back to find Caroline sitting on my desk. I looked

at this virginal innocent. "You are not going, Piggy. Put that in your pipe and smoke it. You can't be out with an old letch like Joe Kennedy." She began to weep. I was spoiling her chance, she said. Who did I think I was? "I'm your guardian angel," I said, "and if you persist in going, then I am calling your mother in London to come immediately and take you back home."

Caroline went on to marry Prince Veriand Windisch-Graetz, making her "Princess Piggy" in my eyes. She had several adorable sons. She later wed the socialite Howard Cushing and then Bill Graham, one of the sons of the *Washington Post* dynasty. She then became the inamorata of David Frost. She came into her own as a West Coast representative for *Vanity Fair*, then *The New Yorker*, and now for Tina Brown's *Talk* magazine. For years she has covered L.A. for Tina. Everyone in publishing knows Caroline Graham.

When I see her these days I always remind this brilliant magazine executive of how I once saved her virginity until she could better lose it on her own terms.

I WAS GOING ALONG HAVING a ball writing about how the Aga Khan had himself matched with his weight in gold or diamonds from his adoring subjects—examining how far his famous playboy son, Aly Khan, had fallen from his supposed role as spiritual leader to millions of Muslims—describing how American deb and rich girl Peggy Bancroft had become the Duchess d'Uzes—noting that the Vatican had to give a special dispensation so the fifteen-year-old Princess Ira von Furstenberg could marry a prince of the Hohenlohes—writing about New York's glamorous Gloria Vanderbilt and how she had an all-white vinyl living room at 10 Gracie Square with black bearskin rugs scattered on the floor—speculating as to how the Duke and Duchess of Windsor were invited hither and yon with hosts picking up their plane fare and hotel bills—and other deathless matters of the Jet Set.

Cassini's other PR world surged around the column as he pushed for his clients relentlessly. (It was said that rival columnists Dorothy Kilgallen and Bob Considine kept a tally of how many times Martial & Company clients turned up as social items in Cholly Knickerbocker. They bitched continuously to their Hearst bosses about how unethical this was.) Ghighi was now handling many accounts: Vat 69 Scotch, Buitoni spaghetti, Alitalia Airlines, Fiat cars, Pirelli tires, Lanvin perfumes, Orion Shipping, Harry Winston jewels, Cinzano aperitif, Evyan perfume, the Mexican government for tourism, NYC's Patrolman's Benevolent Association, Rogers Peet men's clothes and the Brazilian Coffee Institute, to name a few.

Igor and Oleg had also invented a private place for the elite to dine and dance without hoi polloi looking on. In this beginning, burgeoning age of disco, Le Club was a huge success and people clamored for me to get them in. But because of Martial's many clients, there was always a waiting list to join. And now, as the new First Lady's designer, Oleg was on everyone's most wanted list. The Cassini brothers were flying higher than the Wallendas.

There had always been rumors that Ghighi was also doing PR work for two Caribbean dictatorships—Cuba under Fulgencio Batista and the Dominican Republic under Rafael Trujillo. (Playboy Porfirio Rubirosa was a former son-in-law of Trujillo and he had introduced his pal Igor to the dictator as an "influential American journalist.")

I couldn't pin down anything as to Cassini's relationship with Batista. By 1959, the latter had been overthrown by Fidel Castro's Agrarian Reform revolution and had departed Cuba to live in luxury in Portugal. Ghighi, like all the conservative Hearst columnists, was devastated by the rise of Communism in Cuba and often covered this in his column, blaming the fall of Batista on *The New York Times* reporter Herbert Matthews. Whether he actually reaped some riches while Batista was in power, I would never know, but most of his intimates assumed that to be so.

Still, there wasn't any question that Ghighi had a lot going with the Dominican Republic's Trujillo. There were stories that mostly all Ghighi did was write letters describing his fictional positive conversations about the Caribbean country with important people such as Vice President Nixon and with then Senator John F. Kennedy. And there was a really famous anecdote to the effect that when *The New York Times Magazine* was about to print a devastating article on torture under Trujillo, Ghighi got an advance look at the piece, then flew to the Dominican Republic and personally assured the *generalissimo* that he had influenced the *Times* to remove all mention of the telephone batteries wired to men's genitals, which was a well-known Trujillo torture device. The teller of this tale would laugh and say, "After receiving this reassurance, Trujillo would beam at Ghighi and load him down with cash. Trujillo didn't have a clue as to the reality, which was that Cassini had absolutely zero influence over the *Times*. And there had never been anything about genital torture in the piece!"

No one could expect Cassini to admit to all this, but in time it was revealed that he or his minions had been paid PR fees by Trujillo to try to influence public opinion and get U.S. economic sanctions lifted. One sum mentioned was $500,000.

When Trujillo's limousine was riddled with bullets in 1961, it was to Igor Cassini/Cholly Knickerbocker that the fledgling Kennedy administration turned for help. Although Bobby Kennedy wanted to "send in the Marines," Cassini wisely advised that the U.S. do nothing because he felt in spite of the assassination the situation would stabilize. And it did.

Eventually, *The New York Times* ran an editorial on Cassini's having been called by Allen Dulles on such a serious matter. They headlined it "How Not to Conduct Diplomacy." I recall Ghighi coming into the office with the newspaper in his hand. He said to me, "Can you believe it? This *is* the most powerful nation in the world with all facilities for information-gathering, yet whom did they call that morning? A society columnist. I wonder who they called in other crises?"

Cassini would soon be wondering who to call in his own

crisis, and we would all be up to our hips in FBI men. The investigative reporter Peter Maas wrote a story for the *Saturday Evening Post*, examining the connection between the Dominican Republic and Igor Cassini. Ghighi's chickens were coming home to roost.

Certain senators and even the Cassini-friendly Kennedys were unable to ignore this rock after it was overturned. I recall the FBI coming to my apartment and asking me a lot of grim questions. They'd say repeatedly, "Nothing, Miss Smith, nothing is off the record to the FBI." Then they'd stop me in everything I said with, "It doesn't matter what you believe or imagine or think you know. We only want facts." I had to shrug and say that I had none because my role with Cholly Knickerbocker had never had anything to do with Martial & Company or Ghighi's other businesses. If Cassini's clients were often in the column, I was just printing what he told me to. They'd interrupt. They were only interested in a connection to the Dominican Republic, because if Mr. Cassini had one he could be in violation of the Foreign Agents Registration Act, wherein all representatives of foreign governments must register with the Justice Department, disclose their connection and say how much they spent and for what. This case was also piquing the interest of the IRS because no taxes had been paid on supposed Dominican Republic money to Cassini.

Finally, the FBI said they had no further use for me. I was clear and free. "Why?" I asked.

"Well, we looked at your bank account and it is obvious nobody has paid you anything like the amounts we are interested in." One of the agents finally smiled and added, "In fact, you are underpaid for what you do."

Igor and Oleg both tried to plead Ghighi's case privately to the new president and to his brother, the attorney general. Even Ghighi's wife, Charlene, wrote a pitiful letter to JFK. But Ghighi was indicted on February 8, 1963. He resigned from Hearst's Cholly Knickerbocker column and Martial & Company's clients all fled for the hills. I worked on for a while, trying to help him clean everything up. Ghighi kept up a wonderful jaunty attitude. Not everyone deserted him; many people thought this was just Uncle Sam swatting at gnats and others hated the Kennedys and felt he was being persecuted. So he continued to be invited, to go out every night and to wear a smile. Eventually attorney Louis Nizer* advised him to plead *nolo contendere* (no contest) and pay a $10,000 fine. He did, but he was quite effectively ruined. He closed the Park Avenue offices and bid me farewell.

When Ghighi and Charlene made plans to pay their annual Christmas visit to her father, Charles Wrightsman, in Palm Beach, old Charlie asked them not to come. "It might embarrass us with the Kennedys." Shortly after this, the beautiful Mrs. Cassini took an overdose of pills and died. I remember writing a letter for Ghighi to a judge after that, vouching for his skill at parenting, recommending that he be given full custody of his son, Alexander. He had been my boss and I had looked up to him. He had always been so dynamic, so strong, so courageous, so funny, and so independent. I just couldn't bear it that he'd had to ask *me* for this petty favor. But he won custody and departed to live in Europe.

In time I became friends with the man who blew the whistle on Igor Cassini—Peter Maas. I have dealt with Peter many times since I started writing my own column, for he has written best-selling hits, one after another. Maas takes total credit for my success. He says, "If I hadn't caused you to lose your job on Cholly Knickerbocker and forced you to go out on your own and become your own byline, why you'd still be writing for Cholly, making $200 a week! You owe it all to me!"

I suppose I do. But I never took any pleasure in Ghighi's downfall. Cassini is back in the U.S. now, where he is famous on every golf course and his two almost grown sons by his last marriage are golf champions. He has white curly hair, but is

*The famous lawyer and I remained friends until his death. It was Nizer who told me, "No murder case, no violent crime is as nasty as the average American divorce."

slim, trim, athletic and sexy. In his eighties, he abounds with energy. And he told me recently there will soon be a movie made about the fantastic lives of Igor and Oleg Cassini. I never doubted it for a minute and had suggested it myself in a column I wrote back in the eighties. (I want to be played by Oscar-winner Hilary Swank.)

Soon after Cassini resigned, I went to Hearst's Joe Kingsbury-Smith, at Ghighi's recommendation, and asked if the company would make me Cholly Knickerbocker? He said no. "You have done a good job. You are talented. But you have no cachet, no image. We are giving the column to another Hearst columnist, Aileen Mehle, and we'll call it Suzy Knickerbocker! Sorry."

I saw their point. And I saw that Lizzie Knickerbocker was not to be. My fate lay elsewhere.

SMILE!

YOU'RE ON

CANDID CAMERA

O UT OF A JOB AGAIN in February 1963. Second banana slips on another peel. Fired again "through no fault of my own." My resumé was beginning to sound awfully suspicious. But a Texas pal, Bill Anderson, with whom I had worked at NBC, now wanted me to join him at Allen Funt Productions.

Of course I knew of Allen Funt, the roly-poly creator of the super-successful *Candid Camera*, a hit that began in 1948 and still has tentacles in today's TV. Brooklyn-born Funt had begun as an ad man with a gimmicky mind. During World War II he had worked on "concealment techniques," which proved to be the basis for his future success. Luring the unsuspecting into situations, he'd leap out and say, "Smile! You're on *Candid Camera*!"

Funt was a legend, a demanding, irascible boss. Anderson bombarded him, singing my praises and maybe it was Bill's lanky Texas style, his twinkling eyes, his great sense of humor that disarmed his fearsome boss. "You could get a great job from Allen," said Bill. "Nobody in this production company knows what they're doing. Only the *Candid Camera* people operate out of their long success. But Allen needs someone to develop new show ideas and make them happen. He pays better than anyone; he has to because he's so damned hard to work for."

I thought I was finished with TV and it with me. I knew Allen Funt's terrorist reputation. His brilliance lay in his understanding of the negatives of human nature and the raw sadism of humor that comes with watching others be embarrassed. He was a giant control freak, said to be desperate to be loved but forever shooting himself in the foot so nobody could love him.

Bill was amused by his own methodology in touting me to Funt. "All Allen has to hear is that there's someone out there who is superior and he doesn't have them and he moves the earth to make them his." I also knew Fannie Flagg, who worked for Funt. She performed as a kind of clever, flame-haired, funny shill, luring people to believe in her for the hidden camera. (Later, Fannie would "graduate" and come into her own as a best-selling writer. Remember her wonderful Southern book and movie *Fried Green Tomatoes*?)

When I went to see Allen I was in good shape because I didn't really want the job. I didn't like or trust him as he bent over his massive desk, his bald head shining, his powerful hands splayed out on the blotter, his piercing eyes fixed on me. Where had I come from? What did I want in life? What were my sex hang-ups? ("Just kidding," he said immediately in a way to make you know he wasn't.) I nonchalantly told a bit about myself, saying I had no particular skills or aspirations, but was a hard worker. He seemed to feel I was hiding something from him and then, naturally for him, he felt obligated to try to own me. He offered me the astonishing salary of $65,000 a year. I would start immediately although he had no idea what he wanted me to do. He placed me in an office right next-door to his. This was either to keep an eye on me or to establish my rank and his fickle favoritism. I was soon to discover that he was lonely and needed company, an audience. He also spent a lot of time checking up on his workers to be sure they were busy and not ripping him off. With nothing really to do, I began to go to work a half hour early every day in order to rap out a fast letter to my mother. I had been able to type ninety words a minute since age sixteen and it was easy for me to keep to a guilty habit I had developed because I had moved 1,500 miles away from home with the intention of never going back there to live.

Allen was astounded at my typing. He was sure I was writing a novel on his time. He'd stand in my doorway, glowering and asking, Could he see it? I'd say, "...the letter to my mother? You want to see that? Allen, it isn't nine o'clock yet. Just relax."

"You write your mother every day?" he'd ask, accusingly.

"Yes, almost every day."

His features would soften. (Maybe somewhere he had a dear mother that he, too, had neglected.)

I began to besiege him with daily memos and ideas for unusual, unique and fabulous TV shows, trying to earn my salary. But mainly he liked me to come and sit with him and watch his big tropical fish tank, which was his pride and joy. He had a lot of toys. The fish were his captives like the rest of us. He'd ask me to sit in on production meetings for projects I had nothing to do with; then he wanted me to dish the people working on same.

My own solace in the office was Bill Anderson, smart and human. Bill pointed out that Allen was a special kind of bully, cajoling and seductive with women but extra hard on the men in his employ. It was nothing to see some poor soul, who had been hired at a huge salary, suddenly discover himself with a large mortgage, his kids in private schools and his balls in Allen's pocket. These guys emerged from Allen's office after lots of dim but perceived yelling with the door closed, tears staining their faces. I was frightened of Allen Funt, but determined not to let him know it. "Don't give in to him; then he'll kill you!" Bill advised.

So I offered Funt one of the best performances I ever pulled off in the business world. Imitating Elaine Stritch, I pretended to be the important and independent person he thought he had hired. Because I had arrogantly told him during my job interview that I wasn't a fan of *Candid Camera,* his special baby, he never stopped trying to put me on the program. He'd show me

the weekly takes and ask for my input. Then he'd say why didn't
I appear on camera next week, act as the come-on, the Fannie
Flagg of the piece, lure some poor soul into making himself look
foolish. I told him I wasn't a performer and couldn't do it. I know
now I was holding onto the little shred of dignity I still had as a
responsible TV producer. I was, after all, still living in the Fred
Friendly era of decent TV ethics and felt I should be vigilant. I
didn't want to be on-air trapping and making fun of innocents.
And I was afraid if I went along with anything Allen wanted,
he'd have me where he wanted me. I tried hard to stay on the
"high road" of documentary development.

Finally, Allen and Bill Anderson came up with an idea
that I thought was grand and ambitious. We would become observers of the activities of a group of pre-school children in a
private day school in Connecticut. We would film these same
children over a period of time, observing their changes and development and eventually turn it into a show separate from *Candid Camera*. This wasn't to be comedy; it was scientific, proving
how boys develop more slowly than girls, that children start
reading and developing skills exactly when they are ready, etc.
We would act as observers: We'd never address the children unless they asked us a question; we'd never try to influence them
or interact with them. Bill and I were thrilled to have a chance to
be "educational." And "serious." We seemed to have unlimited
expenses and Allen was going to leave us alone. We had the
trust of the private school.

It was a big relief to be actually working and out from
under Allen's thumb. Allen seemed happy; he hadn't known
what to do with me for months. Now I was in place. We began to
bring home the most incredible footage of "our kids" at play.
We filmed interchanges that were to die for—precious moments
of children at their most unselfconscious. One day we focused
on a delightful little boy and girl. He was whispering in her ear.
She was smiling like a grown-up. When we viewed it, the little
boy was saying, "I'se your little tiger, darlin', and I'se going to
eat you all up."

I was relieved to be busy. I had hated "making work" to

earn my salary. I knew it drove Allen crazy to have me in my office writing memos and letters, reading books and dreaming up projects he would never do. He wanted me to come and schmooze with him, to hear his complaints, his experiences, his feuds, his feelings. How his wife was sick and didn't understand him; how his girlfriend was too demanding and wanted to marry him; how his children didn't appreciate what he did for them. One day he impulsively called me in and indicated a pile of new clothes. "I know you have good taste. I was given these. I hate all of them. Go back to Brioni of Rome and exchange them for the kind of clothes I'd like or should wear. Use your own good judgment." I was incredulous. He was asking a highly paid professional to act as a servant. But I realized he was simply trying to get some juice out of me, to use me for something he wanted and he hoped I'd refuse so he could fire me. I simply said, "Okay. Glad to." I picked up the clothes and left the office, went to Brioni, quickly made the exchanges, danced off to Voisin for lunch and spent the afternoon in the Metropolitan Museum. When I came in at five and handed him his new clothes, he looked pleased. "That was a tough job," I said, tongue-in-cheek. But he didn't complain. He beamed. He'd gotten his money's worth out of me for one day and I'd had a pleasant afternoon off.

So Bill and I were happy to travel to Connecticut, to film, to screen, to select, to read child psychology and become amateur experts on child behavior. We were in hog heaven, or piglet heaven, I guess. In the meantime, there were also many adventures in the production office. Famous people were always showing up. Stars galore wanted to be on *Candid Camera*. And I should add that Allen had charm to spare for the outside world and his peers. People who didn't know him thought they liked him. They saw Dr. Jekyll. We worked for Mr. Hyde. As for *Candid Camera,* the famous show often did something worthwhile.

For instance, the former president Harry S Truman frequently came to New York to visit his daughter Margaret, his son-in-law Clifton Daniel and his grandsons. He would walk briskly around Manhattan with his secret service entourage and *Candid Camera* would follow. We caught many funny and poignant exchanges between the thirty-third president and New Yorkers. It was *Candid Camera* at its best.

One day Allen invited Bill and me to join him for a visit President Truman and his aide were making to the office. We had a delightful time listening to Funt and Truman chat and all of us accompanied our distinguished visitor to the elevator. Standing there I tried to think of something sensible to say to a man I admired so much. I remarked, "Mr. President, I want to thank you on behalf of everyone for what you did after World War II with the Marshall Plan, saving Europe as you did."

Truman stared at me and then burst into a big smile. Addressing Allen, who was momentarily silent, he said, "Now here is a young woman who knows what she's talking about. Yes, and also thank you for addressing me properly. Just because I am no longer in the White House doesn't mean I do not have the respect of this title. I am *still* Mr. President." He then expounded for a moment on being referred to now and then as the "ex-president." "I am not the ex anything," said the feisty Harry Truman. "I am the former president." As the elevator doors closed, Mr. President waved good-bye to us with his walking stick.

"Well," said Allen, grumpily, as we turned away, "you sure know how to turn it on with old men." Then he commanded me to come to his office. I sighed: Another heart-to-heart with Allen Funt. Maybe I had upstaged him.

Once we were settled, with the tropical fish waving their azure fins, Allen got right down to business. His girlfriend was pregnant. His wife refused to give him a divorce, said she never would. He was at his wit's end. "You are sophisticated," he said, mistakenly, "you've been around. So what can you do to help me?" I didn't much care that my boss was at his wit's end, but I liked his girlfriend and felt for her.

"Are you serious, Allen? Is she willing to have an abortion?" He said yes. So I said I'd think it over. I didn't weigh the moral implications of the matter. I thought if a woman wanted an abortion, she should be able to have one safely. But I did know this was against the law. So I went to a doctor friend and laid out the problem. He sighed, "Now Liz, you get out of this.

Forget you ever knew about it. Have this woman call me. I'll talk to her."

Before long, the girlfriend was back visiting the office, full of smiles and with a trim waistline. The doctor and his wife had taken her to their country home, where the operation was performed. They looked after her for several days. The doctor finally agreed, after much urging from me, that the bill would be $700.

I went to Allen's office and asked him to take care of it. He exploded. He was "being taken," the cost was outrageous, my physician was a "bloodsucker," he'd call the police on him.

I looked at him and said, "Allen, you are a shit." I slammed the door. Later that afternoon he sheepishly dropped $700 on my desk. I got a messenger and sent it to the doctor. The matter never came up again.

One morning, happily prepping for another week of filming "our kids," I took a call from the school principal. How could Mr. Anderson and I have betrayed them in such a manner? We had signed agreements with them. They would sue us were it not for the bad publicity that would accrue. We were no longer welcome in Connecticut! I was dumbfounded. But it turned out that Allen had been filching our film. He had been sandwiching parts of "our kids" into *Candid Camera*: selected cute sayings, adorable happenings and mishaps caught on film. He was stealing from his own future program, or maybe he never intended there to be such a program. Allen Funt was a law unto himself. I no longer remember Bill's reaction or mine beyond a bitter disappointment, disillusionment and embarrassment, which we could never explain to the wounded school and "our kids." The documentary could now never be put together. We were not sued, but the school, of course, withdrew permission for us to use any of our footage anywhere. I knew the end was near for me with Allen Funt Productions and I had only been there for months.

I had no idea how traumatic that end would be. One Friday, I was lunching at Fontana di Trevi with my friend of Lena and Cholly days Saint Clair Pugh. We were sitting near the front of the restaurant when we heard something. It was like an ocean wave that was gathering momentum as it beat toward shore. A murmur, then a rising wail, a cry—I still can't describe it, but I get chills remembering it.

Disbelief changed into credibility. "The president has been shot! The president has been shot in Dallas!" Saint and I dropped our napkins and flew out onto West 57th Street without bothering to pay our check. We began rushing toward Fifth Avenue, which was ever the center of the universe. We paused in front of one of those giant Magnavox showrooms, solid plate glass for two stories, hundreds of TV sets all tuned to one Walter Cronkite. This was an unbelievable and surreal American moment, like something out of a Fellini movie. Walter would tell us the little he knew. We would then move on to another TV set, where he would tell us something else. I recall thinking, "Why did it have to happen in Texas?"

Saint and I plowed on to Fifth Avenue and 57th. At Tiffany's the corner was clotted with people weeping and hugging one another. Total strangers comforted total strangers. Nobody seemed to be going anywhere. The world hung in limbo. I returned to the Funt office, which was near Fifth Avenue. Inside, almost everyone had left their cubicles to watch the many TV sets in the main room. People were crying softly. Cronkite then announced that the president had been pronounced dead. A wave of anguish rose in the room.

People sat on the edges of desks, stunned. Many went to the coatracks and began preparing to leave. Allen had, throughout, been totally out of sight. No one was even thinking of him.

Suddenly he burst out upon us screaming, "Okay! Okay! He's dead. They say he's dead. So all of you get back to work now. Instantly—back to work!" We all looked at him. One or two Funt sycophants, the people we all knew were informers and "secret police," scurried back to their holes. But ninety-nine percent of the workforce ignored the red-faced Mr. Funt. We put on our coats and silently began leaving, while he continued to yell and berate us. Bill and I left with the rest. We never really looked at or acknowledged him.

I went to my apartment in Murray Hill and promptly went to bed. For three days I watched TV, drank vodka and ate out of cans. I remember rising groggily out of a sick sleep early Sunday morning to watch Lee Harvey Oswald being brought down in the Dallas jail. I wanted to get a look at this creature. But Jack Ruby lunged out from the side of the screen, fired and erased Oswald. It was all "too much for TV" as they say!

When I went back to work after the funeral of the thirty-fifth president, I was numb like the rest of the nation. I wrote my letter of resignation and put it in my top drawer. Some weeks later I presented it, having put a P.S. at the end: "Just add me to the long list of those who have worked for you who can't take it any longer."

And so, I left the best-paying job I had ever had.

PART
FIVE
a Memoir

THE *COSMO*

YEARS

LIKE MY FATHER WHO DIDN'T remember when he
hadn't been married to my mother, I find it difficult to recall
a time when my life wasn't dominated in one way or another by
the dynamic Helen Gurley Brown, the creator of *Sex and the
Single Girl*, the veteran innovator-originator of *That Cosmopolitan Girl* and today the international editor of the magazine
worldwide. I was to serve in her benign dictatorship of love and
sex for eleven years and would remain her friend ever after.

After leaving Allen Funt, I determined to return to magazine freelancing with a vengeance. It may seem a glamorous career with a byline and interesting people along the way, but I
would come to equate freelancing with picking and chopping
cotton. It was hard to get assignments, gain access, please editors and meet deadlines.

The so-called New Journalism had come into being and I
had a nodding acquaintance with it through my friendship with
the men on *Esquire*—Clay Felker, Harold Hayes, Byron Dobell,
Bob Benton, David Newman—and I was always hoping I might
become as well-known and respected as the forerunners of this

movement of lively conversational writing; Tom Wolfe, Jimmy
Breslin, Pete Hamill, Gay Talese, Nora Ephron, to name a few.

I had done a few good things for *Esquire* and for
Felker's a'borning *New York* magazine, which first appeared as
a supplement in *The New York Herald Tribune*. This was just
before the elegant owner, Jock Whitney, threw up his hands and
closed the world's most glamorous New York newspaper.* But
my New Journalism efforts were vitiated by a desperate need to
make a living. Sloan had died in 1962 leaving nothing and I
wanted to care for my mother. My parents had made many sacrifices for me.

So now, having walked away from a lucrative TV career,
I took jobs from any magazine that asked. The New Journalism,
however, demanded single-mindedness and fealty to ideals of
purism too rich for my blood. A certain snobbism reigned and if
you wrote for women's journals, house organs, etc., you didn't
qualify as serious.

Something brought me to the attention of the then editor
of *Cosmopolitan*, a general interest magazine that had fallen on
hard days. Some people think *Cosmo* was always a "women's"
magazine. Not so—in the early sixties it was more like the *Saturday Evening Post*, with a movie star profile on one page, followed by a piece on fly-fishing. All such publications were
about to bite the dust. But, again, the idea of a regular salary appealed to me.

Cosmo's beautiful entertainment editor Lyn Tornabene

---

*Mr. Whitney was my idea of the last of the great gents, described as "an
aristocrat with the soul of a democrat." This polo-playing philanthropist
had said, "Wouldn't it be wonderful if I could somehow manage to give
away more than the Rockefellers?" He had put up the dough for David O.
Selznick's* Gone with the Wind. *He had married Babe Paley's sister Betsey
Cushing. And one of the best compliments I'd ever received had come to me
soon after his death. In La Grenouille restaurant, the witty writer Garson
Kanin had held my hand, rubbed his fingers down the length of mine and
told me I was the only person who would be able to write a perfect biography of Jock Whitney. What a flattering moment!*

wanted to retire to Connecticut with hubby and child. So they asked me to replace her. In my other magazine experience, say at *The Texas Ranger* or *Modern Screen,* I had done exactly as I was told by someone in command. I had line edited, corrected copy, written captions and headlines to size, occasionally made a creative suggestion. But *Cosmo* needed imaginative skills, independent judgment and originality. I was to be "in charge" of entertainment. So I asked Ms. Tornabene to help me set up an operation and suggest procedure. I'll never forget her candid response.

"Why should I do that? Why help you succeed? I don't want you to do a good job. I want to be remembered as the best."

It was a great lesson in competition. Such candor! Lyn was immune to all my shit-kicking charm and I laughed, seeing the beauty of it. I realized how people resent their successors but will put on a hypocritical face of being "helpful." I saluted Lyn and she left. Later, we became friends and she'd write the best biography ever of my idol Clark Gable. So I forgave her everything.

I started playing catch-up as hard as I could—going to movies like crazy, writing reviews, assigning profiles, inviting writers I admired to work for *Cosmo* and trying to "keep up," a journalistic art that comes and goes.

We heard rumors that the Hearsts would wash their hands of *Cosmo.* Then that Helen Gurley Brown would come in to make it over, clean house. Who was HGB? She was the shockingly dirty-minded ex-secretary and ad copywriter who had penned the sensational bestseller. I had hardly believed my eyes when I read *Sex and the Single Girl*—it was so advanced, candid, pragmatic and startling for the time. HGB seemed definitely to be a scarlet woman. What could the Hearst bosses be thinking of?

In my years observing, covering, knowing thousands of famous people, I am always asked, "What is so and so really like?" Next to the horrifying question, "Got any good gossip?" I find this other phrase the most bothersome. But Helen still stands alone at the top of the public's wish-to-know list: at least in my experience. For me, she has beaten out Elizabeth Taylor, Princess Diana, Jackie O, Madonna, et al., when it comes to public curiosity.

Well, in 1965, HGB took over *Cosmo* and I was about to find out what she was really like. We all began job-hunting elsewhere, using the pitiful remnants of our puny expense accounts to take the knowing, the connected, the employed to lunch for obvious reasons.

The day came when the wispy, soft-spoken, shy Mrs. Brown was brought to my desk and introduced. She had a self-deprecating Arkansas charm and a kind of sweet, dithering Billie Burke manner. She seemed so helpless, I thought I'd save her the trouble of firing me and resign. But soon she asked me into her corner office, transformed with scarves over pink lights, pillows, candles, kitty cat knickknacks and needlepoint.

"Well, Lizzie dear, what shall we do with you?" She went on to say she loved my writing and would I consider staying on to help her turn *Cosmo* into what it should be—a glorious, unfettered, sexy and seductive paean for aspiring young women who wanted to unleash their ambitions, have sex with the same careless abandon as men, make silk purses out of the sow's ears that we all mistake for romance, marry millionaires, etc. Would I?

Would I? I leapt at the opportunity. Then, I would remain firmly caught in HGB's tender trap of candor, affection, fun and friendship forever after. I promptly set myself on a high horse to correct Mrs. Brown's many perceived "errors" and to give her the benefit of my experience. I argued, fought and asserted myself with her. She viewed me with dazed, admiring eyes and gave attention but no credence to my numerous critiques of her various philosophies and shocking ideas for *Cosmo*.

This kind of love-hate, argument-rationalizing went on for years and eventually I realized she was seldom wrong in her own incredible intuition. I look back on myself as *Cosmo*'s entertainment editor and I see an absurd jerk. I was callow, opinionated and self-important. But Helen treated me the way she had learned to treat men. She was patient, kind and she listened—a rare thing. She would appear to register my negatives while politely erasing them as she fussed over and petted me. She complimented me and then went on doing it whatever way she had planned all along. It was a battle in which we tested our wits, I had a loud say-so and then we did it her way. She was also the toughest, most demanding editor I have ever had. We fought like tigers over what I called matters of taste, lack of refinement, ethics, manners. Articles under her rigorous pen were scourged of negatives and clichés. It was verboten to write an unkind word. "You are censoring me," I'd scream.

I felt she needed me to straighten her out on matters of which I knew best. But in time I came to see her as the Oracle at Delphi to a mass of U.S. females who desperately wanted her kind of liberation, inspiration, emphasis on sex and love and hope for womankind. And, as Women's Liberation evolved, I came to see she had long been ahead of the pack *in her own way*. She simply wanted to do it her way—to have men, love, romance, sex and the big job in a manner that kept it all together. She was for "having it all" before anybody else knew the phrase.

I was headstrong, impetuous, impulsive, emotional and unstable and Helen brought out the lecturer side of me. I could never stop talking to her, interrupting her, bombarding her with ideas. She remained as patient as if I were a millionaire she intended to marry. I visited upon her all my pent-up frustrations, my sordid thoughts, my personal hits and errors. She listened and was curious, but she didn't seem to judge. Her firm disagreements were couched in such pleasant terms you thought she had agreed.

Sometimes during a raving criticism, she'd compose herself and become the voice of reason. "Oh, I do understand you hate these Frank Scavullo covers. Crass and vulgar, you say. You want soft, erotic girls with flowing hair as in this European magazine *Nova*. I'll tell you what. I'll replace Scavullo with the kind of covers you want as soon as our newsstand sales fall off."

I would collapse, victorious. But sales never fell off. I came to see that the covers I hated were what sold *Cosmo*. Not to forget the lurid but appealing headlines written monthly by

Helen's movie producer husband, David Brown. And Helen's workaholic attention to detail. My romanticized female probably wouldn't have sold an issue, let alone all those tubes of Revlon lipstick that crammed the advertising pages under HGB.

Helen's was the mailed fist in the velvet glove and she had it on the *Cosmo* girl's pulse. She was so successful in holding to her own vision that it became useless to argue. Many of my friends found HGB outrageous and embarrassing. Her success, against all odds—including the oddness of her entertainment editor—was its own answer to her detractors and critics.

And here's a cautionary tale about Helen: When another editor, Roberta Ashley, and I dreamed up an anonymous pillar called "The Gossip Column" by a fictitious Robin Adams Sloan, no one was more delighted by our commercial success than HGB. She contributed and cheered us on in our moonlighting. But in 1976 when I was invited to write under my own name for the *Daily News*, Helen took Roberta's side in a legality that went to arbitration. (I had decided I could do the Liz Smith column *and* retain a franchise in Robin Adams Sloan.) Helen appeared as an imposing witness for Roberta. She said I couldn't do both things. (And here I was convinced I could *do anything*.) I had the formidable writer Nora Ephron appearing for me, telling the adjudicator that of course I could write several gossip columns with one hand tied behind me. I feigned nonchalance with Helen as if I didn't care that she was on Roberta's side, not mine. But it hurt and I lost the arbitration and had to accept a settlement. This would have torn another friendship asunder, but some months after, Nora and I were together at a movie premiere. I saw Helen roaming the aisles looking for a place to sit. I waved. "Come sit here with us!" Nora, who had gone to bat for me in blood, was aghast and rigid with anger—not at Helen, but at me. "I can't believe you are such a sap."

I tried to explain that I respected Helen for doing what she felt was ethically correct. Nora lived on this story for ages; she said it illustrated perfectly what an ass I can be, but HGB and I went on with our friendship. Helen had encouraged me to stay on at *Cosmo* and double up with a contract for *Sports Illus-*

trated. So I had bylines both places in the mid-sixties, traveled for both magazines and there was never a moment's conflict. Later I asked why she let me do this. "I didn't want to lose you," she said.

As our friendship progressed, I began to badger HGB to treat herself more kindly. "Why don't you make the Hearsts give you a car and driver? At least take a taxi! For Pete's sake, Helen, Diana Vreeland has a losing magazine in *Vogue* but she has such luxuries."

Helen thought. Later, I asked again if she was still taking the bus. She said, "Well, now I taxi one way and take the bus home." I screamed. "Well, I need to see my *Cosmo* girls and know what they think, what they wear, what their lives are like." When Hearst gave her a 25th anniversary Mercedes and driver, it barely changed her penurious ways. In the car, she was always preoccupied, wondering how to give the driver the rest of the evening off.

One year, walking along the Croisette at the Cannes Film Festival, I unexpectedly ran into Helen. "Come with me to Hermès," she said, "I have to buy a gift." In the store she paid a handsome $75 for a tie. I then took her to a special place called De Blausse where they made divine items for petite sizes. I would go in just to moon over the merchandise I couldn't get into. "These polo shirts are only sold here, Helen, they are perfect for you. Please buy them in all colors; there's nothing else like them." She looked, drooled, but refused to buy. "Too expensive!" she said, "Helen, you just paid $75 for a man's tie. This is for your life. This is a great chance."

"Oh well," she said. "The tie is a business expense for one of David's friends. But I could never spend that on myself." I despaired. For years David has insisted that Helen goes behind him picking up his tips to bellhops and waiters. For years, David has given her diamonds, rubies and emeralds, but Helen mixes them in with a $200 junk bracelet I once bought her in Paris. After David became a multi-millionaire from *Jaws*, Helen wept, asking if now he'd leave her for a younger woman? He didn't but she has continued to pinch pennies and scorn excess. After thirty-four years at the helm of *Cosmo* entire, she stepped down, but she still works as if possessed. She has written two books since "moving on" and the last one, *I'm Wild Again*, was so candid, ribald and in-your-face that I wrote of it, "Helen will be ridden out of town on a rail after this is published." This, however, was the quote she liked best and wanted to use.

I BECAME A MENTOR WHILE working for *Cosmo*. I "discovered" a talented, handsome good-looker from Louisiana named Rex Reed. He had been born in Fort Worth, so I warmed to him. Working for a press agent, he sent me some of his movie reviews.

I took them to Helen. "This guy can write. Let's give him some review space and I won't do all of the reviews."

Helen said, "Aren't you cutting your own throat?"

I shrugged. "Naw!"

Rex wrote his first review of *Lilith* for us and was soon on his way. One night he went out with Ava Gardner and a beau and slipped into the bathroom every few minutes to jot down notes. When he told me of the experience, I said, "Write this exactly as you told it to me and let me send it to *Esquire*." He did. I did. And Rex became an enormous byline and TV personality. Then he went to the *Daily News* and did astounding profiles for them for years.

Later, this bread cast on the waters floated back my way. Rex spent his years at the *News* telling his boss, Mike O'Neill, to hire me to write a gossip column. It finally came to pass. In the meantime, for all his successful pummeling on my behalf, I still consider my greatest claim to fame being that I was almost named in Rex's father's divorce suit.

Down the years I often went out with Rex and his visiting dad, Jimmy. We became correspondents, Jimmy Reed and I, and then Jimmy married a woman Rex didn't care for. When the marriage faltered the wife threatened to name me as co-respondent. She said her husband kept love letters from me in his underwear drawer. Well, it was true. I may have written Jimmy some loving notes. Mr. Reed was so mortified at this threat that he settled the divorce out of court. I always tell Rex I could have been his stepmother, but that doesn't mean he gives me any respect.

I CAN'T PRETEND EVERYTHING I'VE done professionally has always been one hundred percent kosher. There was the writing of anonymous gossip for the nonexistent Robin Adams Sloan. So many people contributed to this column that I distanced myself from items I didn't like. But writing anonymously is wrong. And then there is the matter of Nicky.

In 1968, Helen wanted an exclusive with a call girl. "You know everybody; I'll bet you know some call girls—not that I mean anything insulting by saying this." So I tried to oblige. I went to heavy-hitter guys I knew and tried to get set up with a prostitute. We had some abortive tries, where the girls never showed. We offered to pay the going rate for their time to talk but this just made them suspicious. I said to Diane Judge, my occasional roomie, "Too bad you haven't made money from your nefarious carryings-on. I could interview you, but you are sexually liberated for your own pleasure."

Diane thought. "Remember Nicky? The pseudo-socialite you met in the Hamptons? She has a lot going. I'll bet she can help you." I protested that this wouldn't be correct. Diane popped another wine cork and said, "Helen will believe whatever you give her. She's more naive than you are."

So I called Nicky and we met. "Fascinating idea; let me kick it around."

Time passed and I was desperate. The more I talked to Nicky about love for sale, the more knowledgeable she sounded. Finally I said, "Nicky, let's playact. You pretend you are a call girl and I'll ask questions in character. We'll tape it."

The Q & A turned out great and became a *Cosmo* article. I overrode my ethics and decided Nicky was either in the life or about to be. Nicky offered chapter and verse as to how "high-class" call girls pass themselves off as models and socialites... what they charge... what they sometimes settle for... how they deal with the old, the ugly, the unwashed... how they avoid the cops... how gullible they find men in general... how even the most cynical guy may want to pretend it's not for money... how many call girls prefer their own sex because they trust other women, etc.

When I had asked Nicky if call girls fake orgasm, she yelled at me. "Of course! Just as wives and girlfriends who never get a thin dime do, night after night, time after time." When I offered Nicky the $200 fee we had slotted for the article, she was insulted. "No call girl would take money from another woman!" she said, slamming the door on me.

Well, I wrote it up and Helen loved it. The piece received wide play as something fresh and new about the world's oldest profession. People talked about it because sex was becoming the watchword. And then, after some time had passed, I received a call to go to lunch with the movie director Alan Pakula, who I knew slightly. "I have a proposition for you," said Alan. My heart began to race. Maybe he wants to put me in a movie, wants a screenplay, is leaving his wife and wants to tell me about it.

Alan and I sat down in the popular restaurant Pearl's on West 48th Street where the clientele usually included William S. Paley, Marlene Dietrich, Robert Mitchum and Lauren Bacall.* Pakula got right to the point. He pulled out my *Cosmo* article and said, "I am going to make a movie with Jane Fonda called

*It was in Pearl's where Lauren Bacall would see me and ask, "Liz, am I speaking to you?" I'd say, "I hope so, Miss Bacall." She'd then say, "Betty, I'm Betty." "Well, hello then."

It was here also that Robert Mitchum said to me over six martinis, and sincerely, that he did not know anyone in Hollywood who had ever used co-caine. I didn't argue. And it was here I met the great Marlene Dietrich who still resembled the incredible icon she had made of herself. If you are curious about this legend, don't do research. Read her daughter Maria Riva's book: the finest, most detailed biography ever of a great star.

Klute and we need you to work on this film as an advisor and expert on call girls. How they operate, what makes them tick, all the stuff you have in here."

I rapidly reviewed my options. I could go on faking, pretending I had a real call girl (maybe I had) and say yes, I was an expert. Who would know the difference? But I said, "I hate to tell you this, but the article isn't authentic. The girl interviewed may or may not be a call girl. I lost my moral compass when I did that, so I am no expert on call girls." Alan's mouth dropped open. Then he began to laugh. "Wait until I tell Jane. She just loves this piece. She thinks we have it made with you. Well, tell me how and why you did it and what became of the divine Nicky who is now a character invading my dreams. Let's just relax and have some fun."

We did. When Pakula was shockingly killed in a freak accident on the Long Island Expressway not too many moons ago, I wrote some tender words about him in my column. He had gone on to glory after *Klute, All the President's Men, Sophie's Choice*. But I wondered if this exquisite dreamer of cinema dreams had ever recovered from his dream of Nicky, who either did or did not really exist.

DURING THE LBJ YEARS, Helen decided she wanted an in-depth piece about the two girls in the White House—Lynda Bird and Luci Baines Johnson. I cheerfully rang my lifelong schoolmate, Horace Busby, aide to the president, sure I would get everything I needed. It seems to me I am always meeting or knowing people at the top, people who are *so* important, they are virtually useless to me as sources and subjects.

Horace had started kindergarten with me at E.M. Daggett in Fort Worth. We had gone on together through grade school, high school and the U of T. Horace whispered into the phone, "Don't call me here again, I'll call you." When he did he said he couldn't help me, as LBJ would have his scalp. But, he added, he wanted to see me and soon asked me to dine with him in New York.

I was in my cute boots and miniskirted phase and I was looking forward to dinner with a presidential aide at someplace like "21." Horace phoned again. "We have to eat in the hotel!" Disappointed, I still tarted myself up and kept the date. After all, dinner in the St. Regis wasn't bad. But when I arrived he ordered me up to his room. "I can't leave the room. I am on stakeout on the president's orders. But damn, why didn't you get here sooner. I was just on the phone to *him*. If only he'd called to find me with a girl in my room!"

As we ordered room service and talked about old times, Horace told me a lot of gossip about the Johnsons and the Kennedys before them. It seems the job of LBJ aides was to keep a record of all the rumors and scandal that had accompanied Jack Kennedy on the campaign trail. "We followed him. We would find maids in hotels and motels who claimed Jack just stepped up behind them as they were making the bed and then—well, you know."

I asked, "Why did you need this kind of information?"

Horace said, "Oh, well, we just had it, you know. We had to have it in case we ever needed it." I felt disillusioned. Then I asked again why he was in the St. Regis.

He said, "There are others like me all around the world. We are each in different places known to the Vietnamese, hoping that Ho Chi Minh will give us a peace feeler to end the war."

I gasped. "But Horace, isn't this top secret? Why would you tell this to me?"

He smiled. "Who would believe you?"

Who indeed.

THE YEAR BEFORE I LEFT *Cosmo*, Sonny and Cher and their press agents invited me to join a three-day concert swing around the Eastern seaboard. These pop cult stars were hotter than hot. Their TV show, where Cher put Sonny down, was a massive hit.

So I happily accepted and we were off, never knowing

what city we were in, but living on the jet, in hotels and backstage where I took copious notes. Chastity was on the trip, a little blonde charmer, and sometimes I baby-sat with her backstage. Cher didn't have much to say; she seemed indifferent, as if on autopilot. She was nice but reserved. She had a beautiful body, which I observed closely to see if she had scars from breast surgery. But I never saw any. On the other hand, Sonny was a whirling dervish, gyrating, talking, advising, giving orders and running everything. He was the control freak supreme. The contrast between these two people was startling.

At the end of the tour, it was a relief to say good-bye to Sonny and Cher. I came home and studied my notes, which were all about him. But what could I write about a bland and almost self-effacing Cher? Finally, I told Helen that I couldn't write the article. "These two people won't still be together by the time we get on the newsstands. They are going to divorce. She hates him. She won't go on." Helen asked if Cher had indicated or said this. "No," I had to admit. But we backed off and advised the PR firm we wouldn't be doing the story. We tried to reimburse them for my expenses and apologized for taking the stars' time. They were furious!

Three months later, Sonny and Cher had separated and they would divorce. Cher made remarks about feeling like a freed slave. My intuition had paid off. And Cher became a much more cheerful person after that. Like the phoenix, she is still always rising. In 1999, the fifty-three-year-old Cher put out a hit record called "Believe," the biggest success of her career.

SHRUNK BY

MILDRED

DURING THE MAKING OF THE film *Play It As It Lays* in 1971, people on the set were always talking about Mildred Newman and her husband, Bernie Berkowitz, two New York psychologists who had helped many of the famous to improve their lives. Joel Schumacher, doing the costumes for movie producer Dominick Dunne, was soon going to Mildred. Many other people I knew talked openly about their group sessions down in Greenwich Village. Rex Reed was especially positive about all that had come his way from Mildred.

Mildred and Bernie then published a book called *How to Be Your Own Best Friend* and it became a bestseller. Mildred was by now the mother hen to a large group who all seemed to thrive under her tutelage and treatment. So, of course, I began to want to be in that number. I only knew Mildred socially at first. I didn't go to her until I found myself on the rebound from an unhappy love affair. Then I needed relief.

Mildred had been a disciple of Theodore Reik and her methods defied ordinary psychoanalytical strictures. I don't know exactly how she did it, but eventually she imbued me with a confidence I'd never had before. "Let's examine what you describe as your envy and jealousy of your peers. And why you don't feel you have the right to be as successful as everybody else." And pretty soon I was feeling better. So I have always said that maybe it's just the process itself, or maybe Mildred keeps fairy dust she sprinkles on you, or maybe her unorthodox family type TLC is in a class by itself.

It became the fad, as day follows night, for people to deride the Newman-Berkowitz technique, to make fun of their popular success, to say they betrayed all the rigid rituals of psychoanalysis.

Pish! Tosh! or Oh, Fap! as the comic strip character Major Hoople used to say. What Mildred does, works. It worked for me. Soon I found I didn't care about my broken heart anymore. And soon I found I was getting out of my own way when it came to work, deadlines, writer's block and my (sob! gasp!) fabulous career.

Nora Ephron hurt Mildred's feelings when she included a character based on Mildred in her true-to-life novel *Heartburn*. I had enjoyed *Heartburn* and I tried to talk Mildred into just accepting this fictional depiction as part of her growing and ongoing legend, but she wasn't listening to me. (So much for Liz as psychologist!)

So having lived through Mildred's unhappiness over the Ephron book, I know she probably won't like it when I write about her here. All I can say about the Mildred Newman treatment of my own neurotic personality is that I love this woman—and, hey, it worked for me!

NOT SO INCIDENTALLY, I HAD played a role in Nora's novel because I had played a role in her actual bust-up with the Watergate journalist Carl Bernstein. We had been friends for years before Nora and Carl married in a real blaze of glory. This glamorous romantic duo had often been guests with my beloved Lee Bailey and me in Bridgehampton. Although at the time I noted that Carl sometimes had his eyes on more than just Nora, I knew they were in love and I reveled in their romance. Once during a summer's dinner while Lee was in the kitchen and I was pouring drinks, I chastised Carl for coming on to another guest, the vivacious Lucie Arnaz. I said, "Carl! Nora is right across the room." Well, Don Juan Bernstein just laughed and kept on keeping on.

I also had occasion to find Carl rather happy-go-lucky and careless at other times. One night a group of us left a Plaza Hotel gala and feeling no pain, we decided to take a horse-drawn carriage through Central Park. (This was unusual in that real New Yorkers seldom stoop to such tourist behavior.) I was jammed into the backseat with Nora and Marie Brenner. The driver went inside the lobby for change. And Carl decided he would get into the driver's seat. He picked up the whip and flicked the horse. Nora was saying, "Carl—don't do this!" But the horse panicked and backed up. The carriage wheel caught on the curb and we turned over on our side, though the horse remained standing. This was not funny for Marie, who was on the bottom. Miraculously, her mink coat padded her from serious injury.

Nora was furious with Carl and I can't remember how the evening ended as we all scrambled out of the carriage in a state of embarrassment. We were supposed to be grown-ups. I remember I was cautioned not to write about it for fear that Carl might have a lawsuit. (I added it to my "Did you ever" list of unusual happenings: Did you ever turn over in a horse-drawn hansom cab?)

But I thought Nora and Carl had a very happy marriage. He was famous—with Bob Woodward—from exposing Watergate and bringing down Richard Nixon. Carl and Nora were then living in Washington, and had two little boys, one recently arrived.

The stories about Carl's involvement with a married woman—Margaret Jay, the wife of the British ambassador—were epidemic but I discounted them. I couldn't bear the thought. I was now writing a column for the New York *Daily News*. One day Nora rang me up and said in her characteristic determined kind of way: "Liz, I have a story for you. Carl and I are going to divorce! Please write it." I gasped—not Carl and

Nora, not when they'd just had a baby! But I didn't ask too many questions, forgetting my reportorial duties, caught up in empathy. I did write on December 19, 1979: "The four-year marriage of writer Nora Ephron and reporter Carl Bernstein...is over. But definitely—finis, the end and out...Writing this scoop makes me feel sick."

LATE THAT AFTERNOON CARL CALLED me. He said, "I understand you have something coming in tomorrow's column about me and Nora. I want you to take it out. It isn't true."

I said, "Carl, Nora gave me the story."

He insisted, "It isn't true. We're not divorcing." He got very angry when I refused. (What, I wondered, had *he* responded to the Watergate gang in the White House when he began ruining their lives with his truth and they were threatening him and telling him he had it all wrong??)

My item ran and caused a sensation. The couple did divorce. Nora then wrote a book, because as her screenwriter mother had told her, "Everything is copy!" Carl objected strenuously. What's more, he went down through the ages, objecting not only to the book, but also to me for having "broken us up."

One night at a party I ran into Carl and he forced me up against a wall, started weeping and told me I had ruined his life. "And I always loved you before that," said the man who had won a Pulitzer for *The Washington Post* and brought down a president.

Through the years, Carl began to use me as a kind of lightning rod for his frequent lectures on the perils of gossip journalism. I became the Great Satan of infotainment for him. When *Prime Time Live* did a story on me for ABC, Carl was interviewed and opined that I made more money than Pulitzer prize-winning journalists. He said this was a disgrace. I agreed with him, but I kept taking the money.

Carl had once given me one of the best lines ever about why people become journalists. He said some people just have the "truth-saying instinct" and it leads them on. I have used that quote of his in many a speech and written piece. And I didn't give up on Carl even though he has given up on me. I still think he was a great reporter, a good writer and I like him very much. I always give him credit for his "truth-saying" line, for he is one of the great "truth-saying" reporters of our time, even though he didn't seem to want me to be one.

THE SPORTING

LIFE

I WAS BEGINNING TO FEEL like a real New Yorker in the sixties, writing piece after piece for *Cosmopolitan*, taking free trips to glamorous places, going to movies any time I wanted and spending summers with my friend Lee Bailey, the designer and cookbook king, on Long Island. The Hamptons were still beautifully bucolic. The Long Island Expressway had just been built.

I have mentioned Diane Judge before as part of my fifties theater crowd. She and I were sharing a terrific apartment at 38 East 38th Street. She had become a very good freelance writer. In this apartment, we "writers" gave bang-up "fried meat and whiskey" parties or we'd serve Diane's Jailhouse Chili. Henri Soule of Le Pavillon kept sending me cases of his favorite wine, Château Petrus. We served this incomparable vintage with chicken-fried steak. But Diane was usually off in Spain having a romance with someone who owned his own winery, or dabbling with a Polish prince, or touring Morocco, or covering the Cannes Film Festival. "Better living through publicity," Diane called it, and she had the secret down pat.

I took trips, too, but mine were always overhung with obligation. I was seldom carefree and I would rush back to New York as if the city might disappear without me. On the other hand, Diane would turn a short magazine assignment into a six-week adventure running from Pamplona to Barcelona with Trevor Howard. Or she'd be golfing in Biarritz with Howard Hawks. She might be watching a snake charmer in Casablanca one afternoon and suddenly realize that she had been away from the States for three months. She never let business interfere with her pleasure, which I guess is a great philosophy if you grew up in Paterson, New Jersey, in a house with no indoor plumbing. I admired the good-looking redhead for how she had erased her Jersey accent, pulled herself up by her bootstraps, and was not only well-read, but an opera buff. She wrote a mean magazine piece and had also worked her way into being a theatrical press agent. Eventually, she became the PR director of the Hotel Delmonico on Park Avenue. She had presided over the Beatles' second visit to New York after the Plaza had refused to take them in a second time. She knew how to enjoy herself.

When Diane wasn't in Europe, she was out dancing her shoes off at night, experimenting with the beginnings of the sexual revolution—sex, drugs and rock 'n' roll were most definitely on the menu. I was stuffy. I usually had a deadline or I was worrying about paying my income tax. So for most of the fourteen years Diane and I shared the apartment, I usually had it to myself. It had a nice fireplace and a beautiful vaulted ceiling in the living room with great bookshelves. The tiled and stylish kitchen had once been a bathroom. In fact, the entire apartment had been the bedroom of Millicent Rogers, the U.S. Steel and Standard Oil heiress, when she was a child.

So life was going along, I was a *Cosmo* girl and the restaurateur Romeo Salta had taken a shine to me. I was lunching in his café when a quirky-looking craggy-faced Irishman came over to say hello. He was George Trescher and I was aware that he was friendly with my agent. George said politely that he was the PR director of *Sports Illustrated* and how much he admired my writing. Would I be interested in going to work for Time, Inc., on *Sports Illustrated*? "You could write a few articles a year for us under contract."

I'm afraid I said right up front that I didn't read *Sports Illustrated* and didn't know beans about sports and didn't understand people who doted on it. "Isn't that a small-minded approach?" asked George. "Shouldn't the sports world figure in a well-rounded, civilized approach to music, art, drama, literature, whatever?"

I saw his point, and also that I had hurt his feelings. "I'd be a washout for you; I'm too ignorant about the sports world," I said apologetically. George said they were actually looking for a kind of junior grade Charlotte Curtis to cover the "soft" and social and human side of sports. Charlotte was a big *New York Times* byline, someone I truly admired.

The upshot of this? After getting the assurance from Helen Gurley Brown that I could be a contract writer for *S.I.* and still keep my *Cosmo* job, I went to see George's boss, the legendary Andre Laguerre.

"The War" wasn't Mr. Laguerre's name for nothing. This rotund Frenchman was a holy terror at Time, Inc. He never joined the rigid in-house old-boy network nor obeyed the unwritten rules of the Henry Luce Empire. He was a law unto himself. And though *Sports Illustrated* had been eleven years in the red, Laguerre was putting the controversial project into the black. He was an old-style gent whose chief interests were fine horseflesh, good food and plenty of drink. And he was definitely a man's man. Uncomfortable with women, he had found the perfect hiding place. *Sports Illustrated* had only a few females working for the magazine then—fashion editor Jule Campbell, the one-day-to-be-recognized editor Pat Ryan, a few researchers and suddenly...me.

At first I wasn't afraid of Laguerre. I had never experienced his sting. And he bent over backwards to treat me well. Although everyone else on the premises of the Time/Life building on Sixth Avenue seemed to be obsessed with sex, Laguerre behaved as if it didn't exist and if it did, he didn't want to know about it.

I was handed to an editor named Fred Smith, who was energetic, smart and clever. Mr. Smith and I were to travel together so extensively, after my hiring, that eventually people we met the world over assumed we were husband and wife. Once when we were trapped over JFK Airport by a blackout, we had to fly to Toronto to land. The fact that a model named Suzy Smith was traveling with us on a photo shoot caused no end of grief. The Toronto Hotel, overcrowded, insisted on putting "the Smith family" into one room, and refused to believe we were three separate entities.

It became my distinction to write the first "nudity" story in *S.I.* for the first swimsuit issue. And so I went down in history, if not quite elsewhere. Fred Smith and Jule Campbell told me to do something about the new nude *zeitgeist* on America's beaches. I was not aware that there was such a thing, indeed, I don't believe there was. But it sounded good, new, fresh and shocking.

And I had been to the South of France only recently. There, I'd seen woman after woman sunbathing and swimming topless. It had shocked me, but I hadn't let on. Now, I had the basis for my article, which would accompany the historic moment when Jule produced California model Sue Peterson* in a revealing nude-colored body stocking under a white fishnet jumpsuit. My story added fuel to the fire of the photographs. It was titled "The Nudity Cult" and included references to Rudi Gernreich's new topless bathing suit and my own idiotic prediction that soon U.S. women would be topless on the beaches.

I pretended to *S.I.* that I had a great knowledge of Gernreich as a fashion pioneer, because after all, I knew his fabulous model Peggy Moffit. She often visited some of my neighbors on 38th Street. They were also in the fashion biz, and were so chic that their entire apartment above me was painted black. Diane Judge and I often "listened in" to their interesting more-than-

The beautiful Miss Peterson had good luck from her swimsuit cover. She married S.I. writer Jack Olsen, who went on to become a true crime specialist.

two-to-a-bed evenings. (We had landlord troubles over our own rowdy parties. One night, the heiress Gloria Vanderbilt was descending our stairs, laughing, and was confronted by the building's owner. "Why don't you go home, you slut!" he yowled at one of America's most famous poor little rich girls. Gloria said, "Oh, you are a hoot!")

It didn't matter that my prediction of Americans getting naked and throwing chili on U.S. beaches never came true. My article was just one drop of gasoline on the fire of subscribers who cancelled *S.I.* in outrage because their fourteen-year-old son had seen the cover. But there were hundreds of others who took up the magazine because of the sensation. As Michael MacCambridge writes in his *S.I.* history, *The Franchise*: "Suddenly a trifle had become a tradition." (I must add that when *S.I.* held a celebration to mark the 25th anniversary of its inventing the swimsuit issue, they forgot even to invite me to the party. But then there was something so *S.I.* about that omission, even in 1989. After all, I was still just a woman.)

Under the firm hand of Fred Smith, who was always sure I was about to disgrace him and Time, Inc., and with the encouragement of my now good friend George Trescher, I began to write a number of articles a year for *S.I.* I had one of those fabled Time, Inc., expense accounts that journalists used to crow about. Always flying first class, staying at the best hotels, I enjoyed the largess, but never became adept at the art of putting a new portable typewriter on my expense account because I had gotten drunk and thrown my old one out the window. No, that practice was for the big boys.

I was given an office that I seldom used. When I came to *S.I.* I just wanted to sit on the floor in Jule Campbell's office and hear everything that was going on. Or go and dish with Trescher, who I discovered was putting *S.I.* on the map in a manner no promotion director had done before. If we printed the slightest thing of national interest—on the environment, say—handsomely bound copies landed on the desk of every member of Congress. George gave us class and was indefatigable.

Once someone complained about him to Time's headman—the elegant and revered Andrew Heiskell. Mr. H. tapped his finger on the bridge of his nose, sighed and said in a dispassionate tone, "Well, I wish I had one hundred more just like him!"

S.I. was a total world unto itself. It was a religion there to be eccentric, outrageous, irreverent. Great sportswriters were on board—my Fort Worth buddies Bud Shrake and Dan Jenkins, Tex Maule, Jack Olsen, Roger Angel, Frank Deford and Roy Blount. Some of them were hard-drinking, hard-driving, sports-soaked professional fanatics, competing for Laguerre's attention and approval. It was a world of testosterone at the top of the Time/Life building.

And the greatest thing about all of this? It happened just before Women's Liberation. It was a last gasp world of male superiority, masculine ego and grown-up adolescence run rampant. So what did it mean to the few females on the premises? All I can say is, we had a wonderful time!

We were so few that we were like rare Dresden china objects. Doors were opened for us. Bags were carried. And I grew so used to being "taken care of" by Fred Smith, or some other sportswriter who had been sent along to cover the meat of the story while I gathered the metaphorical endive for the salad, that I quite forgot for five whole years how to do anything for myself. I never drew or carried the cash we needed. I seldom used a credit card. I never had to make my own reservations. I never handled my passport. Fred kept it with his.

I covered the absurdity of mule races in posh Grosse Pointe; wrote of how folks entertained in Louisville for the Kentucky Derby ("Oh, honey," drawled Mrs. Pruitt, "you just put a ham at one end of the table, a turkey at the other, and a lot of cheese and beaten biscuits in the middle."); described the festivities surrounding the opening of a new Robert Trent Jones golf course in Sotogrande, Spain (where they had marble dust in the sand traps and no actors were allowed to join or play). I wrote of the rigors of the Maryland Hunt Cup Steeplechase and its social strictures; looked at Juárez on the eve of the Olympics; spoke of the rites and rituals of the California young at the Riverside stock car races; covered Portuguese bloodless bullfighting; inspected the Houston Astrodome before it opened; basked in the Arizona desert at Carefree; observed sailing races from a muddy Block Island; watched dog grooming at Westminster; discussed the use of plastics in sports equipment (Diane still has the plastic see-through bowling balls, whose main defect was that if left in the sunshine they sparked fires). Once I interviewed a painter who only did horses. When I asked how much he would charge to add a chicken to his canvas, he laughed and said, "Oh, about twenty-five dollars."

I also went on some "hardship" assignments. One of these was sailing on a three-masted schooner through the Exuma Islands, where I learned to scuba dive and bone fish and was forever warned: "Don't swim in dark water or after sundown." It was on this trip that Grace Kelly's favorite photographer, Howell Conant, took pictures of our scantily clad phalanx of models with a new camera that was half-above, half-under the water.

Another time in the Bahamas, I reported on the technical underwater filming for the James Bond movie *Thunderball*. I was ushered into a dressing room where the incredibly sexy, young Sean Connery was being given a massage. I don't remember anything about what I asked or he answered. But I still hear the drone of his Scots burr and then he sat up, the tiny towel slipping off his loins. He was as unselfconscious as a beautiful animal and he bid me good-bye, flexing his "Scotland Forever" tattoos.*

It was on this trip that we were taken from our mother

---

*Years later writing my gossip column, I received an irate personal phone call from Mr. Connery. He was making a film with a young woman who some people felt had slept her way to the top. Connery did not like the item and told me in no uncertain terms, "I would like to stick your column up your ass."

I replied, "This is the best offer I've had all day." He hung up on me. I never got to remind him that I had once interviewed him in his altogether. I always hope I won't run into Connery anywhere. He's such a he-man and he did tell Barbara Walters that he didn't see anything wrong with hitting a woman.

boat and put in a dinghy to go to a small island sticking up in the middle of the Caribbean. "Now," said our movie dive-master, "we all fall backwards out of the dinghy and swim down to a hole. It's about five feet on the side here and we swim through it, holding our breath. We'll come up inside the island into a cave with air."

I protested. Not even for the article could I do that. I didn't swim well enough. "You don't have to," said the master. "We'll drag you."

I said, "No, I'm too scared."

"Okay," said the tough guy. "We'll swim in and see the *Thunderball* location and you will be left here in the dinghy. But there are big sharks around. Big enough to bite this dinghy in two when they see a pretty little thing sitting in it—alone."

I quickly changed my mind, held my breath, fell over the side and was whisked down to the "entrance." Here, these wise guys had affixed a four-foot dead shark stuck on a spear with its wicked jaw wide open at the hole we were to swim through. I didn't faint. It is difficult to faint underwater. But the sporting life wasn't for sissies and I refused to give the guys the pleasure of seeing me react.

We came up inside the cave into a paradise of light. This place was later in the movie in a scene where 007 is doing his damnedest. I felt thrilled to have been there, too. Me and Sean Connery.

THERE WAS LOTS OF ROMANCE in and out of the offices at *S.I.* I gloried in my friendship with the diminutive but handsome writer Bob Ottum. He'd sit in my hotel rooms and polish what I had written until the editors thought I was a lot better than I really was. Collaborating was almost a must on some of these trips.

And it was wonderful to be under a Spanish moon above the beaches at Marbella with a sexy European genius like Ernst

Haas. He was taking our photos and would soon film the creation scene for John Huston's *The Bible*. And nothing and nobody was ever as much fun as those naughty, dirty-minded, foul-talking good old boys from Fort Worth, Dan Jenkins and Bud Shrake. They and the women in their lives have been my friends ever since.

S.I. had a fabulous editor in Ray Cave, who was Laguerre's protégé and he'd soothe me when the boss barked at me after lunch. (Mr. Laguerre was quite different from his courtly morning self after imbibing a number of martinis at noon.) Laguerre would sometimes call a clutch of us into his office to brainstorm. I seldom had an idea, for I knew zilch about sports and even adjacent activities had to be suggested to me. I would depend on Fred or Jule for fuel. My own suggestions came out of my Texas past. I'd say we could cover the Rattlesnake Roundup in Sweetwater or go to the Cowboy Hall of Fame in Oklahoma. Laguerre, who loved thoroughbred horses and polo and the sport of kings, just like my father, would look up at me in pity. "Remember, at S.I. rodeo is *NOT* a sport; it's an obscenity." Sometimes I'd be so ineffectual and quiet in these meetings that Laguerre would call for me to stay "after school." Then, he'd ask me lots of gentle questions like: Was I happy there? Had anyone been mean to me or bothered me? Was I doing what I liked? I might grump that my pieces were expendable and always first to be shelved for a hot basketball game. He'd nod and say, "You'll get your space. You'll get your space."

In time, Laguerre gave up on Time, Inc.'s policies and he departed to edit a monthly about fine horseflesh called *Classic*. S.I. has remained a profit moneymaker for Time, Inc., but once Laguerre butted heads with management and departed in 1975, I felt the magazine's élan left with him. He had made sports sophisticated, intellectual, colorful and subtle. After Laguerre left, however, I sighed with relief and felt I never had to make myself read *Sports Illustrated* again.

But I made an unforgettable friend at S.I. in the person of

executive editor Richard Johnston. He, of course, was the odd man out of step. He was a snappy dresser, tall, mustachioed and rather funereal looking—something like a riverboat gambler. Inside, he was all fun, games and girls, girls, girls. He never bored me with sports talk, because having come from *Life* magazine, he had other interests. He made me his pet.

When we went to the divinely overblown Forum of the Twelve Caesars for lunch, his talk was incredibly single-minded. He talked incessantly about sex and he thought, mistakenly, that because I also worked for *Cosmopolitan*, I would know all the answers. What do women want, he asked, I suppose not knowing that Freud had already asked the question. We kept each other company through many lunches and cocktails. He was definitely one of the last of his breed.

Historian MacCambridge tells a good one on Dick. His dearth of sports info, his civilized look as "an erudite gangster," came into play making him into an offbeat *S.I.* legend. Interviewing the youthful horse specialist Whitney Tower, who had worked in Cincinnati, Johnston was said to have leaned back, put his feet up on his desk and said, "Ah, Cincinnati. Are all the good whorehouses still in Kentucky?"

One day we were discussing why there were no women sportswriters. Dick said, "Well, there is one. But when she came to interview, she was so aggressive, such a know-it-all that I took her to lunch to soften her up. I said I was having an artichoke. She asked, 'What's an artichoke?' I said, 'Never mind, I'll order one for you.' When it came, I was about to explain how one eats an artichoke. She launched into some crap about boxing. So I never told her how to go about her new luncheon item. She was too pigheaded to ask. She ate the whole thing, thorn ends, leaves and all the fur. I got a big kick out of not hiring her. She was nothing like you—nothing like you."

"Well," I said, rather appalled—remembering how I hadn't known myself how to eat an artichoke until recently— "I'm not a sportswriter. I'm just a workhorse feature writer."

"You're a lady," said Johnston and then he promptly told

me all about a new operation against impotence, where a man could pump up his own penis.

I was ready for Women's Liberation when it finally arrived for I had worked at *Sports "Illuminated"* (as my then housekeeper, Alice West, always called it) and I'd had the best of all possible changing worlds.

"EAT YOUR

HEART OUT!"

I TRIED TO IGNORE WOMEN'S Liberation when it started really happening in the seventies. I adored Gloria Steinem, but I just didn't get what she was driving at. I'd worked my ass off in a man's world and I thought success for women was a normal uphill, terrifying, selective process—you had to simply win against all odds.

I met Gloria early on in my career when she was a lowly editor for a humor magazine called *Help*. She was then dating my U of T pal Bob Benton. Gloria wrote balloon captions to go over famous photos. This process was called by the Italians *fumetti*. She'd have John Gilbert kissing Greta Garbo from upside down and Garbo would be saying, "Can't you do anything right?"

A few years later, I was working pro bono on a fashion charity and up to me came a gorgeous, glamorous woman dressed like a butterfly. Gloria Steinem batted her eyes and said, "Liz, you don't recognize me!" My dear Gloria was then dating brilliant guys like Mike Nichols and Herb Sargent, the head writer for *Saturday Night Live*. She was carving out a career as a freelancer and also rising in the social firmament. So when she suddenly forsook all that, plus a big commercial career as a writer, and became the leader of millions of downtrodden women, it took a bit of adjusting. I had read Betty Freidan's *The Feminine Mystique* in 1963. It hadn't made much impression on me.

But ten years later when Gloria said to me critically, "Liz, you want to be the only Jew in the club!" I immediately saw her point. I dropped most of my objections to the liberation of my fellow females and tried to get on the bandwagon. I tried hard to open my mind to "sisterhood." Never having had any sisters, having assumed that women were just competitive "inferior" creatures, having shown them my heels during my entire career, I had a lot to learn. Gloria was patient.

She then invited me to attend a meeting to be held in upstate New York in a house owned by the *Village Voice* writer Jill Johnston. (Jill was a radical feminist-lesbian advocate. She would later make herself infamous by "debating" Norman Mailer at Carnegie Hall, rolling around on the stage with another woman as part of the "debate.")

I made my friend, the press agent extraordinary Patricia Newcomb, go along with me and we arrived at Jill's to find the property awash in women. Some were well-known; a few were already famous as feminists. Gloria certainly was well-known; Kate Millet had written a book called *Sexual Politics*; Jill represented the underground press; there was the great novelist-philosopher Susan Sontag; activists Brenda Feigen, Letty Cottin Pogrebin, Robin Wagner, etc. We were herded inside for a consciousness-raising session where each of us was invited to speak our mind. I plunged right in and numbers of my "sisters" were delighted to correct, advise, and show me how stupid I was. At one point I was defended by the impressive Miss Sontag, who interrupted, "Leave her alone" and then to me, "You have a right to your feelings."

Jill had started things off by complaining that Sontag had her teenage son there and his male presence was disrupting the atmosphere. Susan said her son was flattered to be so perceived, but Jill was insistent and finally Susan made the boy go off walking in the woods so the *zeitgeist* wouldn't be upset. As it was, I felt the atmosphere had become very sexually charged— something like I imagine a women's prison might be.

Now we "took a break." The women fell into separate groups and there was much networking. I tried to stay close to Gloria, thinking she would protect me. She had become an extremely heroic person to me. When we came back for more, Kate Millet was sitting cross-legged in the middle of the floor. She was weeping copiously. She had discovered during the break that we were *not* going to all spend the night here together in Jill's house. She cried, "What was the point of meeting at all only to run off and leave each other?" I blanched. Like Monty Woolley in *The Man Who Came to Dinner*, I would rather have jumped naked into a barrel of rattlesnakes than spend the night where we were.

Gloria calmed everyone down and we went on. Many spoke. Many argued. Then the very tall Jill Johnston began to pace. She was wearing big clumpy boots, which made her resemble the Frankenstein monster. She surged back and forth excoriating Gloria for being beautiful, glamorous and misleading the movement, for making it hers. At one point she said, "You know, Gloria, that you would be sleeping with women if only you'd let yourself!"

At this, Steinem drew herself up and snapped, "You're the only one who thinks so, Jill—the only one who hopes so. Just…just…just eat your heart out!"

I broke into wild applause and a few others joined me. But the dam had burst between the feminists and lesbian feminists. The meeting began to break up and Pat and I fled back to Manhattan, unsure what we thought. We'd had a glimpse of the future and it required some mental adjustment.

Of course, all of this makes me sound antediluvian and I admit it. I worked hard to get in step and one night when I gave a very pissy dinner party for my small circle of VIP friends, I tried not to flinch when Gloria brought along a famous fat black lesbian as her "date." David Brown, who adores beautiful, glamorous thin females, made it his job to spend the evening talking

My mother, Sarah Elizabeth McCall, in 1911, wearing her Mississippi State College uniform. She was determined to get out of Mississippi.

a Memoir

My father, Sloan Smith, and mother on their wedding day, 1914, Ennis, Texas. World War I was raging in Europe but they were in love.

My brother, James McCall, at age 5, holding me, little Mary Elizabeth Smith (aka MES), age 3 months, Fort Worth, Texas, 1923.

Daddy and MES, still with no hair. He already had me around his horses.

*I*n the Rio Grande Valley. Daddy, James and baby MES on a vintage fender.

$\mathcal{M}$y beautiful
nanny, Dott Burns,
James, MES and
Mother. Soon after
this, Dott would take
me to the movies.

$\mathcal{G}$randma Sally
Ball McCall with
James and me at 1919
Hemphill Street in
Fort Worth.
She said we were
descended from
George Washington's
mother, Mary Ball.
What did we care?

$\mathcal{D}$addy by his favorite magnolia tree with his "best boy" in her authentic cowboy clothes.

$\mathcal{M}$y lifelong idol, the movie star Tom Mix. This photo hangs in my apartment.

That's me on the left, dressed as my Uncle Willie, the filling station owner, in rubber boots, leather bow tie and coveralls. My brother James, sitting in the middle, looks on with neighbors.

Oh, those wool bathing suits in August! James and MES had been joined by baby brother Robert Jerome (Bobby) in 1927.

*M*ES in a Daddy-inspired English riding costume. I preferred the Western style.

*C*ousin Mary Emma Whaley takes gawky me to see the Alamo. She lived with us off and on through numerous boyfriends and husbands.

*I*n the Air Corps: Greene Simpson, John Hart, cousin Bryson Sherrill, my brother James McCall, Rector Genarlsky. Only James and Bryson came back from World War II.

*M*y lifelong friend, the irrepressible Louise Lewis. We were born three months apart. Her family had a profound effect on me. She inadvertently introduced me to my first scandal.

*"B*ig Mama," Martha Tipton Smith, my narrow-minded paternal grandma, with the high school graduate she always disapproved of. 1811 Jennings Street, 1940.

$\mathcal{M}$ES with hair "horns." (It wouldn't be the first time.) Definitely a bad hair day at Paschal High School, Fort Worth, Texas.

$\mathcal{L}$iz-to-be with her beloved cousin Bryson Sherrill, Jr. He was the original "hot pilot."

*L*iz and roomie Nita Mae "Tootie" Boyd at Hardin-Simmons University in Abilene, Texas, 1941.

*D*earest Nita Mae. She cried when she laughed, which was often. The genuine article, she is now in both the Cowboy and Cowgirl Halls of Fame.

*A*t 20, still hoping to be Tom Mix. West Texas.

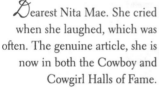

ABOVE LEFT:

The "Cowboy" college tackle from San Angelo, Ed Beeman. I determined to make him mine.

ABOVE RIGHT:

"*Doncha* know there's a war on?" Beeman in flight school, soon after Pearl Harbor.

Ed and Liz, engaged—sort of. I still clung to my bobby socks.

*O*ur wedding in Gonzales, Texas, 1945: Mother Elizabeth, brother Bobby, Grandma Martha, Daddy Sloan, bridesmaid Nancy Foley, Ed, Liz and bridesmaid Jean Wingo.

ARMY AIR BASE
ALAMOGORDO, NEW MEXICO

This is to identify:

MARY E. BEEMAN

Bearer of Restricted Badge

Mary E. Beeman 563
Signature

586
RESTRICTED

Thomas C. Connett

CAPT. A. C. PROVOST MARSHAL

This pass not good after:

*M*ary E. Beeman, war worker, 1945. Not a happy camper.

*O*ur house on Florida Street, Alamogordo, New Mexico, where we were knocked out of bed by the first atom bomb.

*L*iz, Ed and Mrs. Moscowitz, the former Copa show-girl. We shared our house with this glamour girl and her husband.

*T*he gay divorcée at the University of Texas with new Plymouth, gift from Daddy Sloan. He soon took it back.

*M*y father, Augustus Sloan Smith, from whom all blessings flowed— and a few other things, like his temper.

*R*unning for office at the U. of T. My campaign manager said,
"Your name is a natural!"

An editor of *The Texas Ranger*, a columnist for *The Daily Texan*, a big deal on campus.

Daddy, me and Mother— so proud of our handsome war hero, James. Gonzales, Texas, 1947.

"*W*hich way's town?" Posing for the great Cris Alexander soon after arriving in NYC. About 1950.

*K*aye Ballard, a brilliant musical comedy star, fresh from London, and about to change my life. 1952.

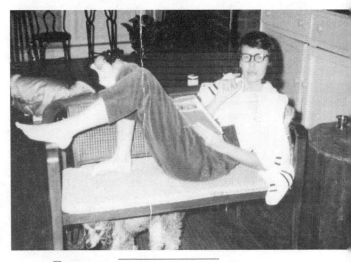

*T*hin and poor, recovering from dental surgery and car accident. Greenwich Village, 1950.

*T*he Smith siblings, Liz and Bobby, usually broke and hungry, but as James wrote us, "You sure are looking good!"

*B*obby, my favorite roommate, trying to make it in the Big City. Cigarettes and whiskey and wild, wild women would do him in.

*F*ifties NYC—
John Keffer and Weldon
Sheffield of Texas with
a girl who thinks she
is Grace Kelly.

*T*he unique actor's
agent/literary agent,
Gloria Safier,
who became my
main mentor.

*C*holly
Knickerbocker's "ghost
writer" Liz with El
Morocco's Jimmy
Mitchell. (Already a
fashion victim.)

My one true secret weapon, Charlotte Curtis of
The New York Times.

"*Marry* Freddie?"
My second
husband, Freddie
Lister. We were
living beyond our
means and beyond
ourselves.

*M*y sometimes apartment mate, Diane Judge, living it up in San Sebastian with actor Trevor Howard. (She was never at home.)

*W*ith Igor "Ghighi" Cassini, the society columnist. I would work for him for five fascinating years. Late Fifties.

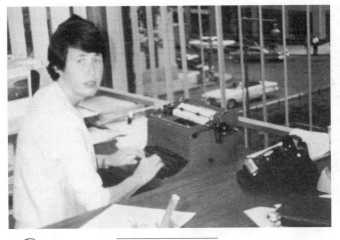

*O*ffice on Park Avenue, somebody else's byline—high cotton! What was not to like about being Cholly Knickerbocker? 1960.

The swinging Pop Op Sixties —Joel Schumacher, the sexual outlaw, with acolytes, me and Vicky (Mrs. Herman) Levin.

I "discovered" him. Later, he "discovered" me. The talented Rex Reed in the Sixties.

Park Avenue hostess Dorothy Strelsin and two nobodies—yours truly and an undernourished Richard Gere.

I never thought to co-star with Ethel Merman, but in 1978 we book-toured together. She was mad for mothers.

I made my own Sarah Elizabeth happy at last by writing *The Mother Book*. Under a pecan tree in Gonzales, Texas.

*V*isiting "Petruchio," Richard Burton, on the *Taming of the Shrew* set in Rome in 1966.

*Y*es, he asked me back to hi motel. With Robert Redford in Lockhart, Texas, 1974.

*M*y fan, the ebullient movie producer Sam Spiegel. He raised hell that my column wasn't up front in the *News*.

*M*y first 33rd-floor high-rise overlooking the Empire State Building. Beginning the Liz Smith column at the New York *Daily News*, 1976.

The man who first put me on TV doing gossip, David Frost, 1978. We were forerunners of the movie *Network*.

The powerful press agent, Patricia Newcomb, Marilyn's last flack. She gave me real access to the stars.

One of the loves of my life, Lee Bailey of Bunkie, Louisiana, gives me a lesson in how to fry chicken. The Hamptons, the Seventies.

The fabled Elaine Stritch, the mad professor Iris Love, the cookbook/ lifestyle king Lee Bailey and me on Sagg Pond, Bridgehampton. Adelaide and Phryne sit guard.

I Love writers!!!

Truman Capote, who didn't always tell the truth.

The mysterious but delightful Renata Adler.

Semi-tough Dan Jenkins from my sporting past.

The mighty Mailers, Norris and Norman.

Anna Wintour, Fran Lebowitz, Harry Evans. They all want me; you can tell.

Admiring the zipless Erica Jong.

Mr. Roman à Clef himself, Dominick Dunne.

The wicked, witty, wonderful Nora Ephron.

Oscar-winner Bob Benton. I should have married him.

James Brady took these knees to La Grenouille during the mini craze.

Midnight in the garden of John Berendt.

I did it for charity, then *Spy* magazine did it to me. The infamous Sitting Bull Toteboard photo.

*A*rchaeologist Iris Love and her pupil "do" the Parthenon. The Acropolis. Greece. The Eighties.

*I*ris, Helen Gurley Brown, Ivana Trump and a nearly naked me in Palm Beach before Donald took Mar-a-Lago away from us.

I watch Malcolm Forbes gaze at Elizabeth Taylor. Were they "an item"?

Working Girl

In the clutter of the 26th-floor office with helpers Denis Ferrara and Saint Clair Pugh.

Robert Mitchum makes yet another woman hysterical on WNBC's "Live at Five."

My boss, Rupert Murdoch, and I pretend we're intellectuals at a literacy benefit in 1999.

Anchorman Jack Cafferty and I try to teach Barbara Walters a thing or two about TV.

With Mike Wallace hosting Skitch Henderson's 80th birthday at Carnegie Hall. Dahlings, we looked marvelous! Our combined ages were 150.

Showing off and showing up for a Princess Yasmin Khan Alzheimer's benefit.

*V*incent Roppatte, the natural blonde-maker, romances his number one client, Diane Sawyer. And to think, I made this happen.

*B*eing led by the world's best ballroom dancer, Oscar de la Renta. Le Cirque 1992.

*M*y dream! Leading Oscar! (Barbara Walters' birthday party.) Sixty men looked on.

*J*oel Schumacher and Liz swing on a star, Julia Roberts, at the 150 Wooster Street Cafe.

A Chorus Line anniversary in Shubert Alley. Saint Clair Pugh watches my dance.

A Few of My Favorites

Flanked by one woman convicted of murder, Jean Harris, and another who covers murders for ABC, correspondent Cynthia McFadden.

Raquel Welch, Kathleen Turner, Helen Brown, me, Barbara Walters. Waiting for borscht at The Russian Tea Room.

NYC know-it-all Suzanne Goodson, excellent writer Marie Brenner and their ardent fan.

My fairy godparents Pete Peterson and Joan Ganz Cooney, proving you can't be too thin or too rich.

My own personal socialite, the closet intellectual and hostess Louise Grunwald.

My all-world champion favorite guy, the genius director Mike Nichols. The year 2000.

with this woman, who turned out to be brilliant even if not beautiful or glamorous or thin. So, the evening turned into a smash hit and sent everyone out talking about Women's Liberation.

I began to participate whenever Gloria asked me. I went to events with Flo Kennedy and Bella Abzug and others who were leading the charge. I gave my money; I tried to support *Ms.* magazine to the max. (On one occasion much later I pushed Gloria's then beau, Mort Zuckerman, into a corner and made him promise to bail the dying publication out. And to his undying credit, he did.) And although only months after the meeting in the woods, I was offered the moon to write about it satirically, I realized that I shouldn't. Such a magazine article and its impact might strike at the roots of a fragile plant that was trying to become the tree of women's liberty. I realized that women did need liberation from the mores of the past, even if they didn't always need some of the foolishness of the movement as it evolved.

When people say to me cynically that nothing good ever happens, nothing in the system ever changes, nothing is ever accomplished by radical revolution, I disagree. Women's Liberation happened—in spite of people like me. It happened to all of us. It isn't perfect yet, but the situation is a far cry from what went before. Gloria and her sisters—and yes, her lesbian sisters—made a big difference in the way women are now perceived and treated. Laws have been made to protect women and some of the world has shifted its perception of what is fair between the sexes.

The revolutionary writer Susan Brownmiller recently published a feminist work titled *In Our Time*. She said to me: "We had a feminist movement that was filled with bitter ideological antagonisms, crazy intrigues, and jealous backbiting and yet it managed to transform the world."

ELIZABETH

THE QUEEN

LIKE EVERYONE ELSE IN THE world, I read about the affair Elizabeth Taylor was having with her costar Richard Burton on the set of the infamous *Cleopatra* in Rome back in 1962. I read the memos sent by the 20th Century-Fox executives where they advised each other, "Liz and Dick are fucking each other's brains out." Eddie Fisher was summarily discarded and so was Burton's long-suffering wife, Sybil. Then, Elizabeth and Richard (as they preferred to be called) got married in Canada about a year later.

I was galloping along as *Cosmo*'s entertainment editor but I didn't have a clue I'd ever get to these two superstars. By now, they absolutely *hated* the press, which had put them pretty much through the wringer. And wherever they went, they were still mobbed by crowds of the curious, and by fevered paparazzi.

Enter the Burtons' well-loved, low-key press agent, John Springer, a legend in his own time. He said he had talked them into seeing me—well, more or less. He wasn't sure, but he thought if I went to Paris, they'd talk to me. There was another famous PR old-timer hovering over their production of *The Sandpiper*, and Morgan Hudgins would be the go-between. Mor-

gan, who had flacked for difficult "really big" stars like Clark
Gable and Grace Kelly in the past, was clued in to expect me.

I flew to Paris with some trepidation. I had never met either of the tempestuous "most famous movie stars in the world"
and the whole idea was nerve-wracking. Mr. Hudgins, a genial
old sweetheart of a guy, gently escorted me over the wires and
cables of the darkened set made out to resemble a Big Sur hippie
cottage on the beach. (Filming in Paris was to please the Burtons
though it didn't make much sense for anyone else.) Here, I saw
sandpipers in their cage waiting to do whatever trained sandpipers do. And I met the director Vincente Minnelli, a soft-
spoken soul with embroidered crowns on his velvet slippers.
Although he had been a legend of creativity at MGM, I didn't
envy him his job. Finally, I was escorted to chat with Burton;
Miss Taylor hadn't made up her mind yet whether to give an interview or even to emerge from her dressing room. She certainly
wasn't inclined.

Burton was impressive. He was warm, friendly and intelligent. He actually seemed to like meeting the press in a con-
trolled situation. He made cogent, sensitive remarks, dressing
them up with elegant quotes from Shakespeare or Dylan
Thomas or Robert Lowell. I showed him a clip I had where Elizabeth was purportedly evaluating what all the men in her life
had offered her. Burton seemed vastly amused by this. He commented in a worldly manner about the sensation of their love
affair, the hoopla of their having married, the continuing excitement centering around them as a couple. He was quite frank. But
nothing could make up for no Elizabeth. When she eventually
sauntered out and came over, she was polite but very reserved.
He told her about the clip I had. She demanded to see it. They
began a faux argument over it. Minnelli then invited them to
come onto the set and act.

Morgan Hudgins came to me and wanted to know if I
"had enough?" Well, I had only been with them together about
seven minutes. I didn't think so. I had tried to get acquainted. I
hadn't asked any real questions. He shrugged. "That may be all
you get."

I had flown to Paris—for what? Then I saw Irene Sharaff. The famous Broadway designer had done the costumes for *Cleopatra* and was now doing the scaled down hippie look for *The Sandpiper*. Irene didn't care for many people. In the New York theater, she was famous for her cutting snobbery, but because we had the same agent, Gloria Safier, she liked me well enough. She hissed: "I have told Elizabeth what a terrific person you are. Richard agrees; he liked you on sight. They want you and me to go to lunch with them in La Grand Cascade in the Bois."

I couldn't have been more flabbergasted. Morgan's mouth fell open and he looked at me with a more discerning eye. He whispered, "This is a miracle. Go. Enjoy. Don't take any notes."

As Richard handed me up into a forest green Rolls-Royce, he asked if I spoke French. Meaning to say "a little," it came out instead, "Un petit pois!" (A little pea!) He found this amusing and off we went in a flurry of Pekinese dogs, curses at the traffic and hilarious showing off by the newlyweds, who spoke to one another partially in Welsh and with one engaging insult after another. The lunch in the all-glass Cascade was dazzling. Wine flowed as if Jesus had turned all the water in Paris into *vin du pays*.

Everything on the menu was ordered, it seemed to me, tasted, discarded, tossed around, eaten off each other's plates. Anecdotes tumbled over one another and I discovered Burton's pet peeve. Waiters. "Point killers!" he insisted. "They stand around and then when you are telling a story, they interrupt at the punch line, asking, 'Is everything all right?'"

At four in the afternoon, director Minnelli was telephoning, begging us to return to the set. By then we were all four quite tipsy so I don't know how much use we were at moviemaking. I toddled back to my hotel and wrote up everything I could think of about meeting the Burtons. And so began a saga that hasn't ended to this day.

FROM PARIS I WENT TO interview this incredible couple in Rome where they took me to a restaurant that served a poached

egg in a baked potato. I interviewed them in New York at the
Plaza Hotel where Richard bitched and complained that Elizabeth used him as an interpreter for her French hairdresser. I interviewed them in London—on yachts, in jets, in limousines—
and another time in Paris where *her* leading man was Warren
Beatty (the movie was *The Only Game in Town*) and *his* leading
man was Rex Harrison (Richard's movie was *Staircase*, about
two aging homosexuals).

Richard always gave me time and quotes, but Elizabeth
was maddening. Her idea of a good answer to a question was
"yes" or "no." She wanted to avoid any real query. At one point,
deserted in her dressing room while she stayed on the set for
hours, I copied down the name of every commercial item on her
makeup table. *Cosmo* had a ball printing a list of Elizabeth's
"beauty aids." She was outraged when next she saw me. "You
got paid for writing that list up and I didn't even get a free lipstick out of it." Another time she asked me to bring a basket of
makeup things she needed from America. In the mix were false
eyelashes. She threw them into the trash contemptuously. "I
have never worn false eyelashes. I don't need them!"

It was after this second stint in Paris that I wrote my very
best story ever on the Burtons. *Cosmo* carried it in August 1969.
It was all about eating—what they might eat, what they had,
what they wished they had, what they yearned for, what was
available. It was never enough. In spite of how it may sound,
this article was a real tour de force. I believe it summed them up
for all time. They fought continuously; they contradicted, corrected and ragged on one another. If he told a long tale, she
would sigh and ask, "Do you ever give yourself the creeps,
love?" But I felt it was Richard holding them strongly together,
confronting producers, directors, screenwriters, agents and
travel schedules. He was a fine actor but he had wanted stardom.
In her aura, he had it. And I still believe she taught him a lot
about movie acting, which is quite a different thing from the
stage. Elizabeth remained her spoiled and charming self. She
wanted this bauble; she wanted that one. She made the producer
Marty Ransohoff take her to a jewelry store where she picked up

a $25,000 diamond bird and pinned it on. He blanched, but he paid. She walked out and probably never wore it again.

I became good friends with the Burtons' two indispensable aides-de-camp, Richard Hanley and John Lee. Richard had studied these men closely before he played a gay man in *Staircase*. He trusted them implicitly, for Hanley had known Taylor since she'd been a child and was like a father to her. She often went and sat on his lap.

In one interview, I encountered Burton after lunch. He was rude and obstreperous. I read him a squib about Dylan Thomas and he flew into a rage, berating me for denigrating one of his idols. I pointed out that I hadn't written it; I merely wanted his opinion of it. He continued to attack me. Later, I realized that before lunch was better than after—not so many drinks. And I noticed that Elizabeth had begun to keep up with him, drink for drink. This was not good and I wasn't surprised when their fighting turned physical and they divorced, nor when they remarried, nor when they divorced again.

Around 1980, I interviewed a sobered up, reserved and ailing Burton in New York and noted to my dismay that he had no snap. He was now wed to Suzy Hunt. His revels had ended. He had grown tired of his life with Elizabeth, but he missed her all the same. He had other women but they didn't count. Perhaps he even missed her raging jealousies.

Then the two of them, unable to let well enough alone, decided to costar in Noel Coward's *Private Lives* on Broadway in 1983. It was a farce. But scandal, curiosity and publicity paid off. They carried the whole disgraceful thing off with some panache and I saw then what I still believe to be true—that he had passed, after he stopped drinking, into a kind of never-never land of living without her for his own peace of mind. But she would always fight to get him back. And I have no doubt if he hadn't died in 1984, she would have done just that.

She and I went on being friends. Although she pronounced me a "bitch" at one perfume press conference, I knew she was kidding. She knew I was on her side. And she became an endless unending story—always good for a headline. When she asked me to "handle the press" for her at one of her White Diamonds press conferences, I went against my own good judgment and stood on a stage with her "against" the ravages of the New York press corps. I shushed them, quieted them, picked out the ones to ask questions and generally made myself very unpopular with my peers. Why? I didn't like to say no to her. And it never occurred to her that she had put me in a compromising position.

When she decided to marry the construction worker Larry Fortensky, I asked her to let me be the only press present and told her we would sell the story to the highest bidder for charity (AIDS). Elizabeth envisioned making millions, but *People* magazine won the bid and she earned only several hundred thousand dollars for the international pickups. The Herb Ritts photos made much more. The wedding itself turned into a circus on Michael Jackson's ranch. And as Elizabeth appeared, deeply tanned, in a bright yellow Valentino gown at the outdoor aisle, on the arm of Michael Jackson, there were about eighteen helicopters overhead. They made so much racket that no one—not even Nancy Reagan in the first row—could hear the ceremony and then a camera-bearing man parachuted down not ten feet from me just as the couple was saying, "I do." Security nabbed him and carried him away.

During the wedding supper, Elizabeth sat closer to Michael Jackson than to her new husband, telling me that she and Michael "understood each other because we were both child stars!" I missed some of the festivities because I was running in high heels between the house and the entrance gate, slipping outside and down the road to the TV trailer Fox maintained for live broadcasts. It was lucky for Dr. Mathilde Krim that I was doing this; for the AIDS doctor—an honored guest—had lost her credentials and couldn't get into the ranch until I took her in.

Then I went to Elizabeth's sixtieth birthday at Disneyland February 27, 1992. She said she'd liked best my T-shirt gifts, which showed a glorious recent photo of her and read, "This is what sixty looks like!" But not too long after, Fortensky was history and I was with Elizabeth in her Bel Air house after a hip operation that left her drastically limping and ill. Then I was there again after she'd had another operation to rectify it. Now she was on top of the world once more, saying she'd never marry again, stating how much she wanted to work. She was selling her next birthday as an AIDS benefit, but before this happened she was diagnosed with a brain tumor. She attended her own party in L.A., taped for ABC TV, the night before her operation. Later, she posed for Harry Benson with her shaved head and the successful scars.

She goes on and on. Now she is a Dame of the British Empire. She has raised millions against AIDS. She has dragged me into raising millions against AIDS. I remain happy to be in her corner. When Richard Burton died, I sent my sympathy note to her; I didn't know the last Mrs. Burton. But I had known the Mrs. Burton who had counted.

READIN' . . .

WRITIN' . . .

NO ARITHMETIC!

NOW AND THEN I HAVE met famous people the same way other mortals do—by chance and with no credentials to back me up. One such happening took place in 1966 when Diane Judge had been hired to promote a resort called the Sunset Lodge and open there the first discotheque in Montego Bay, Jamaica. She lured our pace-setting pal Joel Schumacher, the actress Marisa Berenson, retailer Geraldine Stutz and her then husband, the artist David Gibbs, and others to fly down as guests of the owners.

There in first class I spied the famous author James Jones. Kneeling beside him in the aisle, I whispered, "Mr. Jones, your book *The Thin Red Line* is the greatest war novel ever written. I am a big fan." The tough guy beamed, asked my name and where was I staying in Jamaica? Then he introduced me to his wife, Gloria. In turn I met Rose and Bill Styron with whom the Joneses were keeping up. I was blown away at suddenly being on speaking terms with two of the greatest American fiction writers. (Mr. Styron had his epic *The Confessions of Nat Turner* about to be published, and his classic, *Sophie's Choice*, lay in his distinguished future.)

The day after landing, I received a phone call at the Sunset Lodge. It was Jones. He and his crew didn't like their accommodations in Jamaica and wanted to join my gang at the Sunset Lodge. They did—and a bang-up time resulted. Jimmy Jones and Bill Styron were still drinking and living it up in those halcyon days and so a riotous time was had.

It was during this trip that I met a beautiful brunette who was the sultry girlfriend of one of the world's greatest saxophone players, Paul Desmond, and she became a true asset to our revels. One day on the beach she gazed at the sparkling horizon as we girls were discussing sex. She sighed. "You know, I have been everywhere, met everyone, had a lot of love affairs. Sometimes I think I'd just give anything in the world for a good old-fashioned face-to-face fuck!"

So, we all remained friends ever after. Gloria Jones, Rose Styron and this lady I won't name are all remarkable women, well worth knowing for their own accomplishments. And to think, this came about from a simple compliment, uttered by a true fan. I always advise the celebrity-smitten not to bother the famous, for usually nothing will come of such aspirations. But in this case I proved my own theory to be wrong.

I realize I have loved meeting and knowing famous writers more than any other type of celebrity. And I have been lucky to know so many, beginning with the mysterious, recently resurrected Patricia Highsmith. I met this creator of *The Talented Mr. Ripley* in Greenwich Village in the mid-fifties, just before she forsook the U.S. and moved to England. She was already known for *Strangers on a Train*, which had been made into a hit movie by Alfred Hitchcock in 1951. A successful TV producer named Jacqueline Babbin made the introduction and Highsmith was a very odd bird, even in her youth. She took to me because we had both been born in Fort Worth, but it wasn't possible to really know her. Once we exhausted Texas memories, she was off again into her own odd world. But one couldn't blame her for being aloof and forbidding. Like many people, she had a serious "mother has rejected me" problem.

Other writers have offered me glimpses of real friendship and understanding. One recent morning, waiting for a cab, a man called to me from his own taxi at a red light. "Liz, it's David Halberstam." This giant reporter of our times wished me well in the new century and then leaned out to say, "You know, you and I used to be the new kids on the block. Now we are old-timers. How did that happen?" I said I guessed we were just lucky. He concurred and waved good-bye. I was bemused by this meeting. I admired Halberstam, who had made the Vietnam War his own question mark, who had driven presidents and sec-retaries of state wild with his revelations and who—just like Liz—was wondering where the time went. When I got to my of-fice, I found a beguiling photograph of Gay Talese, another writ-ing idol of mine, greeting me from Beijing. He, too, wondered where the time had gone. I felt pleased to have been a part of the times of Halberstam, Talese, Mailer, Wolfe, Jones, Styron, Capote, Doctorow, Vonnegut, Conroy, Caro, Crichton, Laurents and so many more. One of my idols is the critic essayist John Leonard. Let me pick a few women, as well—Renata Adler, Barbara Goldsmith, Marie Brenner, Lillian Ross, Lesley Blanch, Elizabeth Hardwick, Alice McDermott, Barbara Tuchman, Nora Ephron, Mary McCarthy, Edna O'Brien, Anne Tyler, Shana Alexander, Joyce Carol Oates, Barbara Taylor Bradford, Mary Higgins Clark, Susan Isaacs, Nancy Mitford, Susan Cheever, Erica Jong, Lillian Hellman, Wendy Wasserstein. I could go on and on. My passion for writers had begun in earnest at age six-teen with Christopher Morley. I was amazed to find out when I came to New York that he was considered merely a "popular" novelist. I thought he was an important philosopher. In time, my tastes improved. One of my friends today is the respected *Canon of Western Literature* author and Shakespearean scholar Harold Bloom. We carry on a lively old-fashioned correspondence.

From the beginning of writing a syndicated column I in-dulged myself, giving attention and space to writers, to books and to magazine articles. I found as much to gossip about in lit-erature, book publishing and the rise of media journalism as in society and show business. Like my idol, Walter Winchell, I tended to range all over the place looking for news. And I like to think my interest in talented and even hopeful writers alike has created some focus and demand and has helped the causes of literacy, culture and the better educating of ourselves.

FIRST CLASS

TO RUSSIA

ONE OF MY *COSMO* YEARS' perks came in 1974 when I was offered a first-class trip to the U.S.S.R. to hobnob with Ava Gardner, Jane Fonda, Cicely Tyson, Jimmy Coco, the great veteran director George Cukor and, again, Elizabeth Taylor in Leningrad. Twentieth Century-Fox was involved in an international partnership to make Maurice Maeterlinck's *The Bluebird* into a movie...once again.

Considering the volatile cast, the hazardous nature of U.S.–Russian relations at the time, the language barrier and all the rest of it, I should have been apprehensive about the success of such a venture, but not old Sunnyside-Up Liz. I always assume everybody else knows what they are doing and that, in the end, things will come together. So let's just say right up front that nothing about this trip came together very well.

It started off fine. What's not to like about flying first class to Paris and staying in the George V hotel overnight to get one's bearings before embarking for Leningrad? And I had pals along. Rex Reed, Diane Judge and I enjoyed each other's company and competition; we were each writing for a different venue. I knew I could have a fabulous reunion with my old friend Miss Taylor. I was dying to meet Ava Gardner, who I felt I knew anyway because of her lifelong friendship with my aide Saint Clair Pugh. (He had written me a glowing letter of introduction to her.) I thought I would have a good meeting with Jane Fonda, who I had interviewed back when she'd done *Barefoot in the Park* on Broadway. The gifted comic Jimmy Coço was playing "The Dog" in this movie; he was a friend. The Oscarnominated Cicely Tyson was playing "The Cat." I knew both these excellent actors from my life in New York. And the person in Leningrad who was my real pal was Mr. Cukor, the famous "woman's director" who had made history at MGM and was well known for directing Kate Hepburn and Spencer Tracy in their costarring films. I had met Cukor during my visit to Hollywood in the fifties and we had become close. Like most of the women who came into his orbit, I worshipped him. After all, he had been director number-one for *Gone With the Wind*, before Clark Gable had him replaced. He had made movies with Greta, Tallulah and Marilyn as well. At this time he was already seventy-five years old and would make only one other film before his death in 1983.*

As we three ink-stained wretches flew out of Paris with a big basket of goodies from Fauchon in our arms, who knew that we were entering a snake pit of complexities: rabid bitching from the American, British and Russian cast and crew who were filming in a veritable Tower of Babel; the intermixed hopes of 20th Century-Fox, Soviet Lenfilm and Tower International—a company owned by U.S. tycoon Cyrus J. Eaton, who was determined to achieve detente with Russia; the universal hatred of one and all for the American producer who was eventually replaced; the various illnesses already afflicting most everyone, plus the trauma of arrivals and departures by those of differing cultures and ideologies. (It was said that Jane Fonda and her then activist hubby Tom Hayden had been very disappointed in Russia because they "couldn't find anyone to convert to Com-

---

*Rich and Famous, *starring Candice Bergen and Jacqueline Bisset, 1981.*

munism." Somebody remarked that Jane had found Russia "too
decadent and Westernized for her Marxist tastes.")

Upon arrival, our basket was promptly snatched away
from us by men in Russian uniforms, never to be returned. Its
fruit, brandy and candy went the way of all flesh. The Russians,
some carrying machine guns, weren't happy that we had "journalist" stamped on our passports because they assumed all journalists to be "political." We tried to tell them we were just
"entertainment" bozos but they didn't get it, not having much
entertainment in Russia. I was singled out by the man going
through my luggage. Why did I have so many books? Was I
planning to sell books in Russia? It was forbidden. And we better not have any Bibles either. That was a serious offense. (We
didn't have any Bibles though later I felt I could have used one.)

Now we discovered that one of *The Bluebird* stars had
flown, and yet another was on the wing. Miss Fonda had already
come and gone before 20th's embattled flacks could get Rex,
Diane and Liz there to interview her. We learned also that Elizabeth Taylor was not in the best frame of body or mind, having
broken up with Richard Burton for the first time. She was in
Leningrad with a used-car salesman named Henry Wynberg.
She was bathing in bottled distilled water because Leningrad's
product often ran bright green and smelled of sulphur. When
told that Lincoln Steffans had once said of Russia, "I have seen
the future and it works," Miz Liz snorted. "Had he seen the way
the Russians often reverse their hot and cold water faucets?"
Elizabeth had brought a load of Fortnum & Mason food with her
to Russia plus 2,800 pounds of luggage, but was still often heard
to complain that one could "starve to death" on the spot. Later I
would concur with her assessment; when we left Russia a dozen
days later I had lost twelve glorious pounds. Now it seemed
Elizabeth had amoebic dysentery, had lost twenty-eight pounds
and was in the process of being transported to a hospital in London. Ava Gardner was still present and accounted for but the
woman once described by reporter Helen Lawrenson as being
"her customary self, as amiable as an adder," was bored out of
her mind by Leningrad. She had reportedly gone one night to a

hotel and made her Russian non-English-speaking driver come
inside and dance with her to the strains of forties hot licks like
"Take the 'A' Train" and "Marie." There was a sign on Ava's
hotel door that read KEEP OUT.

It was April in Leningrad and beautiful. I carried a copy
of Harrison Salisbury's book *The 900 Days: The Siege of
Leningrad* and kept avidly reading about how over 1,500,000
had died defending this city from the Nazis. But the Russians
didn't want the world to know how decimated Leningrad had
been. Everyone I encountered begged me to give them the book,
which was unobtainable in Russia.

We were set up in a "modern" hotel built by the Finns on
the Neva River across from the Battleship *Aurora*, a shrine to the
Revolution. We assumed our rooms were bugged and every day
our InTourist guide would be changed, so we could never get too
friendly, nor could we corrupt any of them with our American
decadence. Most of the guides were wonderful, dying for a taste
of what we had to offer from the West. We'd brought lipsticks,
chewing gum, cheap cigarette lighters and we passed these
around. But one guide, a devout Communist, was determined to
treat us to her ideological contempt for capitalism. We pretended
to be amused by her dedication, but it was somewhat disquieting.

She was writing her college thesis on the U.S. playwright
Edward Albee. Delighted, I told her I knew Albee, and would be
happy to send her anything she might need when I got back to
New York, including getting him to answer questions. She was
highly insulted. She didn't need my "help." Russia had libraries
and all the information it needed. She also brushed aside our offers of U.S. junk. It was sobering.

The people bugging our rooms must have been a bit confused. They may have thought we had all escaped from a lunatic
asylum. At night, we often went to Cukor's suite where Jimmy
Coco would cook pasta in an electric fry pan he'd brought
along. He would also entertain with bits from Broadway shows.
One of his big hits was to re-enact Rita Moreno's turn from *The
Ritz*, wherein she'd been a crazy Puerto Rican singer in a gay
bathhouse. Coco had her role down pat. Screams of laughter em-

anated from Cukor's rooms. The "key" ladies, who sat guarding the end of each floor, looked at us with total contempt as we emerged limp to go to our own rooms.

Cukor just couldn't get enough of Coco, as Googie Gomez. Jimmy was playing a dog in *The Bluebird* in a complete dog costume. Both he and Cicely Tyson had tails on their costumes, which gave them no end of trouble, and I kept thinking of *The Bad and the Beautiful*.

In that Vincente Minnelli–directed movie, junior producers Kirk Douglas and Barry Sullivan were ordered to make a "curse of the cat people" grade-B movie. They studied the moth-eaten costumes with whiskers, tails and ears. They elected instead to make a nuanced *film noir* where no one wears a costume and there is only a suggestion of dark feline menace. It became an artistic success! (My movie lore never failed me, not even in Russia.) I went on to suggest to Cukor that he free Cicely and Jimmy from their ridiculous costumes. He said, "Are you the person who directed Spencer and Kate in *Pat and Mike*? Stick to writing for *Cosmo*."

It was with some chagrin that we learned Elizabeth Taylor had indeed flown the coop. "But she'll be back!" they assured us. Meantime, one of the only stars available to speak with us—Miss Tyson—complained that a vegetarian, such as herself, could easily die in Russia from lack of greens. She had arrived as exotic as a cinnamon stick, wearing stunning Halston clothes and Elsa Peretti bracelets, ordering the people around her not to smoke, speaking of her "mystique" and the necessity to live by her "artistry," offended by the lagging nonprofessionalism of the filming, saying, "This is my last brush with the Hollywood star system!" She added as she jogged and exercised desperately that she would "never again complain about any condition in America, regardless of oppression and injustice, not after being here!" Jimmy Coco, on the other hand, just laughed and kept camping it up to amuse his cohorts. He said, with good humor, "I don't care *where* I am mistreated as an actor. It doesn't make much difference." (Eventually, he too left the cast.)

So we were missing two big stars from our mix, but we

still had Ava to beard in her den. Cukor soothed us. "We'll just make something up," he said cheerfully. "And, anyway, Ava is here and she is the greatest of them all."

Miss Gardner was indeed. On the set the first morning, she was in full makeup, ready to go, resembling a grand fairy princess. She'd already had a tantrum, saying she would not work if Rex Reed was allowed on the set. (She had never forgiven him for spending a social evening with her and writing it up when she hadn't known he was a journalist.) Rex happily went off to the Hermitage instead of coming to the set that day.

Cukor forced Ava to come and meet Diane and me. We were in the usual movie "stage wait" in any case. The director playfully twisted Ava's arm behind her back and said, "Ava, my darling, come and meet these lovely ladies of the press." Ava smiled, grimly. She was totally gorgeous, having just come from a beautifying rest cure in England's Forest Mere. No wonder Frank Sinatra couldn't get over her. I timidly extended my envelope, and said, "Miss Gardner, I have a personal note for you from Saint Clair Pugh of Smithfield."

She took it then, smiling for real. George tried to wrest it from her. "Who is he?"

Ava said, "Just a wonderful old beau of mine." She read the note and we exchanged pleasantries about Saint. She was charming. But when I requested a real sit-down interview, she declined graciously. She just couldn't. But she had a few things to say about working in Russia. "I wouldn't put up with this if I were drunk. And don't you drink the water here because you'll get 'Czar's Tummy.' You do have to drink a certain amount of booze to survive. But I want to look my best, so I lay off. As a result I get the trots and giardiasis, which is Russian for blowing up like a balloon."

I saw her often after that. She and her Jamaican maid would drift through the hotel lobby smoking Marlboros. Ava usually wore green espadrilles, blue jeans and a sweatshirt that read "Southern Comfort." She was always very nice but uncommunicative. She simply didn't care. She had nothing to gain, nothing to lose. Cicely Tyson said, "That woman has real soul!"

One day we passed on the back stairs. I didn't try to detain her, just said "hi" and moved on. Ava stopped and said, "Liz, we've got to stop meeting like this." We laughed and I gave her the high sign.

Years later, she became good friends with Elaine Stritch in London and Elaine proudly reported that Ava would always rave about me. (Well, one way to be a popular journalist with difficult stars is to leave them alone. But it isn't a very successful way to be a journalist.)

I kept hanging on the set soaking up "color," hoping a movie star would give me a break. One day Cukor said imperiously to his Russian codirector, via interpreter, that he wanted a ramp built so Ava could ride in and up it on a white horse. Lots of Russian jabbering and the interpreter said, "Yes, Mr. Cukor, we can do that." Cukor said, "When?" More jabbering and finally: "In about six weeks." Cukor exploded. "I was thinking about perhaps this afternoon!" (He'd been at MGM where they could produce 500 extras in Confederate uniform on demand in an hour.)

The movie, of course, was going from bad to worse, with Cukor shooting around the absence of Jane and Liz. When released in 1976, it was one of the great international bombs and I believe only a handful of people have ever seen it, in spite of its star power.

With no stars to talk to, we used our time sightseeing. We were in Leningrad during the famous White Nights and would emerge at 11:00 P.M. from the ballet to a bright but somewhat cloudy evening as if we were lost in a haze of frozen daiquiris. The spring flowers were wonderful but the thing I missed most in Russia was…advertising. Store windows had nothing to offer. Sometimes they'd be full of gravel and miniature tractors, selling—what? There was nothing to see, nothing to buy. In our hotel we were happy to get a pair of fried eggs and cabbage soup, for although we were on some VIP list, we never saw any caviar and decided it was a myth.

We argued with our InTourist guides, begging to be taken to churches, all of which were in disrepair and ruin. They were then full of old people praying. The guides would shove them around and push them aside; talking loudly over the sermons, showing us vaulted ceilings, etc. They bragged the most on "desanctified" buildings that had been turned into swimming pools. But we also spent days in the Hermitage and the Pushkin to make up for that.

In the palaces of Catherine the Great and her son Paul, we slid footpads over our shoes to walk on the rosewood parquet, which was being painstakingly restored by old men who had been doing this work since the end of World War II. We saw the china service sent to Peter the Great by Marie Antoinette. It was vast, filling one big room. We were told it had been stolen and carted off to Germany in World War II and had been returned by Russian soldiers, each one carrying a single cup or saucer or gravy boat. This made good sightseeing propaganda, though it seemed a bit far-fetched. And we were shown where the Germans had been stopped during the siege and how, when the Russians drove them back, their stoves were full of smoldering Rublev icons, the most sacred objects in Russia. Reading *The 900 Days* added poignancy to all of this and I was glad I'd come to Russia even if it looked as if *Cosmopolitan* and 20th might have to whistle for a story on the filming of *The Bluebird*.

I had one perfect moment in Russia. Cukor took me to the studio commissary. "Have you ever had gray ice cream?" he asked. No, of course not. He ordered and sure enough we were served one of the most delicious vanillas ever. But it was gray, as gray as the suit on Gregory Peck in *The Man in the Gray Flannel Suit*. Cukor had also said to me, "Be sure to come and see me if you are like every other American here, about to be sick. I will prescribe my all-purpose cure for you. Midol! It works for everything." Later he would congratulate me and always refer to me as "the girl who didn't get sick in Russia."

So, Ava refused to talk. Jane never appeared while we were there. Likewise, Elizabeth never returned from London until much later. I did finally write my piece for *Cosmo*, somehow. In order to do it, I had to fly on to London and interview Elizabeth in the Dorchester Hotel, which wasn't the same as being in Leningrad. We had fantastic room service, which did not resemble starving in Russia. She had two of her children there—Christopher and Liza. Out of deference to them, I didn't quiz her too much about the mysterious Henry Wynberg.

Terrible tales were making the rounds. She, said to be pining for Burton, had nevertheless thrown herself into Wynberg's arms. She was diverted by his outrageous ways. Rumor had it he would throw her, fully dressed, made up, ready to go out, into the shower, paying no mind to her magnificent gown. He'd turn the water on and have his way with her. (I rather liked that one; so imaginative.) Rumor had it that she was into recreational drugs with him. Well, what was the use of my asking questions about such lurid whispers? She'd just have screeched with laughter, or thrown me out. After Henry left us alone together, I tried to delve into her feelings and being with tact. She dismissed the negatives about *The Bluebird*, saying simply to me, "Liz, no one ever sets out to make a bad movie. Remember that!"

When I got up to leave her suite, I decided to make a grand exit, wishing the star an extravagant good-bye. She was lounging on a couch, looking ravishing and rather amused. I had my hand on the door for my big farewell. I said something smart and turned the knob and stepped out—right into a closet. I emerged sheepishly back into the room as Taylor and her kids exploded with raucous glee. It's always good to get something back on the Fourth Estate.

MY LEADING

MEN

I CAN'T BEGIN TO FIND SPACE to write about all the sexy major stars I've known in this odd career. But let me offer thoughts about two of the best in the leading man category.

Probably the *über* press agent Pat Newcomb introduced me to Warren Beatty in the late sixties. She was that rare thing—an honest name-dropper, for she knew everyone. Before meeting Warren, I recall visiting Pat in her PR suite at some grand Paris hotel. She said casually, "Warren is in town…"

"Warren?"

"Yes, Warren Beatty."

Not long after there was a knock on the door. I was surprised when Patricia held her finger to her lips and said, "Shhh, it's probably Warren." Then we heard him whispering his name. But she refused to budge. The tapping finally stopped. Later, incredibly, someone else famous came by. This time it was Rex Harrison. He, too, knocked to no avail, saying in his unmistakable sexy-Rexy voice, "Pat, it's Rex!" Soon, he, too, went away. I was stunned. I'd known a lot of women to go ga-ga over stars, but I'd never known one who was trying to avoid two big ones in a single afternoon. "I have a date later," said Miss Newcomb. "I'd never get rid of either one of them."

Despite this rare strikeout, Hollywood always abounded with tales about Warren's romantic escapades. One such tale had him romancing one of the most beautiful women in the world—a redhead who'd been wed to a munitions king—and yet another beauty who was well-known, too. Neither woman could have possibly had the slightest interest in the other. But it was said with authority that Warren had enticed them into bed together, with him.

Asked about such adventures, Warren always professes amazement and shakes his head. Sometimes, through the years, I thought I had a special insight into this mysterious man. It came from reading an unpublished manuscript of what it was like to make love to him. This was written by a girl-about-the-world and maybe she wrote it as fiction. But whenever I see Warren, my mind replays the episode and he remains one sexy dude in my head. I was delighted when I interviewed Annette Bening in early 2000 and asked how she coped with Warren's sexy past legend. Did it bother her? This formidably intelligent star laughed. "No, you don't ignore it. I think if you're with somebody for a while, you can't expect to take away his past. You have to know it and respect it. We both have friends from before we knew each other, and that's a big part of our lives. Whatever got him to where he is now is fine with me."

Before Warren married Annette, he and I enjoyed many professional talks—and sometimes personal ones. He would always hint and pretend that he had absolute insight into my private life. And he could be elliptical and maddening if one was trying to get something to write about *his* private life.

Late in the eighties, a Warren observer told me that he'd said there was one particular woman in the world he wanted to sleep with. He was "just curious." It turned out to be me. I laughed at this ridiculous fiction, but admitted I liked the idea. And when *Esquire* magazine asked about it, I said, "He's not picky."

All this myth-making is typical Warren legend. Even today, this very happily married hubby and father likes to sidle up at the end of parties, slide his arm around you and say quietly, "Are you going home with me?"

He's still irresistible.

ANYTIME I'VE SEEN ROBERT REDFORD in the last twenty-five years, he has been wearing cowboy boots. So, there's that—the old Tom Mix syndrome. And then he has always been as truly golden as the 14-carat hair on his arms and hands. And that sunburned grizzled look, no longer as devastating on the screen as it was when he was knocking us dead in *The Way We Were,* is still great in person.

Lois Smith, his steadfast PR rep, introduced us when his stardom was still ascendant—just as he hit the peak before *Butch Cassidy and the Sundance Kid.* Having fallen for him onstage with Elizabeth Ashley in the 1963–64 Broadway production of *Barefoot in the Park,* it was wonderful to have an "in." Lois kept putting us together for interviews on and off movie locations and eventually environmental charity events.

Redford is bright, independent, hardheaded, intelligent. He has done exactly as he pleases, accomplishing most of his goals. And he managed through a highly visible career to keep his private life, family, marriage, divorce, his move to Sundance, Utah, and the creation of his own film festival, several subsequent love affairs and a disdain for "Hollywood" all under his own control. People know very little about Redford and that's just the way he wants it.

At the peak of his screen power, he was making a movie, *The Great Waldo Pepper,* down near Lockhart, Texas. Lockhart lies in a triangle between San Antonio and Gonzales and my darling mother lived in the latter small town at the time. I asked her to come sixty miles to San Antonio and we'd have a visit while I was interviewing Redford on location. As I left for Lockhart, she was going shopping and we were to meet for dinner at the famous La Fonda restaurant that evening. I had a good day interviewing Redford, watching him film a plane crash. I was a little shocked at the peremptory manner he used on an extra who dared approach and ask for an autograph as he came out of camera range and took my arm to walk to lunch. "Not now," he snapped at the man. "Maybe later." (Well, of course no extra should ever impose on the star or the latter would be overwhelmed and go crazy. But at the time I still thought of my hero as being someone like Jesus who could walk on water and turn the other cheek. It was surprising to learn he could be testy!)

The day's filming ended. By the time Redford divested himself of his flying helmet and goggles and emerged from a dressing room, he was in his own Levi's, boots and a snap-button Western shirt looking like he'd won the West. I started to say good-bye, but he said, "Come back to my motel with me and let's talk some more!"

This kind of rare invitation from a star was just too much to resist. Of course I went. We sat down in a combination of two rooms where the star was staying and also had made an "office." Redford flopped down in a chair, propped his boots up and began to talk. "I thought it would be fun if you stayed here and had dinner with me and we could go on talking," he said, accepting from his departing secretary a great big red-and-white bucket of—ta-da!—Kentucky Fried Chicken. "Here!" he said, offering me the bucket. "Which do you like best—regular or extra crispy? We have both."

I said, "I like to mix them up." (Redford and I had already agreed on the merits of the Forever Yours candy bar over the Milky Way even though the Mars candy company had paid us no never mind and quit making the Forever Yours.) Well, tempted wasn't the word for what I was. I am a very big fan of the Colonel's.

Here was the most beautiful man in America in his Western duds, legs up over his head, munching a crunchy drumstick. He wanted me to stay and have dinner with him in his motel room! I gulped and stammered that my mother was waiting for me in San Antonio. He seemed disappointed, saying, "Are you sure? I thought we could talk a little more." I just couldn't believe this was happening to me.

In fact, as I drove back to San Antonio thinking about him sitting there alone, swirled in a haze of fried chicken, I wasn't feeling too great about my mother, though none of this was her fault. I realized that my movie star was just bored, in the boonies, feeling talkative.

Still, I've never gotten over it. It makes a great line for the party game "I Never"—true or false? It's true: I once elected to have dinner with my mother rather than with Robert Redford in a Texas motel. Yes, I'd definitely win that round.

LOVING LEE

YOU MAY WONDER IF DURING all these comings and goings, to-ings and fro-ings, I had any personal life outside of work. Did I ever! Men, women and dogs, in the words of James Thurber, kept me occupied. But my lodestar was someone I wanted to marry—someone who didn't want to marry me.

I first saw my darling Lee Bailey in the early fifties. He was sitting on a lawn in Amagansett, Long Island. He had sexy broad square shoulders, a trim waist and an attractive thatch of flat chest hair nesting in the V of his polo shirt. His chest had sapped whatever had once been on his strong, almost Roman head. He laughed. "Yes, it's been like this since I woke up at nineteen to find all my beautiful red hair on the pillow!"

Lee spoke in the casual, slurring and lovely—to me—cadences of the Old Confederacy. Ashley Wilkes himself never exuded more class, style or gentlemanly virtue. Having grown up on *Gone with the Wind*, I fell for Lee instantly.

He told me his grandpa had owned the only movie theater in Bunkie, Louisiana, and he'd grown up on a steady diet of Mae West, the Marx Brothers and all the rest. So, we had that in common. He described his absent-minded grandma tending her garden while a cat tangled itself in her dragging corset strings. Lee had been partially raised by a former slave named Parsons, a man with only one arm and one job—to look after young Master Lee. I was enchanted.

Lee had actually graduated from New York's Parsons School of Design but said he'd never be a decorator. He was living in New Orleans, building sets for advertising. I noticed that in spite of his lack of stated career goals, everybody seemed to look up to Lee, to seek his approval. He had reserve, gravitas and authority. He made me think of the William Steig cartoon, "All Who Want the Answer Must Come to Me."

He also had a unique vision, a refined simplicity, and he knew a lot about flowers and food. But what I liked best was his sardonic humor, his appreciation of really low jokes like the ones I'd been force-fed in Texas. I said to myself, "Self, I'm going to marry this man." (I spent the next thirty years, off and on, trying.)

After our first meeting, I didn't see Lee again until the sixties when I discovered him "having a cocktail" (as he liked to put it) in the living room of the agent Gloria Safier. He had moved to New York. I have already discussed Gloria, a legend in her own little world, a mover and shaker, the only one of our mutual friends who was an unqualified success. Let me add, Gloria made enough money to have a "salon." Her weekends of marathon drinks, the manufacturing of meals, the throwing out of leftovers, the inevitable nightclubbing, theater, gossip and general carrying on, supplied us with the glamour, contacts, sophistication and connections that we "wanna-bes" craved. And she nagged and motivated us. "Don't just sit there complaining—go get a job at Bloomingdale's selling ties if you can't do any better!"

In the hurly-burly of these formative and exciting years, Lee and I blended. We had in common our love for Southern lore, the mores of black people, tall tales and what Tom Wolfe would call "the glories of boiling lard." (Southern cooking.) We liked to both laud and make fun of our "Suth-run" backgrounds. But now we had New York before us and with Gloria's guidance, we began to climb. We were learning Manhattan's ropes. Ambition and laughter dominated everything we did. But Lee was more casual than some of us, more mature. While we clawed our way up, warbling endlessly about our "careers," he watched, waited. He spent time as an advisor to a national paint company, tried his hand at being a photographer's agent.

I was infatuated. I wanted to get serious with Lee. He'd just pat me and say, "Now, now—if you don't calm down, I'm going to have you 'fixed.'" Or he dubbed me as being "just like a swimming pool, which realtors call 'an attractive nuisance.'" Lee wasn't about to give his life over to a ditsy nutcase like me—someone who was wild, crazy and forever emotionally involved with too many people, too many things. He liked standing back. And so our "love affair" progressed into something else. Without speaking of it, we kept our mystery for one another, spending most of our time together. We were loving, loyal compadres. Together we became "superior" in our own eyes. And as a team, we gained some minor notice as host and hostess, letting down or pulling up the drawbridge, refining our worlds. For several years we stayed in Gloria's summer shack in Quogue. Here we sometimes shared sandy weekends with the likes of Lena Horne or Vivien Leigh. But then, Lee inherited a small sum of money and he built us a simple house he designed himself in nearby, then bucolic Bridgehampton.

It rose like an elegant boxcar on the Sagg Pond shore, a throw from the ocean. Lee made gardens and lawns. And we began an orgy of inviting, pouring, chopping, blending, mixing and matching people. In the process of also flailing around to make a living, we lived it up on weekends in the Hamptons of the sixties and seventies, not leaving there until the mid-eighties crush began to diminish that lovely spot.

Our house was a locus of things and important people to come—fame, fortune, success loomed. We had Helen and David Brown visit us before *Jaws*, and also the next year when they had become multi-millionaires. We entertained Broadway names from Arthur Laurents to Elaine Stritch to Jerome Robbins to Cheryl Crawford to Jimmy Kirkwood to Truman Capote to

Peter Larkin. We had many writers whose bylines were just waiting to happen. (I recall one poetic guy, the mild-mannered Tom Harris. In addition to *Black Sunday,* he would write *Red Dragon* and *The Silence of the Lambs.*) We entertained Barbara Howar when she still counted as a luminary at Elaine's restaurant. (Entering one of our parties, the blonde bombshell indicated her strong, rugged and silent date Herb Sargent, "And you already know Mount Rushmore!")

These people were like "old-home" week. Personally, we were after really big celebrity fish. We lay quietly concealed on Lee's roof to watch as Greta Garbo and Gaylord Hauser made their way from our neighbor's—Francis Carpenter—across our lawn to the ocean. We never met "Miss Harriet Brown," but we observed.

Lee refined himself into a cottage industry. He wrote *Country Weekends* for Clarkson-Potter and then seventeen more books—how to cook, how to plant, how to entertain, how to live. They are *all* still in print. He went on TV, wrote for magazines, opened shops in Southampton, Henri Bendel, Saks, then franchised his name. He became a true national guru of good taste and better living before anyone had ever heard of Martha Stewart.

But in 1987, Lee sold the house and we put away our photo albums with their all-too-prophetic jokey titles: "In Happier Days"—"The Jet Nothings." We had danced a million miles, swung, twisted, hully-gully-ed, rocked and rolled, skinny-dipped the Atlantic and escaped the beach patrols. We had drunk a million cocktails, including vodka stingers blended with hard peppermint candies when we'd run out of *crème de menthe.* We had eaten everything that hadn't eaten us, gained and lost thousands of pounds and climbed in and out of a few beds and windows. Philosophically, we "had et our load," as our friend Wydell Martin's daddy used to say after dinner in Louisiana. We'd become championship drinkers but now, without resorting to A.A., it seemed better to open Poland Spring water. We had lived our dream, become "sophisticated," "successful" (so that we didn't have to look at the prices on menus), and yet we'd hung on to "our roots." Why, we couldn't have dug them out if we tried.

Today, Lee lives alone in Manhattan with his border terrier, Mercy, in a beautiful Chelsea garden penthouse. There's a view of the Hudson River and from his spare, pared-down interior to his exploding fruit trees and flowers on the terrace, Lee lives like an Italian padrone in Tuscany. I still live like a college sophomore in the same cluttered Murray Hill apartment* where I have had an office for over thirty years. We are only blocks apart. But we know we did just right. We mingled our diverse styles—Lee's reserve, Liz's general hysteria. Our love, our friendship, we discovered, was not for everyday, but for great occasions. And it still is.

*Now I have two of them in the same building.

THE SEXUAL

OUTLAW

L ET'S GO BACK A MINUTE. It's 1963. I am sitting at cocktails in the Hamptons with a clutch of good-looking young people who are on the rise. We're all there in the twilight looking tan, relaxed and rich. But most of us are sweaty from "climbing" and none of us have much more than a thin dime in our pockets.

As an aspiring freelancer, I have just done a map for *Esquire* on where to go to see celebrities in Manhattan. Suddenly one of the guys attacks me for "invading the privacy" of two rich men named Tug Barton and John McHugh. Putting them on the map was an offense against the Manhattan gods.

I started to answer back but suddenly a tall, handsome drink of water does it for me. He says, "Oh, pul-eeze! Leave her alone. Tug and John just love publicity about how they serve caviar with men in white gloves standing behind every chair. No matter how they bitch, why else do they invite Margot Fonteyn, Rudi Nureyev and Princess Margaret—*not* to get publicity?"

As cocktails break up, I run down the front ramp as this guy and his group are leaving. I grab him by the back of his old leather flight jacket. "Who are you?" I ask.

"I'm Joel Schumacher. I work for Geraldine Stutz; I go to the Parsons School of Design and I also do the windows at Henri Bendel," he tells me sweetly. And the rest became history.

Lee and I, the perennial host and hostess to the up-and-coming, more or less adopted Joel for our own. He was light-years younger than we were but he became one of our best friends.

Joel and his pals lived in a cache of tourist courts on the Montauk Highway. But they only put their heads down in the Cozy Cabins to sleep, for they were swept up by people better off who loved their engaging and youthful company. They liked to dance, drink, gossip and eat the hors d'oeuvres and dinners of their social betters. Lee and I sometimes called Joel "The World's Tallest Child." I personally referred to him as "Baby Ray," after a character in a children's reader of the thirties. He called himself "A Sexual Outlaw."

Joel was soon winning design prizes and was hired by Revlon at a huge salary during one of that cosmetic company's forays into fashion. "The Youthquake" was on in the sixties/seventies and Joel was part of the new gilded youth set, along with Halston and others of that ilk. I remember going to Harlem discos with Joel and Halston; it was like being escorted between two Russian princes. They were tall and sexy, wore beautiful boots and were terribly arrogant and funny.

Joel had grown up a fatherless child in Queens. His widowed mother worked hard to give him a good start, but he was precociously into the glamour of the movies and from there into the fast life of New York and Palm Beach. After his dear mother died in 1965, his overnight success at Revlon fell into the "too much, too soon" category. Diana Vreeland and *Vogue* couldn't do without him. *W* idolized him. But Joel soon met one of those "Dr. Feelgood" drug prescribers and I'd find myself sitting all dressed up in my apartment, waiting in vain for the date Joel and I supposedly had. Drugs had entered our lives. Finally, I stopped seeing Joel because he was so heartbreakingly unreliable.

Then one night he came across a dance floor at the St. Regis, took both my hands and said, "Darling, I've kicked

everything. I just went to Fire Island and lay on the beach for
months and screamed, but now I'm clean. I am sane at last. I'm
broke, of course. I put all the money I made from Revlon into
my veins. But now I am okay." We picked up right where we
had left off before amphetamines, because Joel was "family" to
me in a way I could never explain. I felt he was my own flesh
and blood.

　　Around this time, my roommate, Diane, must have been
entertaining a long-staying houseguest from Spain. I needed a
temporary place to live and Joel invited me to share an apartment
he'd rented in the East Sixties. He had gone to our mutual friend
Gerry Stutz and she had taken him back to do the Bendel windows. He was living a very reduced lifestyle, determined to pay
back the $50,000 he owed the IRS and others. Living with Joel
suited me fine; it reminded me of life with Bobby in the fifties. We
were poor and happy. I learned a lot from Joel. He was unusually
independent and brave. If I complained that someone had said
something nasty about me—that I was ambitious or jealous or
selfish—Joel would just laugh and ask philosophically, "And
what if you are? Isn't that okay?" (This didn't totally apply but
was a damned good lesson for a scaredy-cat like me.)

　　"Are you tempted to use drugs?" I asked him.

　　"No, I just dream of food and having enough of it!" said
Joel. We spent our mutual pennies on the ninety-nine-cent special and chop suey at a joint upstairs on Third Avenue and 59th.

　　Joel asked me to help him make up a budget so he could
give the major part of what he earned to his creditors. He said he
had $2.00 to spend a day, after paying his rent. He could walk to
work, walk everywhere. I protested he hadn't left himself
enough to eat on. "I'll go to parties and eat cocktail crap!" he
said. "But I have to have seventy-five cents a day for myself."

　　I was suspicious. "Why?"

　　Joel shrugged. "Well, I am wearing blue jeans and my
black velvet blazer, so I can get away with that, for work or for
evening. But my boots—I have to have my boots shined every
day so people won't know I'm so down and out. I need fifty
cents for the shine and a quarter for the tip."

Although Joel was one of the smartest people I'd ever met and one of the funniest and most beguiling, I didn't pay much mind when he began telling me he intended to make a career in the movies. "Sure, sure, you can do that—and I'm Lana Turner!" I'd scoff. But soon Joel had written the screenplay for something called *Sparkle,* about a trio of black girl singers. And soon he and his partner Howard Rosenman were making this movie. He may not have known a thing about writing in the literary sense, but his visual talents were incredible. *Sparkle* went on to be a forerunner to *Dreamgirls* and suddenly my Joel was in the movies. He moved to Los Angeles. I moved back to 38th Street. Joel began doing costumes and sets for Woody Allen. He continued to write screenplays, finally demanding that they let him direct one of his own works for television. He began to direct feature films and his pop culture sensibility, his cutting-edge ideas and his fearlessness paid off. He made hit after hit: *Car Wash, St. Elmo's Fire, The Incredible Shrinking Woman, D.C. Cab, The Lost Boys, Flatliners, Cousins, Dying Young, Falling Down, The Client, A Time to Kill,* two *Batman* films, *8 MM, Flawless* and *Tigerland.* He became exactly what he had dreamed of being, the dream about which I'd been so skeptical. And he has seldom made a movie that has lost money. He is one of the big success stories, rags to riches, self-made man stuff. Sexual outlaw—"born without the marrying gene," as he describes himself—makes good!

In 1997, the *New York Observer* took Joel and me to task. They portrayed us in a front-page cartoon as "Batman and Robin," depicting us as two mutual back-scratchers who enjoyed the *quid pro quo* of our professions, me praising Joel's movies and he supplying me with gossip items. This hurt our feelings terribly. It was completely untrue.

I didn't always praise Joel's movies. Sometimes he made films I didn't much like. Many of his movies were dark and cynical. But, unfortunately for me and for Joel, I had loved *Batman and Robin* and I'd said so in print. (I think I was about the only one, which made matters worse.) As for gossip, Joel and I had a deal. After I began writing a column, he never told me anything

I could use about anybody. It was useless to ask him for gossip as he had earned the trust of countless stars and celebrities by keeping their secrets. His attitude about this was something I totally respected. In fact, the matter seldom came up.

So can gossip and speculation as printed by the *Observer* be hurtful? You bet. It hurt both Joel and me and there was nothing we could do about it, but try to rise above it. It caused a subtle separation to take place between the two of us. I suppose the worst thing was that after a thirty-five-year friendship, it took our carefree, longtime, artless relationship and turned it into something a little self-conscious.

I had hardly conceived of Joel's becoming a major film director and neither of us had a clue that I was going to become a national name as a gossip columnist. Neither of us engineered or expected what had happened. I suppose one of us will have to give up working and retire before we can entirely be ourselves again.

JOEL OCCASIONALLY TOOK ME OUT socially with Woody Allen and Mia Farrow when they were still together. He and Woody had become real friends after Joel did costumes and sets for *Sleeper* and *Interiors*.

Woody was a connoisseur of food and wine. Joel and I were connoisseurs of nothing and would, at the time, drink anything. So I recall several spectacular feasts in Pearl's great Chinese restaurant and in the splendid Maxwell's Plum. (Like most celebrity marriages, neither place still exists.)

Woody and Mia always appeared as vastly underdressed ragpickers, no matter the occasion. They seemed afraid of being touched, talked to or stared at by the great unwashed. Yet they went around town in a white Rolls so as not to be unnoticeable.

In spite of not always liking what I perceived personally about Woody—and taking Mia's side of things in the Great Unpleasantness—I haven't wavered in my critical admiration for Woody's talent, his genius, his offbeat films. But Woody isn't easy. I'll never forget expressing my admiration for what he'd done in *Everything You Always Wanted to Know About Sex* . . . —a groundbreaking 1972 comedy.

Woody listened to my compliments on the use of the actors as sperm about to be ejaculated in a "parachute jump" sequence, but then interrupted. "Now, look. Your comments are nice, but a total waste of time. I already know what I did in that movie. It is behind me. What I need from you is 'input' that has nothing to do with me. I am wide-open for other stimuli, for what's happening, what's going on now. Tell me things I don't know. Talk about yourself, your life. Do some of those tales about when you and Joel were living together and how you did all those bad 'little kid' things to get attention. But don't talk about me and my past work. I don't get anything out of that!"

This was one of the most unexpected comments ever from an actor-director-ego. We are all overfamiliar with the insecure talent who says, "Well, enough about me, let's talk about you. How did *you* like my latest film?" Woody doesn't need that. On the other hand, in general, he is so private, so exclusive, so rigid, so untouchable that I wondered how he ever gets any real input from a world he seems to have rejected and only sees from the back of his Rolls.

I WASN'T YOUNG WHEN SEX, drugs and rock 'n' roll began to invade the lives of Americans and so I erred (or stepped wisely) on the side of caution. I had always had friends who loved marijuana but I couldn't stand it. I didn't really know how to smoke anyway, although once the actor Tony Perkins took me into a bathroom at a Diane von Furstenberg party and diligently tried to teach me. Managing, unlike Bill Clinton, finally to inhale, I got the kick from it. But I still didn't like it. I knew I would never do it again. And anything "stronger" scared the hell out of me. But, of course, trying to stay young and keep up with my youthful friends, I'd be lying if I said I never tried a few things.

Cocaine was an exaggerated high and I solved the problem by vowing never to buy any no matter how tempted I might be. So I never did and as a result I was offered damned little of it. But there was one drug I tried in the Hamptons in the seventies with incredible results.

Joel Schumacher and I were houseguests in East Hampton of his mentor, the famous decorator and furniture designer Angelo Donghia. We were invited to a party at the home of a couple named Pines. Joel had worked with Mrs. Pines many years before at Henri Bendel when he was a window designer. Before the first of these parties, Angelo suggested I take a tiny pill, which he called THC. He said, "It's synthetic marijuana and it makes you very happy and is quite harmless." As Angelo was the very soul of dignified decorum for the most part, and older than Joel, I asked myself what harm could there be?

I took the pill. We set out in a Jeep for the Pineses' house and just as we arrived the pill kicked in. I felt very warm and cuddly and terribly amorous. Seated at dinner next to a man I'd known for ages—the film producer Marty Bregman—I came onto him. He must have thought I'd lost my mind. He even said to me at one point, "Liz, no—look, my wife is here at another table." I went right on trying to feel him up and smooch with him and fondle anything I could get my hands on.

I don't quite know how Marty, a well-known producer/advisor to Al Pacino, got rid of me that night at the Pineses' but I guess Joel and Angelo saw that I was making a nuisance of myself and took me off his hands.

I was faintly mortified the next day but thought if I never mentioned the evening again, it would go away and I could pretend it had never happened. And indeed, I haven't ever brought it up with Marty who, when he sees me, always has a faint grin on his face. I know he considers me an absolute fool.

The summer rolled on. Most of my friends in the Hamptons were on everything except the Pony Express. I just rose above it and sometimes asked one of them after a wild night: "Please, write on a blackboard the following—'I will not drive after taking quaaludes.'"

I, however, was relatively pure. I stuck with an occasional drink or the old Southern standby, two aspirin and a Coca-Cola. One night Joel announced that, again, we were going to the Pineses' for dinner. "They just love you, Liz. Can't wait to see you again. They think you are so sexy." I blushed. Then Angelo said, "Here take this little THC and see if you can have some fun." I don't know what possessed me, but I took it. Again, nothing happened. Then, as we arrived at the Pineses', our host was standing on the lawn by one of his giant modern sculptures.

Mrs. Pines had married well. Her husband was a well-known art collector and he was much older than she was. In fact, he was just plain old. I unloaded myself from the Jeep and made a beeline for Mr. Pines. Like Bottom's Ass in Shakespeare, THC made me fall in love with the first thing I saw. I don't recall much else about the night, but Joel swears I said to the genial and ancient Mr. P., "Why, Mr. Pines—I hear you are hung like a horse!" I'm sure I didn't. But I did carry on with him all night and am told he had a simply wonderful and unusual time.

Occasionally when I am spending an evening with a lot of dull dogs, I find myself wondering why THC never really caught on as the drug of choice. It seemed harmless except for its home-wrecking possibilities.

And then there was LSD. I figured if a person as exalted as Cary Grant had tried it, I should. The actress Holland Taylor and I ingested something we'd been told was LSD and decided to stay firmly in my Murray Hill apartment for safety's sake. We were playing records when the walls of the apartment seemed to flap down, exposing us just standing there on the 33rd floor. We were afraid to move from the middle of the room. So we didn't. Our hands and feet seemed to flow like rubber sculpture. I felt that I had become one of those shaped-like-a-hand chairs by Mexican designer Pedro Friedeberg. Holland said her bones were gone and she could not support her body. I rang up Joel. He said, "Drink a cup of tea and take a Valium. You'll be all right. The walls of the apartment are still there, take my word for it."

The next morning when Saint Clair Pugh reported for

work at my apartment, I crept slowly out of bed and literally
crawled to my desk to write the column. I never did that again.
And somehow the experience caused me to lose respect for Cary
Grant. He fell to the bottom of my list of beloveds.

Holland is one of my intellectual actor friends. She won
the Emmy in 1999 for playing a sexy judge in *The Practice*. At
age 56, she brandished her Emmy and said triumphantly,
"Overnight!"

THIS IS AS GOOD A place as any to remember my late friend
the writer Tommy Thompson, a guy who had known and interviewed just about every film star in the spectrum for *Life* magazine before he began doing books and made himself really
famous. (Tommy wrote the best-sellers *Blood and Money*, *Ser-
pentine* and *Celebrity*, as well as introducing America to Doctors DeBakey and Cooley, the Houston heart surgeons. He was
ahead of his time with heart-stopping nonfiction.)

When I was still sharing the apartment with Diane on 38
East 38th Street, we gave a party one fine night to send Tommy
off in style to Los Angeles where he'd decided to live. He arrived at our door carrying what looked like a doctor's case of
pharmaceuticals, including a bottle of liquid amyl nitrate. (This
drug, usually in "poppers," was the drug of choice for the dancing guys and dolls in Studio 54 and other discos.) I had cooked
chicken-fried steak in honor of Tommy's Texas upbringing and
the great games keeper Mary Ann Madden of *New York* magazine pronounced the dish simply awful. "It tastes like burnt
nurse's uniforms," she said. My publishing pal Joe Armstrong
strongly protested. But food hardly mattered. We were playing
music and passing Tommy's case around the room. Some of us
were not partaking, just passing.

I had dressed that night in what I thought was a beguiling
pair of leather pants. (I'd never had a pair before and haven't
since.) I had my eye on a writer-editor named Alex Ben Block,
who would later work for *The Hollywood Reporter* and at Mor-

gan's Creek. Tommy began handing the bottle of liquid amyl ni-
trate around and it was almost impossible to escape its fumes.
But I was firmly avoiding drugs. Anyway, the night wore on.
Some people were stoned.

Alex and I did a little in-house wrestling, which gave me
a terrible whisker burn, and the evening died. After everyone
left, I must have tossed my glamorous leather pants into a corner
of the closet. Mary Ann Madden, who had a late date with an
off-duty cop, sent flowers the next day and a note reading,
"You're all under arrest!" But now I began to smell something
terrible whenever I opened the closet. It had the odor of rotting
apricots. I finally discovered it was my leather pants on which I
had wiped my hands after handling the bottle of amyl nitrate. I
took them with tongs to the garbage.

Tommy came to visit me in Vermont not long before he
died all too young in 1982. I remember him rising up on water
skis out of Lake Champlain behind my boat. He had the body of
an Adonis. Unfortunately, too many of the Adonis persuasion
were soon to die—just as Tommy did—from AIDS.

CHRISTIAN

SOLDIERS

AFTER MY FATHER DIED OF a series of small strokes and emphysema in 1962, I went home to be with my mother for a while. I arrived in Gonzales to find Sloan all laid out in his coffin, embalmed, ready to go, wearing his only good suit and with his hands folded one on top of the other. Under his shirt collar was threaded his favorite bow tie, but it wasn't tied.

I looked down at him and all I could see were my hands. His hands were *my* hands, exactly. Except for the cotton-rubbing calluses, they were mine. It was eerie. I wondered how many other things about me were exactly like him—and I didn't really want to know.

As for the tie, nobody could tie it, not the undertaker and neither of my two brothers, who both tied bow ties all the time. They said they just couldn't. Feeling that I was still his "best boy," I caught up the ends and tied it perfectly, then gave it a fluff to mess it up a little bit. Sloan hated anything that smacked of ready-tied or was "too perfect."

Then I kissed his cold, marbled cheek. There was nothing of the energetic dynamic Sloan in that cheek. Bobby, James and I took the occasion to rail against embalming, the outrageous price of coffins, funeral homes and so forth. James said, "Cremate me. And play 'White Heat' at my funeral." (He now had three wonderful kids and was working for the State of Texas as an auditor.)

Bobby said, "Just burn me up or throw me away." (He now had three wonderful kids and was working as a TV newsman when he was sober.)

Mother went "Tch, tch!" at us. When we said we didn't like funerals, she told us they were important and "you are not supposed to like everything."

My brothers left for Austin and San Antonio, and Mother and I had a fine time together for a week, the best of our lives. And afterwards, she blossomed and became even more of a social butterfly in her little town. She didn't have to worry anymore about riding in the "Come and Take It" parade in her Sesame Club's open convertible and passing her own house, only to find her husband on the porch reading the paper with his back to the street. His iconoclastic antisocial ways had been so embarrassing. She put on a good show of grieving, but I could tell she was relieved not to have to be cooking anymore. "He had gotten so he woke me up a half an hour earlier every day asking for breakfast. First at 7:30, then 7:00, then 6:30, then 6:00! I drew the line at 6:00!" I pointed out that she could have told him to go chase himself, make his own breakfast, go down to the Bus Stop. She looked at me as if I were nuts. Sometimes she'd put on an act and say how much she missed him. "I miss his guidance," she'd say.

"Oh, how pretty," I'd rejoin. "I guess you miss his gambling away every penny he ever made, never buying you a house, leaving you nothing and being demanding and impossible?"

She'd just smile. "We had a wonderful love affair," she said, "and we had you children."

My mother had a perfectly fine second-act life as a widow. She was a joy to behold. She cracked jokes. She threatened people in the most casual way when they couldn't give her dough for her library.

Then, in 1979 my pal Howard Rosenman was down in Shiner, Texas, producing the film *Resurrection* with Ellen

Burstyn. He called to say he was having a great time, only a few miles from Gonzales. I urged him to go see my mother and so, soon he was in Gonzales eating supper with her once a week. I went down to visit while he was there and I noticed a certain frisson of exotica at the dinner table. Good china, best silver, fried chicken, the works. Mother was wearing her best bib and tucker. Howard was carrying on, lecturing about religion, the meaning of his film, how he'd served in the Six-Day War, his family in Israel and on and on.

After he left, she said, "I need to have a talk with you." So we settled down in the parlor under the reproduction of the *Christ Child* by Raphael and she opened up. "Now I know you love Howard and so I want you to seriously talk to him about becoming a Christian."

I looked at her. "Mother, Howard has his own religion. He isn't an Orthodox Jew, but he *is* a very devout Jew. His family is Orthodox. I can't ask him to give up his religion for yours."

She said, "Yes, you must. The Bible says you must be evangelical and win souls to Christ. And he is ready to surrender to Jesus. I just know he is."

"How do you know this?" I asked.

She said, "Why, he talks so knowledgeably about the Holy Land. He said to me the other night that you can just feel the spirit of the Christ in Jerusalem. He is ready, I tell you."

We argued for several days and I began to get it. She was totally infatuated with Howard. He paid attention to her. He was big and curly-headed and sexy. And he was intellectually knowledgeable and liked a good religious conversation or argument. He was also an expert on Israel. I said to her, finally, in exasperation, "Figure it out for me, Mother. Why is it so important for Howard to become a Christian?"

She said, "Because, I want to see him again in heaven."

I was bowled over. I kept trying to tell her I wasn't the evangelical type. I couldn't ask this of Howard without embarrassing him and me. I just didn't have the courage. She kept insisting. Finally, I saw Howard in New York. "Howard, you've

got to help me. My mother wants you to become a Christian."
He threw back his head and howled.

When I told him that I thought she had a big crush on him
and wanted to see him in heaven, he fell silent. He said, "Maybe
you could just tell her you asked me and I converted if it would
make her happy and she'd have peace of mind about it. Bless her
heart; she is such a wonderful woman. I just love her."

I said we were skating on thin ice here. I wasn't much of
a Christian myself. But I didn't want to tell a lie about something so serious to her. My mother asked me to bring Howard to
Jesus until she died. I would say I had broached the subject.
She'd nod: "He is considering it. He is taking it seriously. I
know. I know. He is just on the verge."

She died in 1987 when she was almost ninety-five, sitting
down on her living room couch to watch her soap, *As the World
Turns,* and play a game of solitaire. She'd just had her hair done
because she was expecting James to visit her. A massive stroke
instantly removed all her worries. And she looked fabulous.

I called Howard to say she was gone. This time I didn't
speak of his "conversion," but he said, "I hope she went knowing I'm still considering it. I'd like to see her again, too."

PART

SIX

a Memoir

PART

SIX

WHAT'S IN

THE *DAILY NEWS*?

(I'LL TELL YA WHAT'S

IN THE *DAILY NEWS**)

IN LONG ISLAND'S HAMPTONS OF the sixties and seventies, we were much given to games and one I remember
was "Overheard." On a piece of paper you wrote what you
wished people would say about you. These were collected, read
aloud anonymously, while various smart alecs guessed the name
of the wisher. One of mine was typically idiotic: "There goes the
happiest married Pulitzer prize–winner in the world!"

My close friends invariably "got my number," so all
chortled with glee and said, "Lizzie! Lizzie! Of course." I was
mortified. And I was stumped as well. I had very little luck being
either happily married or even long connected to a significant
other. And the Pulitzer was out of the question.

I decided maybe I should set my sights a bit lower. I was
earning about $65,000 a year freelancing for magazines, work-
ing my ass off, being an editor for *Cosmo*, but I remained only a
mid-level byline despite having sparkled occasionally. I had
worked diligently for Clay Felker's original *New York* magazine
when it was folded into the old *Herald Tribune* newspaper. I

* Guys and Dolls, *by Frank Loesser.*

wrote for Clay the very first article ever on the advent in New York City of something unusual called "the discotheque." And I had analyzed the scandalous gossip columnist Alex Freeman of *The National Enquirer*. (This man had been the Matt Drudge of the sixties.) I'd had bylines right along with the best of them, but I wasn't famous. I suppose I was happy enough. I loved my little circle of friends and my life on Long Island on what were mostly happy weekends. (And looking back, later, I realized that even the unhappy weekends were invariably only the result of too much alcohol, or recreational drugs. Ah, the people who would be CEOs and celebrating happy anniversaries and with money in the bank if only they'd never heard of booze and stimulants.)

My friend Rex Reed was pushing the idea that his newspaper, the tabloid New York *Daily News*, should hire me to do a gossip column. "They don't really have anybody except Aileen Mehle—Suzy, that is—and she mostly sticks with society. So I showed the editor, Mike O'Neill, these great little columns you've been writing for the *Palm Beach Social Pictorial*. He likes them. He wants to talk to you."

I laughed it off. I had observed that the three major columnists of the *Daily News*—Ed Sullivan, Danton Walker and Bob Sylvester—were dying out. No one had replaced them. But I had no real idea that my type of weekly Palm Beach column, which I wrote strictly for fun and because I loved the *Pictorial*'s owners, would work in New York. I always dragged my feet when confronted with any change or challenge. But finally I kicked myself and went to see the genial Mr. O'Neill. It was now 1974. I actually said to him: "I don't believe people are interested in gossip anymore. It's something that has become passé. The great ones—Winchell, Kilgallen—are all dead and the gossip column's time has passed into history." (You can see why I was never asked to enter the crystal ball business.) O'Neill said, "You may be right."

Two years passed. Then O'Neill called again. "Come back and see me. We want to kick around the gossip idea." By now he knew me pretty well. I had started ghostwriting in partnership—Robin Adams Sloan's "The Gossip Column"—a syndicated pillar of questions and answers. O'Neill knew of my participation when the *News* bought the column from the syndicate. "Liz, we think you can now do something spectacular under your own byline."

Again I demurred. But he insisted. And I started thinking. I could use this economic sinecure, this ongoing job as a columnist, this prestige and this power. I began to dream up names to call such a mythical column, jotting down corny stuff like "Gotham City"..."City Lights"..."This Is the Week That Is," etc. I was introduced one day to *Daily News* editor, Sheward Hagerty and he casually showed me a column mock-up. "Well, what do you think about this idea?"

He was holding a beautiful block of dark typeface. At the top in bold print were the words **LIZ SMITH.** I was sincerely shocked. I'd never thought of such a thing. All the old greats, even Winchell and Kilgallen and Earl Wilson, had their bylines but their columns had other titles like "The Voice of Broadway" or "It Happened Last Night."

I was bedazzled. I kissed *Cosmo* and the darling Helen Gurley Brown good-bye in preparation for my new life as a gossip columnist. I signed a contract with the *Daily News* guaranteeing me something like the same dough I was already making. I couldn't believe this was happening to me. I wasn't sure I could do it. I had no mechanism set up for it, no army of tipsters, press agents or feeders in place. I didn't recall "how" it was done exactly, although I had been flirting with the idea for much of my life. And had ghosted Cholly Knickerbocker for five years.

The *Daily News* hired me as outside talent—on contract. I would not belong to the newspaper guild and they wouldn't pay medical or retirement. One thing I did was to move from my town house apartment at 38 East 38th Street to a brand-new building three blocks away. It had just gone up at 38th and Third. They called it the Murray Hill Mews, but it has nothing in common with any mews I've ever seen. It boasted twenty-four-hour doormen and concierge service. So I moved in and my new life began. Out my windows I had a splendid view of the Empire State Building, and to the south I could see the World Trade Center and a fraction of the East River.

The Liz Smith column began to appear on February 16th, 1976, back on page 22 in the paper. Suzy was, for instance, up on page six. To my heartbreak there was an error in an early column. I had sent through an opening quote by one of my favorites— La Rochefoucauld. Someone in editing had "corrected" and misspelled it.* So it wasn't my fault. But I discovered that indeed it didn't matter. You could blame copy editors and whoever, but it was still under your byline. It was *your* fault! The slip between cup and lip of getting a gossip column of ninety lines into print with no typos, no misspellings and no errors was about to become the nemesis of my life. And I discovered that every column made somebody mad; even the most benign item might turn around and bite you. Soon after, I formulated my theory that writing a gossip column is like riding a Chinese tiger. You can never dismount.

The column was only a few months old when I received a gruff call from the famed movie producer Sam Spiegel, the man who had brought *On the Waterfront* and *Lawrence of Arabia* to the screen. He was a special pal of mine and wed to the vivacious Betty Spiegel, a woman he would seldom let enter his Park Avenue apartment because he didn't like her wild party ways. Sam said he feared Betty or her friends might destroy one of his objets d'art. "So we don't live together." But he liked being married; it kept the other women he was seeing from trying to marry him.

"What in hell is your wonderful column doing buried back in the ass end of the paper?" he yelled at me. I said I was glad to be there at all and I had no say in its position. "Well, I might have something to say," grumped Sam. He claimed he was calling the editor to complain. I had several thrilling shows

*To make matters worse, The New Yorker selected the La Rochefoucauld error to make a comment saying that I would be even better if I knew how to spell. Boy, did that hurt my feelings! My first mention in The New Yorker and I was the butt of the joke.

of support like this. The great Rod Serling telephoned. "Who are you? Where have you been all my life? Your column is the most refreshing thing." These were welcome respites from the almost literal brickbats that afflict any daily writer of a column. I never knew if Spiegel called or not, but about four months after it began, the *News* moved me up to page 20, then page 8, 7, and 6. Suzy was placed slightly behind me.

Since she had never spoken to me again from the day I was hired, this was sweet—I guess. I didn't wish her ill; I actually admired her and always had. And I couldn't blame her for not wishing me well.

When he had first talked of hiring me, I had asked Mike O'Neill what this would mean for Aileen. He said, "Oh well, we gave her every chance to write about entertainment and she is only interested in the jet set, Europe and high society. So you can't blame us for wanting something else." (As it turned out, Suzy did blame them and years later when then publisher Jim Hoge forgot to note that her contract was up, she whizzed off to the *New York Post*. And from there, in time, she went to *W*.)

I know it's hard to keep up with all this shit. Some of us ink-stained wretches have been all over the map for years. For instance, I have written for the *New York Journal American*, *The Herald Tribune*, the melded *World Journal Tribune*, the *Daily News, New York Newsday, Newsday* and the *New York Post*. And I have freelanced and had a byline in *The New York Times*. Three of these newspapers and *The New York Mirror* no longer exist and we are all just lucky that we even have three newspapers still left in New York City as I write this.

And so began my saga at the New York *Daily News*, or what I began to call "Twenty Years Before the Masthead." Actually, I would work there for nineteen years, but as we say when discussing the ages of movie stars—"Who's counting?"

MAGIC XX

IN 1977 I BECAME FRIENDS with a person I had long admired from afar. She'd been on the front page of *The New York Times* twice, in its magazine once, been the subject of a CBS documentary and was about to appear as a profile in *The New Yorker*. She was an archaeologist who had, on the day man first walked on the moon, discovered the long-lost Temple of Aphrodite on the coast of Turkey. In her junior year abroad, she'd found a section of the lost Ancient Via Cassia between Orvieto and Florence in Italy and soon after, on Samothrace, she had found the marble base of the Winged Victory, or Nike, that stands at the top of the stairs in the Louvre in Paris. She had already written that the Metropolitan Museum's famous, popular "Etruscan warriors" were fakes. And this maverick had "excavated" with dynamite. She came from two powerful family backgrounds and lived in Brooklyn Heights. Her telephone number was actually MAGIC XX. And, in a time when *Charlie's Angels* was all the rage, she didn't have a clue who Farrah Fawcett-Majors was.

I was dining at the home of an anthropologist, Miriam Slater, when I heard a great entrance commotion on the stair. I looked up to see a blonde, athletic and slim woman in a chic dress, speaking in an animated manner. Her intelligent face had a simian cast, as if she were some glamorized character from *Planet of the Apes.* She was explaining why she was late.

My life was humming along just fine at the time, but I did occasionally stop and ask myself: "Is this all there is—gossip, show biz, limitless entertainment and trivia?" So I was enjoying a night out in the company of people who discussed history, art and scientific discovery instead of movie grosses, ratings and gossip. I was immediately taken with the dramatic personae of Iris Love—a Givenchy-clad scientist with a name befitting a movie star. Dinner was a wildly entertaining affair with Iris and my hostess arguing about the merits of archaeology vs. anthropology. Miriam said the latter was foremost, the study of mankind. Iris said the former was more important, studying the creations of man.

The evening ended with Iris taking off for Bali and me going home to study up on her accomplishments. She'd taken exception to standard authorities, who had said the famed Temple of Aphrodite in Asia Minor had never been located at Knidos, Turkey. She won the right to excavate there, spent her own money on the effort and, using a small charge of dynamite, cracked a stone as big as a garage off of the actual foundation of the Temple, proving she was right. Here had stood the larger than life-sized nude cult statue of the goddess of love by Praxiteles. Iris went on to discover what she insists is the head of the Aphrodite, which had been carted off to the British Museum. She was a gadfly, forever jousting with the Turkish government, museum establishments or the academic world.

I guess I had a secret yearning and need for a more intellectual and cultured kind of inner life that drew me so strongly to Iris. Many weeks later, I used the MAGIC XX phone number and went to Brooklyn Heights to meet her aunt and uncle, the Freeman Loves, with whom she lived when in the U.S. She'd been something of a prodigy, born into New York families fractured along lines of gentile and Jewish intermarriage. Her mother, Audrey, was a Guggenheim heir. Her father, C. Ruxton

Love, was a haut WASP whose family settled in Brooklyn during the Revolution. The twain had met and produced the rebellious Iris, who was hazed when she attended the Madeira School. She was told by classmates that she was Jewish. As she'd been christened in the Episcopal Church, she didn't know what they were talking about. At school break, she asked her father, "Am I Jewish?" He said, "Never mention that to me again." She asked her sister Noel, "Are we Jewish?" Noel rejoined, "Well, *you* are—what the hell do you think the Guggenheims were?" Iris then confronted her Guggenheim grandmother, who smiled. "So you found out."

I really liked this mixed-up person who had grown up with the Metropolitan Museum as her baby-sitter. I couldn't get enough of her adventures, her tales of derring-do, her prodigious plans for the future and her brilliant and engaging intellect. She rose every morning convinced she could move the world if only she had a lever. She retired every night amazed at how little she'd done. Iris had been honored by the Italian, Greek and Turkish governments. She was forever writing, lecturing, taking photographs and traveling. And she was very social; she never missed a party, an opening, any occasion. She loved celebrations, putting on costumes, noting birthdays and dancing to almost anyone's tune.

Iris began to spend more time in my apartment-office than she did in Brooklyn Heights. It was more convenient to Manhattan occasions and she loved the hustle and bustle of my frenetic work-life. Finally, deep friendship and romance won out over common sense and I invited her to move in and stay when she wasn't out of the country. In this manner, I inherited her two dachshunds, Phryne and Carlino, who were great characters in themselves. When we could find dog-sitters, Iris and I often traveled together. I took several marvelous yacht tours with her multitude of rich Greek friends. I began to call members of the Goulandris, Varides, Zoulas and Coumantaras families by their first names. I traveled so much in Greece and Italy as her pupil that I felt I had a Ph.D. in the classics. At one point, Iris took a group of us to the very top of the Parthenon. She sim-

ply spoke to the director, who took us up for a view seen only
by a handful of Greek workmen, the sculptor Phidias and the
architects Ictinus and Callicrates. Because of Iris, I've been to
restoration rooms in Zürich and Geneva and seen miracles happen as craftsmen put back together what time had sundered. I've
seen treasures unknown to the public in the basement of the
Athens National Museum. And once, on a trip that would have
tried the nerves of any pilgrim, Iris drove me into the wilds of
Arcadia to the rare, all but deserted Temple of Apollo Bassae.
"Most people think they've seen Greece if they see the
Parthenon. This was its contemporary, discovered by a Frenchman in the 1700s."

The Pulitzer prize-winning *Wall Street Journal* writer
Manuela von Holterhof once bet Iris and me we could not hit the
highlights of the Louvre for her in only sixty minutes. She timed
our rush past the *Mona Lisa*, the Nike and the Venus de Milo for
a national magazine. This was stressful to Iris who could spend
sixty minutes looking again at the first displayed sculpture in the
Greek and Roman wing, even though she'd been examining it
for years.

One big mistake many of us made with Iris was trying to
bring her into the twentieth century. We should have known better from something in her *New Yorker* profile. It noted that
above the desk in her Vermont house was a copy of a letter to
the IRS. "Once again, circumstances beyond my control have
prevented my being able to file my taxes."

My office became a separate headquarters for what we
called "Iris business." When she was traveling, as she usually
was, I paid her bills, handled her mail, social calendar, clip-
pings, photos, her archaeological library and her burgeoning
family of dogs. I had learned something I didn't really care to
know—that dog responsibility centers on the alimentary canal.
Dogs must be fed, natural events must then either be arranged
for or picked up after, vets must be seen, animals transported
and on and on.

I sometimes felt like the Indian god Vishnu. I had many
hands—one writing the column, another doing live television

for WNBC TV, another looking after "Iris business," another worrying about the dogs in what became The Dachsmith–Love Kennels of Vermont. I simply didn't want all of that responsibility on top of my own rather demanding career. Iris, insatiable for adventure, would sometimes disappear for weeks on end. Once she took off for China and there was silence for five weeks. She phoned then from Chungking to say she might stay on and excavate more of the large warriors of Xi'an. I pointed out there'd be no glory in that for an American. She conceded I was right, but before leaving China, she translated all the new Shaanxi Museum signs into English to the delight of her Chinese hosts. She traveled extensively with her good friend Steve Ross, the head of Warner's, and took both Barbra Streisand and Faye Dunaway on guided tours of the Greek islands and Turkey.

I would become irritated and irascible at the problems she left behind for me to solve, but then, I had heard the "poor little rich girl" stories of Iris Love's childhood and it was this child who had touched my heart. Iris always loved everything about the idea of "family"— anybody's family. She was related to a clutch of Loves, but had been raised only with her older sister in a Park Avenue apartment where she saw Mummy and Daddy briefly at night as they dressed to go out. She never ate at the table with them except on holidays and her childhood had been spent in the company of Irish maids, German cooks and her English nanny. This wasn't really pathetic, but the photographs of Iris as a charming, wistful, towheaded child always got to me. I desperately wanted to take care of her and make it all up to her and I often said I didn't need to have children, for I had Iris.

So I had lovely times with Iris, who might have been a headache, but literally never was a bore to me. Finally, we branched out into bigger, then into separate apartments, but somehow Iris and the dogs always managed to invade my space. I enjoyed her house in Vermont with its view of Mt. Abraham and all the attendant joys of a state that reminded me of America in the twenties. Iris then decided to become a dachshund breeder—totally succeeding by producing at least three Westminster champions, Tyche, Ajax and Diomedes, each of whom became the "number one dachshund in America." I was proud and gratified by these honors. And I loved the dogs, but I couldn't handle it all. After fifteen years of close companionship, I convinced Iris to take over the dogs on her own and to move somewhere far enough away from me that I would not be running her life. We have remained close and still take trips together. In 1998, Iris took a gang of us to see the bronze Warriors of Riace in Calabria. She wore many amulets and charms against the bad luck sometimes attributed to these massive Greek-made beauties who were fished out of the sea.

I had learned not to be too skeptical of Iris's Mediterranean superstitions and auguries against the evil eye. I still keep worry beads on my desk and wear the *malocchio* against the evil eye and sometimes I find myself using the Greek five-fingered open palm to insult insane drivers.

Nothing beats Iris for rousing adventure. Recently we were lunching. I cut off one of her long tales and said, "Don't begin the story back when they invented language. Get to the bottom line." Iris continued to take her time with long pauses. I realized that knowing her for almost twenty years, much never changes.

She told me that day she believes she knows where the head of the Winged Victory, the Nike of Samothrace, may be found. My jaw dropped! Iris went on, "Let's plan to go to the Mediterranean some summer soon and I'll show you where the head is." So there is always another MAGIC XX adventure on the horizon and even though I can already envision going bankrupt, schlepping Iris's bags and cameras and standing around waiting for her endlessly, I probably won't be able to resist.

THE TRUMAN

SHOW

SOUTHAMPTON ONCE HAD A GREAT grocery store on Main Street called Herbert's. I often ran into Truman Capote there and one day he called to me across the aisles. "Liz, say hello to the man on your left—the one holding that incredibly vulgar big sausage." I turned and Bill Paley was smiling at me. The founder of CBS did indeed have a huge salami in his hand. Truman thought this juxtaposition was just adorable. Maybe Mr. Paley did, too. We shook hands and even after he fell out with Truman later, Mr. Paley always sought me out at parties, cuddled me up under his arm when I sat near him and acted as if he liked me. (I think it was more a case of "When I'm Not Near the Girl I Love, I Love the Girl I'm Near." But there was no doubting that the legendary Mr. Paley had his charms and plenty of S.A.*)

Truman was already super-famous by the time I met him in the seventies in the Hamptons. In Texas, I had been awed by the young genius who had produced *Other Voices, Other Rooms* and then publicized himself to fame with his own provocative

*sex appeal

photo in a "come hither" pose. He'd had his big Hollywood fling with the John Huston movie *Beat the Devil*, starring Jennifer Jones and Humphrey Bogart. He had risen socially by giving his famous black-and-white ball in honor of Kay Graham of *The Washington Post*. He had already written *In Cold Blood*, which made real-life murderous drama into a new kind of journalism. Truman was also famous for being famous, for being a character, an audacious, outspoken, campy homosexual who had gained social acceptance in a straight world.

At some point in my freelance career, I asked Truman to give me an interview for a piece I wanted to write on Jackie Kennedy and invited him to come lunch with me at Lee Bailey's house on Sagg Pond. I'd made chili. Truman drove up in his convertible with a big Isadora Duncan–type scarf flying in the breeze. But he didn't like the saltines I served with my chili. He said, slyly, "I do see some lovely little Carr's Water Biscuits peeping out of the cupboard. May I have those?" Truman was very observant.

The interview was a flop because Truman didn't want to talk about Jackie. He was besotted and smitten with her sister, Lee Radziwill. He'd gone so far as to secure a starring role for her as "Laura" in a David Susskind–produced TV drama of the movie classic. Truman wrote the teleplay on the condition that his Lee would star. (It was old-fashioned Hollywood-writer blackmail at its best.)

While I tried to steer him to Jackie, Truman told me how fragile, ethereal, lovely, smart, beautiful and witty Lee was. "Compared to Lee," he said, "Jackie is just a cow." Well, okay, I filed that away, but I couldn't get Truman off of Lee and onto Jackie.

Truman decided to befriend me. He was very nice to me but I feared he thought I was gullible. (I often felt that way around him, for he had a quicksilver mind and tongue.) But I had something he wanted: popular access in the media to newspapers, magazines and TV shows. So he thought nothing of using me as a conduit to get out whatever he felt might accomplish this or that. And he was full of gossip—mercy, was he ever full of it! The only problem was to differentiate between his many imaginative lies, and the truth. (I did think that he wrote in an almost mythic manner about people and as in most history, the myth becomes the reality, so maybe his writing in this imaginative romanticized way didn't matter in the end. It's the myth people remember.)

I was later present at the creation of Truman's downfall. In 1975 he published a section of his long-awaited book *Answered Prayers* in *Esquire* magazine. It created a social firestorm, in Manhattan at least. "La Côte Basque," as the story was called, contained thinly disguised real people doing and saying embarrassing things. Some of these people were hardly disguised at all. William Paley, a man with the most devastating social ambitions, certainly recognized himself as the person "with the mouth-watering cock," and others such as Gloria Vanderbilt, Anne Woodward and Slim Keith recognized themselves as well. Some of them had been Truman's nearest, dearest, most intimate friends. The intimacy was over the minute the printing presses turned.

People in New York couldn't talk about anything but how Truman had shot himself in the foot and whether what he wrote constituted genius, à la Marcel Proust, or just plain betrayal, à la *The National Enquirer*. Truman was sure he had written social history of literary import and he thought the fuss would blow over. But no—Babe Paley, Bill Paley, Gloria Vanderbilt, Slim Keith and many others stopped speaking to him. Only C-Z Guest, his longtime socialite pal, stayed the course, saying, "Truman is a writer. Writers write what they know. These people knew Truman was a writer when they began telling him all their most deadly secrets."

But C-Z couldn't talk the Paleys into not being angry with Truman and I didn't have any luck either, though I approached Gloria Vanderbilt's husband, Wyatt Cooper, and went directly to Slim Keith to beg her to reconsider. No dice!

Truman had gone to Hollywood to escape the tempest. He was staying with Johnny Carson's ex, Joanne. I flew out to interview him for a *New York* magazine piece on the controversy. Truman was indignant. He couldn't see that he'd done anything wrong. "Hadn't these people ever heard of a-r-t?" He was an artist. They were the paint on his canvas. And he wouldn't believe me when I told him people were up in arms, finished with him. "What did Diana Vreeland say?" he asked of the *Vogue* high priestess. I said I didn't know. So Truman called her in my presence from the El Padrino bar of the Beverly Wilshire. She fended him off with a typical switch-play detour.

"Oh, Truman, you do write so fetchingly about the little tiny vegetables served by the rich!"

Truman handed me the phone, triumphant and vindicated. I wrote my piece for the February 9, 1976, issue of *New York* magazine. The article became in itself something of a classic, having as it did a fabulous Edward Sorel drawing of Truman as a bulldog biting the wealthy bejeweled hand that had been feeding him.

After that everything went downhill for my friend Truman. He began to drink and drug and I was alarmed at his physical condition. He started going every night to Studio 54 with the Andy Warhol crowd and he'd dance around in an old porkpie hat like some demented teenager, roaring with delight every time the mechanized man in the moon raised the Studio's coke spoon to its nose.

One night the writer John Berendt* and I were at Truman's United Nations Plaza apartment high above the East River. We were admiring his collection of decorative snakes in the living room when in came Truman carrying a large fishbowl full of white powder. He sat it down in front of us and announced, "This is the world's purest, best cocaine. You have never had anything like this before." Our mouths hung open, for if it indeed *was* cocaine, it was about $35,000 worth. Then, as suddenly as he'd offered it, Truman snatched it up and marched away with it, saying, "No, it's too good for the likes of you."

This was drug drama at its worst and John and I were

Later to write the astonishing long-lived best-seller Midnight in the Garden of Good and Evil.

pretty worried about Truman. But soon Truman had me on the phone in the down-to-earth realism of his despair. Gore Vidal was suing him for libel for having repeated an old chestnut of a story about how Bobby Kennedy had Gore thrown out of the White House for being too familiar with Jackie Kennedy. Truman wailed, "Why is Gore doing this to me? He just wants to destroy me. Everybody has known this story since before JFK was killed. Everybody has repeated it. And it's true; it happened. But now Gore wants enormous damages from me and I haven't got any money. And I have lost the manuscript for *Answered Prayers*. What will I do?" (Rumor had it that: (1) Truman had never really written any more of this book; and (2) the manuscript had been stolen from him by a jealous lover who was a carpenter or plumber or some type of "rough trade.")

TRUMAN ANSWERED HIS OWN QUESTION. He would be okay if he could only convince Lee Radziwill to testify in his behalf that the Gore-Bobby incident *had* ACTUALLY HAPPENED. But he hadn't been able to get Lee on the phone. (I assumed she was now one of the social set who had stepped over the line at the Alamo of "La Côte Basque.")

Truman then had a brilliant idea. I should call his friend Lee and convince her to testify for him. "Me? I haven't any clout with Lee. I hardly know her. I spent one evening at dinner with her once in North Africa. I don't think I am her cup of tea."

But Truman was insistent. "She'll speak to you. She's afraid of you. Please, please, please."

So I found myself calling Lee and when she got on the phone I explained Truman's pathetic predicament and how he needed her help. And I cited his great love for her and their long, deep friendship. Lee ignored that and said softly, in her characteristic breathy manner, "But I don't want to be involved." Oh yes, the hottest places in hell are supposed to be reserved for those who don't want to be involved. So I argued. Lee was adamant; she wouldn't testify for Truman. She wouldn't call him. And then she delivered the *coup de grace.* "What does it matter, Liz? What does it matter—after all, they're just a couple of fags."

I don't know what I said, but I hung up dumbfounded. This was a woman Truman had loved so dearly; a woman I felt he secretly wanted to be. She was his ideal. He had done so much to try to make an acting career for her. Finally I told Truman to forget it. "Lee won't testify." Like some prosecuting avenger, Truman insisted I tell him everything Lee said. I refused at first. But he wouldn't let me alone, so finally I delivered the low blow.

I was sorry ever after, because Truman really disintegrated then. He went on the Stanley Siegel TV show so drugged out and demented that they had to take the camera off of him and hustle him out of the studio. And he took his revenge on Lee. He went on TV and radio and told a very nasty story of her trying to have a love affair with a famous married man who was a devout Catholic. According to Truman, she asked the man for religious instruction while she set out to seduce him.

It was almost a relief weeks later when Truman went back to L.A. I could hardly cope with his downhill slide. He had called Mr. Paley and asked him if he had really read the *Esquire* piece and couldn't they get together as old friends to talk about it? Mr. Paley said to him, "Truman, my wife is dying of cancer in the other room and I am too busy to talk to you." Truman had worshipped the Paleys and he'd thought because Bill told him everything man to man, that it was okay for Truman to unilaterally decide when it was all right to print such confidences. After this, Truman left New York again for L.A. He died of natural causes in the home of Mrs. Carson in August 1984.

On the heels of his death I suddenly remembered *Laura.* The plot of this movie concerned a rather cold and glacial young woman, deeply enmeshed in the superficial life of Manhattan. She is worshipped by a possessive, adoring writer of great influence, played by Clifton Webb as a not too thinly disguised homosexual. The writer had championed Laura, defended her and had "made" her success. She was his ideal woman though she could not return his love.

I guess I'm just a sentimental fool but I always felt Truman died of a broken heart.

TO SIR,

WITH LOVE

IN 1976, *NETWORK* BECAME THE landmark prescient film where TV news is sullied forever after by Faye Dunaway's success when she takes over the nightly network news, adding astrologists and gossip columnists. The Paddy Chayefsky–Sidney Lumet film resonated but it took Great Britain's David Frost to make it all become a reality. I knew David because he'd been the ongoing romantic interest of my onetime Cholly secretary Caroline.

Nobody had seen the likes of David's particular brand of satire before 1963 when he imported his hot hit *That Was the Week That Was* to the U.S. It had grown too controversial for the BBC and would become, in America, the high I.Q. inspiration for the eventual *Saturday Night Live*. When David's show first found itself on the air, Steve Allen did a warm-up for it. Someone asked, "Do they get this show in Des Moines?" Allen answered: "They *see* this show in Des Moines, but they don't *get* it!"

Frost made TV history making fun of presidential candidates, moralists and hypocrites. He went on later to seriously interview in-depth almost every single famous person of our times, saying that only General DeGaulle had stiffed him. "He promised me an interview on the third morning when he rose up again, but he never turned up."

Frost's biggest moment came when he famously paid Richard Nixon $600,000 to talk to him exclusively after Watergate. Criticized for "checkbook journalism," David asked Nixon all the toughest questions, caused him to apologize to the American people, scooped *The New York Times* and left an enduring record of the 37th president in his disgrace. Without such "checkbook journalism," Nixon might never have spoken openly of Watergate, which was the news event of the decade, and we'd be left with only Nixon revisionism.

Now it was 1978, soon after my "overnight" success as a gossip columnist for the *Daily News*. David was back in New York to do *Headliners with David Frost* as an NBC summer replacement. He invited me to breakfast at the Plaza and I couldn't imagine why. I thought perhaps he had news to impart on Caroline.

"I want to make you a star!" said David, stirring his expensive scrambled eggs. "Let's just get this decided. You'll say yes. Once you agree, we can stop talking business and only talk about sex." I could hardly believe David thought I might succeed on-air as a purveyor of TV gossip. Sure, Winchell had tried it during TV's infancy, but it hadn't caught on.

David described the first show. Kelly Garrett would sing our opening song, we'd have some variety performers, show biz stars and then David would ask some embarrassing questions of a news heavyweight like Richard Helms of the CIA. Midpoint, Liz would do two minutes of gossip. And so it came to pass. David Frost was the most benign of producers. He never worried and refused to let me be nervous. I came up with deathless junk for the show. Our first effort featured a young actor who danced in a white suit. He had just made a movie called *Saturday Night Fever*. We didn't know we were making history, giving the world John Travolta.

Sir David Frost has written over seventeen books, produced seven movies, had endless TV shows of every stripe and is one of the wittiest and most versatile talkers of the twentieth century. (Make that "of the twenty-first century also.") He was recently saluted by the Museum of Television and Radio, and I was in the audience asking questions. And he was the first person to put my gossip on television. A very great man in my book! Although purists think he has a lot to answer for.

BEFORE MY REAL TV CAREER began, back in the sixties and seventies, I was flattered to be asked to guest on the David Susskind TV show, along with others like the outrageous golden Greek playboy-writer Taki Theodoracopoulos or the *Ad Age* columnist-novelist James Brady. Susskind would get us in a semicircle and go "tch-tch" because we were all gossips and he liked to affect a grand demeanor. We made him look almost statesmanlike.

One day we were on with David's super-guest Joyce Haber, dish queen of the *L.A. Times*. Joyce wrote snobbishly about Hollywood's "A" list and "B" list. She became so attached to the "society" part of movie royalty that she forgot to cover the lowlifes of the movies. She had a lot of power and David was kowtowing to her.

The show had an associate producer, Gloria Rabinowitz, who stood offstage under the cameras, watching us. Taki, Brady and I were having a high old time discussing Elizabeth Taylor and Frank Sinatra. We were speculating. Had they ever really had a love affair as some people said? We rambled on. It was juicy.

David, afraid he was ignoring Joyce, suddenly interrupted and began asking her to describe the Hollywood "A" list. Joyce spoke in plummy tones, "Well, there's Greg and Veronique Peck, then there's Anne and Kirk—Douglas, you know. And there's Bob Stack and his wife and, of course, there are the Armand Deutsches."

I knew who the Deutsches were. Mr. Deutsche, a producer, had been the little boy Loeb and Leopold were actually supposed to kidnap, torture and murder in Chicago instead of

Bobby Franks, who became their victim. The Deutsches had money. They were friends of Nancy and Ronnie Reagan. And Joyce was impressed with them. She talked on and on about them.

We came to a taping break, then from under the camera and sound boom there came rushing at us, like a crazed virago, producer Rabinowitz. She hissed at David, "Fuck the Armand Deutsches!! Just fuck them! Get back to Elizabeth Taylor and Frank Sinatra! Are you people crazy? Who wants to hear about the Armand Deutsches?"

And that is one of my favorite moments in the history of TV.

YEARS LATER IN A BIG party at the Metropolitan Museum, Jerome Zipkin—a friend to the Reagans and me, but considered a pompous ass and a fiend by many—took my arm. He said, "I want to introduce you to the Armand Deutsches." I began to laugh and told him my Susskind story. He marched me right up to the Deutsches and ordered, "Now tell them the story." I did, reluctantly. I'm glad to say they turned out to have a sense of humor and "Fuck the Armand Deutsches" went into the gossip slang lexicon.

HOW I REALLY

GOT INTO TV

AND THE CHARITY

RAT RACE

EVERYBODY IN THE WORLD YEARNS to be on television. Right? Well, not exactly. I was pretty cavalier after my brief stint for David Frost, when a nice guy from WNBC kept calling, begging me to come do gossip on the local news. Desperately busy with the newspaper column, I put Bob David off.

Then, in 1978 a newspaper strike hit and the *Daily News*, hoping to keep itself visible, *ordered* me to go on local TV and give out dollops of my column. Although strikebound in New York, I still had to write a full ninety lines every day for syndication across the U.S.

So, I went to WNBC in a kind of "command performance" and there I would stay, eventually on the groundbreaking hit *Live at Five*, for eleven years. In fact, it was TV, not the column, that turned me into an NYC household word and the move burnished and enriched the column immeasurably.

For over a decade, I had a really charmed experience almost every day. There was nothing not to like in going each afternoon to the most glamorous spot in New York—Rockefeller Center. I'd go to the sixth-floor studio, have hair and makeup, stroll on the set, show off, grandstand, mimic, tell jokes and offer bits of trivia. A man named Earl Ubell had dreamed up the chatty, informal, funfest that would be *Live at Five* and a young genius named Ron Kershaw (a sports fanatic much like Roone Arledge of ABC) took the ball and ran with it. After Ron came a succession of spirited, talented news directors—Jerry Nachman, Mark Monsky, Norman Fine, Terry Baker. All of them bent over backwards to keep me happy.

It had been suggested that I might want to study with the NBC vocal coach to get rid of my Texas accent. But Kershaw just snorted: "No way. Keep away from that woman. She'll ruin your natural ways." I was perfectly willing to be improved, but it wasn't in the cards. I wrote my own scripts, showed up on time, schmoozed with everybody and was on the air for two and a half minutes, offering something that I hoped was funny, amusing, gossipy or inconsequential. Now and then I did an interview with an actor: Jane Alexander, Bette Davis, Bob Mitchum, Liza Minnelli, Bob Hope, Kate Nelligan, etc. Or with a Manhattan socialite like Brooke Astor, Alice Mason or Judy Peabody. I talked with Sidney Sheldon, Truman Capote, Jackie Collins and Norman Mailer about books. The producers loved it that I could "get" high-profile personalities their "booker" couldn't. And when possible, I did give WNBC real news scoops, as when the Hunt brothers cornered the silver market and we had it first. Or during the torrid days of the ongoing Ivana–Donald Trump separation and divorce, when I had exclusive after exclusive.

I'd be finished by 6:00 P.M., made up and raring to go to cover the evening's events. What I did on TV was simply "perform." I didn't take it too seriously. I wore funny hats, talked in accents, offered props and gave gossip. All of this worked fine in the informal *Live at Five* setup. News anchors Sue Simmons and Jack Cafferty were my particular cohorts, easy to work with, full of sass, jokes and good humor. Daily, we were announced into being by the miracle voice of Don Pardo, who would shoot to fame on *Saturday Night Live*. We were such a hit that in August 1981, *New York* magazine dubbed us "The Hottest Show on TV." *Live at Five* with Sue, Jack, Liz, Pia Lindstrom, Katie Kelly, Chauncey Howell, Dr. Frank Field and all of Channel 4's

reporters would be a forerunner of the many "happy talk" informal, pre-6:00 P.M. TV shows to come. (At 6:00, the station grew
more astute and serious with the capable Chuck Scarborough.)

I occasionally resorted on-air to using a story or tidbit I
also put into my column. This caused Carol Sulzberger, the wife
of the then owner/publisher of *The New York Times*, to telephone
my *Daily News* editor, Mike O'Neill. "I don't want you to let Liz
repeat stories from the column on the air. You must make her develop original material for each medium. I'm reading her, I'm
watching her, and I like to be surprised." Mr. O'Neill didn't much
care what I did, but Mrs. Sulzberger was a VIP to be heeded. He
said, "I think you'd better do as Carol Sulzberger says." I had to
laugh—I didn't even work for the *Times* but a family member was
monitoring how I performed on the air. I loved it!

ONE DAY IN MAKEUP, MY colleague Carol Jenkins asked
if I could get my friend Lena Horne to appear for her at a fund-
raiser for the local chapter of Literacy Volunteers of NYC. The
charity, which tried to teach illiterate adults to read, was in dire
straits, about to close down. I tried, but Lena couldn't work it in.
I was so guilty at failing Carol's request that I agreed to go with
her to a Literacy meeting. The rest would be history—*my* history, it seems.

This was in 1979 and we were at a Park Avenue apartment with about thirty other people. I was desperately casting
about for a way to crash out of the entire experience when a nice-
looking young man stood up to speak. "Victor" looked to be right
off Madison Avenue: well-dressed, articulate. But he had escaped from high school unable to read and nobody had been the
wiser. He had some kind of job he was faking his way through.
He handed letters to his secretary, saying, "Read this to me." He
also had his wife read to him. But finally he'd gone to Literacy
Volunteers and an Exxon executive had tutored him at night.
"Now," he said proudly, "I am reading Gibbon's *The Decline
and Fall of the Roman Empire* and I have never been happier."

So I was hooked. I signed on to do a benefit for this group, which was losing its headquarters. *Daily News* columnist Beth Fallon helped and we secured their office space. We did a modest fund-raiser on the Brooklyn waterfront and raised a whopping $10,000. I repaid Beth by sending her bags of her favorite food—Chee-tos.

I have to confess: Sometimes I struggled to escape my charitable duties. But eventually I developed my own philosophy, the antithesis of Nancy Reagan's "Just Say No!" My motto became "Just Say Yes!" Yes, to all kinds of volunteerism, to going the extra mile and to backing up to the hairbrush of obligation. This way lies madness, but satisfaction, too.

We became bolder in fund-raising. My good friend Diane Judge, who seems to show up in my life at the most opportune moments, was at this time the theatrical press agent for Michael Bennett's 1983 musical hit, *Dreamgirls.* The quirky and gifted choreographer-director-producer from Buffalo had become the king of Broadway after his work on *Company, Follies* and *A Chorus Line*, which was still playing the Shubert Theatre. Diane went to the Shubert's Bernie Jacobs to ask if he and partner Gerald Schoenfeld would give us the theater on a Monday, provided Bennett would direct for us. The Shuberts, as Broadway called them, said no, advising that Michael "never does benefits."

Diane shrugged and went to Michael, who asked us to dinner. We went to his apartment for a rowdy, gin-bedazzled evening with Michael and his gifted assistant, Bob Avian. Michael instantly agreed to take the project on, and suddenly the Shuberts, advised of their golden boy's yes, fell in line. We had the theater and Shubert Alley. Now all we needed was a show and to sell tickets.

Michael called our show *Broadway Salutes Liz Smith*, saying I had a strong connection with New York theater; my column supported it, now it was time for the theater to support me in return. With back-breaking effort—and the magic of Michael's name—a revue came to fruition.

Carol Channing, Susan Sarandon, Treat Williams, Dorothy Loudon, Maureen Stapleton, Bobby Short, Marvin

Hamlisch, Hinton Battle, Kevin Kline, Bernadette Peters, Mandy Patinkin, Liza Minnelli, Elaine Stritch, Tommy Tune, Twiggy, Barbara Walters and the cast of *A Chorus Line* all appeared onstage. Lena Horne presented our successful student "Victor" with the "First R" award.

It was Michael's idea to have Liza Minnelli lead the chorus line for the closing number, "One"—the irresistible, gold top-hatted bit that ends the show. Then he decided that I should join the dance as well. I really wasn't up to it, but I was scared of Michael. As he threw me to the wolves, I tried my best. I was up there in rehearsal sweating with Liza, who was laughing at me. Mary Tyler Moore had dropped by to see what was going on. She said wryly as I came offstage, after fouling up the number for the umpteenth time, "Liz, you'll have to do better than that." I felt like Rhoda on a bad day.

I shall never forget Michael's last direction before the show began. "When you come out at the finale to join the chorus line, Liza will dance over and take your hand. Keep walking toward her. But I want you to enter thinking of Betty Grable in the days of 20th Century-Fox. Turn just your head toward the audience, lift your face up to the people in the balcony—and smile! Like a star." Somehow I Method-acted enough to do this and the whole night came off brilliantly.

My mother, brothers and their wives were in the audience. When introduced, Mother stood up and waved a little Texas flag. Nothing was *de trop* that night. My good friend, the grand star Claudette Colbert, pronounced it "the greatest show I have ever seen in a theater."

I had no illusions about this success. Some thought I had great power to get those stars, but most of them were too busy before Michael Bennett asked them to join us. It was his triumph—and also part of his pragmatic cleverness. Some months later, he produced another grand event in Shubert Alley and at the same theater when *A Chorus Line* became the longest-running show on Broadway. Michael winked at me on that occasion and said, "I used your fund-raiser as a dress rehearsal for this. And to get Bernie and Gerry used to the idea of spending a lot of money!"

Michael promised he would mount another fantastic evening for Literacy. But this most dynamic energy force became ill too young and died of AIDS, leaving a vacancy the theater can never fill.

So, because success inevitably breeds more work, for the last twenty years and even now, I have been a prisoner of literacy, which has changed its name from LV to Literacy Partners. We have given Wild West parties and black-tie dinner dances and auctions at Christie's and Sotheby's and now we offer annual "famous authors" reading from their work in Lincoln Center each May. Our last fund-raiser brought in over one million, three hundred thousand dollars and I like to think we have become one of New York's most popular charities.

Barbara Bush put literacy on the map as her White House issue, and after my friends Parker Ladd, Arnold Scaasi and Clare Gregorian joined our efforts, we went from high to higher. Mrs. Bush has often appeared in person to support us. My cohorts do the hard work. They just wind me up from time to time to front the whole thing. Our goal is to teach one million New York adults who can't read or write at the fifth-grade level how to do so. And our work has become a role model for the entire nation.

Arnold and Parker also dreamed up an idea to begin The Liz Smith Fund, which would raise a few million dollars, invest it and give the organization an earning income in the years ahead, so that Literacy Partners wouldn't just disappear if I fell in a hole. People in the know pooh-poohed this effort and said we would never raise even a million. So far we are nearing the $5 million mark and are forging ahead.

So, because of that adorable rat fink, Carol Jenkins, I always associate my *Live at Five* decade with my Literacy career. (Carol promptly disappeared from this charity and went about her own pursuits, leaving me stuck.)

FUNNY THINGS HAPPENED AT *LIVE AT FIVE*. I have wonderful videos of myself goofing, stumbling and fouling up on-air. One day I referred to Woody Allen on the air as an "alcoholic" when I was trying to say he was a "workaholic." I put my head down on the desk and pretended to weep for the audience. There is, in the end, nothing like live television. (Years later, I would see Diane Sawyer repeat this gesture on her first day with *Good Morning America*.)

One of my pet fragments on *Live at Five* was a story that caused me to break up on camera. I reported Rose Kennedy's reaction to news that her daughter-in-law Joan Kennedy was living in Boston, while Teddy Kennedy was living in Virginia.

"Virginia?" asked Rose. "Who is Virginia?" (In these post–Bill Clinton/Monica Lewinsky days, that reportage may seem tame. It was raunchy for the eighties. I can remember when we had to refer on-air to "The Best Little Hoo-House in America.")

My nadir on *Live at Five* concerned the Oscar-winning actress Maureen Stapleton. When I first met Maureen in the fifties, she was wed to the stage manager Max Allentuck, and they used to come to Kaye Ballard's to play poker. Maureen drinks a bit. She used to prop her feet up on the table, and as she never wore underwear, this was not an edifying sight.

Hundreds of years later, Max Allentuck was dead, but Maureen could not make herself forget that during the run of *Lute Song* on Broadway, a young actress named Nancy Davis had the temerity to romance him. During the Reagan years, Maureen woke me regularly after midnight to rail against "that Nancy Reagan." She wanted me to "do something about that bitch." I would try to be calm in my sleepy stupor and ask Maureen just what she thought I could do to punish the First Lady for her youthful indiscretions—indeed, if she had committed such.

Nothing came of this, of course, but I am still never surprised when Maureen rings from her country home in New England, demanding that I "fix" Nancy Reagan.

Maureen won the Oscar for *Reds*, and we decided to invite her on *Live at Five* because we knew she'd be a great guest. I was to do my regular "news" stint early in the show and then return to interview Maureen toward the end. I sailed out and did my gossip bit but somebody intercepted me as I was returning to Makeup. Diverted and distracted, suddenly feeling as if I had finished, I picked up my junk and went downstairs, grabbing a cab back to my office. As I stepped out of the taxi a mental warning sign was flashing "You are supposed to be on the air *now* interviewing Maureen." It was, of course, too late for me to go back. I ran upstairs and switched on the TV. There was Jack Cafferty in my place, talking to Maureen. He was saying, with some wariness, that he didn't know what had happened to me, but he'd fill in. With this, Maureen leaned into the camera, asking, "Liz, was it something I said?"

I guess this was the low point of my public TV career. The next day I went on-air noting that people often forget their spouse's birthdays, they forget their umbrellas and briefcases, but I had forgotten an entire person—and a brilliant and gifted one at that. I apologized to Maureen and sent her champagne and candy. She called. "I prefer getting all these gifts to being interviewed by you."

The producers thought it was just great. "It shows we are all human. The audience eats this stuff up. They can't believe it's happening before their very eyes."

Jack Cafferty, a great pro, simply grinned at me and grumped, "They are never going to ask you to anchor *NBC Nightly News*, Liz."

Around this time, my friend Maureen pulled off one of the funniest remarks ever heard from the lips of an actor. After *Reds*, her devoted agent, Milton Goldman, took her to a party. She began to imbibe heavily and he was worried. He got her coat, came and draped it over her shoulders. He whispered in her ear, "Darling, let's go. I don't want you drunk here with all these theater biggies. You are one of America's greatest actors, you have won the Oscar, let's get out of here!" Maureen pulled back, looked at him, and tears came into her eyes. "Milton," she said, "you are so sweet, so dear. Milton, if you should ever decide to fuck a woman—I'm your man!"

KENNEDYS

FOREVER

THE KENNEDYS PLAYED THROUGH MY columns for years when I wrote as Cholly Knickerbocker and then as Liz Smith. When Jackie moved to New York after JFK's death, I made a vow that I, for one, wouldn't make her life miserable unless she did something to frighten the horses.

She and her children deserved a break. So, she was widely reported on by everyone but me. Her chief tormenter was *Women's Wear Daily*. This fashion newspaper was obsessed with what she wore, how she ate at the counter at Hamburger Hamlet, the size of her sunglasses. They were always thrilled to observe that she often took taxis and talked to the drivers.

There were always great rumors about Jackie in New York—some of them most diverting. For a minute there, she seemed to be having a walkabout with the famous masturbatory and sexy writer Phillip Roth. It was told, however, that one evening, he casually draped his arm over the back of a sofa where she was sitting next to him and he touched her. She was said to have given him a battering look and moved away, saying, "...and you thought you could make love to the wife of the

President of the United States." This story ran like wildfire through Manhattan.

But the better anecdote is the one Roth tells of this experience himself. He says he and Jackie were gazing out of her Fifth Avenue window, looking down on Central Park, when he decided finally to steal a kiss. Jackie drew back, looked sternly at him and said, chidingly, "Aw—what did you have to go and do *that* for?" End of romance!

These possibly apocryphal tales thrilled New Yorkers who think they must know everything and that they literally "own" anybody famous.

My personal relations with the former First Lady fell into the clever-handling-of-those-devils-in-the-press category, a subject Mrs. Kennedy/Onassis came to know only too well. In public gatherings I usually left her alone and seldom went near her. But she would often come to me. If I tried for some substantial exchange, she'd change the subject. I counted about a dozen separate times she said to me, "Oh, Liz, I love your hair. Who does your color? The cut is so great." I would respond dutifully that I owed all of my fun as a blonde to Vincent of Saks Fifth Avenue and she would seem to mark this as if for some future use.

Eventually I discovered she'd actually talk if I didn't ask questions and would turn the subject to books. We both admired Frederic Morton's works on Vienna and the history of the Hapsburgs. I also have several charming letters from her. She wrote in her own unique hand with a personal vivacity that was disarming. She would thank me for items written about her authors or her favorite charities, such as the Municipal Arts Society. She ignored the items in my column about Judith Campbell Exner, or whatever might be unpleasantly known of the Onassis years, etc. So I often wondered how she really felt when she had to place the black-and-white ribboned Medal of the Municipal Arts Society around my very own neck. I knew she might prefer to wring it instead. But never at a loss for poise, she just smiled and sailed on.

Jackie had once told her good friend Mike Nichols that

all the press were "cowboys" and stars—celebs—and famous people were "cattle." (I was a cowboy at heart, so she had that right!)

One of my favorite stories of Jackie concerned a time when the director of the Metropolitan Museum decided to mount a fund-raising campaign for the erection of the Temple of Dendur—a very minor old pile of stones given by Egypt to the U.S.

Tom Hoving exerted his charm, but Jackie was said to be implacable and refused to be involved. She was reported to have commented: "I don't give a shit about the Temple of Dendur!" Gossip, gossip, gossip—it was all gossip, of course, but we ate it up. Every morsel.

Now and then, however, in my seemingly unending claw to the top, I had actually experienced a real Kennedy story rather than just a rumor. In 1968, my old buddy Patricia Newcomb, then head of publicity for 20th Century-Fox, sent me to Tunisia to do interviews with the European cast of *Justine*. (This was back in the good old days when entertainment editors thought nothing of accepting first-class tickets to gain access to movie locations and it was the last gasp of 20th luxury under Darryl Zanuck's reign.)

Miss Newcomb, a delightful creature with a dazzling smile and a brain to match, knew everybody who was anybody. She had seen it all with Frank Sinatra and Dean Martin. She was the person who had attacked the press in the driveway of Marilyn Monroe's home on the morning the star was found dead, shouting that they were "vultures!" It was a memorably loyal performance by a devoted flack, who had seldom met a big star she hadn't liked. Then, she had been close to Ethel and Bobby Kennedy after JFK died, and she was given a job under Edward R. Murrow with the U.S. Information Agency. There were rumors that Pat had been "paid off" by the Kennedys to keep quiet, but the reality is that Miss Newcomb was a natural clam about her famous friends and clients. She is another one of the few who has never tried to cash in on what and who she knows. (And I still think she knows a lot about Marilyn and the Kennedys that she isn't telling.)

Anyway, there I was in Algeria and my friend the great English actor Dirk Bogarde invited me to dine. I took Pat Newcomb with me to Dirk's rented villa. At the table were Mr. Bogarde, his longtime manager Anthony Forward, the divine writer Kathleen Tynan, wife of Ken, and most surprisingly, the Princess Lee Radziwill.

At this time, I had never met the delicate fairy-tale sister to Jackie and was fascinated. Conversation came around to marriage. Everybody but Dirk and Pat had been wed at least once. The twice-married princess, however, seemed upset and unhappy, almost angry. At one point she asked me, "Have *you* ever been married?"

I replied I had twice failed the Myrna Loy test.

"But would you ever marry again?" Lee demanded. I said, indeed I would, noting that I was not only an incurable romantic, but also an adventurer.

The princess didn't quite "lose it" at my answer, but she exploded in miniature. "I can't believe it! Why would anyone want to get married more than once? I was talking to my sister just the other day and I asked her the same thing. How in God's name could she ever contemplate marrying again after having been the wife of John F. Kennedy? How could she?"

Conversation switched to Anouk Aimee's behavior on location when she had been handed a flyspecked cardboard box containing couscous and a greasy lamb chop in the 99° desert heat. But the princess stuck in my head. She had been extraordinarily emotional and I especially thought it odd of her to criticize her famous sister in front of a professional gossip and a lot of amateurs who weren't bad either.

I mentioned Lee's behavior to Pat who, with the reserve I notice beautiful women often exhibit when speaking of other beauties, said only, "She is usually a very calm, serene person. But wasn't that some dinner we had?"

I returned to Paris and the beautiful suite Fox had arranged for me at the Hotel de Crillon overlooking the Place de la Concorde. (It's not every day a girl from Texas gets to look out a window right onto the spot where Marie Antoinette lost her head!)

My then agent, Roz Cole, was wiring, calling and screaming. Jackie Kennedy was going to marry the Greek millionaire Aristotle Onassis. America's most famous widow seemed to be going for the gold. I had already written in my column that Ari seemed smitten by Jackie and had been seen playing in a sandbox in Hyannisport with her children. But who knew? The world was disbelieving—and oddly enraged. My agent snapped, "Rupert Murdoch will pay you $10,000 to write a worldwide feature on Jackie and Ari if you can turn it in within twenty-four hours."

I said truthfully that I didn't know a thing about their marrying and not enough to produce such a story from a Paris hotel room. "Make it up!" shouted the agent. So I began to make phone calls and to type. Then I remembered Lee Radziwill's high dudgeon and realized that once again I had been present at the creation. Now, it fit right into what I'd heard—that Lee was furious because Jackie had snatched Ari away when Lee had eyes for him herself. Using this as a lead, I made many phone calls and wrote the story, which was whisked away from me page by page by bellboys who did something in those pre-fax days to get the copy to the U.S.

Room service had a ball with me, and the fabulous person I had gone to Paris to be with got fed up and stormed out. Hell hath no fury like a romantic who finds their loved one pounding a rented French typewriter, concentrating on a deadline. Many great love affairs have ended over the demands of the rolling press. But I had a worldwide scoop and the story did me nothing but good. Writing it, I found I knew more about Jackie and Ari and all the rest than I had realized I did.

The Kennedys were in the American bloodstream and no number of antibodies could clear them out. "Kiss me, kill me, fuck me," as the old love chant went in the sixties, nothing can cure us of the Kennedys.

SCOOPING THE

WORLD WHILE EATING

A SNICKERS

ONE OF MY BIGGEST SCOOPS—a story that put me on the map around the world—happened in March of 1976, when my column was only weeks old and I was sitting in my office pretty much doing nothing. I characterize this behavior as "eating bonbons," or a Snickers bar, and having a story drop in one's lap. Actually, I work pretty hard, but eating bonbons is a metaphor for some of the lucky breaks that have come my way.

For years I had known the Washington gossip writer Kitty Kelley. She was a pert little blonde, saucy, amusing, very intelligent. She told me when we first met that her next project would be a book on Jacqueline Kennedy. By then I had exhausted myself on Jackie. I hoped never to have to write about her again.

So I told Kitty she could have all of my Jackie files. I was never going to use them. She came and carried them back to Washington in a small trunk. Her Jackie book was eventually published and it was only a fair piece of work. I said to Kitty, "If you ever want to be taken seriously you must write a book with a historical index. Try to act as if you are a serious writer, whether you are or not." Then Kitty told me she was going to undertake the saga of Frank Sinatra. I was surprised. It seemed so difficult and dangerous and I knew Sinatra would make her pay. He had made me pay and he had never even met me, just taken offense when I had called him a "bully" of others, such as Barbara Walters, Tom Brokaw, Maxine Cheshire, Jonathan Schwartz and Barbara Howar. I had defended all of them after his attacks.

Kitty said defiantly that she wasn't afraid of Sinatra. Okay, I gave her my background files on him as well, and arranged as many interviews as I could for her with the rare people who would talk. This book showed Kitty's mettle as a reporter. She was fearless, indefatigable, dogged and determined. She had joined up with the respected photographer Stanley Tretick, and he helped her document her interviews and get interviews. (Stanley was as respected as Kitty was feared. He had taken some wonderful pictures of President Kennedy and his children.) The combo worked. Kitty's book on Sinatra was a blockbusting classic. Maybe Sinatra and his family don't like it, but it is a very good book, delving into all kinds of matters no one ever thought would see print. For instance, people talked openly and frankly to Kitty about Dolly Sinatra having been a Hoboken neighborhood abortionist, and so much more.

Now we were professional friends, Kitty and I. Occasionally she'd call and give me a good item, but I felt I very much had her on the debit side of the ledger. (I am always so terminally naive.)

One day Kitty called. "I'm sending you a story that's so hot, it sizzles. It will fracture *The Washington Post* and *Newsweek* because they have just paid a lot of exclusive money for rights to print what I am going to give you for nothing. This is material from the coming Bob Woodward–Carl Bernstein book *The Final Days,* about what happened to Nixon at the end of his office before he resigned. Go with it and God bless you!"

I wrote up Kitty's info. I should be honest and say I mostly just "copied it up." The New York *Daily News* was aghast when they received it. "Do you have any idea what you've sent us?" asked editor Mike O'Neill. We went front-page the next day with the stories of Nixon and Kissinger praying on their knees, with Nixon talking to portraits in the White House, Mrs. Nixon drinking—and all the rest of it. This advance stuff on the Simon & Schuster book, which few had seen, broke around the world on the wires. Suddenly, I was noticed.

I couldn't claim any effort in securing this story. Yet I went around New York accepting congratulations, having people listen to my opinions for the first time. At a cocktail party the day the story was published, *Newsweek*'s then editor, Ed Kosner, attacked me. He said I had "stolen" his story, ruined his magazine's paid-for-exclusive and that I should be "ashamed." I was only slightly "ashamed," mostly because I'd had so little to do with getting the story. But I wasn't about to tell him that. I said, "Tough darts!" to Kosner as I passed on in triumph at the party because a scoop is a scoop and it goes to the one who gets it in print first. I didn't care what he had paid for the story; he didn't get in print first!

A more satisfying run-in was with Carl Bernstein, who was then a friend and had coauthored the book *The Final Days*. He phoned, laughed and said, "Well, congratulations, Scoop! You did it. You have Kay Graham's and *The Washington Post*'s nose out of joint. We don't know how you did it, but you did and that's what counts. We tried to keep it secret. We sold our excerpt to the *Post* and to *Newsweek*, but you have it for free, for nothing and first. Congratulations!"

I appreciated Carl's attitude. But I didn't have the heart then to 'fess up that I hadn't done a damned thing. I had merely sat there in my office, opening a Snickers bar and the story dropped in my lap.

Shortly after this, I began to discuss the realities. I tried to divest myself of some of the glory for what I thought of as Kitty Kelley's scoop. But it didn't seem to matter. Nobody listened. Nobody cared. And the thing to remember was, that no matter whose scoop it was, they wrapped fish in it the next day. The *Daily News* editors seemed to think it was amusingly naive that I would deny any authority in the matter. Several said to me, "Get off it. Take the bows. You got the story—somehow, how-

ever and for whatever reason. You deserve the credit. You had
the sources. Now it is history and nobody cares about the sordid,
gory details." And Kitty didn't seem to want any credit; she was
already busy with her plan to make millions from her next best-
seller and she knew I would be duty-bound to help her.

I remember going to dinner in The Quilted Giraffe with
Kitty and her literary agent, Lynn Nesbit. Kitty was "thanking"
me for the help on the Sinatra book. I was thanking her for my
scoop and she was pooh-poohing it.

Then something bad happened to Kitty and Liz. The
writer Sidney Zion effected a meeting for me with Sinatra. This
led to the end of our long, ongoing "feud," or whatever it was.
Kitty was disappointed in me for "being suckered" into meeting
with Sinatra.

Kitty had by now embarked on her book about Nancy
Reagan. I liked Mrs. Reagan and had already defended her
against those who felt she was costing America a lot for new
china in the White House. I tried to say in my column that it was
all donated, so who cared? I also defended Mrs. Reagan in the
matter of her falling out with presidential aide Donald Regan. I
said people who didn't believe that a certain amount of "pillow
talk" dominated the American presidency were not being realistic. Mrs. Reagan had her faults, but I simply didn't find her to be
the dragon lady of the Reagan years.

Kitty was enormously offended by my more balanced
point of view. She began to say I had "sold out" to Frank Sinatra
and to Nancy Reagan. I became a bum in her eyes. And when the
Nancy Reagan book came out, Kitty let me have it in spades.
Somehow, in her fury against Mrs. Reagan, Kitty decided that
women who went to Smith College (as Mrs. Reagan had) were
"suspect" in their femininity. Kitty wrote: "Homosexuality was
an unspoken fact of life in the all-female environment of Smith
College." The book, which had much excellent material, was
somewhat marred by this inane thesis that if Mrs. Reagan wasn't
having an affair with Sinatra in the White House then surely she
was a lesbian who had gone to Smith College. And after all, even
if I hadn't gone to Smith, wasn't my name Smith? Mrs. Reagan

must have been a bit shocked to find me so important in her life story. She scarcely knew me. And Kitty seemed to drag me out of left field into Mrs. Reagan's milieu, even mentioning in a fantastic aside that I had been "living openly for years with another woman in New York." I didn't quite get this stupid and arcane implication, but on the other hand, I did. (Kitty had known my friend Iris Love for years and it was never any secret that Iris headquartered herself, when she was in America, in and out of my office apartment.)

Kitty ended her book with the story of a lunch Barbara Walters had given at the time Nancy Reagan's autobiography was published. Barbara had assembled some of the biggest names in journalism—Diane Sawyer, Connie Chung, Aileen Mehle, etc. Kitty cited me as having ended the lunch by anointing Mrs. Reagan in an ass-kissing manner. "Now you belong to the ages!" she said I had said.

Well, it was true. Kitty was often accurate. I had said exactly those words, but as a kind of embarrassed joke. We had all been asking Mrs. Reagan questions and we'd run out of steam. There had been a rather long silence at the table when nobody seemed to know how to wind up the proceedings. Then I made a feeble jest. But satire, sardonic remarks and irony don't come off well when repeated in print.

Never complain, never explain, as Bette Davis and Henry Ford are variously credited with saying, so what's the use? Kitty had paid me back for what she said was my finking out and becoming a "tool" of Nancy Reagan and Frank Sinatra.

I was sorry I lost Kitty's friendship. I still think she is a top-notch reporter, albeit a rather unkind and reckless one. And she did once give me a scoop that did nothing but advance and augment my career. For that I will always be grateful.

MY LOVE

AFFAIR WITH

FRANK SINATRA

SPEAKING OF FRANK SINATRA, I had been in love with him since dancing to the Tommy Dorsey Orchestra at the Lake Worth Casino back in the late thirties. These were my high school years in Fort Worth and Sinatra was Dorsey's vocalist. Our local boyfriends were livid that we looked over their shoulders longingly, failed to hear what they were saying and always wanted to edge closer to the bandstand. So far, so normal. I was just another bobby-soxer who wanted to scream when Sinatra sang. I didn't because I was determined not to be one of the mob. I wanted Frank to realize *my* sophistication and understand *my* appreciation for his very great talent.

I looked up at him in the flesh, standing before Tommy's trombone in his skinny, big-eared way, and sighed. Then came the movie years where we could sit in the dark to our heart's content, memorizing his every look, action and inflection. I never, ever sang a Sinatra song after that—even under my breath—that I didn't try to employ Frank's phrasing. And my later "career" as an amateur singer with the Skitch Henderson New York Pops Orchestra for benefits in Carnegie Hall only happened because I was still/always imitating my idol. Skitch would say, "You know, Lizard, you can sing sort of like Sinatra. Too bad you don't have any voice or range."

So, my life went on and I fell into journalism and show biz. By those days, we all knew a lot more about Sinatra—what an ego he had, pal of presidents, chief of the Rat Pack. But early on we had devoured the Lana-Ava years, and then the Lauren Bacall–Juliet Prowse years. Then, I was a relatively anonymous writer. But, when I became a gossip columnist for the New York *Daily News,* a responsibility devolved upon me. Certain things were a "must" if you had the byline. I was expected to take sides, take stands, make enemies, be brave and fearless, take my knocks and raps, never wince nor cry aloud. I tried, but as a devout coward that part was hard for me.

Through the years, however, I had learned inevitably about a different Sinatra from the one I worshipped. Now he was a tough-talking guy who called women "broads" and "hookers," who hated the press in general, and often meted out punishment and revenge for himself and his friends.

My column was not very critical of celebrities. I tried to give everyone a break. I liked actors and understood that like all true paranoids, some of them actually had enemies. But when a phenomenal celebrity rose on the horizon, a person with real power, who threw their weight around, I would occasionally tilt at windmills. I had come to feel that the federal government, the Pentagon, politicians, televangelists, *The New York Times, The Washington Post, Time, Newsweek* and Frank Sinatra were all big enough that in criticizing them, I would not destroy them. They were able to take care of themselves. And I began to be offended by Sinatra's chutzpah, his hubris, his attitude toward women, his laxity in regard to the Mob. His volatile temper reminded me of my own feisty little father and that wasn't something I enjoyed being reminded of.

So I defended Maxine Cheshire when Sinatra put $2 in her cocktail glass and said that was her price. She was a good, if annoying Washington reporter, who was fearless herself and often dug into hornets' nests. I defended the disc jockey Jonathan Schwartz, a number-one Sinatra fan, when Sinatra had him fired for breaking a release date. I defended Barbara Howar after she asked him a simple, unadorned question at Reagan's inauguration, and he called her a "two-bit hooker," smashing her down verbally while she was just trying to earn a living with *Entertainment Tonight*. Then when he began attacking Tom Brokaw and Barbara Walters in particular, saying she should turn in her press card, I termed him a "bully" in print, and inquired why he so often attacked women. Sinatra immediately attacked *me* with great gouts of venom from the concert stages in New York, from Carnegie Hall itself.

I was a "dog; all you had to do was hang a pork chop out the window" and I'd chase it. I was invariably described by him as "fat, old and ugly." He said I preferred "Debbie Reynolds to Burt Reynolds." I thought the Debbie/Burt wisecrack was pretty funny. I *did* like pork chops. But I was hurt by "fat, old and ugly." I knew Frank and I were very much the same era. (He was only seven years my senior.) I didn't figure I was any older, heavier or uglier than he was. Neither of us was in the raving beauty class.

I knew lots of people who loved Sinatra and knew him well. Important folks like TV star Arlene Francis and her actor husband Martin Gabel, TV director Billy Harbach, TV producer George Schlatter and Manhattan socialite Judy Green. They were forever urging Sinatra to "let up on Liz." I was told that one of his major problems with his wife, Barbara, was her wish that he "make up with Liz." One night, Martin Gabel stood with him in the wings at Carnegie Hall and urged him to give it up. "Frank, you are a gentleman and you are making a big mistake. Liz is a wonderful girl. If you only knew her…" Sinatra went onstage with smoke coming from his ears and did fifteen minutes on me, until a lady in the audience yelled, "Shut up and sing!"

But it was my pal Sidney Zion, the revolutionary political columnist and tough guy, who put the cherry on the sundae. He simply never let Sinatra alone about "the Liz biz." He argued and cajoled. One day Sidney took me to Gallagher's Steakhouse on West 52nd Street where we examined the steaks that hang in

the window, like decorations. He said, "Liz, I think he's soft-
ened up. He's about to give in. He is curious now. He can't
imagine how you can be as good as we all say you are, and he
can't believe he has made a mistake in judgment." I shrugged.
By now, Sinatra was part of my fame. He had made people interested in me who had never heard of me before. He had joined
the dubious pantheon of my known enemies.

I answered Zion, "Forget it. He'll never like me. I worship his talent, but why would he care about that? It won't happen." Sidney drew on his cigar and smirked. "Wanna bet?" Sure
enough, three months later, Sidney called. "Sinatra's coming to
town. He wants a meeting with you."

I snorted.

"No kidding," said Sid. "He thinks maybe he done you
wrong and anyway, I think he admires you as a standup girl who
won't be intimidated by him."

A day came when Zion whispered into the phone, "Put
on something pretty and be ready to be picked up at 5:30. We're
going to Jimmy Weston's to meet Frank." I dressed seven times
that afternoon. I threw my clothes around like a demented debutante. I was a girl on a first date. I didn't know what to think. I
was scared. Finally, I managed some demure outfit and climbed
into the limo with Sidney. "Just be yourself. You look nice. He's
going to love you!"

We stumbled into Jimmy Weston's on Manhattan's East
54th Street. The place was a throwback to the grand old crummy
nightspots, bars and restaurants of the fifties. It smelled of old
beer and fried shrimp. It was tawdry and rundown. But it signaled Sinatra's loyalty to Weston. We approached one of the
doorless "rooms"—a small banquette walled off for privacy—
and from the entrance shot Sinatra with his hand out. "I'm so
glad to meet you. Thank you for coming!"

"And it's so nice to meet you, Mr. Sinatra," I stuttered.
He turned aside, taking my arm and guiding me into the seat.
"Francis," he said emphatically. "Call me Francis." We made
small talk with Sidney beaming. We were into chitchat: how is
so and so (he and Sidney discussed pals) and why was Frank in

town? Etc. Suddenly, Sidney was up and out. "Well, I'll just leave you two to get acquainted." I glared at him and insisted he stay. He smiled, sucked on his cigar and disappeared.

I was alone with Frank Sinatra—the man who had tried to run down tabloid columnist Lee Mortimer in his car. The guy who had "ruined" the career of comic Jackie Mason and crushed syndicated columnist Dorothy Kilgallen by calling her a "chinless wonder." He had made many women cry with his cruelty. But, here was Francis looking at me intensely with his soft blue eyes, ordering another gin and tonic. He began asking questions. I talked and asked him questions. I told him of my love-struck days when he was with Dorsey and how I had followed his career from afar after the Paramount Theatre era. How much I loved him in movies, and how he was the greatest singer of his time. I tried to stop myself, but I couldn't. He took it very well. Of course he was used to it; his fans did it over and over.

He sat and nodded and asked more questions. Where had I come from? Why had I become a gossip columnist? What was it like to grow up in Texas? I told him about reading Mezz Mezzrow, the musician who wrote the first enlightening words in my life about jazz and the life of a musician. He knew all about Mezz and "The Race." He told me of his love for Billie Holiday and Lena Horne and about the long phone conversations he still had on a regular basis with Irving Berlin. I was able to brag that Mr. Berlin had sent me a note reading, "I see your column every day, kid. Keep up the good work!" We discussed our admirable mutual friend, journalist Pete Hamill. We talked about Elizabeth Taylor and Lana Turner and other movie stars. We talked about Ava and how Saint Clair Pugh had known her all his life in Smithfield, North Carolina. I told him of my adventure when Artie Shaw tried to take me home with him and I couldn't go because I was intimidated by Ava, Lana and Kathleen Windsor in his past. Sinatra loved that!

"Why that old letch!" he exclaimed. He didn't care for Artie Shaw, though he thought his music was great. We talked philosophy, history, art, books and our dogs. I admired the Alexander the Great seal on his gold ring and I asked, knowingly, "No more worlds to conquer?" He liked that, and launched into his view of history. We had another drink.

He said, shyly, "I'd like to help you with your charity for literacy. I am impressed by that work. Just call on me anytime, and also, if anybody ever bothers you just ask me and I'll fix it for you."

I fixated for a moment on sugarplums of money dancing for literacy, and then on the idea of certain people with their legs broken before I snapped back to reality and said, "Thanks, but—"

Sinatra interrupted. I needn't explain; he understood. I couldn't take favors from him. But I wasn't to consider anything a favor. He just liked to "fix" things for his pals. All of a sudden I was his "pal." I almost fainted.

I loved him. I had a feeling for what it would be like to be in his strong and capable arms. (He wasn't so frail and skinny anymore.) And he was the most immaculate man I'd ever seen, beautiful French cuffs, a fantastic silk tie, wonderful hands with clean strong nails and sexy wrists. (I'd always been a sucker for wrists.) I loved his smell, the scars on his face. I imagined a headline or two:

SINATRA ATTACKED BY OLD BROAD IN SALOON!
SINATRA CHARGES GOSSIP MOLL WITH SEXUAL
HARASSMENT!

After two hours we both knew we had to go. We ambled toward the door. On the street, an old woman screamed and threw up her hands yelling, "Frankie!" She moaned.

He took her in his arms and kissed her. "Darling, you look wonderful," he said. Then he took me home while we chatted all the way. We kissed good-bye in the drive-through of my apartment building.

As his chauffeured car drove away, I realized I had thrown all judgment to the wind. I was Sinatra's slave. Co-opted by a couple of gin and tonics. I was his for the rest of my life. And neither of us had even mentioned our past differences. We were too genteel for words.

The next day as I swooned about my office in a kind of daydream, the most beautiful orchids arrived with a handwritten note, offering his private phone number and signed "Francis Albert." Then came a letter thanking me "for the moment." I think that was signed "Albert Francis." Through the years after, I received a number of fabulous notes from him and occasionally more orchids. I was invited to his seventieth birthday party in the Waldorf and seated only a stone's throw from his selected lady of the night, my own friend Claudette Colbert. I sent him stuff about his hobby, miniature trains. I sent Mrs. Sinatra a pin that read: "I Am Married to a Train Nut." We became pen pals from afar. Every day I prayed Frank Sinatra would never insult anybody else I loved or admired or do anything untoward that I would have to write about. I was lucky. He never did.

Once when I was in Palm Springs, I posed on Sinatra Way under the street sign. After he received the snapshot, he professed great fury that I had come to town without calling him.

I saw one of his last concerts in Radio City Music Hall, with four of the best seats in the house provided by Frank. I took his old enemy Barbara Walters. When I told him later, he just laughed and said, "That's swell."

So I stopped being a real journalist when it came to Frank Sinatra. Love is funny that way.

FASTEN YOUR

SEAT BELT

I HAD BEEN HOPING TO meet the fabled over-the-top Bette Davis after seeing her with Leslie Howard in *Of Human Bondage* back in 1934. From age eleven, I had followed her life and career and had much background on Bette because of my friendship with her onetime Warner's *Dark Victory* costar, the Irish actress Geraldine Fitzgerald.

But connections can be everything in a life like mine. And mine to Bette came when I realized that her lawyer, Harold Schiff, was dating my friend Shirley Herz.

Harold Schiff told Miss Davis I was okay. She was inclined then to like me because he did. By now, her heyday was long past. It had been years since her Oscar wins, years even since she'd put an outrageous advertisement in the Hollywood trades saying she was an actress who wanted to work. It had been years since she'd appeared on the Broadway stage in *Night of the Iguana*, a 1961 theater opening I never forgot because of the tumultuous applause at her appearance, which caused her to completely step out of character and bow to the audience. It was a long time since her greatest career effort, *All About Eve*, in 1950.

Bette Davis was a wizened little old lady by the time I encountered her, but she hadn't lost her bite and bark.

In one of her final films, *The Whales of August*, she made everyone suffer. Her iconic costar, the sainted Lillian Gish, the sweetest and kindest of souls, told me privately that during filming, "Bette was the meanest, most unforgiving, least generous actor I have worked with in a ninety-year career."

It was 1985 when I telephoned Miss Davis to say I was in possession of a story about a book being written by her daughter, B.D. Hyman. *My Mother's Keeper* would soon be published and turned out to be the sad tale of a child disillusioned by parental fame. B.D. had become a born-again Christian and found herself more estranged than ever from a mother who didn't care to be "saved." I thought Miss Davis might hand me my head for even asking, but instead she gave a kind of glorified yelp over the phone, then said dramatically: "Ah-ha! Liz, you've got me. You've got me. You have nailed it down. Yes, there is such a book and yes, I am devastated and unhappy about it. But my darling daughter has married a fool who has influenced her against me. So there is nothing I can do but grin and bear it."

She went on to give me quite a good interview and I got several columns out of it. I was surprised at how resigned Bette Davis was. In this instance, she had abandoned "control." She presented herself as a victim of circumstance, much concerned about never again seeing her beloved grandchildren. She liked the way I wrote about it all, and so when the Film Society of Lincoln Center honored her with their Lifetime Achievement Award in 1989, I talked her into giving me an interview on *Live at Five*.

She arrived on the set fully made-up, dressed to the nines. She had on a smart little hat with a veil and although a stroke had left her face drawn to one side, she was most definitely still Miss Bette Davis. It was the only time I ever saw the WNBC crew in awe of a guest. These hard-bitten burly souls danced around her like elves. She surveyed the studio, hand on hip. She began to direct changes in the lighting. She wanted this camera to be there. Everyone obliged. Her lighting changes made me look like fifty miles of bad road, but she was beautifully lit. On air, she was chiefly concerned that the man who had made her hat receive a lot of credit. Still, it was a big day for WNBC-TV and she was a great "get" for me. Nobody thought she would ever do local television.

But the night of the Lincoln Center awards, things unraveled. After the awards she was seated with her agent, my pal Michael Black,* at table number one in Tavern on the Green. Michael went to the men's room and I began to joke with her. Big mistake! "Onstage tonight, you really took the audience along with you," I offered. "But you didn't seem a bit nervous."

She said emphatically, "I was nervous—very!"

I persisted, "Not you, no—not you—never."

Her eyes blazed. She ordered me from the table. I had bitterly insulted her. How dare I say she wasn't nervous! Again, as so often in my dangerous career I had said too much at the wrong moment to the wrong person. Michael came back and tried to reason with her, but she was furious. Not wanting to further taint her triumphal night, I left.

Miss Davis died in 1990, without forgiving me. I was sorry, having admired her to distraction. It remained for Michael to tell me his own defining Bette Davis story. It seems the star moved into an L.A. apartment. She had a young paid companion and told the girl to secure a certain parking space in the basement. It wasn't available, belonging to two men living on the same floor with Miss Davis. These movie fans learned of her wish and gave up their space to her. Then they invited her to dinner. Miss Davis went and a delightful time was had by the foursome. Time passed and she invited the men to dine with her. They were thrilled and arrived, bearing wine. As they departed,

*Michael Black had trained with the legendary agent Sue Mengers. He gave me one of my favorite expressions—"Suckez les oeufs!" This is what he and I always say to one another or to others we want to gently put down. Michael says, "It rings through my head whenever I have a particularly idiotic actor I am dealing with."

warm with the prospect of a future friendship, Miss Davis herself showed them to the door. As they stepped outside, she said firmly, "Okay. You've had me to dinner. I've had you to dinner. That's it; that's the end of it—now we are even." She shut the door firmly.

Ah, Bette Davis—great at exits.

THE TOWERING

TRUMPS

EVERYONE REMEMBERS EXACTLY WHERE HE or she was when President Kennedy was shot. But I, typical gossip columnist that I am, remember exactly where I was when I first heard the word *Trump*. My friend and literacy ally Parker Ladd and I were in a car heading up Park Avenue. As we neared the statue of old Commodore Cornelius Vanderbilt that forces New York taxi drivers to turn right and then left at what used to be the PanAm Building and still is Grand Central Station, Parker said, "Have you ever met Ivana and Donald Trump?" I said I hadn't. He explained that Donald was a building tycoon and she a Czech ski champ, a blonde who talked a mile a minute with a deep accent. She had just bought some couture dresses from our mutual friend Arnold Scaasi.

I was always interested in Arnold's clients ever since he had made those outrageous see-through-the-back pajamas that Barbra Streisand had worn when she went up to get her *Funny Girl* Oscar in 1968. The cute little guy from Canada had made fashion history by changing his name from Isaacs to (backwards) Scaasi, and he charged the ladies of Manhattan and points west thousands for a dress. (He had once pinned a piece of glittering material at my shoulders, nipped it in on the sides and said, "This is how it will look." It looked divine and I asked what it would cost me. "Well, I could make it for you at cost, but if you were someone like Carroll Petrie or Edna Morris, it would be $8,000." I screamed, "It took you ten minutes." Arnold smiled. "Well, it took me years to be able to do it in ten minutes.")

Anyway, Parker gave me chapter and verse on the Trumps and the wide swath they were beginning to cut in New York: how certain uppity types didn't approve of them because it was all *nouveau riche* money and yet, they were attractive and had three divine little children and—he added—"Mrs. Trump— Ivana—is really a very sweet, dear person. I think she's getting a bad rap."

A bad rap! I sat up, being a sucker for anybody who is being pushed around by the Establishment. I immediately decided I liked Ivana Trump from afar and was curious. Before long, I met Mrs. Trump, and then I met her tall blond husband. I found them both refreshing, if a bit presumptuous and naive socially, and I began to note their comings and goings. Little did I dream that their eventual "going" would be something of my "coming" to the fore in newsprint and other media. The Trumps were to have a profound effect on my career.

But before that, I became involved with the entire Trump family. I liked them—the daddy, Fred, who had slugged his way to the top in the Queens building business; his other mild-mannered son, Robert, and his adorable charity-minded wife, Blaine; Mary, the matriarch mother, a truly divine lady; the two sisters—Mary Ann Barry, a New Jersey judge, and the other, Elizabeth Grau, a banker. I began going to many of the overachieving Trump family's anniversaries, weddings and birthdays.

Donald became bigger and bigger. He was the king of hyperbole and he had just the requisite touch of Elvis vulgarity to endear him to the common man. Whenever he emerged from his chauffeured car on Fifth Avenue to go into his new Trump Tower, or to the recently bought Plaza Hotel, or turned up at the fights or at his new casino in Atlantic City, he would be mobbed by the public. They adored him. Because of Donald, I'd find myself sitting at dinner next to Mike Tyson or Don King, or Adnan Kashoggi, or Mike Douglas or Don Johnson.

Donald would always gather me up under his arm and say to whoever might be near, "She's the greatest! Isn't she the greatest?" This was silly and embarrassing and he did it with everybody else as well. Although he was phobic about germs, he was a natural-born toucher and hugger. I enjoyed talking to him, arguing uselessly that he should build low-income housing to help New York's less well-heeled, or turn floors of his buildings into rooms for the poor. He laughed at me and I never believed a word he said about how rich he was, how he'd bested the competition and what he intended to do next. It was his singular and special brand of conversation, overlaid with hype. As for Ivana, I liked her, too, but never knew what she was saying. She talked in a machine-gun patter that was mostly incomprehensible, but then some of it was very funny, as when she referred to her husband as "The Donald."

The Trumps were always inviting me to go somewhere on their jet plane. I flew with them to San Diego, to a big party Barbara Walters and Merv Adelson were tossing just before that marriage came apart. I flew down to Palm Beach after the refurbishing of Mar-a-Lago and spent an all-girls weekend there with Ivana's mother, her girlfriends and ladies such as Helen Gurley Brown, Georgette Mosbacher, Shirley Lord, Barbara, et al.

Ivana and I went in the Trump helicopter to Atlantic City and we bounced around in a terrifying fog that made me wish I'd never heard of the Trumps. If I was going to be punished for the sin of accepting free trips from rich people, now seemed to be a perfect time for it. But we landed and I went on to interview Ivana for WNBC's *Live at Five*. She was seen on TV as a top executive in the Trump organization, while Donald stood on the side beaming and nodding. He also offered her up to me as running everything at the Plaza Hotel. It all seemed harmless. The *Daily News* and WNBC-TV were more than happy to lap up every word on the ubiquitous Trumps and as my so-called "expense accounts" from both companies combined wouldn't have bought me a month's worth of hamburgers, they didn't question my ethics.

I didn't question my ethics, either. So far as the philosophy goes, I have always felt that the chief thing for a columnist to have is access. Then after you get it, you can weigh how far you want to go, whether you need to blow the connection by telling "the truth—the whole truth—and nothing but," or whether you can straddle a true middle course in reporting. I put my tongue firmly in cheek in everything I wrote about the Trumps. I would poke gentle fun at them because they weren't, after all, popular with their betters—New York's movers and shakers. (These threatened people looked down on any new money that wasn't their own.) And when push came to shove, I found my bosses at the *News* and WNBC didn't really want to be confronted with the question about *how* I got where I was going. They weren't as rigid as the paragons running ABC, NBC and CBS, nor like *The New York Times* and *The Washington Post*, where they have hard rules about not accepting anything from a subject. No, tabloid heaven's motto was "Go for broke," so long as we didn't have to pay for it. (This is the real and absolute "don't ask, don't tell" dogma of minor media. It's about not even bringing up the subject of taking favors that might rebound to a story, good or bad.)

When *New York* magazine selected its twenty "Most Important" New Yorkers in April 1988, editor Ed Kosner said that the list was a fantasy. But he invited me to describe the greatest fantasist of all, Donald Trump. The magazine defended naming him, along with such paragons as Brooke Astor, "Because his buildings and his book and his ego are so much bigger than life."

In my article, I spoke of Donald's rabid detractors and his love-hate relationship with the hoity-toity and the adoration of hoi polloi. I said if he smoked, he'd have his cigarettes monogrammed like so—$—with Ayn Rand's dollar sign. But I added that jealousy and spite played some part in making him the city's biggest target. Yes, he bragged and blew hard, but in my book he wasn't a real phony or a fake. I found him incapable of dissembling or doing the hypocritical things a lot of other rich New Yorkers do—such as blathering on about "giving back to the community." Donald had never gone hog-wild giving money away to charity in order to pander to the public. No, it just wasn't his thing. Likening him to the rich young ruler who asked Jesus what he might do to be saved, I noted that Donald wasn't ready to be "saved." (Jesus said, "Sell all your goods and give them to the poor"—and the young ruler went away sorrowing for he was very rich.)

I noted that Donald Trump had attacked a paralyzed, stultified New York bureaucracy and given commerce, construction and business a real shot in the arm. I asked, "If you love democratic capitalism, how can you hate Donald Trump?" I spoke of the other ruthless tycoons I'd heard opine that Trump couldn't last. I said I hoped he wouldn't self-destruct. And I added that one reason I liked Donald was because he reminded me of my tall, good-looking brothers in the days when the world was their oyster. I added that I knew they were really good guys under their egos—good guys with soft centers. I thought Donald had a soft center, too. "And, anyway, I can't resist a man who calls me 'honey-bun.'" I noted that someday I might hear that standing in the White House receiving line.*

THE INTERNET GOSSIP COLUMNIST JEANNETTE Walls says in her excellent book, *Dish*, that Donald Trump "botched the story of his own divorce when he refused to talk to Liz Smith, and the columnist took up the cause of his wife, Ivana." This is an interesting theory but it's not quite as simple as that.

In the fateful year 1990, I began hearing tales that all wasn't well in the Trump marriage. I called Donald and asked,

*In 1999, Trump supporters launched thedonald2000.org, a Web site dedicated to urging him to make the race sometime in the future. He took it seriously for a little while, but finally came to his senses.

"If rumors of your rampant cheating on Ivana are true, why don't you decide to talk to me about it and let me print it in a way that won't be too inflammatory or sensational? Actually, I'd rather see you fix the situation with Ivana so these rumors stop." (You well may ask—where does a gossip columnist get off talking and lecturing to famous people like this? My answer is—I don't know. We're like mothers. We can't be stopped.) Donald didn't deny the story, but said, "Liz, I'll think about it."

That would certainly have been enough for most gossips to rush into print. But I liked the Trumps. They had three little kids and I didn't want to be the one to notify Ivana that her husband was playing around. It just wasn't my style. I figured my warning shot would bring Donald to his senses. (Such fools we scriveners be.)

The Trumps went underground for a while. It seemed to me Ivana hadn't been seen in weeks. Then I went to some big "do" in the Plaza and a woman swept into the ballroom, brilliantly dressed, coiffed and made up. I stared. I thought it looked like my old friend Ivana, but then decided—no. Too good-looking, younger than Ivana, none of Ivana's world-weary sharp features and—egad!—I got a look at her décolletage. Ivana had never had such knockers. I turned to ask someone who this woman might be? Suddenly she was making a beeline for me and threw out her arms, crushing me to her new grapefruit-sized bosom. From the mouth of this dazzling vision came the unmistakable rat-a-tat-tat of Ivana.

Now I knew. Ivana had gone away and had a face-lift, a bosom inflation and heaven only knew what else. She looked sensational—and very different. I decided right then that the rumors of trouble must be true. Soon stories were circulating about Ivana and "the other woman" having a catfight on the ski slopes of Aspen.

I sat down and wrote Donald a letter. Now I put a little pepper in the birdshot. "Give me this story or you are going to be in someplace a lot worse than the Liz Smith column." I thought this was true and honestly good advice, yet as I mailed the letter, I felt like the Toothless Tiger and laughed at myself. If

Donald wasn't ready to 'fess up, and I had no actual proof, there was damn little I could do about it.

Now it was February and suddenly Ivana telephones. It is urgent that we meet. "Please don't tell anyone, but go to the Plaza direct to the such-and-such suite and go inside and wait for me." She sounded utterly distraught.

When Ivana stepped into the room, she threw herself, sobbing, into my arms. Donald was having an affair. Donald didn't love her anymore. Donald hadn't wanted to sleep with her, saying he couldn't be sexually attracted to a woman with children (shades of Elvis!). She had gone to California "to have some work done," but Donald didn't even like her after that. Nothing was working for her. I reacted sympathetically to this broken-hearted woman who was telling me that this man who didn't want her was her whole life!

I gave her the old run-don't-walk-get-yourself-to-the-analyst routine. I said, "Don't wait. The sooner you start, the sooner you'll get over it. No one can make anyone come back to them. So start the process whereby the analyst convinces you that you are too good for the person who doesn't want you anyway." I told her that even then, I was afraid it took about a year to get over being dumped, but then I knew it always took at least two years if you didn't have help. Ivana half-listened. Mostly she wept.

She said she'd picked up a phone months back to hear Donald talking to a friend about "Marla." When she asked him about it, he said "it was a girl who had been after him." Not important. Then in Aspen, someone pointed out Marla in the food line at Bonnie's restaurant. Ivana said to her friend, "Will you give her the message that I love my husband very much?" Then, Ivana claimed, she walked outside and "Marla charged right behind me and said, in front of my children, 'I love Donald. Do you?' Donald was just looking like nothing was happening. Later, he told me I was overreacting."

Now all of her friends began to commiserate with Ivana and she just couldn't take it. She'd tried for two months, but now she had hired a lawyer, Michael Kennedy. She told me she was afraid of Donald, of what he'd do to her. How he had all the power and could "ruin" her. She said he would take away her friends, "like you and Barbara." I said this wasn't true, but she wasn't listening. No, she didn't want me to *print* the story she'd told me. She had just needed a shoulder to cry on. (Damn!—Another one of those "don't print that" episodes.)

I kept trying to soothe Ivana and advised she call the PR guy John Scanlon. He was good at swaying public opinion. I knew Scanlon socially and liked him, but his operations were usually above the level of a gossip column. He was into influencing the *Times* or networks. I left the Plaza and in my office called Ivana's attorney, Michael Kennedy. With his ever-present helpmate-wife Eleanore, the Kennedys were personal pals to Ivana. (Kennedy had been described by *New York* magazine as "experienced, elegant and deadly." He had won legendary cases against the CIA, the FBI and was called "The Incorruptible.") Both Scanlon and Kennedy were now afraid that Donald would break the story to his own advantage. I feared this as well. I said they *had* to let me print it, since I already knew it. They agreed and they convinced Ivana.

Jeannette Walls says in her book: "Liz promised Ivana and her lawyer that she would treat Ivana well—and she lived up to her word." I admire Ms. Walls as one of the best dishers ever to serve up the dirt. But I didn't have to promise anybody such treatment. I already *had* the story from Ivana's own mouth before any caveats. (The only warning was not to mention lawyer Kennedy's name yet.) I thought at this point that I could tell the true news of the Trumps's trouble in paradise, as well as speak of Ivana's very sincere heartbreak, and that I could present Donald's side of it as well. It hadn't yet occurred to me that I would be forced to "take sides."

On Friday, I secretly sent my take of the separation to Fran Wood, my gifted editor at the *Daily News*. We were set to print on Sunday. Every time you file a story on a Friday that won't appear until a Sunday or Monday, you are walking on eggs. It may get leaked. I sent a dramatic note to Fran: "I only got this by swearing in blood to do it their way, and Ivana's lawyer doesn't want his name revealed yet. After Donald gets off the plane (from Japan) Sunday night, I'm afraid he's going to kill her—or me. But that's show biz. My chief hope is that we can keep someone on staff from leaking to the *Post* or *Newsday*. The lawyer, however, says so far there are no calls or nibbles, so maybe nobody knows she has this lawyer yet. I will be available until the wee hours."

On February 11, 1990, everything hit the fan. The Trumps were page one with the headline "Love on the Rocks" and the paper put my photo on there with them.* The headline: "Ivana Trump Is Devastated 'that Donald was betraying her.'" And Ivana whomped up a big sympathy rush from the statement that she could remain Mrs. Trump if only she'd agree to an open marriage where Donald would be free to see others. I added that Ivana had too much self-respect for that.

I spoke personally to Donald aboard his plane that Sunday. His fabled PR rep, Howard Rubenstein, had already said they wouldn't "dignify idle gossip with a response." But there was nothing "idle" or merely "gossip" about this story; it was direct from Ivana. Then, I got a response from the man himself. Donald told me, variously, "It is better for Ivana and me to separate at this time. I am leaving because I want to leave. Ivana is a wonderful woman and a very good woman and I like her. We might even get back together. I can't say we won't. Who knows what could happen?" He characterized the other woman in the case as "just friends and that's as far as it goes." Donald did deny, however, that Ivana helped build his empire, and said, "I could have gotten any good Swiss hotel manager to run the Plaza." He also said he had an ironclad pre-nup with Ivana for $25 million. She also could have the house in Connecticut and he'd take care of their three children.

*It may surprise newspaper readers to learn that editors do exactly whatever they please with your copy no matter how "important" you may think you are. They write the lurid and luring headlines. They decide when to splash the columnist's photo with it. And they press and press for more, more, more!

Charges and counter-charges flew. I'd write one thing in the *Daily News*; the *New York Post* would write another. The nastiness was only beginning. Photographs of Marla Maples, the Georgia peach, began appearing everywhere. I noted at this time that Donald was "long gone" and ready to sample new publicity, new delights and a new freedom. "Let's remember, he is quite young, only forty-three, and hasn't been single since 1977." But I did defend Ivana in what I stated were "personal opinions"—to wit, that she'd been a dedicated wife and partner, working eighteen- and twenty-hour days, always on call, always at her best. And I said that Donald liked nothing better than a public fight, one he intended to win.

Only four days into coverage of the Trump split, the late Pulitzer prize-winning reporter Mike McAlary sounded an alarm. He wrote for the New York *Daily News*: "We have already given the so-called situation more attention than it merits." I don't know if the knowledgeable McAlary thought I was just forcing Trump coverage down the throat of our newspaper, the *Daily News*, or what? Maybe he wanted to twit the editors as much as he twitted me. But the *News* editors were now begging for a Trump "scoop du jour." Later, McAlary would blast me from hell to breakfast in a satirical column. The editors of the paper refused to run his column. Hearing about it on the grapevine, I called and begged them to relent, to let McAlary have his say. Editor Gil Spencer drawled on the telephone, "Liz, the paper is having a wonderful time with this story. Newsstand sales are booming. You have done us the best turn of your career—and remember, McAlary is not *yet* running this newspaper!" (I was sorry. I have always been curious to know just how deep McAlary dished me.)

Everywhere I went I was under siege by insiders and VIPs, all wanting in on the latest dirt. They were sure I wasn't writing everything I knew and that I'd give them the real lowdown. At cocktails in the home of Shirley and Richard Clurman, two media mover-shakers, Mike Wallace ordered an entire room of *New York Times*, *Time* and *Newsweek* types to "Be quiet, so Liz can tell us everything about the Trumps!" I could hardly believe it. I was a star and I hadn't even twinkled yet. People couldn't seem to get enough of the Trumps and what happened next made it even more so.

Pre-separation, Ivana's friends had planned a February 14th birthday lunch for her at La Grenouille on East 52nd Street just off Fifth Avenue. Guests were to bring a gift of friendship in the shape of a heart. All of Ivana's in-laws had accepted in spite of their love for Donald.

I went blithely off to lunch on 52nd Street as an invited guest. I didn't even think to take a notebook. I took some heart chocolates instead. But outside La Grenouille, pandemonium was building. Inside, thirty well-wishers toasted Ivana in her red dress and she alternately laughed and cried. Her mother-in-law spoke touchingly and so did her sister-in-law. People like Carolyne Roehm, Anne Bass, Shirley Lord, Carroll Petrie, Judy Taubman, Georgette Mosbacher and Laura Pomerantz chatted among themselves. Somebody remarked, "We should go en masse to Donald and ask him to conduct the rest of the divorce in private."

When it came time to leave, the crowd outside had grown to *Day of the Locust* proportion. The police had cleared all cars from the street except private limousines. People were standing, packed wall-to-wall filling 52nd Street. Ivana said she couldn't face it. Barbara Walters took her arm on the left and I took her arm on the right. "We'll just go out with you... and, Ivana, don't forget to smile like Jackie Onassis!" We were crushed through the door. Somehow, Barbara was swept aside as we emerged. (Lucky B. W.!) So there Ivana and Liz were on the front page of the New York *Daily News*, caught by the energetic lensman Richard Corkery.

The picture became infamous—gossip columnist possessively spirits Ivana through the crowd. I felt like an idiot. I reminded myself of Hope Emerson, the prison matron in the *film noir Caged*, escorting a prisoner to jail. It wasn't really anything I'd sought, but I was right there—in the middle of the soup: well-meaning but stupid. It made me part of the story. The *News* described it on the front page: "A crushing crowd yelled to

Ivana Trump, 'Get the money!' Inside posh La Grenouille, her friends, including our Liz Smith, moved her to tears with their warm support."

There is no going back from a telling front page like that one. It made Ivana into a media goddess. (I have to admit, Corkery had made both of us look very good!) And now I was in Ivana's corner whether I wanted to be or not. Had I lost credibility as a journalist? Yes, of course. Were lots of other journalists mad as hell at me because I was getting so much attention? Yes, of course. Were some very nice friends of mine now saying I was an "asshole"? Yes, of course.

Next came "The Best Sex I Ever Had" headline in the *New York Post*. Ivana wept buckets even though she was told Marla had denied ever saying such a thing about The Donald. Old Miss Lonelyhearts here advised Ivana in print: "They used to quip 'Love is the delusion that one woman differs from another.' This saying could also apply to your footloose, immature husband."

Meantime, the broadcast media didn't want the Trump story to die down either. For three months, I would be awakened every morning at 7:00 A.M. by my *Live at Five* producer Bohdan Zachary demanding breathlessly, "What ya got for us today?" I was on the tube, endlessly discussing it. And threatening Bohdan's life didn't help. He called incessantly. I was to make something up if I didn't know anything new to say. I didn't do that, but I did do what I could with what I had. I made bricks without straw, all right, for at least three months. This was a story that wouldn't die down—one of the first of the coming avalanche of media overkill, those "to the max" situations that would culminate in the disgraceful overcoverage of John F. Kennedy, Jr.'s death a decade later.

Donald fanned the fire. He could never shut up and let well enough alone. He had taken on Cindy Adams of the *New York Post* to tell his side of things. Cindy was funny about it all—yet people imagined we were in a feud because Donald was talking to her. Everybody loves a feud. But actually, it was Donald who had turned himself into my enemy. He demanded on

February 24th that the *Daily News* fire me. Word went around that he intended to buy the paper for this purpose. The publisher and editors just laughed in his face.

TV loved the Trump story almost more than the tabloids did and we began to get a lot of national high-minded coverage. ABC and other networks looked down their noses at the rest of the media, then offered "expert opinions," from the likes of Dr. Ruth and Zsa Zsa Gabor. The networks cannibalized everything they seemed to be criticizing, expressing disdain for the tabloids and local TV, while stealing from all of us, and representing all the very scoops they so claimed to despise.

At this same time, my friend Malcolm Forbes died of a heart attack. But Malcolm's going couldn't compete with the ongoing Trump madness. And I will deal with it later.

I was amused at the admirable braininess of Alexander Cockburn in *The Nation*. He wrote that "Manhattan's answer to 'Götterdämmerung' is the fissure between the Trumps, and its Wagner is Liz Smith." Maybe he didn't mean it as a compliment, but because Mr. C. had always referred to me mockingly as "the divine Liz" and because I wished I were a fraction as smart as he is, I pressed it in my scrapbook.

Jeannette Walls has described the tabloid war that ensued. "A lot happened in the world that week. The Berlin Wall was toppled and Germany was reunited. Drexel Burnham Lambert, the wildly powerful junk bond company, that spearheaded the eighties financial boom, collapsed. And after twenty-seven years in prison, South African civil rights leader Nelson Mandela was freed. But for eleven straight days, the front pages of the tabs were devoted to the Trump divorce. *Time* and *Newsweek* did cover stories. Even *The New York Times* stooped to cover it."

Time magazine now decided that gossip was news. Or, as I had put it, "Gossip is news running ahead of itself in a red satin dress." *Time* posed me for a photo with all the *Time* types who had worked on their big cash-in about the Trump split. I was shown sitting with two Pulitzer prize-winners, William "O. Henry" Porter and Carl Bernstein. These giants should have been ashamed for what they let happen to their story in *Time* magazine's pages.

I expected them to take a dim view of what I did for a living. But Carl, who had become the self-appointed Savonarola of journalism, took the dimmest view. He had already expressed himself, saying the Trump story was "the Three Mile Island of journalism, a meltdown waiting to happen."

At that time, he had blasted me, and my "smarmy sort of New Journalism." (The Trump story was about adultery, disillusion, betrayal, the end of romance, divorce and money. Subjects that Carl personally knew only too much about. I didn't find it particularly "smarmy," nor was there anything new about this kind of gossipy journalism.)

Time interviewed me, of course, for its cover story on the rise of gossip. The first questions asked were whether I'd had a face-lift, whether I dyed my hair and whether I was gay. I would never ask anybody any of those questions. Then *Time* had the audacity to make fun of *me* for being "trivial."

Time seemed to feel the gossip boom was brand-new and had just happened—because of the Trumps. But it had been well-reported that the entire genre (so ravishingly evident in the Winchell/Kilgallen/Hedda/Louella years of the forties, fifties and early sixties) had received a big shot in the late sixties and seventies. Chappaquiddick had become the—you must excuse me—high-water mark of more candid, juicy reporting by a press tired of covering up for politicians and the like. Watergate had created a new interest in modern investigative journalism. Sally Quinn said, famously, that, "After the heroin of Watergate scandal we were then hooked on the methadone of gossip!"

My own words and thoughts and answers to *Time*'s questions about gossip appear in their cover story. But they are presented as the melded work and thought of *Time* researchers and of writer Bill Henry. Tch-tch.

The Trump saga marched on. I tried to stop writing the Trump story at the end of February. But by mid-March I was back with an exclusive from Marla Maples's dad. And on March

21, I reported on a fax from Donald in which he said I should be ashamed of myself.

The anger between Ivana and Donald became like overboiled coffee and now little dollops of crême de la Marla appeared in the gossip column. I had become a part of this spectacle but my editors just shrugged. "If this isn't a tabloid story, then there are no tabloids," said one and they assigned many other reporters and photographers to the Trump watch. My producer at *Live at Five* said our ratings were up fifty percent. I have to give him credit for our coverage; he'd bug me so aggressively that I'd go out and get something new. I said, "This is the biggest story I've ever seen that isn't important—next to Elizabeth Taylor and Richard Burton."

Donald Trump was now enjoying his new sex symbol image. Before, he'd been just a braggart and a show-off, but the tabloids were making him look like a stud, catnip to women. His second book was coming out and he found time to slip into it this charming sentence: "Liz Smith used to kiss my ass so much it was embarrassing."

I was sitting on-air with my TV colleague the rambunctious Sue Simmons. She asked how I had liked what Donald had written about me. I stupidly asked, "What?" She repeated it. I blushed. "Oh, that Donald, he just doesn't know when he is really liked or when people are being nice to him."

Well, you know what? Everybody prospered. Donald married Marla and got a wonderful baby daughter out of it. Ivana settled for the pre-nup money but won out in the court of public opinion and when she went into the Ivana business, she did well (ghosted novels, clothes, makeup, a column, what have you).

The Donald-Marla marriage in the Plaza was a thing of beauty and Marla insisted I be invited to cover—and sat me right near the altar. And by now you know that Donald and Marla are divorced. She settled for practically no money because she didn't want a replay of the "Ivana bomb squad disposal method" used by Donald. But Marla *was* now a name. She *had* appeared in a Broadway musical, maybe her fifteen minutes isn't up yet? No, it isn't. She is now involved happily with a son of Norman Mailer!

Ivana is her usual bubbly, charming self and we are still friends, but then, now *she* and *Donald* are friends—as the parents of three heirs need to be. Mr. Trump himself made a big financial comeback, which nobody thought he could. Today he travels only with beautiful young women to keep his image in shape. And he is building the tallest structure in the world near the United Nations, a feat guaranteed to make thousands furious and to make him very happy because of it.

I had never fallen out with the Trump family because they wisely stayed on the sidelines throughout. And it wasn't long before Donald started greeting me warmly and kissing me again when we'd meet in public.

I could never dislike Donald, even in his worst moments. And I treasure three letters I have received from him since the unpleasantness. They were unsolicited, on his heavy cream-colored, engraved stationery with his characteristic bold signature. Here's one April 5, 1991: "Even though you crucified me over the last year, you really are a spectacular woman!" And another, "You are honest, fair—and a Great Lady; not to mention an excellent writer." And one I framed. (I had written positively about how he had preserved Mar-a-Lago so accurately.) Donald writes: "Dear Liz, I think I am beginning to love you again. Sincerely. Donald."

Oh yes—in all the hoopla, did I benefit from the Trump story? Well, when the New York *Daily News* fell on hard times in 1991, I was wooed and won by New York's most elegant and best-edited, best-written tabloid, the upscale New York *Newsday*. I am sure they wouldn't have wooed so hard or offered such a great contract if I hadn't just been through the War of the Trumps. At that time some people said I was the highest-paid print journalist in the world. And some said I was now the most powerful. I don't know about the first assertion, but I can't complain; I did really well for myself. As for the second assertion, I say, "Bull!" There are no really powerful print journalists these days. Even if they aspire to be, their position would be vitiated by the fact that there are now so many voices vying to be heard, in print, in television, on the radio, on the fascinating but totally unreliable Internet and—for all I know—in outer space.

THE CHAIRMAN

OF CAPITALISM

TO ME, THE MOST FASCINATING thing about my late friend Malcolm Forbes was that he owned the letter Albert Einstein wrote to Franklin D. Roosevelt advising him that there *could* be such a thing as an atom bomb. This letter was the beginning of the famous Manhattan Project that helped us win World War II, and it let the nuclear genie out of the bottle for good.

This letter can be seen in the Forbes Building at 60 Fifth Avenue in NYC, along with many other priceless missives that Malcolm collected. Forbes was born to privilege and tried to rise to the occasion by public service, running for governor of New Jersey. He didn't make it. I haven't really analyzed Malcolm too deeply, but I think that one day, after not getting to be governor, after a long marriage, five kids, grandchildren and after becoming very rich from *Forbes* magazine, he threw up his hands and decided to do exactly as he pleased with the rest of his life. After that, he worked and played with equal vigor. It was in this last ten years of his life that I knew Malcolm as an adventurer who had the loving companionship of his children, his former wife, loyal employees and hundreds of friends, old and new.

It is disheartening to me that Malcolm is only remembered as a rich man who dated Elizabeth Taylor, refused to "act his age" by riding motorcycles and was a closet case. When he died suddenly in 1990, much hateful homophobia, shared by some gays and straights alike, began to surface to smear him. I never saw this gay side of Malcolm—and wouldn't have cared if I had known about it—so I can't really comment on what I don't know. I am just sorry he isn't remembered for the more pertinent contributions of his life.

This is what I wrote in February 1990 about the death of one of my own best celebrity targets: "The world has lost a colorful subject, but I have lost a good friend and someone I truly respected. Malcolm enabled so many of us, including the public, to live vicariously as if we were at the top of the heap along with him. He was a sincere capitalist ideologue, who still believed anyone who wanted to could make it. Yet his brand of super-capitalism was defined by a compassionate and dispassionate nature and a good sense of humor."

I frequently wrote about Malcolm for himself alone, but when his friendship with Elizabeth Taylor was revealed, he became infinitely more interesting to all of us in the press.

The Elizabeth-Malcolm "relationship"—whatever it may have been—certainly put these two show-offs on the map. And that's where both liked to be. Elizabeth has always managed to keep herself in the limelight. Malcolm, in his later years, learned how to do that, too. The two of them were natural-born publicity hounds.

They met when Elizabeth first launched her perfume Passion. Malcolm had been invited to introduce her so they knew each other in a casual way. Then they began to surface together, and finally the tabloid press made them "an item." Elizabeth liked powerful, wealthy men and in her developing consciousness for the AIDS fight, it wasn't lost on her that Malcolm could be an enormous benefactor. This he became—presenting her with a one-million-dollar check at a party given on his New Jersey estate. He also gave her many expensive baubles and she was used to men giving her "trinkets." She, in turn, gave him more public recognition than he'd ever had before. They co-hosted charity galas together, they went riding on motorcycles and up in hot-air balloons. They took trips on the Forbes yacht and went to Asia together. They were very good for one another's "business."

The fact that the tabloid press can never accept a relationship between a man and a woman without bringing sex into it may just be an indication of how fatally romantic the tabloid press really is. Platonic friendships don't exist in Tabloidland. But, of course, the friendship between Elizabeth and Malcolm *was* platonic, affectionate and very much a true friendship. When he died, she said simply, "A light has gone out in my life."

I was often around Malcolm and Elizabeth during their white-hot publicity time. They sometimes kissed rather chastely and held hands. She seemed to depend on him. He was always thrilled to be in her presence. If one asked if they had any future serious plans, they'd just giggle like kids. Now I do think he'd have married her in a second if he'd had the nerve. But she wasn't about to barter away her single state and give up on the possibility of romantic love. So, I doubt this matter ever actually came up between the two of them. Malcolm was a bit shy. It would have been daunting and hurtful for her to have to say no to him. My bet is, he never asked and she never encouraged.

After Malcolm's death, I was amazed when both she and I were accused of being part of a "cover-up," a calculated effort to convince the world of Malcolm's heterosexuality. But Elizabeth never, ever uttered one word to me that indicated she and Malcolm were anything but friends. And I never wrote about them as a romance, only as a pair of famous, wealthy people who were having a very good time together in a fair exchange.

I couldn't have been induced to take part in a "cover-up." I didn't know anything about what Malcolm was purported to be covering up. I saw Malcolm arrive, alone, at black-tie parties, get off his bike, doff his helmet and go inside. I knew his kids, his grandkids, his whole family and I didn't question his private life. I never saw Malcolm in the company of the young male entourage that his critics claimed he'd had in life.

Malcolm took me on several delightful trips. One was to his island in Fiji with the *Architectural Digest* editor Paige Rense and her then husband, Arthur Rense. We stayed in authentic grass huts, snorkeled, sunned and attended Fiji ceremonies. The Fijians were then said to be the world's most peaceful people. Since those days their quarrels with the Indian population of Fiji has sullied their good reputation.

Malcolm loved his own Fijians. They were then all peace-loving Methodists for whom Malcolm brought a bagpiper to church to play "Amazing Grace." We had flown 25,000 miles on the Forbes jet with some of his sons, daughters-in-law, his PR guy, his regular helicopter pilot who had broken his hand and could not work, his secretary and staffers. Malcolm exercised his droit du seigneur—he slept in the only real bed on the plane. In Fiji, he'd appear at sunset to throw out quantities of hard candy to the island kids. It was very noblesse oblige, but it was Malcolm to the max, and it had an innocent, paternalistic charm. (Malcolm was providing the entire island with jobs, health care, work and retirement.)

Another time, Malcolm invited me to go ballooning in Normandy. His château offered one big house party, dominated by defunct kings, princes, dukes of Europe, plus the financier John Gutfreund and his wife, Susan, the charming Betsy and Walter Cronkite, and the down-to-earth Joy and Regis Philbin. Malcolm gave us the total Forbes treatment. He had bagpipers playing at dinner and men in red coats blowing big gold hunting horns. I stayed in a bedroom dedicated to Napoleon III. I was in hog heaven when the Gutfreunds arrived from Paris and Susan asked me what one was supposed to wear to dinner. I figured if a very rich woman whose neighbor is Hubert de Givenchy didn't know what to wear to dinner in Normandy, then I was home free. I told her that the night before I'd seen the King of Romania in a red shirt by Ralph Lauren's Polo.

That same night at dinner, I advised Malcolm: "You have a perfect photo op here. You must get Lucky Roosevelt, Anne Eisenhower and Jean MacArthur together in one picture with yourself!" Malcolm was thrilled by this suggestion. He almost fired his PR guy. "Why didn't you notice we are here at the site of the Normandy invasion and I had an Eisenhower, a Roosevelt and a MacArthur all together?" (Mrs. Roosevelt was a U.S. Chief of Protocol. Ms. Eisenhower was the granddaughter of General Ike. Mrs. MacArthur was the widow of General Douglas MacArthur who had presided over postwar Japan and carried on the Korean War, until Harry Truman fired him for insubordination.)

I hated ballooning. It was eerie and beautiful to hear the gas hissing into the globe overhead while the rest was silence. But it was scary and I was ever on the lookout for power lines, even when flying with some world champion. Still, it's a wow of a memory to recall floating up over the castles of Normandy with balloons shaped like witches on broomsticks, châteaux, Faberge eggs and the like, all following silently. It was the landings that were a bitch—being dragged in the overturned basket over manured cow fields before we could stop. Having to drink brandy with the farmer whose field had accepted you. But only a total nerd or sissy would refuse to go up when even the octogenarian Mrs. MacArthur was often seen stepping into a basket with Malcolm.

When we weren't ballooning, we were free to sightsee and there are few things to compare with going to Caen to have the Bayeux Tapestry explained to us by Professor Iris Love. (Regis Philbin, now a big ABC star from his *Who Wants to Be a Millionaire* quiz show, sometimes says, "I've made a popular success in life in spite of knowing more than I ever needed to know about the Tapestry and the invasion of 1066.") Other times we visited Mont-Saint-Michel and let the ocean close in, saw the beaches of Normandy and the Eisenhower Military Museum in the presence of an Eisenhower herself. All this was terrific, thanks to Malcolm.

Another time I went on the Forbes yacht, *Highlander*, up the Hudson River because Malcolm was trying to impress Elizabeth Taylor. We walked all over the Rockefeller properties without Ms. Taylor complaining about her stiletto high heels. Malcolm had just given her a lavender-painted motorcycle so there was lots to talk about.

One of my own favorite *Highlander* photos is of Mrs. Douglas MacArthur and the great actress Lillian Gish and me. We set out to prove to the world there were some people older than Liz. I spent much time trying to convince Jean MacArthur to let me interview her. No way. She did like to talk privately about her famous husband but refused to read the William Manchester book I recommended on his life, *American Caesar*.

"No, there might be something in it about my general that I did not like!" She did tell me she had given his museum in Norfolk the wristwatch he gave her after they escaped from Corregidor during World War II. It is engraved, "To My Best Lieutenant!" I went many times to the Waldorf Tower to dine with this petite little widow who was always one of Malcolm's VIPs. She never missed a Forbes party. Mrs. MacArthur would say as we ate fabulous room service, "I'd prefer to have chili with our friend Joel Rice." Mr. Rice, a native of Aransas Pass, Texas, was famous for his fiery food. One night as Mrs. MacArthur and I chilied down on his terrace, I noted Lillian Gish was also there. I signed the guest book then, "Please invite me back sometime when you have a more mature crowd." *Les Girls*—Jean and Lillian—thought this was quite funny.

Lillian, the grandest star (next to Mary Pickford) of America's silent film era, was another Malcolm VIP. We were at a party where the ninety-something Ms. Gish refused to sit down. Betty Bacall noted the actress Anne Jackson sitting on a couch. "Get up, Anne, and give Lillian your seat!" Anne pretended amazement. "Why—is she pregnant?" Lillian adored this story and later, being saluted at the Plaza Hotel, she asked me please to tell it in my speech about her.

In August 1989, Malcolm gave his valedictory party to end all parties—a celebration of his seventieth birthday at the Forbes castle in Tangier, Morocco. As I have said, he had a head for public relations on a big scale. I knew he liked me for myself, but he liked me much better for having a major column. Malcolm's self-aggrandizements were pragmatic and good for his empire. Fun and business as one. He didn't tell you what to write and you were free to fire at will.

The guests were to arrive in Tangier by chartered jets, their own jets, their own yachts, however they liked. Most of the 700 internationals took Malcolm up on his offer of transportation. A few souls like Kay Graham of *The Washington Post* insisted on paying their own way. I went as his guest and had a good time, but the effort—with Miss Taylor as its centerpiece—was not perfect. Sometimes the logistics broke down. Still, the press in general reacted with outrage that Forbes was spending his own money on such luxury and that some of us (most of us) had elected to go along for the ride.

I thought my report of the party was fairly critical. I said, in part: "Believe me, friends, if you feel envious or scandalized, a lot of this outing—as wonderful as it was—seemed chiefly designed for the press to overreact to it. And some of it was like accompanying 700 people on an unair-conditioned bus trip to Ardmore, Oklahoma—during the dog days.

"Even for the stars of the trip, there was much 'hurry up and wait'—wait for the 700 to organize so their planes could leave, wait for them to find their seats (many complaining that they didn't get into first class or aboard the Concorde with Barbara Walters), wait in line for an hour to inch into the Forbes Palace Mendoub on the night of the gala, wait to fight for a seat assignment for a dinner that wasn't even served until after 10:00 P.M., wait for a car or bus or a "huff" (which some of the guests left in) to take you back to your hot, tiny hotel room that smelled of fish and fresh paint, and where the water taps were often empty...and, once back on the ground at JFK, there was an hour and a half scramble in the sultry dark for luggage, with nobody to carry it through Customs or to your vehicle. (Certain fragile ladies without strong-armed escorts were quite nonplussed by this abrupt ending to the fairy tale.)"

I did add that there were many plusses. When it comes to Morocco's culture itself, it is impossible to overstate the "Lawrence of Arabia" glamour and color. Chanting women in gold-embroidered veils, dashing men holding rifles astride gilded saddles on fine horses, wonderful otherworldly camels chewing their cuds into eternity, whitewashed buildings and date palms swaying under a half-Mediterranean, half-Atlantic moon. Then there was Fiat's Gianni Agnelli at the helm, steering his beautiful two-masted scarlet-sailed schooner right across the drift of British press lord Robert Maxwell's big awkward white steamer in order to land the Agnelli guests in style at Rupert Murdoch's yacht for lunch. Everyone loved King Hassan's lunch, given in the Tangier Country Club. Again, it was Morocco itself that captivated us by unbelievable spectacle; charging horsemen, firing rifles, rich kingly tents boasting elaborately beautiful cushions, silver platters of greasy lamb and couscous, and a serving of orange juice, scented coconut milk and Coca-Cola only. No alcohol. (This was, in fact, a hard weekend for drinkers—they ran out of vodka, gin and juice even before dinner was served at Malcolm's party.) People who had grown rich overnight, or by years of hard work, were reminded once more of how the other half usually lives—sober, hungry, cramped in economy class, schlepping their own luggage in unairconditioned terminals. I don't think it did these grand personages any harm, but some said they felt "used" in yet another publicity blast for Malcolm, his magazine and Elizabeth's perfume. They said they hated the numbers of imported paparazzi. Malcolm and Elizabeth even did their birthday cake speeches with their backs to the guests, addressing the TV cameras and the press. (Miss Taylor was reported taking a break from personally greeting all 700 guests by sitting in an anteroom swearing, "I don't believe he made me do this!") A reporter asked if she'd ever been to a party like this before and E. T. said, 'No. I never have. And I never will again!'"

My pet memory of the forty-eight-hour event was arriving at the King of Morocco's party and being told by David Frost that at a recent other gathering, sixty-one guests were assassinated in an attempt on the king's life! I decided that instead of being berated by critical stay-at-homes in the press for accepting Malcolm's invite, I should receive combat pay.

Malcolm shrugged off my critical column: "Well, I'm sorry. But I was trying to give everybody a good time. And it did win us millions of dollars worth of publicity for the magazine."

As I've said, I was embroiled in L'Affair Trump at the time Malcolm died in February of 1990. I was saddened, but did think it was lucky that he'd given himself such a fabulous birthday only months before.

On the day of his memorial service, I went alone to St. Bartholomew's Episcopal Church on Park Avenue. I wanted to grieve and be quiet. At the door I saw Sirio Maccioni, the owner of Le Cirque. He summoned an usher, whispered to him and we went down the aisle—way down the aisle! He took me almost to the very front. I was a little embarrassed since I had only intended to slip into the back and lick my wounds. Suddenly I find myself in the second row being seated next to Brooke Astor. I felt this was a mistake, but I couldn't object. Mrs. Astor and I whispered discreetly to one another. The music was playing softly.

Suddenly down the aisle came Richard M. Nixon, alone, but under escort. He was placed directly in front of us. The church was fairly quiet. Nixon turned in his seat, lasered in on me and spoke up heartily, as if we were at a party. "Hello there. You know the story on you in *Time* magazine—yes, the story on gossip—I thought that was terrific. Good for you for the work you have been doing." (The Trumps? And gossip? Ex–President Nixon was keeping up with all that?) I murmured my thanks. Nixon turned back to the front. Then he turned back again. "Oh, Mrs. Astor—I almost didn't see you there. How are you? Did you see the *Time* piece on Liz and gossip?"

Now I was ready to go under the pew. But about that time, they delivered another VIP. Elizabeth Taylor was seated next to Nixon. She turned, winked at me and whispered softly, "Isn't it sad? Didn't you just adore Malcolm?" And then, Nixon, mindful of her celebrity, chatted Elizabeth up for a while. The service began and Malcolm's children each stood to do him justice before the bagpipers played that final sad thing they do.

As we left the church, Mrs. Astor was holding my arm. She said, "Well, Liz, I thought you were a liberal Democrat. I didn't know you were so friendly with Mr. Nixon."

I said, "I'm not. I don't know what that was all about. I have only met him once before in my life."

But I did feel the whole thing would have appealed to Malcolm. The world's biggest movie star, the world's most disgraced U.S. president, the world's best-known, best-loved philanthropist and a gossip columnist, all seated together at his memorial, making small talk.

I'd had another brief collision with the ex-president who had resigned his office because he was a liar, a cheat and about to be impeached. I was at a party for Ambassador Jeanne Kirkpatrick in the Sign of the Dove restaurant on Third Avenue. Nixon came in and "did" the room. Then he saw me and came over, holding out both hands as if we were old friends. (I thought suddenly of his daughter Julie, who always refused to speak to me.) Nixon was saying, enthusiastically, "Say—I see you on TV all the time, on WNBC, and enjoy you so much. I have been wondering and wanting to ask you. Do they pay you a lot for doing that—an awful lot, I hope!" I said I was probably overpaid for my seven and a half minutes on-air a week. Nixon nodded enthusiastically. "Good, good. You make them pay you all you can squeeze out of them." I felt really creepy being lauded by someone who I had wanted to see driven from the White House. It seemed so insincere. Yet here he was, not doing anyone any harm, acting like a true New Yorker, hoping to rehabilitate his reputation, praying we all had short memories. My guess was that he had very few friends and the people he sometimes glimpsed in public life were so familiar to him that he felt he knew them.

At any rate, when Le Cirque moved from Park Avenue to its new quarters in the Villard Houses on Madison Avenue, I found myself there prominently painted into a group portrait of former Le Cirque regulars. I am seated for posterity—next to Richard Nixon. And now, every time I go in and out of the restaurant and look at the painting by Robert Cenedella, it makes me smile.

Me and my pal, Dickie.

INDIANS AND

CHIEFS

IN THIS OLD WORLD THERE are Indians and there are Chiefs for a very good reason. Without us Indians, the Chiefs would have no one listening, admiring or following them. A heady mix is therefore good. Most Manhattan hostesses realize this. They select a good quota so that the Chiefs will have Indians hanging on their every word. And they select enough Chiefs so that the other Chiefs feel properly in their milieu and are glad they came.

Nobody wants to go to an all-Indians, no-Chiefs event. And nobody who is a mere Indian, as most of us are, should want to go to an all-Chiefs get-together, because these often implode, and become black holes as Chief after Chief destructs with too much VIPness.

This may not make any sense. But I went to Egypt in 1990 with an all-Chiefs-and-me entourage and the trip was indelible, unforgettable and some of it was trying. By the time it had ended, I felt totally reclusive, more and more inclined to the Indian way of thinking and more and more exhausted by the rigors of dealing with the Chiefs.

.   .   .

NOW THIS STORY INVOLVES MY very own super-Chief friend, Barbara Walters, someone extra-special in my life. It is not meant to be critical, merely observant.

Barbara and I had known each other slightly in the days when she used to host the *Not for Women Only* talk show on NBC. I was an occasional guest as an entertainment writer and editor. Barbara was already famous then as the cohost of *The Today Show*. She had done all the groundbreaking, backbreaking, throwing herself on the barbed wire of male dominance so that other women might advance in TV. But today, she is nonpareil. I consider her the biggest star and the grandest VIP in the world. Barbara is more famous than the famous people she interviews and usually she has more impact than all of her peers put together. This doesn't always make her popular; she's a big target. I do think that without Barbara and her moneymaking, news-making abilities, the ABC network might not have survived quite so well.

There are lots of myths and misimpressions about my Barbara. I see her as a really nice human being, curious, emotional, generous to a fault, softhearted, mercurial. She can be moody and impatient and competitive. She has lots of perfectionist trouble in making up her mind and sticking to it. She's a big "what if—" or "maybe I should have—" kind of woman. The worst thing I can say about Barbara is that now and then she forgets that we are not blood kin and she treats me the way people tend to treat their close relatives. I am actually flattered by this maternal or sibling interest and I kind of enjoy the warm, homey way it makes me feel when she snaps at me, saying, "Oh, don't be idiotic. You are just wrong about this!" Or when she takes something I mean as a joke the wrong way and her feelings are hurt for ten seconds. But Barbara is incapable of staying mad or holding a grudge. I find her an amazing mixture of sweet and sour, a veritable cocktail of super-success and insecurity, but an ultimately cheerful, optimistic and positive soul. She never lets her right hand know what her left is doing when it comes to charity, giving away tons of money to almost anybody who asks her for it and also giving of her time, her talents and her heart to everything under the sun. I admire her.

My devotion to Barbara and my interest in writing about her exploits causes some to lift an eyebrow but I often write about her for a very good reason—*she always seems to be making news*. For years an anonymous woman would call my office and ask if Barbara and I were having an affair. I always knew when she had called, for I'd hear the fearsome Saint Clair Pugh say, "Madam, do me a favor and don't call here again. How dare you?" (But, of course, people are correct to do anything they damn please to gossip columnists because of the vice versa.) I always thought this was a funny, fanciful rumor and Barbara didn't take it seriously.

Years back, a rather nasty book was written about Barbara. I had been interviewed and tried to give my best, most honest impressions. The author described everything I said as "gushing" (one of the worst words in the English language) and it taught me a lesson. You can do your famous friends a lot of harm by speaking positively of them. It's better you should decline to be interviewed. But this is hard for me since I feel I should always cooperate with other writers. And it is impossible for me not to write about Barbara in a book that purports to tell something about my life.

One of the things this guy wrote was that Barbara "couldn't keep help." At the time, after twenty years, she still had her grown-up daughter's nanny in her employ. She had the same cook-housekeeper she'd employed for twenty years. Her office staff had been with her for years. At her parties, well laced with VIPs, you can also see her college roommate, old pals from *The Today Show* era, lowly staff members. I was glad when I started writing my column in the *Daily News* and Barbara took me to celebrate at the Café des Artistes. I became one of her Indians, though she would never see it like that.

.   .   .

BARBARA INVITED ME TO GO to Egypt with her and her
then husband, Merv Adelson, back in 1990, saying she was allowed to bring one extra person on a friend's jet. We would fly
on Linda Wachner's plane, spend the night in Paris, head on to
Egypt, go up the Nile on a brand-new boat, the *Hopi*, and end in
Cairo. After that the entire party would segue to Jordan and on
to Israel. What a chance.

      Linda Wachner owned the jet and was the person on the
trip I didn't know. She was the only woman with a Fortune 500
company. She was into making and selling shirts, ties, bathing
suits, bras, and Speedo sportswear. She would explode after our
initial meeting into one of the real financial movers and shakers
of NYC, and move on from being a Chief in Barbara's social set
to becoming an international Super-Chief. She became friends
with the late Ambassador Pamela Harriman, and is an intimate
to Mercedes and Sid Bass of the Fine French Furniture crowd,
and like that.

      But on this particular trip, my host Linda seemed to me to
be a rather lost-in-the-woods soul. She fretted that she didn't have
a man. Her husband had died. She needed a date. I recall sitting
alone with her in a tour bus near the Pyramids while everyone else
went inside. Linda and I were on a close-to-the-restrooms watch
at the time and we didn't dare sightsee. She asked me would I introduce her to some nice guys, did I know any nice guys, and what
could she do about her love life? I *am* a regular Dear Abby, but I
wasn't much help as I remember. I think I said my own love life
wasn't so ja-da-ja-da-zing-zing-zing.

      When we'd first taken off from New York, I discovered
there wasn't really a seat for me on the plane. Barbara had erred
on the side of generosity. So we noshed on fabulous baskets
from E.A.T., gossiped a lot and I slept stretched in the aisle
overnight under a blanket.

      Linda had booked us into the Ritz. We arrived at 7:00
A.M. and needed sleep. Barbara and Merv were next door to me

in The Duke and Duchess of Windsor suite. Well, because we came in so early, we were presented with bills for "two nights" and these seemed astronomical. I think the D&D suite went for about five thousand dollars. My own single cost me over eight hundred. The women in the party hit the roof over this expense, but the men were shushing them and resignedly pulling out their Amex cards. There was some griping—"Does Linda think we can all afford to live like this just because *she* can?"

I actually luxuriated in my Ritz room. It reminded me so little of the first time I'd been to Paris alone, back in 1956, returning from Rome. I had then stayed at a tiny hotel off the Etoile where the bath was down the hall and the towel the size of a washcloth. I had ridden every tour bus in Paris trying to get the hang of things and left the City of Light having never spoken a word to a single soul except mercenaries. It was lonely. But this was different; I was with the Chiefs in all their war paint.

Who were these people? They were Evelyn and Leonard Lauder of the cosmetic empire and the fabled art collection; Joan and Paul Marks—he was then the head of Memorial Sloan Kettering Hospital and she was a respected sociologist who had been Barbara's roommate at Sarah Lawrence; Linda and Mort Janklow (she the Lincoln Center philanthropist/Hollywood heir to the LeRoy dynasty and he the über literary agent); Blair Brown, the actress of *The Days and Nights of Molly Dodd* * and Mort Zuckerman, the magazine-newspaper publisher; and the lovely person who had arranged our tour for us—the late Micki Sarofim, an Egyptian, whose grandfather had exerted an enormous influence in the Coptic Church.

Of course, our trip was off the record. Me, the only Indian on board rating only one feather, couldn't even write with *that* feather. The trip had started with a bang and went whimpering on. We flew to Aswân and already people were getting a bit testy about their personal water bottles, not wanting others to

---

Blair, a lovely Chief, would go on to win a Tony Award in 2000 for her performance in the play Copenhagen. *On this trip she was being closely examined by our ladies to see if she was "good enough" for Mort.*

swill where they swilled. I loved Aswân but was horrified to discover that the dam had created a body of beautiful water no one could sport about in—because of the crocodiles. And the dogs, the starving dogs of Aswân, did take some of the fun out of it.

We got on the *Hopi*, our new boat, which had the type of rooms one finds in a good motel. We posed for photos as a group, wearing T-shirts that bore our pictures and read "Egypt 1990 Tut Tut." So cute! Soon some of us weren't speaking. But never mind that. When we went to our first *son et lumière* show at night, the description was in German. Most of us didn't have a clue, but Evelyn Lauder, born in Vienna, translated. It does pay to have bilingual friends.

In Edfu, we discovered an entire wall painting that seemed to be dedicated to the making of perfume. For this reason the Lauders lingered and we got a load of Edfu. I much preferred the crocodile city where mummified crocs are stacked up like cordwood.

In Luxor, we learned the value of being with Barbara. The museum opened a wing of "new finds" especially for us and we wandered around in bliss. Everybody in Egypt seemed to remember Barbara, who had been the friend of Sadat back in 1977. Her finest moment!

At night, I found out how much of a Super-Chief my Barbara really is. It seemed everyone jostled every night to sit next to her at the table. I became so disheartened by this maneuvering, and my lack of success in ever landing her that sometimes I would go sit at the corner table with the two ladies who Micki had brought along to do our laundry and ironing. They spoke English and were delightful.

One evening, visiting the Temple of Karnak, there was much joshing after Evelyn Lauder said it reminded her of the American Tel & Tel Building on Madison Avenue. That night I ran into Suzanne Maas, the Texas girl who had married writer Peter Maas. In the small-world department, I tried to introduce her to some of my Chiefs, but they weren't interested in meeting a mere Indian, an American Indian at that. This night I had a moment with Barbara as we walked among the massive columns.

She was depressed she said. She knew now she would never write a real book about her life. And then she said, "Anyway, next year this time I may be dead." This was uncharacteristic, but I chalked it up to the atmosphere. Egypt is a land of the dead, so it's a perfect place to feel depressed. (When I remind Barbara of this conversation, she can't recall having it.) We mostly all came down with the turista in neat relays, so that everyone wasn't sick at once. Linda Janklow and I had fallen absurdly onto a plate of beautiful peeled tomatoes, which we'd been warned not to eat. We did anyway. We paid for it. Dr. Paul Marks would poke his head into the rooms of the dying, but he refused to lay hands on us. I didn't blame him.

Before us, the *Hopi* had had as customers Gayfryd and Saul Steinberg, and Mrs. S. had left us all the fine down pillows she had brought along to upgrade the boat. We who were dying and crawling to the bathrooms were very grateful to Gayfryd for soft, clean, sweet places to lay our heads. (You see—rich Chiefs are good for lots of things.)

Arriving in the Valley of the Kings, I began to notice that almost every man in the crowd turned solicitously to Linda Wachner to help her over obstacles, down stairs, out of buses. It was awfully hot and Linda was light-years younger than I was, but nobody ever said, "Liz, old girl, can I give you a hand?" I finally decided to take this as a compliment. It had to be that they thought I was still young and spry and it couldn't possibly have had anything to do with Linda's owning a Fortune 500 company. (Linda would go on to become one of the most feared and controversial bosses in U.S. business, but on this trip she was a pussycat.)

On the boat at night our guide, Tati, would try to fill us in on what we were to see next, explaining the glories of Egypt and answering questions. Some of our gang were obsessed with the children of Israel in Egypt. (I guess they didn't want to wait for the DreamWorks movie *Prince of Egypt*.) Tati would find herself peppered with questions about Ramses II and how he oppressed the children, forcing them to make bricks without straw, forcing Moses to bring down the Plagues, causing the parting of the Red Sea and all the rest of it. Tati tried patiently to explain that the children of Israel form one of the shortest, least-known chapters in Egyptian history. "If you took one thousand match-sticks and lay them together as the history of Egypt, the history of the children of Israel in Egypt wouldn't even be represented by one matchstick head."

I often felt sorry for Tati, who was a cultured and bril-liant person. She was lecturing us and generally we had the at-tention span of mayflies. On the other hand, the Janklows had been in Egypt many times and they already knew all this stuff. I was blown away by the Egyptian culture; it was so much more grandiose, monolithic, hieratic and impressive than I could have imagined. It was beyond studying. You had to be there. And we were lucky—I believe we were among the last people allowed to actually go into King Tut's tomb and breathe our worst on his "wonderful things." (Tourists now visit a replica.)

In Cairo, at the museum, we had a real New York mo-ment. There on the line waiting to get in were premier songsmith Marvin Hamlisch and his wife, Terre. She was wearing a big picture hat, which sent all of us into convulsive questioning as to whether we had missed some important dress protocol? We were in shorts and T-shirts. I said, "Look, Barbara, our piano ac-companist is here from NYC. I guess he thought we might like to do a few numbers." (Marvin, the millionaire Pulitzer-Oscar-Tony-Emmy winner of Broadway, had often played for Barbara and me so we could make fools of ourselves singing at charity events.)

Now Barbara's celebrity paid off again. A museum offi-cial caught sight of her and waved us to a special entrance. We hadn't asked for VIP treatment, but we got it. We were even al-lowed to see the mummified body of Ramses II—a very little guy for such a powerful figure. (Since then he has been covered up for the sake of a newfound decorum or P.C. treatment of the dead.) I wandered off down a hall with Tati. She stopped before an enormous stone stela. She was reading it. I was yawning. "Here," she said flipping her hand, "here is the only chiseled representation referring to the children of Israel in Egypt. It says they threw their seed upon the ground." I ran, did not walk, back to my gang, who were in an all-gold casket room discussing what the entire thing might be worth to Cartier.

"Come on! Tati has found it for us: the children in Egypt. They threw their seed on the ground." Mort Zuckerman quipped, "Wouldn't you know it?" After this, everybody studied the stela, relaxed and seemed satisfied.

The rest of our stay in Cairo was taken up with buying jewelry. Micki wanted to show us Christian Coptic Churches, but she didn't get much response from us. Now we were taken to some diplomat's house for Barbara and Mort Z. to ask questions about world politics. Walters and Zuckerman both began to "do business," trying to arrange exclusive interviews and everything suddenly became New York normal. Barbara began to speculate about what she'd wear to greet the Queen of Jordan.

A great light fell upon me in the static calm of my big modern Cairo hotel room. I decided I'd opt out of Jordan and Israel with the Chiefs. I was afraid someone might take my scalp. But no, no one even cared when I said I was going to fly to Paris.

As I entered the silent hotel lobby at 5:30 A.M. on the day I was leaving, I was surprised to find Leonard Lauder there. He kissed me and said, "I just came down to say good-bye. I'm going to miss you so much. After all, you are the only person on this trip who ever listened to a thing I was saying." I was touched. I just kissed him and said, "Watch your back."

The Tut Tut Group went on brilliantly without me and I heard there was a row over drawing straws to see who got the best bedroom on a chartered boat in Jordan.

I was so happy to find myself Chiefless in Paris at this juncture that I went crazy and bought myself a Concorde ticket to fly back to New York. Leaving Paris at 11:15 A.M., I arrived in New York at 8:15 A.M.

I had a great adventure in Egypt with the Chiefs. I am still terribly fond of each and every one of them, though some of them no longer speak to one another. And though I concluded that I still believe the Greeks had the greater civilization—be-

cause their world was about democracy and life while the
Egyptian world was all about tyranny and death—I was over-
whelmed by Egypt's beauty. To this day, I treasure the needle-
point pillow Barbara gave each Tut Tut trip member. It reads:
"My name is Ozymandias. King of Kings: Look on my works,
Ye mighty, and despair!"

Despair? Well, no great adventure is worth its salt if you
can't stand back ten years later—and dish it!

BUT PLEASE DON'T PRINT IT!

THIS CHAPTER TITLE IS SOMETHING I have seriously thought of having inscribed on my tombstone. This often unreasonable plea is the single thing that people I am interviewing, questioning or having a simple chat with say to me the most.

The all-American view is that one can say absolutely anything one likes. Engrained in our heritage of free speech, it occurs with taxi drivers who suddenly tell you mid-ride that they are "as good as you are," when you have never suggested they aren't... or it's the lament of some sobbing starlet who has been done wrong...or one of the nation's top anchormen who can't believe you are actually having the effrontery to ask him a question. Yet, along with the freedom to speak out, comes the second freedom—the "But please don't print it!" freedom. People who have just run off at the mouth and blabbed their guts out seem to believe they are entitled then to request a suppression of the quote, the facts or any speculation or curiosity on the public's part.

My favorite in this genre occurred after the death of Ruth Cosgrove, Mrs. Milton Berle. I had always liked the feisty Ruth and I wrote a column saying I thought Milton should have given her a military funeral, for during World War II she was a WAAC. Ruth Berle had joined the war effort because, as she told her girl friends, "Honeys, that's where the men are all going to be—in the Army—and I want to be in the Army with them."

The idea of Ruth, laid out in her uniform, and Milton receiving the folded flag triangle was an irresistible one to me. But instead she had a Class A Beverly Hills show-biz funeral with a eulogy by the brilliant *M*A*S*H* humorist Larry Gelbart.

I was standing in the NBC makeup room some months after Ruth's death when in came a frail Milton Berle. We embraced and he said, "Well, I can't tell you how much I appreciated the nice things you wrote about Ruth when she died. She adored you and I am very grateful." We chatted for a moment and Milton said thoughtfully, "I wonder if I could tell you a story about Ruth. It's just priceless; a real wrap-up on her and I think you'd enjoy it. *But please don't print it!*"

He proceeded to describe an ongoing poker game they often played with pals, one of whom had been the late actor Lee Marvin. Milton said: "We were going at it hammer and tongs and Ruth, who could be a really vicious player, had put everything into a big pot and she threw her cards down, saying, 'Okay! I've won! I've won!' She began pulling the entire pot across the table into her arms.

"I put my hand on her arm and said, 'But Ruth, you didn't win, darling. You see, Lee Marvin here has a full house.'

"Ruth looked down at Lee's cards and then shoved the pot furiously away from herself, exclaiming; 'All right, Milton, all right. But remember, the next time you want your cock sucked, just call Lee Marvin!' "

I laughed for five minutes and so did Milton. But I was really laughing as much at "But please don't print it" as at the anecdote. Where, in what family newspaper or magazine could I have printed that? (Now times have changed and I feel I can. After all, a memoir is an exercise in vulgarity, candor, excess and overkill.)

As long as we're in this vein—and speaking of the legendary Milton Berle—I mentioned in my material on El Morocco that he was always one of the winners in the men's room contest to see who had the biggest organ.

Milton was always modest about his endowment. If anyone brought it up, he'd blush and say, "Oh, shut up." But the best stories told on him were by the Hollywood reporter Jim Henaghan, who said that when Milton was asleep in the locker room of the Hillcrest Country Club, the attendant would charge a quarter to lift the towel from the great comic's loins and let passersby see for themselves.

Henaghan's other story is of how Joey Bishop constantly pestered Milton to show him the real goods. Milton would fend him off, saying, "Get away from me, you little pervert. Leave me alone."

But Joey kept jumping around saying, "Oh, Milton, I just gotta see it for myself. Please."

Finally, one day, feigning irritation, Milton whipped it out to let Joey take a look. Bishop was amazed. "My God. Milton, does it get any bigger when it gets hard?" Milton shrugged: "I don't know. I always black out."

Now and then a "But please don't print it" plea seems worthwhile. Years before it was revealed that the former daughter-in-law of Elizabeth Taylor—Aileen Getty—was HIV-infected, I told Miss Taylor that I had this information. She said, "But please don't print it!"

I always thought that the plight of this young woman who had been married to Elizabeth's son, Christopher Wilding, and had children with him, was some part of Elizabeth's dedicated resolve to fight AIDS. She loved the girl and worried for her grandchildren. Of course, one of the tabloids printed the story soon after. But ain't that always the way? (As I often try to point out to recalcitrant gossip subjects—wouldn't you rather I dealt with it Liz Smith–style? Or you can offer yourself up to the supermarket tabloids. Sometimes they see the light, sometimes they don't.) I just couldn't justify the pain the Getty item might cause at the time. And it wasn't exactly something involving national security, though I concede it was gossip fodder. But then I've proved over and over again that I am a lousy gossip columnist.

THE BAD,

THE BAD AND

THE UGLY

WHERE SHOULD ONE DRAW THE line as to who one will or will not consort with among the vast array of celebrities littering our landscape? This is a hard one and I contend that even the most die-hard ethicist has difficulty drawing the correct line or living by his own prejudices. I have flip-flopped around. I once felt I could easily feed Richard Nixon to the lions personally, but by the time I encountered him, post-Watergate, as a man famously trying to live down his past, I found him rather personable, and at the same time, sad. At any rate, I certainly did not refuse to shake his hand and wish him well.

The same thing happened with Roy Cohn. I had grown up as a youthful radical, despising everything about the Commie-baiters of the fifties. I do mean Senator Joe McCarthy and his henchmen David Schine and Roy Cohn. But by the time I met Roy, who had become a very successful lawyer and influence in New York politics, I found myself unable to turn away from him. He fascinated me the way snakes are said to fascinate birds they are about to eat.

Two guys I like and admire, the late columnist Murray Kempton and the writer Sid Zion, gave me good advice about Roy. In effect, both said—you can enjoy Roy without approving of him. He isn't going to "take you in" and he knows that. But he'll try. And he is a loyal friend to the people he likes, plus being an invaluable source.

Source? I desperately always needed sources. So I settled for that, and to ease my conscience I told him directly exactly how I felt. "Roy, I like you personally but I don't approve of a single thing you stand for. You are politically, ethically and historically a very bad guy in my book. Take it or leave it." He would smile, showing his obvious face-lift scars.

Take it or leave it? He absolutely loved it. He set about trying to co-opt and influence me in really heinous ways. Once he asked me to print an item about how his boyfriend, a certain handsome model, was going to vote for Ronald Reagan. He elaborated that the guy had been chosen by cosmetic queen Estee Lauder to be her company's "man of the year." I knew that Estee hadn't selected this guy to be anything and I also knew that the young man was still an Australian citizen and unable to vote in the U.S. So I laughed in Roy's face, but then I shuddered. What if I had taken him at his word?

I met Roy because he was a devout fan, admirer and aspiring public escort to Barbara Walters. These two had known each other all their lives. Roy was forever saying to the world that he wanted to marry Barbara and had been pursuing her for years. This put Barbara in an awkward position; she didn't like to reject him by saying that the idea was ridiculous. She just ignored it. She was most loyally Roy's friend, publicly and privately. Considering how much Roy played up and depended upon his friendship with Barbara, I thought she conducted herself with admirable restraint.

Roy would call and say, "Want to go to '21' with me and Barbara tonight?" And, of course, I'd say yes. It was a three-way parlay—dinner in one of my favorite places, being with Barbara who I loved, being with Roy who might have a scoop for me.

But Barbara warned me. "He calls me and says the same thing. I accept, thinking you've accepted. We have to let him know we are 'on' to him." But we never did.

One of these "21" nights I arrived to find Barbara and Roy in a heated argument at the corner banquette near the kitchen door. Seated with them at the turn of the banquette was a good-looking young man. Roy sprang up, mumbled a name and put me between himself and the unknown man and then he and Barbara went on with their argument like two siblings on a night when Daddy had given the wrong one the car keys. I was pretty much stuck with the guy, so I "made conversation." He was pleasant but noncommital. Barbara and Roy were locked in their discussion, interrupting each other and waving off the waiter. Finally, desperate, I said the words I try never to ask, "And what do you do?"

The guy smiled. "Oh, Miss Smith, I'm just a TV repairman. I was fixing Mr. Cohn's set this afternoon and he invited me to come to dinner with you and, naturally, I was delighted."

When I told Barbara later that we had dined with a man totally unknown, even to Roy, she sizzled. "Isn't that just like him? Why, I could brain him."

Still, I had some interesting times with Roy. He dropped incredible stuff onto me, much of which I couldn't print—such as his absolutely riveting depictions of J. Edgar Hoover as a closet queen and transvestite long before it became common gossip. I saw that Roy, gay himself, was a rigid homophobe. I knew he owned a number of successful gay bars around Manhattan but he'd never admit it. Okay, that was his way of dealing with his unconventional life.

On other subjects, I'd chide him. He'd laugh. We had two bang-up fights because he was insulting in public, first, to Lauren Bacall and second, to Gloria Steinem. "I hate these phony liberal females," he'd fume. But when I said I wouldn't go out with him again if he reviled another woman in public, he calmed down and said he'd watch it. His quarrel with Bacall had to do with her long association with the Democrats and her and Bogart's stand during the Red witch-hunts. His quarrel with

Steinem was that she walked out of Le Cirque after giving me a kiss, ignoring him. Kid stuff.

But Roy had good gossip and good information that sometimes checked out. And he was a fount of information about everyone who was anyone. As time went by I discovered an essential truth about Roy Cohn. An effective deal maker and "hondler," a rainmaker and arranger, he was not much of a lawyer. I don't think he knew how to write a legal brief. He had others do all the scut work for him. He talked a great game and scared his opposition to death up front.

I went to Washington to cover the Reagan Inaugural for NBC, an experience so exhausting, idiotic, funny, fast and furious that I ran up thousands of dollars in personal expenses and never found time to turn in an expense account. Still, it was mucho grist for the old gossip mill. Roy had me invited into every GOP inner circle. I met the fattest of cats. It was a look at the rich and conservative side of American political life that I hadn't even dreamed existed.

I owed it to Roy and society's Jerome Zipkin, a friend to Mrs. Reagan, that I, a dedicated Democrat, was invited to the Reagan White House. President and Mrs. Reagan were the first residents of 1600 Pennsylvania Avenue ever to ask me. And I went, several times. It was in the receiving line for President and Mrs. Marcos that I had the opportunity to look for the machete scars on Imelda's arms. (She had almost been assassinated in an historical attempt on her husband's life.) There was some flak from my liberal friends that I would accept an invite for President and Mrs. Marcos. How could I go to such an event, they asked? I said, "It was a chance to meet my favorite living dictator." *The Washington Post* chided the Reagans for having a gossip columnist, plus the pop star Andy Warhol, to a state dinner.

But then *The Washington Post*, which took my column in syndication, suppressing it every day so that no one else in the area could print it, linked me up with the wrong New York newspaper. And they also referred in their guest list to a well-known Spanish count named Luis, as "Louise." (Since his wife had long known him as "Louise," there was quite a bit of titter-

ing about that!) And I had the satisfaction of knowing that even
the sainted *Washington Post* makes mistakes.

I NEVER MISSED ONE OF ROY'S self-given annual birthday parties, which took place when I knew him, at Studio 54. It
was here I observed him with the California businessman David
Schine, who had figured so largely in his youthful rise to fame.
Roy and David had gone round the world examining libraries
for subversive material, making asses and nuisances of themselves. And Roy had bent every effort to keep Schine from being
drafted into the Army. They were quite a scandal for their day.
At this latter-day birthday, Schine was with his wife and children and seemed to be a reliable, upstanding member of the heterosexual community. So, what did it mean? It meant that Roy
knew how and when to pick his friends.

　　At this party I brought Roy a magnificent pink-and-green
formal bow tie and cummerbund for his tuxedo. He wouldn't
wear the cummerbund. "Too gay," he said. But he threw away
his black tie and put on my colorful choice. It was on this night
that I joked with the reporter Murray Kempton, saying I'd try to
keep his name out of my guest list. But Murray lectured me.
"No, do not keep my name out. Maybe Abe Rosenthal would
rather not have the *Times* see his name on the list. But I am a
friend of Roy's and although I don't approve of him, I will always be his friend." I felt ashamed of my callow remark.

　　My experiences with Roy kept me waffling about him. I
would attack him to someone, then end up using him in some
manner. I tried to tell him this, but he just laughed and said, "I
know. It's okay. I don't have great expectations of people."

　　Soon, Roy Cohn came down with AIDS. And I won-
dered, as I had before, if all those special VIP trips to the basement of Studio 54 had been the cause. I knew so many who had
died after being taken into the inner circle of Steve Rubell's
hellhole. There were too many available easy drugs down in the

private enclave, too many chances for reckless, unprotected sex. Luckily, Rubell didn't usually invite us ink-stained wretches to participate.

Falling ill, Roy stonewalled to the end, denying he had AIDS until it killed him. He flatly refused to let me see him at Bethesda, where Nancy Reagan had arranged for his treatment. I called often. His last words to me were, "Well, okay, I'm sick. And you are kind to want to see me, Liz, but I don't want you to see me like this. I know where we stand. You don't approve of me. You may not even like me. But we've had a hell of a swell time, haven't we?"

I had to say yes.

WHEN I WAS CHASING SOCIETY FOR Cholly I had found myself welcomed with open arms by the padrones of "21," the former West 52nd Street speakeasy with the jockey statues outside wearing the colors of the Kentucky Derby winners.

I loved going to "21," looking at the football helmets and airplanes on the ceiling and trying their wonderful vichyssoise and billi-bi, a cream soup I had first encountered at El Morocco.

Two interesting things happened to me in "21." I went one night to dinner with the controversial Roy Cohn and my old friend Dorothy Strelsin, the former chorus girl who had married so well. Roy and I were sitting side by side with Dotty across from us, her back to the room. At "21" you are invariably sitting practically at the next person's table, so I was aware of a good-looking couple on my left—James Stewart of Lone Star Industries in Texas, with Mrs. Averill Dalitz, a beautiful blonde dazzler. (Mr. Stewart had just made himself famous in 1980 by suggesting on the Op Ed page of the *Times* that the nation's capital should be moved to Kansas.) I became really interested when the Washington mover and shaker Bob Strauss waltzed in. This genial, profane, astute man had masterminded Jimmy Carter's bid for reelection and it had failed. But he was a Texan and still one of the nation's most powerful Democrats. He sat down across from Stewart and began to talk about subjects so fascinating that I immediately lost interest in Roy and Dotty and began only to listen to Bob Strauss.

He knew I was listening to him because he smiled at me frequently and all but included me in his conversation. When he went to the men's room, Stewart asked the unknown man who was with Strauss what it would take to get Bob on the Lone Star board of directors. The man said he thought Strauss wanted the use of a corporate jet. Stewart said Strauss could have *his* jet. When Strauss returned, the jet went unmentioned but Strauss then agreed to join Lone Star's board.

During all of this, Strauss never lowered his voice an iota and at times he seemed to be addressing the room rather than his companions. At one point, he had some harsh criticism of Jimmy Carter—then said, "I like the little guy but that 'born-again' Christian stuff…" He added that Carter had a "death wish." He stopped. He then looked right at me, inclined his head and said, "Iddn't that right, little lady?" I nodded. I was really into it. I rushed home from dinner and wrote down everything I could remember.

Some people think most gossip reporting is done like this, via eavesdropping. I had a personal rule not to report anything I overheard without advising the speaker. But this time I did a no-no. I felt Strauss might not have known me from a hole in the wall and he might not have realized he'd given me an exclusive interview, but he sure made himself fair game speaking out in "21." I could hardly believe how dynamic and indiscreet Strauss had been and I wanted to tell the world about it.

He opined that with Ronald Reagan in the White House he had sold most of his stocks and he reminisced about his Texas boyhood when the cotton crop was only affected by the weather, not by actions in Germany and Japan and Iran. At one point he reached over and shook my hand and said, "Thank you, little lady."

The column caused all hell to break loose. Sheldon Tannen of "21" telephoned. He said I had "broken the code of '21,' which was like a private club." He chastised me as unethical. I said I couldn't believe Mr. Strauss minded being written about since everyone could overhear him. It wasn't, after all, like the adroitly separated seats in the Four Seasons Grill where people go to talk business knowing no one can overhear them.

But I agreed with Tannen that maybe I should not have done it. I said, "Okay, I won't come in to '21' anymore."

Sheldon protested. "Don't say that. We want you in '21' all the time."

I took him at his word. I couldn't resist "21." My friend former senator Abe Ribicoff also called that day to say the column was sensational and being passed around all over Washington. "You did put the blocks to my friend Bob. But, you know, I think he kind of enjoyed it."

Later, Strauss and I became friendly acquaintances. He took my arm at a D.C. party and marched me over to his wife, Helen. "This is the girl who killed me over Lone Star Cement!"

Mrs. Strauss just laughed and said, "Good...that'll teach you not to be such a big mouth."

After this I tried to keep to my rules, to call my subjects if I had overheard them and ask—beg—plead—for the right to quote them. Of course, it's the perfect way to lose a really good juicy story.

And I did print another overheard. The acerbic *New York* magazine drama critic, John Simon, had said one night during a play that he was sick of homosexuals in the theater and wished every one of them "would die with AIDS." This was so horrible and John Simon, as smart as he is, is such a jerk that I took my source—a major actress—at her word and reprinted what he'd said. Simon had to apologize publicly. But naturally, he didn't forgive me. He had already accused me in print of being "a lowbrow" and I had said I preferred that to being "a highbrow" of his kind. On his thirty-year anniversary with his magazine, Simon was interviewed about his life and times. He wasted a lot of space attacking me in this piece meant to glorify his career. Well, he's entitled. It was his anniversary and his dime.

MY OTHER "21" EXPERIENCE WAS JUST your usual tippy-top type name drop. Or rather person drop. I went in with my friends Shirley and Dick Clurman. We weren't expected and "21" set us up at a tiny table about the size of a dish plate near the bar. Pretty soon I realized why. The main room was rocking and crowded. Frank and Barbara Sinatra had a large round table in the center of the room with Tom Selleck and other biggies.

I never thought another thing about it and became engrossed talking to the Clurmans. They were a couple who knew everything including who'd done what to whom, and why. I often joked that they'd known Ghengis Khan when he was young. Then I became aware of a presence at my elbow and of Shirley, uncharacteristically silent, looking up with awe. I turned. My new "best friend," Sinatra, stunning in immaculate black-tie, was standing there. He said quietly, "Why didn't you come over to my table to say hello? Aren't you going to introduce me to your friends?" I stammered about how I hadn't wanted to intrude. I did introduce him and he chatted with us for a few moments. Then he bent down, kissed me and took off.

Everybody in "21" had a comment on this encounter. Walter, the famous headwaiter, said, "Well, I've seen a lot, Miss Smith, but I never saw Sinatra go to anybody else's table before." I discovered I had new cachet for being in the right place at the right time. I shuddered to imagine what would have happened if Sinatra and I had turned up in the same confined space during the years when we were *not* friendly. I thanked my lucky stars.

The Clurmans simply never got over it. They dined out on it for months. "We were with Liz and Frank Sinatra at '21' and Frank said such and such..." It's no wonder I love "21." That night alone erased all the times I had tried, in my poverty-stricken youth in the fifties, to gain access through the bronze front doors and been told to, "Beat it, kid." Or words to that effect.

A FEW

FASCINATING

WOMEN

ONE OF THE PERILS OF the gossip biz is the inevitable cutthroat competition. As you rise to the top like curdled cream, somebody else is rising right along behind you, or after you, or maybe they were there before you. Well, competition is one of the hallmarks of free enterprise capitalism, so I'm all for it. But we've all been or will be scorched. If you're hot today, somebody else will be hotter tomorrow. It's inevitable.

When I was Cholly's lowly ghost, now and then I'd attend a party where the reigning society gossip queen, Suzy (aka Aileen Mehle), was present. She didn't seem to mind me then. I was nobody. But she was vociferous in her distaste for my famous boss, Igor Cassini. And after his almost twenty-year reign as the Hearst's big social top dog, she wanted to replace him. Because she was smart, beautiful, sassy, witty, funny even—I didn't doubt that she might do so. I'll say this for Miss Suzy. When she wasn't letting some social climber or someone who had displeased her "have it," she was the most congenial and amusing of companions. People hung on her every word and that included me.

When Cassini's wax wings melted under the heat of the

focus of the FBI and he fell, like Icarus, Suzy was right there to step into his harness. Years passed and Madam ascended and ascended. The big names of the international set and even those still holding the tatters of the U.S. social register tightly about them loved Suzy. She treated them fairly. She bruised them but didn't break the skin. She managed total access. There she was on the Riviera with Frank Sinatra; there she was with the Gianni Agnellis in Greece; there she was with whoever was who in New York. Yet she scooped them, described them, lived through their public trials and tribulations, their divorces, their affairs, etc, reporting it all tongue-in-cheek and with verve and dash. I was her professional admirer then and still remain so, though she has repeatedly tried to have me erased and maybe several other things that aren't quite so nice.

She wasn't happy when Mike O'Neill hired me at the New York *Daily News*, where she had gone from the Hearst newspapers, dropping the "Knickerbocker" to become simply "Suzy." She'd been the only game in town for a long time. It irked her to find people talking about a no-talent nobody from Texas. (Yes, she was from Texas, too, but El Paso was far behind her.)

Suzy had a devoted admirer, the press agent who had helped Elaine Kaufman open her famous saloon. He decided to spring to Suzy's defense as my column began to take off in the *Daily News*. Bobby Zarem did his damnedest to bring me down. Sometimes his efforts were funny.

I was living it up on the dance floor at a party given by the NFL's Pete Rozelle when someone cut in on me. It was my big boss at NBC, the handsome Robert Mulholland, head of the TV network. He twirled me around and said, "Well, I have received a letter about you today from—"

I said, "Never mind; I can just imagine."

He laughed. "This time he says you had a woman killed. Really, Liz, I have never employed a murderer before." I sighed. It was just you-know-who up to his usual tricks. I felt I had passed through a real apotheosis—I had been accused of just about the worst thing anyone could dream up. After that, I felt I was safe from harm. And it reminded me that the *Times* editor Arthur Gelb had once told me, "Don't worry. Bobby Zarem writes anonymous letters on his own stationery."

The writer Noel Behn was a denizen of Elaine's and he often joked with me. "Every time I see Zarem he tells me that your column is 'finished.' He says you'll be out in ninety days—in three months—in a year. I tell you, Liz, you just don't know it, but you are all washed up." Noel and I had some good laughs about this for twenty-five years or so, or until his death a few years ago.

Suzy didn't really need anyone to defend her. She was doing just fine, writing about shooting grouse in Scotland and other deathless matters of social import. When the *Daily News* publisher, Jim Hoge, neglected to notice that her contract was up in 1985, she went right off to the rival *New York Post*, and enjoyed a long stint there before ending up finally in the perfect place for her—the fashion bible, *W*.

I was just an innocent bystander back in 1988 when a young columnist on *Newsday* decided to trim Suzy's sails. The late James Revson reported that the venerable Suzy had claimed certain persons appeared at a party in the Metropolitan Museum of Art and yet they hadn't been there. She had obviously written her guest list in advance, believing it would come to pass. (Ah, deadlines are so treacherous.)

Well, almost everybody in the biz has erred like this at one time or another. It was a good journalism lesson, a real "don't do that" for the rest of us, a specific that you can't be sure who'll do what in the future, so never write it as if it already happened.

I confess I took some glee in Suzy's embarrassment. Her predicament was one most of us wouldn't even have known about, but she overreacted. She defended herself so robustly in her own column that it became another life lesson. (Don't bring up Big Bertha to kill a mosquito!)

You know, gossip didn't just get hot toward the end of the nineties. It was a raging furor already in the eighties, because in one single day, I was asked to comment on the Suzy-Revson "feud" by the Gannet chain, the *Washington Post*, ABC News, *Newsday*, CNN, *Good Morning America, A Current Affair, USA Today*, and *The Wall Street Journal*. But I didn't need to drive in any nails, for Suzy was doing her own brand of damage control.

She wrote: "I have survived as a star all these long years...because in my field I am the best and the brightest there is...a class act loaded with prestige...Mount Rushmore, just as majestic. They (my rivals) will be left squirming on the ground."

Well, as I noted at the time, some of us were squirming a bit, but not for the reason Suzy thought. Anyway, it's nice to have a healthy ego and be able to pen your own tributes.

JUST ABOUT MY FAVORITE HOLLYWOOD character ever is the agent Sue Mengers, now retired. She ruled with an iron hand for a number of years before the rise of Michael Ovitz and his ilk.

She long represented Barbra Streisand and this gave her enormous power and leverage. Sue was smart and quick. I remember her standard answer to most questions when I'd ask, "Is so and so going to do such and such?" Sue would say simply, "Don't dress!" This meant don't bother to get gussied up for the opening, the premiere, the start date. It wasn't going to happen.

I tried to talk Sue into being a source since she knew everything going on in her world. But she'd say: "No. Don't even tell anyone you know me. Please don't write anything nice about me. Just forget you ever heard of me." But now and then Sue went against her own good judgment to tell me some inside skinny. She'd never tell me anything about personalities or stars. She would drop industry news instead. Usually it was too "inside" to make sense to the average reader—or to me. She'd lose me in high-level industry chat. "Yes, Joe Blow of Fox will be the next, etc." I'd ask who Joe Blow was exactly, his history, how to identify him. This would reduce Sue to crazed impatience. "Are you in the business?" she'd ask. "If you're in the business, you know what I'm talking about. Get with it. Get in the business."

Such experiences make writing a column a difficult "art." Obviously, I was never really "in the business" enough to make sense of the arcana. And sometimes, just as they say "God is in the details," the arcana is all there is in show biz. I'd have to say, along with Sue, I have always failed at being "in the business."

And perhaps that's why I managed to stay in place. I was usually just as much in the dark as the reader, just as curious, just as entertained on a naive level, just as ordinary as any fan.

I FINALLY MET ONE OF the survivors of the Algonquin Roundtable—the great Dorothy Parker, philosopher of my soph-omoric years. I fear I didn't make enough of an impression for her to bother to insult or take much notice of me, but because of Parker Ladd, I spent a number of evenings in her company. (Mr. Ladd is the good and generous-hearted Vermont native who once headed the Association of American Publishers and so he knew Dottie.) She was living in the Volney Hotel where she begged and entreated us to go home from our evenings with some of the many books she had been sent to review. "I hate these damned books. Get them out of here. Don't you want them?" I tried to oblige, for I didn't think one should refuse any-thing from the hand of Miss Parker, who had uttered one of my favorite lines.

Living with her husband, Alan Campbell, in Bucks County, Dottie had developed a list of hates: his relatives, the Pennsylvania climate, their mutual friends, etc. One day Alan came into the living room and shivered. "Gee, it's awfully cold in here, isn't it?"

Dottie looked at him and sniffed. "Not for us orphans!" She is, of course, more famous for other utterances but that one takes the cake for me. Once I became an orphan, I began to use it myself on any occasion I could muster up.

One evening Parker Ladd and I were with Dottie and he began to beg her to go to a certain party at Gloria Vanderbilt's. Time passed and he didn't let up and after Dottie said she had nothing to wear, Parker announced that Gloria would send her a gown, etc. The gown arrived and was glorious. But on a follow-up night in the Volney when I asked to see it, Miss Parker just shrugged. "She didn't even send me any shoes for it."

There was no pleasing this grand literary figure. Even in death she was a bit stubborn. She specified in her will that she wanted to be cremated, not buried next to her husband in Virginia. Ever pleading poverty, when she died, Dottie left drawers full of uncashed, undeposited checks, but willed all she owned to the National Association for the Advancement of Colored People.

Reduced indeed to dust in June 1967, for twenty years her ashes sat in the law office of Paul O'Dwyer. He had been the attorney to playwright Lillian Hellman, who was Dottie's executor. When Hellman died in 1984, Dottie's ashes continued to sit there. O'Dwyer, whose brother William had once been the mayor of New York, was a sensitive soul. He didn't feel it was right for Dottie to be languishing in his office. He called me for ideas.

I agitated that *The New Yorker* and/or *Vanity Fair* might take over. Dottie had made an impressive reputation working for both magazines. I urged the Algonquin Hotel, where she had been a part of the Roundtable of the thirties, to make a shrine in her name. Many people felt her ashes over the bar would have pleased her enormously! But the hotel found the idea gruesome. I urged the literary organization PEN to do something about the matter. They ignored me. I suggested Gloria Vanderbilt, who had tried to lighten Dottie's final years, take the ashes. And finally I urged the NAACP to act and honor the woman who had left them her all.

This prompted Joseph McLellan of the *Washington Post* to pen a Parkeresque poem. Part of it read:

> *"Your wit may dazzle all New York,*
> *Your songs with passion burn,*
> *But, like the dullest nerds in town,*

You're headed for an urn…
Liz Smith, the columnist has told,
A story grim and dark,
About a girl named Parker who,
Can't find a place to park."

Finally, the NAACP acted and Dottie's ashes were placed on their grounds in Baltimore. I hear that the site is not well kept up. Paul O'Dwyer has long gone to his own reward so he isn't around for me to nag that we should go down to Maryland and do something about it.

Dottie would no doubt complain because she liked to complain. But she had written her own apt epitaph many years before when she was in her prime: "Excuse my dust!"

I HAD A BRIEF SET-TO with the irascible, very famous Lillian Hellman several years before she died. The playwright excoriated me at a Literary Lions party in the New York Public Library for some offense I'd written, but when I reacted with sincere concern, she instantly calmed down and took a shine to me. Ever after, she would ask me to sit down with her whenever we met. "I can't stand. We must sit and talk!"

I fell for Lillian's hard-boiled, wounded old-age charm. She seemed a broken-hearted woman and that appealed to me, though I never believed a word she said and I still think much of her autobiographical writing was sheer fiction.

She was a brilliant mind who had fooled herself into believing she'd had this great romance with the writer Dashiell Hammett. But I always thought his public coldness to her counted against him. Still, Lillian couldn't let the idealization of their affair go. She was clinging to a myth and somehow I wanted to protect her. Whatever her faults, it was a privilege to know such a character. And I loved the play *Cakewalk*, based on a book about Hellman by the young Peter Feibleman, who had shared her later life. To me that was reality.

A FEW

FASCINATING

MEN

I HAD BEEN BYLINING THE Liz Smith column for a year when I first met Norman Mailer at a cocktail party on the Upper West Side. I can't remember the host and would like to bless his name, but I had been watching the Aquarian closely before he turned and came my way. He introduced himself. I made some gushing remarks. "You are one of my heroes!" He wanted to know why and I launched into praise for *The Naked and the Dead*, first encountered in 1948, then went on to tell him how I'd placed *The White Negro* into my file on "The Race." How I had voted for him for mayor when he and Jimmy Breslin launched their quixotic campaign in 1969. I told him I thought *The Prisoner of Sex* was a really wrong-headed but romantic book. ("Good sex makes good babies" indeed!!) And I raved about *Superman Comes to the Supermarket*, which had defined the JFK years.

He seemed genuinely amused by this outpouring, said something nice about liking my column, finding it fresh and engaging. This turned my head all the way around.

Norman and I became friends and he was even more amused to discover we were born almost at the same time in the same year. (Three days apart in 1923.) So he wasn't the only one who was an Aquarian. When you have won the Pulitzer Prize and the National Book Award and everything else, the Rose Award from Lord & Taylor may seem like small pickings. But I was moved when Norman asked me to introduce him for that event when the department store used to honor famous New Yorkers. After that, we really bonded.

There are four men I am just nuts about because they have a way of speaking that is so convoluted and thoughtful: so mysterious in its effect that one can never second-guess where they are going in their argument, or what they might say. This— the mystery talker—is compelling to me. My chosen four are the former senator from New York, Daniel Patrick Moynihan; the onetime head of Time, the elegant and urbane Andrew Heiskell; that brilliant fast talker, William F. Buckley, Jr., and Norman Mailer.

Norman and I have had two contretemps. I always felt his best work was *The Executioner's Song*. So when Larry Schiller* was about to make it into a movie in the 1980s, I involved myself. Schiller told me it would be for TV and I printed that. Norman rang to correct me. "This is a feature film, not TV." On such authority, I corrected the column immediately. Time passed and I spoke with Schiller again. He emphasized, "It's for TV, to star Tommy Lee Jones." I wrote that then without consulting Norman.

This time he was furious. Why did I do this twice, he asked? I said, "You better talk to your producer. You two are on different wavelengths."

Norman fumed. "I will take you out to the greatest dinner of your life if *The Executioner's Song* appears on television. Let's make a bet."

I was baffled. Maybe Schiller was pulling Norman's leg.

Later, my admiration for Larry Schiller grew. He did write the very best book of all about the O. J. Simpson trial in 1996 titled American Tragedy: The Uncensored Story of the Simpson Defense, *published by Random House.*

Maybe Norman was crazy. In 1982, *The Executioner's Song* appeared on NBC-TV to great acclaim. I didn't mention it again to Norman, trying to employ the great broadcaster Fred Friendly's axiom: "To say I told you so would be demeaning to you—and to me."

I forgot about our bet and one day Norman invited me to meet him at Elaine's. "We'll have some dinner," he said. I thought he meant dinner at Elaine's. I was jawing with Norman's wife, Norris Church, and some other pals when, after drinks, Norman rose, said good-night to the group and added, "Liz and I have a long-standing dinner engagement together."

I protested. "No, let's stay here."

Norman guided me firmly to the door. "I owe you dinner for the Schiller business." This was typical Mailer gentlemanly behavior but even though we discussed it briefly at our dinner alone, I never did figure out why these two men, who seemed to admire each other so much, had so much trouble communicating. It seems America's foremost literary tough guy can be naive and sometimes out of the loop. (Well, he *is* an artist.)

Norman couldn't or wouldn't explain it. He probably didn't want to blame Schiller for misleading him. Years later, when I heard he was doing another film with Schiller in Russia, I asked, "Do you know if this is a feature or for TV? And why should I believe whatever you say?" Norman found this funny.

My second bout with Norman came during the exotic Metropolitan Museum wedding of Saul Steinberg's daughter, Laura, to the hotel scion Jonathan Tisch. I was sitting with Norman. We noticed Washington's powerful Vernon Jordan on the dance floor. People watch Vernon the same way they watch movie stars. I wondered aloud if Vernon would ever run for public office. Norman pontificated his psychological conclusion. Back in 1980, when Vernon had been head of the Urban League, a stalker had shot and almost killed him. Norman felt this incident precluded Vernon's ever wanting to run for office.

When Vernon came to speak to us later, I enthusiastically relayed all of this to him as an illustration of Norman's brilliance. (Maybe I'd had a few drinks.) Vernon wisecracked and left us. Norman then took me gently from the table to the side of the dance floor and spoke sternly. "Now, look, when I say something to you, it's to you. I don't want you repeating it. I'd never have said those things to Vernon's face for fear of offending him, and embarrassing myself. Can I trust you to absorb this lesson?"

I began to cry. I had never wanted to disappoint Norman. He, confronted with tears, patted me and said everything but "There! There!" I apologized and he said, "Forget it. I know you. I know you didn't mean any harm."

Vernon had seen this emotional carrying-on and a bit later came and asked me to dance. I waltzed off in his capable arms. "What's with you and Mailer?" he asked.

"Nothing," I said. "I just shot my mouth off and he was trying to restrain me. Really, Vernon, I am sorry. I had no right to repeat what he said about you."

Vernon stopped in his tracks. "You know what, little Smithy. That was a good moment, to have Norman psychoanalyze me and for you to play Johnson to his Boswell."

I have written a lot in my columns about Norman's exploits and also those of his wife, Norris, a gifted writer in her own right. I value their love and friendship and have visited them in Brooklyn Heights. Norman is to me the consummate New York street guy who grew up to have a heart even bigger than his talent. Norris is the Arkansas beauty with a soul of the South and a brain firmly above the Mason–Dixon line. She is the beauty who tamed the savage beast—Norman.

Yet, the moment I cherish most with Norman happened on April 12, 1988. Arianna Stassinopoulos, now a political commentator and talk show expert, was marrying the very rich Michael Huffington of Houston. Norman and I were seated side by side at the wedding dinner in the Metropolitan Club. Norris was out of town. As the former lovers of Arianna rose to toast her, things got funnier and funnier to the two Aquarians who were feeling no pain. There was first the Englishman Bernard Levin, then the internationalist Lord George Weidenfeld and after him, the publisher Mort Zuckerman.

The way Arianna was being praised by this group of formidable men, who had at one time or other been involved with her, struck the Aquarians in their cups as hilarious. We weren't really holier than thou, just inebriated. Then the groom's Texas dad rose up. Mr. Huffington was a man John Wayne might envy. In his he-man way he said, "Well, thank God for Arianna because we were beginning to get a little worried about Michael!"*

Mr. Huffington's comment all but launched Norman and Liz over the edge. And then Norman turned serious. He gave me the piercing look that always thrilled me and made me know I should listen carefully. I thought perhaps I was in for another lecture. "I guess you know," he said, "that you are a very attractive woman." (Yes, I thought, especially when I'm drunk.) "Can you tell me," asked Norman, "why you and I have never gone to bed together?"

I looked at Norman, no doubt bleary-eyed. "Norman, what's the matter with you? You don't want to go to bed with me. Why, you and I are exactly the same age. You can't go to bed with me. You require someone younger. And I require someone younger."

Norman pulled back, pensively. "You're right. And anyway, Norris loves you, so we couldn't, could we?"

I took another sip of my drink. "No—and, anyway, if I go to bed with any of the Mailers, I'd rather it be Norris than you." (You have to give these tough guys a zinger now and then or they don't dance.)

THE YOUNG MARLON BRANDO BECAME known in his youth as a guy who couldn't say "no" to any homely girl. I think

---

*Arianna would divorce Michael some years later, after two children and when his political aspirations came to naught. Michael announced he believed he was homosexual and would become a Buddhist monk. Arianna went on to become a more liberal voice of commentary, leveling her big guns at "soft money."

Vernon Jordan, the aforesaid Washington rainmaker, now in his post-Clinton multimillionaire prime, is the same kind of guy. He can't stand to see a wallflower at a dance.

He is happily married, but Vernon pays lavish attention to the women he meets. He likes to make us all feel good. At a party given in 1998 by Elizabeth Rohatyn in the U.S. Embassy in Paris for her husband, Ambassador Felix Rohatyn, this marvelous *Casablanca* fete was actually marred when Vernon left early. Every female in the room had noted his charismatic presence, his bejeweled cigar shirt studs (so phallic) and when the tycoon Linda Wachner insisted Vernon and her group leave to catch her jet for New York, women all over the room sighed unhappily. We were—to a woman—waiting for Vernon to ask us to dance.

Vernon would scoff at my thesis that he lives to make women—no matter how plain, widowed, deserted, and elderly—happy with a momentary attention. He'd say there are no plain, widowed, deserted, elderly women!

I was dancing with Vernon at a John Kluge birthday gala in the Waldorf where the men were in white-tie, the women in ball gowns. It was one of those last of its kind "dancing on the lip of the volcano" evenings that made some of us feel guilty. "Comes the Revolution, if the Ethics Cops swept in now and arrested us, how could we explain ourselves? I know," said I, "I would say I'm just a member of the press covering this."

Vernon topped me. "I'd just say I am the headwaiter, wearing this getup as part of my job. I'd be the only man here—just as I am the only African-American—to escape the guillotine."

THERE I WAS ON WILLIAM F. BUCKLEY, JR.'S, *Firing Line* with Nat Hentoff and Pete Hamill and the subject came up of Jimmy Carter's brand of fundamentalism. I decided to surprise my Roman Catholic host with a question he'd have to tiptoe to answer. So I popped off, "But, Mr. Buckley, isn't it true that while a lot of people make fun of Jimmy Carter's being a 'born-again Christian,' he essentially believes what Roman Catholics believe—that Jesus is the truth, way and light and a person has to save his soul by coming into acceptance of Christ? Wouldn't you have to say of your own religion, that you, too, are a kind of born-again Christian?"

Mr. Buckley paused only one second before his unanswerable answer: "Well, I do prefer to think of myself as a—congenital Christian."

Although Bill and I are worlds apart ideologically, he has never fallen in my eyes since that brilliant moment.

JIMMY KIRKWOOD WAS THE CHILD of the silent film star Lila Lee and a well-known actor. Having a temperamental, famous and sexy mother formed his psyche. Jimmy went from working with his partner, Lee Goodman, in cabaret to being a very good writer of comic novels and plays. He created *There Must Be a Pony* and *P.S. Your Cat Is Dead*. As he was good-looking, energetic and full of youth, I always imagined that one day I'd be dead and an adorable Kirkwood would speak eloquently at my funeral.

I was rueful in 1988 to find myself onstage at the Shubert Theatre speaking at Kirkwood's memorial. This lighthearted creature had come to glory, winning the Pulitzer Prize with his cowriter Nick Dante, for the Broadway musical *A Chorus Line*. There were so many funny tales to tell about Jimmy that in the end I was choking with tears and laughter. I signed off singing a song I associated with him, "It's High Time," a spirited paean to booze, written by Jule Styne and Leo Robin for *Gentlemen Prefer Blondes*.

And I recalled Jimmy telling of the morning he and Nick got on a plane in Canada for New York after learning they'd won the Pulitzer. Beside themselves with joy and disbelief, they ordered drinks. The stewardess served them the obligatory booze and peanuts. They kept chug-a-lugging, congratulating themselves. Ordering again, the stewardess brought their glasses, but said she was out of peanuts.

Jimmy screamed: "But you must have peanuts! We just won the Pulitzer Prize!"

Jimmy liked to tell how Tallulah Bankhead had called one day to invite him to come meet Eleanor Roosevelt, his idol. (Excoriated during the years she lived in the White House, as a New Yorker, Mrs. FDR later enjoyed almost universal respect for her humanitarianism.)

So Kirkwood put on his best suit and tie and there he was, in Tallulah's library with the former First Lady. Politically motivated since childhood and a raving, ranting liberal, Tallulah told how she had campaigned against Tom Dewey. Mrs. Roosevelt laughed, recalling that Tallulah had said on radio: "Mr. Dewey is for unity. Next he will declare in favor of motherhood, the zipper and the dial telephone. Will all the candidates for disunity please stand?"

At that Tallulah herself stood. "Excuse me, dahlings, but I must go to the bathroom." She proceeded down the hall, which had a half-bath at the end. Clearly visible to Jimmy and Mrs. Roosevelt, Tallulah used the john, then pulled up her pants and returned, still talking.

When Mrs. FDR departed, as if nothing had happened, Jimmy vented his spleen. "How could you? Tallulah, I want to kill you!" Seldom at a loss for words, the star just looked at him and said, "But, dahling, don't be silly. Mrs. Roosevelt has to pee, too, you know."

In the Hamptons we were playing "I never" and others had to guess if we were lying or not. I said truthfully I had been knocked out of bed by the first atomic bomb. Kathy Graham, whose family owned the oldest art gallery in NYC, said she'd had a love affair with a rabbi. But Kirkwood won. He said he and a friend had wandered into a vault at Tiffany, been locked in and had to sleep on the floor overnight. "Fortunately, it was air-conditioned." I never knew whether to believe this or not, but I did—it was so Kirkwood.

Every Christmas would come a card with a photo of

Jimmy and someone famous, such as Elizabeth Taylor or Liberace. The card would read "The Kirkwoods." I loved the year he posed with the two hard-boiled men who ran the Shubert Organization. It was signed "The Kirkwoods." The Christmas cards stopped when this vivacious writer paid the ultimate price for the fame and fortune gained when he'd helped create *A Chorus Line*, which played the Shubert for thirteen years. So many of the principal players in this musical died of AIDS that the Broadway theater is still reeling. Someone, or several someones, had unwittingly passed the killer virus to many in the company. It is one of the theater's most heartrending tragedies and it took my Jimmy with it.

TO BE OR

NOT TO BE

SOME THRILLS ARE BETTER THAN others and one of mine, early on at the New York *Daily News* was to be caricatured and hung on the sacred walls of Sardi's show business restaurant. I had always remembered what John Barrymore had written on his likeness, "To be or not to be, what's the difference?" I wrote, "To be or not to be, but to be in Sardi's!"

Years later, I would think of this when a revitalized *Vanity Fair* put me into their Hall of Fame. I had watched *Vanity Fair* come back to life with interest. The magazine went through early trials as Condé Nast tried to gear it up for the late eighties and nineties and finally Si Newhouse put the British editor Tina Brown in charge. This was 1983. Tina performed wonders and everybody began talking about *Vanity Fair*, including this old magazine junkie.

So I was vastly flattered when Tina asked me to pose for the genius Annie Leibovitz. Annie said, "Bring some cowboy clothes and a lot of pictures of celebrities." I tricked myself out in black with red lizard cowboy boots and plunked a huge square-shaped synthetic diamond on my hand. (The ring was created by the actress Polly Bergen for her jewelry line. The design was so authentic that in two burglaries, this ring was taken twice.) Annie began shooting. She had handed me a professional rodeo lariat and she was leaping around in front of me like a gazelle. I had said before the sitting, "Now, Annie, don't try to get me to take my clothes off, or get in bed with a dog like Debra Winger, or stand half-nude in the water like Norman Mailer or put me in a bathtub of milk like Whoopi Goldberg." She laughed, faintly.

The sitting was over, when Annie asked, "Listen, would you pose with a gun?"

I said smartly, "Pose with a gun? Why I'd wear one holstered every day in New York if it weren't against the law!" (I should explain here that I am actually for super gun control, or else I am for everybody in America being *required* to carry a gun to equalize matters!)

Annie had her assistant tacking up celebrity glosses on a wall behind me. She then handed me a nifty pair of revolvers. They looked to be real. Checking to be sure they weren't loaded, I then began to play with them and the resultant photo shows me whirling my six-guns, threatening a lot of innocent celebrities.

Under this photo *Vanity Fair*'s editors kindly wrote: "Because she's the good old gal of gossip, whose syndicated column always plays fair. Because, besides serving up juicy dish day after day, she roots hard for causes from AIDS research to literacy. Because she's a sharp shootin' rootin'-tootin' Texan who's become a New York institution." It was a high point of personal publicity.* And I liked it even better when the magazine later did their Proust Questionnaire with me. I repeat it because it shows me as I'd like to think I am. Here it is:

---

*Only recently was I made more famous or infamous. Madame Tussaud's Wax Museum was set to open a Times Square NYC version with my exact likeness installed. Therein I will be seen taking notes at a glamorous party wearing an Arnold Scaasi original. I particularly enjoyed being measured by Englishmen with calipers and sorting through trays of blue glass eyes for my match.

Q: When and where were you happiest?

A: Now. Here in little old New York City!

Q: What do you consider your greatest achievement?

A: Clinging to the lower rungs of journalism, making a living and having people yell at me in the street.

Q: What is the trait you most deplore in others?

A: Lying, cheating, fudging, nudging the ethical line.

Q: What is the trait you most deplore in yourself?

A: Lying, cheating, fudging, nudging the ethical line.

Q: Which words or phrases do you most overuse?

A: Great.

Q: On what occasion do you lie?

A: Oh, puh-leeze!

Q: What do you consider the most overrated virtue?

A: Loyalty (it gets people in a lot of absurd ethical trouble).

Q: What is your idea of perfect happiness?

A: Television, a thriller, a candy bar, popcorn, no telephone—all at once.

Q: What do you regard as the lowest depth of misery?

A: Public humiliation.

Q: What is your greatest fear?

A: Dying a lingering, painful death, becoming a pain in the ass.

Q: What is the quality you most like in a person?

A: Intelligence leavened with humor.

Q: What is it that you most dislike?

A: Hypocrisy.

Q: What is your most marked characteristic?

A: Self-defeating generosity.

Q: What is your greatest extravagance?

A: Eating in restaurants, overtipping.

Q: Which historical figure do you most identify with?

A: Voltaire.

Q: Which living person do you most admire?

A: Governor Ann Richards.

Q: Which living person do you most despise?

A: They all jostle together in my head and become one big fat slobby press agent in particular.

Q: What is your favorite journey?

A: The Greek islands. Greece itself.

Q: What is your most treasured possession?

A: My genes from the Tiptons, McCalls, Balls, Smiths.

Q: What do you most value in your friends?

A: Their infinite variety.

Q: If you were to die and come back as a person or thing, what do you think it would be?

A: The three monkeys—seeing, speaking and hearing no evil.

Q: If you could choose what to come back as, what would it be?

A: A cat that does as it pleases.

Q: What is your motto?

A: "Dare to be true."

When Tina left for *The New Yorker* and Condé Nast hired Graydon Carter to replace her, Tina's husband, Harry Evans, invited me to a party to welcome the former *Spy* magazine editor aboard. This presented me with a slight dilemma. Mr. Carter had seemed to be my implacable detractor while he and Kurt Anderson put out *Spy*—a kind of college humor exercise in negativism concerning New York VIPs. *Spy* had singed my tail almost monthly, referring to me on several occasions as being "grizzled," "insane" and "*Spy*-obsessed." They developed a monthly feature, The Liz Smith Tote Board, which listed (purportedly but not always accurately) how many times a month I mentioned certain names—such as Barbara Walters, Elizabeth Taylor, Donald Trump and, once, Jesus. (I took the criticism to heart and didn't include the Nazarene again in my gossip column. I'm nothing if not sensitive.) With this box score, *Spy* always printed a photo I had foolishly provided for them myself. It showed me in a headdress and war paint from a play I had performed to benefit Lighthouse International, the organization for the blind. In that play, *Raindance*, I portrayed Chief Sitting Bull.

So every month in *Spy*, I looked ridiculous, either by my own hand or theirs.

Did *Spy*'s knocks at me really hurt my feelings? Yes, I suffered every month wondering, What next? But I wasn't unaware of the fact that it was something of a compliment to be in the public eye of *Spy* like a cinder. When my assistant Denis Ferrara went to Paris during this period, he told me excitedly, "Everywhere I went when I'd meet English-speaking people and say I worked for you, they'd exclaim, 'Oh, the Liz Smith Tote Board!'" So I tried to be philosophical and tell myself that bad press can be good public relations. (After all, I had survived being The *Playboy* Interview in 1992.)

But could I be nice to the dastardly Mr. Carter, whom I felt had done me so much harm? I decided, oh, the hell with it. Life's too short. And when we came face-to-face at this dinner, he extended himself in such a humble and charming manner, saying how sorry he was for my long maltreatment at the hands of *Spy*, that I thought of my mother always saying I should "turn the other cheek" and "forgive seven times seventy." I just said, "Oh, forget it. Let's be friends and not ever mention it again."

I didn't really believe that a sophisticated smartie like Graydon Carter was actually sorry he'd raked me over the coals for years. He'd gotten good professional mileage out of lumping me with the other visible New Yorkers that *Spy* wanted to twit. But life goes on. Mr. Carter had a divine wife and four adorable children. He had been making a living with *Spy* and now he had his big chance with *Vanity Fair*. I guess we both decided not to let the past be prologue. I have never regretted this pragmatic decision of his and of my own. I have been a friend to Graydon and *Vanity Fair* ever since and hope always to be.

Some people don't like *Vanity Fair*. But in my world it is "must" reading and I never miss it. Sometimes I say under my breath, "To be or not to be, but to be in *Vanity Fair*."

PART
SEVEN
a Memoir

DOUBLE DUTY

COULD ANY GOSSIP COLUMNIST WRITE two entirely separate columns a day over a long period of time? You may think no, or even ask, "Why would they want to?" Well, I did it for twelve months, day after day. And you know what? Almost nobody even noticed.

The *Daily News* was ever seeking to draw attention to itself and the powers that be had long dreamed of putting out an afternoon edition. Finally, in 1980, they invited the media genius Clay Felker to make it happen. I was pleased, having worked for Clay back when he was at *Esquire* and *New York* magazines.

Once Clay began setting up the afternoon edition, I offered to write a distinct and different column for the P.M. paper. He was delighted, but I could see he didn't think I could do it.

Nevertheless, I did and I don't believe, in history, anyone ever did this before, or since. Was this feat ever recognized, put into the record books, noted by the *Columbia Journalism Review*? It was not.

The only two people who gave me any satisfaction for

my extreme effort over that year were (1) Clay (2) the Broadway producer Alexander Cohen. The latter, a voracious newshound, called me at least twice a week during this stressful period to say how much pleasure he derived from having me to read, morning and afternoon.

I was proud of myself because I was also doing live TV three days a week. But when I'd arrive in Rockefeller Center every afternoon to do WNBC's *Live at Five*, there, in what I considered to be the center of the universe, I'd find to my despair that no afternoon edition of the *Daily News* had been delivered. And if the paper wasn't on sale there, where was it on sale? Some people in Manhattan swore they never saw the P.M. edition in its entire brief life.

If I didn't get any glory for doing double-duty, neither did Clay Felker. He was made the scapegoat for the failure of the separate edition. But the fact was, this P.M. paper was never adequately distributed. Even people who wanted it couldn't find it. Again, newspaper bosses and unions cut off their noses to spite their faces.

So the failure of the afternoon *Daily News* wasn't Clay's fault. Nor was it mine. We did our part. In fact, I overdid my part. I've been waiting for the *Guinness Book of World Records* to call me ever since.

THE SINKING

SHIP

THE LARGEST CIRCULATED NEWSPAPER IN the world (at the time), the New York *Daily News* had created me, given me my big chance, stuck with me through everything and metaphorically "put my name in lights." Now, after nineteen years, it seemed to be melting away. Although in 1984 the Chicago Tribune Company, which owned the *News*, had sent in a handsome top gun named James Hoge to be publisher and save the newspaper, it didn't seem to be working.

Successful large tabloids for America's working-class immigrants had flourished as a way of life in New York. But now the new immigrants didn't even speak or read English. An entire generation was getting all its news from television. There were two other tabloids in New York besides the *Daily News*—the *New York Post* and *New York Newsday*—they weren't making money either, but they were fierce competition for us. The *News* was burdened by terrible union problems: extravagant featherbedding, labor costs, overtime, the need for new presses and equipment. The Chicago Tribune Company owners were finding it too expensive to run the paper, too expensive to close it down and impossible to give it away.

For years in Manhattan I'd been running into the tall, good-looking publisher of *New York Newsday*, one Robert Johnson. He would always say in a courtly manner, "Someday, I want you to be working for us. Would you consider an offer?" I would always answer that I was flattered but the *News* had given me my big break and I would never leave so long as they had viable owners and management.

Publisher Robert Johnson was obviously following the disintegrating events at the *News* closely. Long Island's burgeoning newspaper, *Newsday*, had in September 1983, created under him a youthful offshoot called *New York Newsday*. It was just beginning to compete in a very upscale Manhattan manner in the tabloid wars. The L.A. Times-Mirror Company, owners of *Newsday* and this brand-new offspring, was more or less counting on the elimination of the New York *Daily News* to make their own success possible. Later, Johnson told me it had seemed crucial to him to pry me away from the *News*. "You were the most popular columnist in all of the U.S. and we needed you!"

I was still "hot" from the recent Trump divorce story. So Johnson made me a firm offer. It was financially spectacular. So was the figure for a signing bonus. If I came to *New York Newsday*, my column would be handled by the L.A. Times-Mirror Syndicate and would appear not only in all its current syndicated papers but also in the prestigious *Los Angeles Times*. This was no small thing. I had long needed a voice and byline on the west coast.

Now, on the horizon of the sinking ship that was the *Daily News* appeared Robert Maxwell of London. He said he would buy the *News* from its Chicago owners who were wild to get rid of it. The *News* publisher, James Hoge, with whom I had always enjoyed only the best relations, was eager for me to meet with Maxwell, to assure him I'd stay at the paper. I had met Mr. Maxwell before, at the Forbes party in Morocco where he had appeared in a resplendent costume as an enormous Arab pasha—turban, jewels, scimitar, etc. Even out of costume, he seemed very much like a great big fake. But I respected Hoge and he was subtly nudging me toward Maxwell.

The Maxwell yacht, *The Ghislane*, was moored and making big news in the East River. New York was about to gain yet one more flashy public figure in press lord Maxwell. Hoge organized a meet between Maxwell and me onboard. As I went to the boat I remembered I had seen it before, in the Tangiers harbor, when it had been almost run down by the red sails of Gianni Agnelli. This gave me a tiny silent snigger.

Unaccountably, I wore to this meeting a pair of cowboy boots. *Spy* had made so much fun of me for occasionally appearing in Western clothes that I had about abandoned the habit. It turned out that Maxwell made everyone coming onboard shuck his or her shoes. He had spotless white carpets in his floating palace. But no one said a word about my boots as I came onboard. Maxwell and Hoge were both in their stocking feet. My boots seemed defiant and I asked Mr. Maxwell if I should take them off. He waved his hand as if it were of no consequence. We sat down. Maxwell presented himself to me as a dedicated family man, showing me many photos of his children, his wife. He urged me to stay with the *News* and offered a salary only fractionally above what I was already making. It was several hundred thousand dollars below the offer from *New York Newsday*.

He added, beneficently, that if I would stay I could then give parties on his yacht. (I didn't want to give parties. I wanted to make money for my old age, which was already upon me actuarially.) He added in a rather paternal and patronizing manner that if I would re-sign with the *News*, he would—as he put it—"reserve the right to give you a generous bonus every year on your birthday."

My birthday had recently passed, so the prospect of his "reserved right" and a year's wait for it, didn't appeal to me. As my rude boot heels rang down the gangplank, I knew I was out of my old home base. I would accept *New York Newsday*'s offer. Some attempts at negotiation by my lawyer confirmed my fears that the *News* was not healthy and neither was its about-to-be owner.

I TOOK THIS OPPORTUNITY TO run away to the Caribbean. The larger-than-life titan of Time-Warner—the powerful Steve Ross—had invited me to come on a little yacht cruise. It was really Iris Love he wanted, for she had joined the Rosses in many a sail overseas. But Steve was vastly amused by both of us. He called us "the Odd Couple" because he said he had never seen two people who were friends who were so entirely different—and so often in public disagreement.

Steve Ross was dying of an advanced prostate cancer, but he pretended he wasn't. He just said he had a sore back and sometimes favored it. On our first night at sea, I recall we sat down with Steve and his wife, Courtney, in the main salon. The appealing and lovely Anne Ford Scarborough was along for the ride, as well as William vanden Heuvel—a guy who always liked to pretend he was taking your photo when he didn't have any film in his camera. (I guess he thought this was flattering and you'd be too stupid to notice.)

I knew some of the Ross history. How Steve had been ready to marry Courtney, a Texas blonde beauty, when he had met Amanda Burden, the daughter of Babe and stepdaughter to William Paley. Steve had dumped Courtney and wed Amanda instead. This wasn't the kind of story one asked the principals to repeat, but somehow discretion was vanquished and the first thing I knew, Steve was telling the story on himself. Courtney sat near him as silent as a cat. He poured out his heartrending yarn of misadventure. How he had wronged Courtney, how his marriage to the beautiful Amanda had not worked out, how Courtney had taken him back and given him a marvelous daughter.

I thought as I sat there that rich people certainly do have their troubles. Here was a king of the world and he was dying of an incurable disease. And he was still haunted by having done a lady wrong and trying to make it up to her. (He did; he left her an amazing fortune when he died in December 1992.)

Steve was overgenerosity itself. He had given me many large checks from Warner's for Literacy Partners. On this trip he was determined to give everyone onboard some small bottles with sand drawings in them. These trinkets cost pennies, but when the tourist stores didn't have enough for each of us to have a share, Steve would order dozens and send them on after the trip had ended. If you were in a bikini shop and he came in, you had to bolt out or you'd find he had bought you bathing suits in every style and color.

But I digress. When Steve stopped talking about his own life that night, he began to tease me and Iris. "Now what is up with the Odd Couple?" he asked.

I didn't give Iris time to answer. Long-winded, I knew she might go all the way back to the invention of pictographs just to tell about a dinner she'd had the night before. I told Steve I was leaving the *Daily News* and going to *New York Newsday* and my contract was being negotiated as we spoke. He said, "Get me your lawyer on the telephone." I called the hapless Bill Goodstein in New York. He was so impressed that Steve Ross was going to speak to him, he all but *plotzed*. Steve got on the phone with Bill and for forty-eight hours did nothing but negotiate points for me. I should get this and that. Bill should demand such and such. The paper should indemnify me for what's what. On and on it went. I would protest that *New York Newsday* was already being very open-handed, but Steve just said, with conviction, "Nonsense, Liz. You don't understand. Negotiation is part of life and you must get all you can out of these bastards."

I realized how much negotiation and winning meant to Steve. I had seen him that very day in the backwaters of the Caribbean bargaining with little children who were selling twenty-five-cent scarves. Steve would bait them and then set them up. "Okay, twenty-five cents apiece, but I will give you five dollars for thirty." He often won this challenge.

As he waved the irresistible fiver in their pinched little faces, I asked, "How can you do that to them?"

He'd laugh. "It's good for them. They have to learn not to be overcome."

Steve Ross, this Master of the Universe, was criticized for having had Mob connections, for overusing the luxuries provided by his company for personal matters, for squandering Warner money as a favor for charities. Personally, I didn't care if he gave company money away for a good cause—my cause—and anyway, he had to know when not to be "overcome."

On March 24, 1991, I transferred my column overnight from the *Daily News* to *New York Newsday*, which meant it would also appear in the super-successful ad-heavy *Newsday* on Long Island. I didn't miss a day in print. It wouldn't be long until Robert Maxwell had disappeared mysteriously off the back of his yacht in the Mediterranean. He jumped, fell or was pushed. His nude body was found, but the mystery remains. He left the family he had presented to me as a paragon of his own virtue in hopeless turmoil and economic confusion. His sons were charged with some wrongdoing. His wife of many years turned against him in an excellent book she immediately sat down and wrote after his death.

The New York *Daily News* floundered along and almost disappeared. The tabloid was narrowly saved from extinction, then bought and brought back to life by real estate tycoon Mort Zuckerman. I liked Mr. Zuckerman and wished him well and breathed a sigh of relief that the *News* didn't go under. I was sentimental about it. I hate to see any newspaper die.

Now I was working for a good-looking and brilliantly written and edited newspaper, one that seemed rock solid and on the verge of becoming a commercial success. A paper with a hard-boiled, dynamic editor, Don Forst, who interacted with his reporters and columnists and wanted their input; a debonair and classy Bob Johnson as an imaginative publisher, who offered to support my charitable works; and a creative executive Dave Laventhol in Los Angeles, who was my undying fan and intercessor with the monolithic Times-Mirror Company. I was given a fantastic personal editor, a veteran named Mort Persky, with whom I had worked before while freelancing for the *Detroit Free*

Press. I was writing in a paper that boasted the extraordinary talents of Jimmy Breslin, Doug Marlette, Sidney Sheinberg, Gail Collins, Linda Winer, Mike Lupica, Dennis Duggan, Sheryl McCarthy, Bill Reel, Marvin Kitman, Michael Shain, Robert Reeve, Jim Dwyer and the sainted Murray Kempton. Everyone was encouraging, flattering, pleased to have me onboard.

I was about as joyful as a girl in a new romance, planning to live happily ever after. I couldn't know that the romance would only last five years and then my "partner," my newspaper, would be murdered. The Times-Mirror Company would kill its own brilliant baby and *New York Newsday* would win two Pulitzers on the very eve of its destruction.

The real journalism giant killers of the twentieth century would turn out to be hard-boiled business "suits," who do not see newspapering as a sacred calling. But there's no use crying over spilt milk. And on the first day my column ran in *New York Newsday*, disaster was not in the foreseeable future. Everything was coming up roses.

GREAT TITS

BARBARA WALTERS'S BEST GIRLFRIEND in all the world is a petite blonde charmer named Suzanne Goodson. She'd been wed to the *What's My Line?* producer Mark Goodson, and is one of those Manhattan marvels who keeps up with everything.

So in 1992, Suzanne and I tried to think of some way we could celebrate one of Barbara's birthdays without ruining ourselves socially. (As the Baron de Montesquieu said, "Every party is given against someone!" and this model for Proust's Baron Charlus was right. Not only is Paris society that way, but every party in New York is fraught with who does or doesn't get invited, and the fallout can be tremendous unless you are prepared, like Malcolm Forbes always was, to invite a cast of thousands.)

Suzanne and I came up with what we thought was a foolproof party. We'd invite to Le Cirque sixty-odd important gentlemen friends of Barbara's, omitting wives entirely, and we would attend ourselves in black-tie—as waiters. We thought this was terribly clever. We assumed all of the wives had Barbara's happiness at heart just as we did and that they would gladly give up their men for a night. Boy! Were we ever wrong. We ended up being called female chauvinists and a lot worse. But the party itself was a bang-up success.

Sirio Maccioni turned over a private room in the old Le Cirque and we didn't get a single "no" from any of the invites sent to NYC, L.A. and Washington. Everybody kept it a secret from Barbara while a few fuming wives arranged anterior parties for their lady friends and others just stayed home "mad." Several offered to "drop in" at the end of the night, but we said, "No—it's Barbara's night and we want her surrounded by male admirers."

Barbara was delivered to Le Cirque by Joe Armstrong thinking she was having dinner with him, Suzanne and me. We greeted her at the door in our tuxedos with white napkins over our arms. She burst into tears when she saw what was going on and the party got off to a rousing start as guys lined up to kiss Barbara a happy birthday. The look on this superstar's face when she realized it was sixty guys and a girl—and two nondescript "waiters"—was worth anything.

We discovered that night a truism—that important men love the company of other important men, as we cycled Barbara from table to table throughout the evening. A lot of guys tried to get Suzanne and me to sit down, but we demurred. No, we said, we were just serving staff. In the end, of course, this detail broke down as the Forrest Perrin orchestra played; Barbara, Suzanne and I were much in demand to dance. As Oscar de la Renta took my tuxedoed self in his arms, he smiled. "Shall I lead or do you want to?"

I collapsed. No woman would ever want to lead the greatest ballroom dancer in the nation, but later that night, I tried.

Barbara was radiant, basking in the glow of love from so many who were not strangers—Barry Diller, Roger Ailes, Vernon Jordan, Pete Peterson, Abe Rosenthal, Henry Kissinger and her various bosses at ABC. I won't name them all for fear of glazing your eyes. Men rose up to extol her with toasts and Barbara capped the evening by singing a tender "I've Grown Accustomed to Your Face" to the then CBS boss Howard Stringer, who had just told of his unsuccessful bid to woo her from ABC. (Everyone speculated as to how this affected Barbara's boss Roone Arledge who was definitely sitting there.)

The funniest thing that happened was when the tall movie director Joel Schumacher took Barbara in his arms and cuddled her to him. She said to him, "What's your next movie?"

He was already gazing down into her excellent cleavage and he murmured, "Great tits!"

Barbara fell back. "Your next movie is called *Great Tits*??" Everybody fell down laughing. It remained a catch-phrase ever after and now whenever I ask Joel what's next on his plate, he always says, "*Great Tits*—what else?"

The group photo taken by the fabled Mary Hilliard was so great *Vanity Fair* reprinted it. Barbara was disappointed, however, because at the last minute, the tiny titan Ron Perelman had sat down on the floor in front of her, obscuring our guest of honor's glorious legs. (Ron has a way of driving women crazy, have you noticed?) Other than this detail, the party was a palpable hit. A few annoyed wives in the great inner circle never forgave Suzanne and me. But we considered the evening such a success we didn't much care. It made us both fearsome and infamous.

And we knew we had a happy hit when Barbara let one tycoon take her home in his limousine as the party ended. She whispered, "He is insisting. I have to go. But don't leave. I'll be right back!" As soon as she said good-night to the man, she waited a beat, jumped in a cab and returned to rehash the party with Joe, Suzanne and me. By now we had moved out of the private room into the restaurant proper and it was 1:00 A.M. Barbara immediately began to characteristically second-guess herself. "Do you think I should have worn another dress?" she asked. "Maybe this one is too revealing?"

Suzanne's answer went down in history along with "Great tits." She simply said, "Barbara, shut the fuck up!"

.   .   .

EVERYONE HATES "HAPPY BIRTHDAY," WHICH must be the most sung song in history. But given that, I want to comment on what I believe is mostly a New York social phenomenon—the reverence toward birthdays of everyone over fifty. The crowd I seem to have fallen into is death against *having* birthdays, but at the same time, loathe to let one happening to *anyone else* pass unremarked.

This rather awful relentless remembrance is, at the same time, upsetting because no one wants to say his age. It's a no-no even when it is recorded right there in all the almanacs.

On the occasion of my seventieth birthday I insisted on nothing happening. I wasn't too pleased to leave my glorious sixties. The unrelentingly ceremonious Iris Love, who worships any occasion where there is the pop of a cork or the blow of a candle, insisted that at least we should have dinner with a few close friends. I kept saying no. So on the fateful night, I refused to dress up to go to the Russian Tea Room, where Iris had a reservation. I sauntered out in a foul humor, wearing an old sweater and pants to find Iris dressed to the nines in a Dior silk creation. "Don't you want to put on something nicer?" she asked.

"No, I don't even want to go." Iris didn't insist; she actually enjoys seeing someone slip on their own banana peel.

We arrived at the Tea Room and I could hear the murmur of many voices above as I ascended the stairs. "I'll kill you!" I muttered to Iris—and sure enough there they were, at least 100 of them all screaming, "Surprise!" and "Happy birthday!" (Iris and Barbara Walters and Suzanne Goodson had turned out the "usual suspects.")

I don't like surprises, even though I like to give them. So the whole event became a night of horror as I sat in my ratty sweater with people I admired like Henry Kravis and Peter Jennings and you name them. The kind and loving tributes were even more painful. But then, it was a night when Brooke Astor was seated with a table of dynamite guys: Barry Diller, David Geffen and Charlie Rose among them.

Later Mrs. Astor asked if Charlie Rose was straight. I said he was, yes indeed. Pretty soon, Charlie had Mrs. Astor's backing for his successful interview show on public television, so my seventieth was not a total loss. I also learned my lesson. If it's your birthday, dress up—just in case.

A couple of years later, I masterminded my own birthday party in Barbetta on West 46th Street. I announced right up front that I was changing my birthday back to sixty, just as people change husbands, change their faces, change their minds and change their sex. I wouldn't lie about my birthday, but I was *rolling it back*.

It worked. *The New York Times*, the paper of record, reported the event as my "60th Birthday." So much for investigative reporting.

WHY DID

BARRY DILLER GIVE

ME $600,000?

O H, HE'S SEXY! HE IS so smart, he's scary. His balding head has kept him from ever looking as if he is growing older. He has a divine body, and great wrists and ankles. (Kitty Foyle said men have to have great wrists and ankles or forget it!)

The mogul we know as Barry Diller grew up in Beverly Hills. He raised himself up in The William Morris Agency mailroom, opening files and reading management correspondence that went back for years. He went on to study at the knee of Gulf & Western's Charles Bludhorn. Then he invented TV's Movie of the Week for ABC-TV, became president of Paramount Pictures, hired Dawn Steel, raising her to prominence as the first effective female executive in the industry. He headed 20th Century-Fox and then Fox TV. He cashed in on the QVC shopping network. Now he is a brilliant entrepreneur and who knows what's next? I have never understood any of the various businesses Barry has been in since he left Fox and whatever I wrote here would be superseded by events. Let's just say he is his own energy source.

People want him to invite them, to notice them. People yearn for his attention. They hope somehow to access his power.

So why did this guy give me $600,000 and not get anything in return?

We had been friends for years, and Barry had always suffered my gossip column with patience even if he had no use for such stuff. But at one point in the early nineties, he had enormous ambitions for me. Barry had decided I was unique and should cash in on the high regard in which he felt I was held in the entertainment community. "Liz, you are the only one with a real voice and in your business, your voice is important. You also have things to say. Let's think what to do with you."

I was getting slightly weary of WNBC's *Live at Five* and Barry's offer was appealing. At this time, Barry was running Fox TV for Rupert Murdoch. He easily lured me away from WNBC. Then, he cast about for a venue in which he could show the world just how special I was. And he asked if I'd mind having a rather unique producer named...Roger Ailes?

Mr. Ailes was famous from the Washington Beltway. He had been a political expert behind both Ronald Reagan and George Bush. He was known for his bare-knuckled moxie and his conservative fighting spirit. Now he was tired of being called an attack dog; he was going back into TV where he had first been successful as a producer for Mike Douglas. I acquiesced to Barry's wisdom and when I met Mr. Ailes, I found him charming and fun. Again, I became involved with someone with whom I was a world apart ideologically. But something about Roger's courage and energy appealed to me. We were off and running. And Barry gave me a very generous two-year contract with Fox.

Barry wanted us to re-create the old Edward R. Murrow program *Person to Person*: interviews taking place in the home of the subject but conducted by me from a studio. At the time Murrow did his show, back in the fifties, it was new and avant-garde. Remotes were glamorous and difficult. So I went to the Museum of TV & Radio to remind myself of what made *Person to Person* such a hit. I saw that it was like a dog walking on its hind legs. At the time, it was unusual—Murrow's reputation as a serious journalist did the rest.

There he was in black-and-white, his brooding presence very appealing as he sat wreathed in the cigarette smoke that would eventually kill him. I went to Ailes. "This is a bad idea. *Person to Person* was great for its time, but it is now old hat. Everybody does remotes, everybody does celebrity interviews, everybody has seen split screen. I don't think we can pull this off."

We were never to know. Roger more or less agreed with me, but said we had to try and he set to. We lined up Mike and Mary Wallace in their Manhattan apartment and then Wayne Newton in his over-the-top Las Vegas house as subjects for our pilot.

We taped. I realized I wasn't a very good interviewer after all, especially not with subjects who were miles away. Roger did his damnedest to help me and Barry seemed to like the finished shows, even if I didn't. We had a contract for nineteen of these things and hoped to establish ourselves on Fox in the fall. But summer came. Barry had Fox air to fill. He decided to throw our pilots into the hopper and see if people liked them. "Then, maybe we'd make two more a little later." Roger and I felt we'd be wasted in the doldrums and that we couldn't "establish" ourselves by putting out two piddling efforts. We cited to Barry our big number of shows, *guaranteed*! We insisted we wanted to wait until fall. Barry shrugged and let it pass. He probably forgot about us.

The next thing we knew he had departed Fox for greener pastures. Fox was now paying me $600,000 for two years. But nobody in the new regime there ever contacted Roger or me to ask us to do something to justify the contract. It was as if we'd never existed except to Fox bookkeeping. Any idea Barry Diller had left behind him was banished by the new order. (Roger Ailes would move on to become a power at CNBC and then as the head of the surprising and burgeoning Fox News. He has made a silk purse out of a sow's ear and is another one of my heroes!)

I saw that Fox had a kind of *Entertainment Tonight* show called *Entertainment Daily Journal*. I volunteered to work out my very expensive contract on that show. They said okay and it turned into a small but credible gig. However, since *EDJ* was being seen in *L.A.* at one in the morning, it had no chance to last. Few people ever saw it. From there I elected to go on New York's local Fox Channel 5 morning news show *Good Day New York,* which was being run by my former NBC producer Gail Yancosek. Gail used to laugh, "You must be the highest paid local newscaster in the world."

When the Diller contract ended, I signed with the local Channel 5 for much, much less money. But working with Gail and my longtime friend Jim Ryan was a joy and I rose up early for *GDNY* for the past seven years. Except for the alarm clock ringing at 6 A.M., this is like stealing money.

Every time I see Barry, he says, "I could have made you a star, but you are too stupid." Then he adds, "Not that you aren't already a star."

I just say, "Shut up and give me a kiss."

UNBIND MY

ASPARAGUS

I HAVE BEEN WRITING GOSSIP COLUMNS for almost thirty years. People always ask, "What was your biggest scoop?" I have to hang my head. "The Donald–Ivana Trump divorce." (But that wasn't really an important story; it didn't change history except *my* history.)

Or sometimes folks ask, "What is your favorite column you've ever written?" Then I don't blush. I don't stammer. I don't hesitate. I know my favorite. I wrote it in answer to critiques leveled at me by Jonathan Yardley and Maureen Dowd in *The Washington Post* and *The New York Times*. They hadn't liked a report of mine on a book party for Colin Powell. This rejoinder column doesn't have movie stars in it. It didn't break new ground. It didn't make headlines. It was absolutely of no consequence, but it's still my pet. Here it is, circa September 1995.

"The sin of newspaper people is almost invariably the sin of envy," writes David Remnick.

Recently I had the "good fortune" to be the only print reporter covering a dinner in New York given for General Colin Powell by his Random House editor, Harold Evans. That isn't to say there weren't many other media-type guests, but after dinner, and after General Powell's dynamic speech kicking off his book, Harry Evans interrupted the fine time I was having with my dinner partners Barry Diller and Bob Woodward. They were discussing the joys of "vertical integration" in big business mergers when Harry whispered in my ear, "Go sit by the general, ask him questions. You're the only one invited here tonight to report on this party!"

Well had I known that earlier, I would certainly have taken notes, been paying attention and observing more carefully. So I did go sit by the general. He was very nice. I liked him. He said he'd decide about running for president after he got *My American Journey* out of his system. He told me he liked the press. I told him, "General, you'll get over it."

When Tom Brokaw joined us, I ceded my place next to the general and rushed out of the café knowing that now—dammit—I had to write a story, which I hadn't planned. And it was this story that got me in trouble with Maureen Dowd of *The New York Times* and Jonathan Yardley of *The Washington Post*. Both of them seemed mad as hell in print, a few days later. General Powell had dared to act as if he might run without their approval: or without their being present at his book party? Both of these highly placed, well-regarded columnists seemed to take scornful exception to my description of the dinner that had been served in the I Trulli restaurant, down in Manhattan's East Twenties.

We were offered bound asparagus and three kinds of pasta, plus a fruit tart. Wondering what the hell I had to write about, as I taxied to my office in panic, I remembered the great Professor DeWitt Reddick of Journalism 101, the University of Texas: "Details! Details!" he had cautioned. "Good feature writing is in the details!" (Well, I thought, it certainly had worked for Tom Wolfe.)

So, in addition to writing that guests around me were placing bets as to whether or not the general would run, I added a few colorful garnishes about the dinner menu. Big mistake.

It was the bound asparagus that got Yardley and Dowd. Either they hate silly details, or they are genuine asparagus liberators. These columnists most likely belong to organizations like People for the Ethical Treatment of Animals, so they may be all for freeing asparagus as well. Instead of reporting on the party, I should have called Madeleine Albright at the U.N. over human and vegetable rights transgressions. And I wasn't even a good enough reporter to say what the I Trulli asparagus had been bound with? (Proscuitto—it turns out, not even good old U.S. bacon.)

And the three kinds of pasta: definitely un-American. I ask you, if it's against the law to bind asparagus, then why didn't NYC Police Chief William Bratton, a party guest, place the I Trulli chef under arrest right then and there?

But Yardley wasn't just offended by my food comments. He didn't approve of the guests themselves. He wrote: "The guest list as reported by Smith consisted of all the famous and beautiful people whom, if God is on your side, you will never have to meet, much less break bread and/or beautifully bound asparagus and three kinds of pasta with."

Hmm, I know I'm culpable in not having unbound my asparagus, but I thought the guest list was fine. What's wrong with guests such as Anne and Vernon Jordan, Sally Quinn, Ben Bradlee, Bob Woodward, Elsa Walsh, Norris and Norman Mailer, Len and Sally Garment, Carol and Joe Lelyveld, Don and Marilyn Hewitt, Tom Brokaw, Barbara Walters, Lynn Sherr, Leslie Stahl, Jessye Norman, Jennifer Patterson, Howard Stringer and New Jersey's Bill Bradley?

Yardley also referred to "Hollywood saps" at the party, but I'd only mentioned Barry Diller. Does Yardley honestly think of Diller, of all people, as a sap? My, my.

Dowd wrote a satire on planning such a book party. "Liz Smith will rave about the bound asparagus. Wait until she sees the bound book!" (I did see the bound book: It was full of blank pages since the text hadn't then been released.) Well, I'm sorry I mentioned food at all. But as I rushed out of I Trulli, I'd seen the owner sitting alone at the door. He looked dejected and shell-shocked. He had given his all to what Yardley called "publishing twits" and they had laughed, talked loud, gossiped, carried

on and paid little attention to his very nice dinner. I felt rather
sorry for Nicola. I could just imagine some PR person from
Random House saying, "This party will *make* your restaurant."
It had been so crowded and noisy as almost to unmake the place
and poor Nick had turned away his neighborhood regulars.

So I decided to add food details to make him happy. Did
I know this was a crime against nature? Next thing we know
there'll be slogans, marching, picketing and people throwing
things at Korean veggie stands. "Let our asparagus be unbound!" the righteous will yell. And, yes, I'll join them. Never
again will I leave an asparagus bound on my plate, let alone eat
one that can't defend itself, or invade asparagus privacy by writing about one in bondage. It's too S & M.

Probably Harry Evans made a mistake, too. He should
have had the general's book party down in Washington at Kay
Graham's house. That way those sensitive Beltway insiders
would have been in control. They wouldn't have felt left out of
General Powell's plans.

As it was, a gossip columnist had to lead them—right
into the asparagus patch.

THE DANCER

DIES

JOURNALISM IS NEVER SERENE. AND in a world where most things don't last, one usually has no expectations. But seldom has anything surprised me so much as the sudden death of *New York Newsday* in 1995. I thought we were solidly on the way to success. I still think we were. We were told that we were only a million dollars away from profitability, which would come within the year. I also thought if any tabloid newspaper died, it would be either the *New York Post* or the New York *Daily News*. Both were slim, quavering and fighting for their lives.

But the Chandler family that owned the *Los Angeles Times*, which in turn owned *Newsday* of Long Island and *New York Newsday*, decided they needed better dividends. They wanted to close the financial drain of *New York Newsday*. My mentor, publisher Robert Johnson, had felt the heavy hand from L.A. on his shoulder and he had resigned, refusing to do the dirty deed requested of him.

The big, ad-fat, rugged, family-oriented, suburban Long Island *Newsday* would go on, but the good-looking, snappy and unusual *New York Newsday* would die. In my final column on July 16, 1995, I was hurt and angry. I noted that when I'd come to New York wet behind the ears, the city had eight vivid news-papers; the good, stolid, gray *New York Times*; the appealing and urbane *New York Herald Tribune*; the flashy column-heavy, Red-baiting Hearst-owned *New York Journal American*; the Walter Winchell–dominated, sensational *New York Mirror* tabloid; the solid and heavy, moneymaking, headline-brilliant New York *Daily News* tabloid; the then very liberal voice of the *New York Post* tabloid; the dimming and dull *World-Telegram and Sun*—famous for sports and racing news; and the tabloid-sized *Newsday* on Long Island.

I had actually worked for five of those papers and would, eventually, work for a sixth. I had just spent a really happy five years toiling at the new kid on the block, *New York Newsday*, a publication dedicated to covering New York and competing with the *Times* in the international arena. I had worked with daz-zling compatriots.

So we were unlucky: Our newspaper was discarded. But I felt New York City was really the unlucky one. It was losing one of its finest, best journalistic products. *New York Newsday* had been editorially independent. Our L.A. owners didn't interfere with us or inflict ideologies upon us. We stood almost alone in being unhampered by our owners. We were truth-seeking, dispas-sionate, honest, dedicated, with no axe to grind beyond the truth.

For months, I had scolded, cajoled and begged my friends to support *New York Newsday*. The arguments I got back were unworthy, having to do with cosmetics, typography, style or confusing page-numbering. While the city and its other highly competitive papers made fun of my upscale newspaper, calling it "the tabloid in a tutu," the dancer was being murdered.

I felt stunned and shocked. New York deserved a paper, other than the *Times*, with truthful independent points of view too important to be left to the other two "untutued" tabloids, if you will. We had done everything right except make enough money quickly enough.

.   .   .

WHILE *NEW YORK NEWSDAY* WAS dying, naturally I was wondering what was going to happen to me. No columnist can make a dent without a New York outlet. You can be read in seventy other venues, as I was, but it don't mean a thing if it ain't got that Manhattan swing.

The new boss of *Newsday*, Ray Jansen, assured me that the Long Island–based bastion wanted me to stay on and continue my generous contract as it existed. But he hoped I would seek another outlet in the city. There were only two places to go; the New York *Daily News* (again?) or the *New York Post*. Mort Zuckerman, the new *News* owner, said he wanted me but went around town telling everyone I was too expensive. (He never once asked me what I required. In spite of rampant rumors to the contrary, he and I never once negotiated even though we were good friends.) The editor of the *New York Post*, Ken Chandler, didn't hesitate. He wanted me to join his wicked little band of *Post* merrymakers, subject to *Newsday*'s approval. My financial godfather, Pete Peterson, advised me, and my wonderful attorney, David Blasband, ran interference. We made a deal for me to continue with *Newsday* and my syndicate, just as I was, yet receive another salary from the *Post*, and become the only columnist in the history of journalism ever to appear in three separate venues within one metropolitan district. I would be read in five boroughs—in *Newsday,* the *New York Post* and in the superindependent *Staten Island Advance*. Times were changing in the newspaper world; nobody could be quite so stuffy about "exclusivity" as they had once been in the past.

Scared to death, laden with sorrow for *New York Newsday*, I soldiered on and wrote my first exclusive for the *New York Post* on August 31st, 1995. It said: "SPLITSVILLE FOR LIZ: Taylor and 7th hubby separate!"

I was out at dinner when Elizabeth's PR rep Chen Sam called. My stalwart aide, Denis, said to her, "Chen, don't make me call Liz in a restaurant to come to the phone and talk with Elizabeth if it's just something about her new perfume line. Is this a personal story?" Chen said it was and Denis found me. The rest became front-page history, based on a talk with the lady herself. And this is how big scoops sometimes happen if you're lucky.

ON SEPTEMBER 5TH, MY COLUMN began appearing in the *New York Post*, opening with the kind of sophisticated NYC story I liked best—a tale about how every eligible woman in town was hoping to marry the newly widowed headman at *The New York Times*. I had these women doodling "Mrs. Punch Sulzberger" on their notepads. And I commented on the power and appeal of powerful, single, eligible, heterosexual males.

I have been there at the *Post* on page fourteen ever since, following Page Six, Neal Travis and Cindy Adams. The *Post* is a reflection of its powerful owner, Rupert Murdoch—it is scandal-driven, headline-screaming, gossip-laden and naughtily eye-catching and irresistible. My take is that every thinking New Yorker "says" they read the *Times*, but they also read the *Post*—for fun and sensation, for its fabulous sports, gossip, business and book/media coverage and also for a caffeine-type jolt. I like to think I am a leavening liberal voice of reason in this paper's spicy, saucy mix. And so far, I have enjoyed a relaxed and carefree existence with my ideologically conservative bosses and my very famous publisher-owner, Mr. Murdoch. They don't tell me what to write or what not to write. I have to tiptoe around using my own judgment.

This was perfectly reflected when Rupert Murdoch telephoned me personally to say he and his longtime wife, Anna, were separating. He seemed to want me to print it in my column though he did not exactly ask me to. It was a great little scoop, but I asked if I should read back to him whatever I was writing. He said, "No, just do it the way you think is best." Later, Mr. Murdoch called again to advise that the divorce was indeed on. I wrote this again as an item. I'm not sure, but I think no one was more surprised by my Murdoch scoops than my fellow workers on the *Post*. I felt I rose a few notches in their jaundiced eyes.

PART

EIGHT

a Memoir

OFF THE BACK

OF TRAINS

ON JANUARY 4, 1998, a story written about me by the talented Geraldine Fabrikant appeared in *The New York Times* and created a sensation. I suppose I believed that money was the root of all evil but I had often expressed my own smart-alec philosophy, borrowed from the late Ben Hecht, which was that money is something to be thrown off the back of trains. Still, I had no real concept of the actual power of money until I gave this interview.

You can talk about anything these days—your sex life, your face- and bosom-lift, your substance abuse, your cancer, your heartbreak—but what no one is ready for is when you actually discuss money—how much you have or don't have and what you do with it!

I had never before been the center of such a fury. It seemed everyone read the *Times* business section and people were flabbergasted that I had spoken openly to Geraldine about what a poor manager I had been all my life, how my friends Pete Peterson and Joan Ganz Cooney had twisted my tail a few years ago and forced me to start saving. I discussed my life history of professing, hypocritically, to disdain my father's gambling and open-handedness.

While talking to Geraldine about all this I realized I had simply followed directly in my father's footsteps. I was a bigger gambler than he ever was. There is a certain big ego at work in disdaining the intelligent management of one's finances. I made money, it squirted through my fingers for sixty-five long years, just as money had spilled out of the top of Sloan's Luchese boots when he came home from a successful crap game. I looked down my nose and was holier than thou about casinos, wagers and betting, but I had bet my entire life on being able to keep making money without saving any. And I had gambled on good health to make that possible.

This newspaper story was a cautionary tale and it certainly struck a lot of nerves. I came into great demand to discuss money, high finance and to talk about "how to" on TV shows and such. I was asked to explain my behavior as a poor manager when I had friendships with such men as Henry Kravis, Ace Greenberg, Pete Peterson, Felix Rohatyn and Alan Greenspan. I loved it when people began to turn to me as some sort of what-to-do-with-money guru. After all, I still had trouble with the multiplication table and long division and I had almost not graduated from college because of freshman algebra.

I learned a great lesson myself from reading *The New York Times* analysis. I have been trying to behave like a grown-up ever since.

WHAT'S

TYPICAL?

M Y EDITORS WANT ME TO write about a typical Liz Smith day. Had they asked me to write about my favorite kind of *atypical* day, it would have been a cinch. That's the day when I go to work and my desk is full of items already offered, checked-out and written up. I have a cup of coffee, a piece of fruit, a roll, bagel or doughnut, take my vitamins and read *The New York Times*, plus all my competition. Every other day, I try to exercise for an hour and a half. Then I fall to writing the column. The phone barely rings all day, or if it does, it's a big movie star in person with his/her own exclusive. Maybe I go out to lunch with someone great like Beverly Sills just to "catch up" and for talk among ourselves about things that will never appear in a gossip column.

By 6:30 P.M. I am ready to get in bed and watch the evening news. After that and *Entertainment Tonight* I get up and make myself a bowl of Campbell's ordinary tomato soup with whole milk, eat a bag of Lay's potato chips, drink a diet Coke and save a Snickers for later in the 5,000-calorie evening. Then I read and watch TV until I go to sleep. My phone never rings.

But as you may imagine, this idealized day almost never

happens. I am often awakened early as if a fire bell has gone off. Gossip is a crisis business like fighting fires. You can be sure that everything planned the day before for the coming column has fallen apart, not checked out or been rendered obsolete. Denis, Mary Jo, Diane and I rush around all day like chickens with our heads off. We write and we rewrite. We get and make hundreds of phone calls. We are always waiting for the proper time difference to enable us to speak to the West Coast, which is three maddening hours behind us. We tear up the column and do it over and over. We lose our good juicy lead and have to settle for something else. Although we ostensibly file the column for the syndicate editors around noon, we are revising, checking, calling, pleading and changing tomorrow's column up until 4:30 P.M. Then I rush about getting my hair and makeup done because I need to be somewhere that evening to emcee an event, to cover an opening, to do my bit for charity. You name it. On night after night, after days like these, I don't get to bed until 11:00 or midnight.

And let's just draw a veil over the exigencies of having to also "do" television. On those days all bets are off and nobody knows exactly what will happen or what will fall by the wayside. Me, mainly, from sheer exhaustion.

There are some "givens" in the gossip column business. Any big breaking gossip story will usually happen late on Friday afternoon, just as you planned to go away for the weekend. Legit press agents can never believe you would want to miss an opening night *on* or *off*-Broadway. This requires being dressed and wherever at 6:15 P.M. Ordinary dinners and parties usually begin at 7:30 and you're lucky to be out by 10:45. There is, of course, the ongoing worry of what to wear. Here I often fall by the wayside and just put on my now ancient Yves St. Laurent tuxedo jacket.

The Academy Awards come up every March and I am expected to go. Here's how I feel about Oscar: For about fifteen years I would arrive in L.A. the day before in order to set up and cover the events at the Dorothy Chandler Pavilion on the big day. The problem? I had to be in place for a live remote broadcast to New York at 2:00 P.M. when very little is happening in L.A. But *Live at Five* was on the WNBC air live at 5:00 P.M. and had to be served. Yes, there'd be bleachers full of people, yelling and holding up signs. But they had been there for days, saving their seats. And although I would report breathlessly what was supposed to be going on, there usually wasn't a star anywhere near us, within thirty miles. I often likened this to having hair and makeup done to sit down for root canal.

Exactly twice I went to the Academy Awards as an actual guest with an assigned seat in the auditorium. I found I didn't get anything more out of this than the average TV watcher. Then on several occasions I went backstage as "press" and was shunted to the room for print journalists and prevented from ever leaving my post to wander around. Print was low on the totem pole. I graduated to the TV room, where at least I could hang out with Siskel and Ebert and "dish," while we waited for the next winner to favor us with a few words.

What did we get out of this? Believe me, nothing exclusive. I'll never forget when Joe Pesci won for *GoodFellas* in 1990. He came back holding his Oscar and proceeded to give us a profanity-laden statement that wasn't suitable for repeating. I love Joe and knew he was just giving us the razz. We were left with little to transmit but his "bleeps."

I recall standing in the Oscar backstage line to get in, behind Robert and Dorothy Mitchum. When I mentioned this to the irresistible Mitchum years later, he said, "No, it wasn't me. I have never been to the Academy Awards." Movie stars do love to jerk us journalists around and why shouldn't they?

Another time on the red carpet I actually encountered a star, Whoopi Goldberg. While we talked, a tattoo on her breast kept peeking out of her cleavage and then disappearing. I was so fascinated by this I couldn't remember a word Whoopi said.

Now I content myself by going to the *Vanity Fair* Oscar dinner at Morton's and hanging around to see the stars after. It amuses me to watch big, big names rushing to get inside, avoiding their screaming fans behind the barricades. They can't wait to cozy up to the many gossip columnists invited. (Better they should talk to their fans. It would be safer.) I have been soundly kissed and squeezed at Morton's by such as Uma Thurman, Cher, Camryn Manheim, Deborah Harry, Madonna, Nicole Kidman, Tom Cruise, Regis Philbin, Barry Diller, George Hamilton, Sly Stallone, R. J. Wagner, Arnold Schwarzenegger, Sidney Poitier, David Geffen, Harvey Weinstein, Kevin Costner, Jay Leno, Rosanna Arquette and one night, above the din, Michael J. Fox said to me, "You and I are grown-up people. What are we doing here in all of this?" I couldn't answer.

However, going to L.A. on Oscar night has its good points. At the last one, Tony Curtis came up and kissed my hand, apologizing for having yelled at me, "Go fuck yourself!" one recent evening in New York's Le Cirque. (He imagined I had insulted his wife.) Oscar night he was contrite and full of charm. It was gratifying.

AS FOR COVERING NEW YORK, I guess my night at the *Time* Magazine 75th anniversary party in Radio City Music Hall was about as "typical" as they come. Here's what happened.

People fought for these *Time* invitations in 1998. I sat with the young movie idol Chris O'Donnell, who I had interviewed while he was making *Batman and Robin.* My other tablemate of note was Tricia Nixon Cox whom I had, oddly, never met although she lived as a young social matron in New York. Tricia looked almost exactly as she did when she wed Edward Cox in the White House, circa 1971. I was amazed. I wondered if she had a painting, à la Dorian Gray, moldering away in an attic while she held time at bay. One reason Tricia looked so exact was because she had on her Oleg Cassini wedding dress. "It still fits me. Maybe it has come back in style." This blonde babe was very friendly, unlike her more reserved sister, Julie, who pointedly never speaks to those in the press who ever criticized "Daddy." (A large group!) I do seem to have problems with presidential offspring. The sainted Caroline Kennedy Schlossberg never speaks either. In fact, I recently sat at a dinner right across from her. Hillary Clinton had given me a grand salute and a big kiss, but Caroline never makes eye contact with most of us ink-stained wretches. She simply ignored me and refused even to say "good evening." (Something her elegant and smart mother would never have done.)

In my line of sight all of the *Time* evening was the beautiful Sophia Loren. But I wouldn't say she was serene. I didn't blame her. Next to her sat the evening's most difficult dinner partner, Mikhail Gorbachev. He was dour until he rose to make a "little" speech. Then he seemed downright angry. He harangued us for about forty minutes in a language few understood and brought the heretofore charming evening to a shuddering halt. Then, as the event recovered and people began to proceed in a leisurely fashion to the exits, I found myself run down by his thuggish bodyguards as they hustled him away from the proletariat. Like the Russian people, I wanted to say, "Good riddance." (Yes, I know he helped tear down the Iron Curtain, but still, he has lousy manners. Since he lost his accumulated fortune and is *persona non grata* in Russia, he may have a reason to be grumpy.)

The number-one biggest "name" at the party turned out to be Joe DiMaggio, who refused to be seated next to President and Mrs. Clinton, insisting he must sit with his friend Dr. Henry Kissinger. And so he did. There wasn't a famous person at the party who didn't yearn to meet Joe and shake his hand. VIPs turned up their noses at Tom Cruise, Nicole Kidman, Sharon Stone, Norman Mailer, Tina Brown, the Reverend Billy Graham, Anita Hill, et. al. They only wanted Joltin' Joe. I didn't get in line to shake his hand, but months later I was asked to attend his memorial in St. Patrick's Cathedral. His friend who set it up told me, "You were the columnist Joe really respected. He read you every day. He'd want you to be there. He always said you were the only one who understood the character of Marilyn Monroe and the only one ever to give her a break."

JUST

BRAGGING

WILL IT ENHANCE ME IF I run down memory lane telling about scoops and triumphs, awards and the occasional honor, or what was said positively about me? Probably not. Then, to be fair, I'd need to elaborate on the fun often made of me on *Saturday Night Live,* or by Don Imus or Howard Stern.

But I did finally achieve my dream of being in the movies. When I landed small roles in three films, I found it was less interesting than watching paint dry. Because of the column, I am often evoked in contemporary novels and TV sitcoms to advance the plot.

In Sidney Lumet's feature film *Garbo Talks*, I stood at a cocktail party with no lines. The star Ron Silver lurked over my shoulder and has, ever since, referred to me as his "costar"! In Lauren Bacall's *The Fan*, I make a TV pronouncement but end up mysteriously heard and seen only as a reflection in the window. In my big moment, in *Buffy the Vampire Slayer*, I stood outside a high school at the end, announcing sternly into a mike: "Nobody knows for sure what happened here last night, but . . ." This was dramatic, but the producer Howard Rosenman decided to run the movie credits over me as I talked. So much for cinema fame!

I fared better on TV, having an actual "acting" job with my esteemed colleague, Army Archerd, when we appeared as ourselves on *Murphy Brown*. We are in Phil's café-saloon, griping that we can't get anything to eat. The director was the cheerful, energetic Garry Marshall, and though we spent a full day together on the L.A. set, he didn't recognize or remember me when next we met. So much for the Method! In our scene, I am clumsily laden down with a camel's hair coat and that turned out to be rather funny. Both Army and I behave as if adversarial to the star's character, Murphy. This did require some "acting" since there is nothing not to like about the real Candice Bergen.

There *are* two things in my history of which I am really proud. There is a fabulous book in the libraries by David McClintick titled *Indecent Exposure*. It details the Hollywood–Wall Street story of a great business scandal and power struggle that took place in 1977. This revolved around David Begelman, a one-time agent who was then in control of Columbia Pictures. On the verge of having saved the studio and on the eve of an enormous hit with the movie *Close Encounters of the Third Kind*, Begelman was exposed as having forged the name of Oscar-winning actor Cliff Robertson on a $10,000 check. Hollywood's coverup of this happening was intense and some of the important players in this sordid drama were the influential producer Ray Stark, the important agent Sue Mengers, Herbert Allen, Jr., Alan Hirschfield and other moguls of Columbia.

I played a minor role in this, but author McClintick gives me a lot of credit. He notes of journalism's watchdog role that in order for any event to become a major news story, there must be broad public reaction. Otherwise, says David, the event is like an airplane moving along an endless runway, unable to get up enough speed to take off.

McClintick writes that the story of Begelman's forgery had been around for some time but a column I printed in the *Daily News* on January 12, 1978, was an important catalyst in its resolution. *The Wall Street Journal* and *The Washington Post* had done yeoman work in exposing this scandal but somehow it kept being swept under the rug, especially in Hollywood where they know how to close ranks. The *Washington Post* editors had buried their exclusive interview with Cliff Robertson during the Christmas holidays by placing it inside instead of on the front page as the publisher Kay Graham had intended. Reading it, I realized that almost nobody else had even seen it. People were not into newspapers during the Yuletide. I decided enough was enough. So, I rehashed the *Post* story, with credit, adding whatever I knew under the headline AND NOW FOLKS, "HOLLYWOODGATE."

McClintick reports that I had "quickly become the leading newspaper gossip columnist in America and a prime practitioner of the new form of gossip journalism that burgeoned in the seventies and effectively eclipsed the Hedda Hopper–Walter Winchell school…Unlike the old columnists, Liz Smith wrote with a droll sense of humor and a lack of malice. She did not take herself or her work more seriously than the subject merited, but she did strive for accuracy, and on the few occasions when she erred, she corrected herself openly. A skilled reporter by any standard, Smith consistently broke major news stories—not only show business stories. Thus, she had helped to redefine gossip, elevate it to a new level of respectability and broaden the audience for it…By the late seventies, Liz Smith's column was very influential and in a way, essential." Blah, blah, blah— hooray for Liz!

I particularly relished author McClintick's take on all this for he was not doing it out of friendship. He is too good a reporter for that. I knew him ever so slightly through my friend, the excellent writer Marie Brenner. I am very proud of what he wrote in his book about me.

Anyway, I lit a fire under the Begelman–Columbia Pictures mess even though I was under pressure from many powerful people in Hollywood to suppress any mention of it. I couldn't do that and I added fuel to the scandal by getting an exclusive interview with actor Robertson who finally admitted that he had feared for his life in the circumstance of making the forgery accusation and that the FBI had feared for him as well. This finally galvanized the Los Angeles district attorney. Begelman was sentenced to a $5,000 fine, three years probation and the necessity to perform community service. But the stigma of publicity seemed to do him in. Although Begelman survived the scandal, in 1995 he shot himself to death in L.A.'s Century Plaza Hotel. It has recently been revealed that he systematically robbed the late Judy Garland blind.

I GUESS I WON'T SERVE history if I fail to mention my connection with Judith Exner. When she finally died in 1999 of the cancer that had plagued her over the years, Judith's obituaries ran the gamut. The worst were *The New York Times* and its columnist William Safire, a man I admire and with whom I am friendly. But both described Judith derisively as a woman who "claimed" to have had a relationship with President John F. Kennedy. They seemed to take seriously the denials of Dave Powers and others that she had actually played an important role in negative aspects of Kennedy's administration. (I guess the *Times* doesn't believe the White House phone logs and the memos of J. Edgar Hoover and the FBI.)

Judith Exner was an impressionable, fun-loving girl from a good Los Angeles family. In her youth, she was said to have been more beautiful than Elizabeth Taylor. She fell in with a fast showbiz crowd that brought her to the attention of Frank Sinatra. After a brief affair, they remained friends. Eventually, she was in Las Vegas and Sinatra introduced her to the young, handsome Senator John F. Kennedy, who was seeking the presidential nomination. Judith, a somewhat lapsed Catholic, says she tried to avoid involvement with the married JFK, but he pursued her relentlessly. She gave in and they began their affair. Judith fell madly in love. She claimed JFK told her he and Jackie had an "arrangement" and would divorce if he lost the election. And after he was elected, she continued to see him but resisted

JFK's gamesmanship. (He wanted her to fly with him on Air Force One; he wanted her to come to parties at the White House with Jackie present.) She refused but went on believing that he loved her.

Just before his election, Kennedy asked Judith to carry a bag of money to the Mob king Sam Giancana in Chicago, but didn't tell her who Giancana was. Judith had already fleetingly met the Mob boss via Sinatra, but says she didn't make the connection. She began to carry missives from JFK to Giancana and set up several personal meets between the president and the mobster. JFK told her, "Sam is helping us to get rid of Castro." Judith claimed Bobby Kennedy was aware and complicit in all these activities. Many people believe that the original suitcase of money was used to help buy crucial Kennedy votes in the Chicago area. Judith claimed that by the time she realized who Giancana was, she had decided she liked him and felt he was her friend. She insisted to the end that she did not have "an affair" with him, as most people assume, and slept with him only once, after she and the president had broken up when she was in a despondent state.

Sam Giancana and his henchman Johnny Rosselli were both murdered after this. Marilyn Monroe was found dead in mysterious circumstances. Then both Kennedy brothers were assassinated. Judith said she feared for her life in this aftermath and slept with a gun beneath her pillow. When a congressional committee commanded her to testify in 1975, she did so, reluctantly. Feeling hounded by Congress, the FBI and the IRS, Judith agreed to do a book of her life, but opted out at midpoint and left her collaborator to, as she said, "mostly make up portions of it." This book was Judith's downfall. It haunted her down the years and she had to perform a number of feats of revisionist history, which some skeptics still do not buy. She said to me plaintively, "I was twenty-five and in love. Was I supposed to have more judgment than the President of the United States?" Nevertheless, Judith gained the reputation of a mob moll, a party girl, an adulteress and a liar. Most people in those days didn't want to blame John F. Kennedy. Or Bobby.

Judith had gotten in touch with me after Congress itself
had blown the whistle on her relationship with JFK. She told
them as little as possible, but once her spurious book came out,
she found herself despised for having created the first crack in
the Kennedy myth of Camelot. I liked Judith Exner when I first
talked to her on the telephone in the late seventies. My internal
shit detector told me she was not a liar. She seemed to be suffering too much self-revulsion, fear and good old Catholic guilt. So
I wrote many columns about her, attempting to set the record
straight. She would now and then phone and give me an incredible item or story, which would turn out to be true. Over the
years, my office befriended Judith. We tried to help her in any
way we could without compromising ourselves. I talked Kitty
Kelley into writing an update on Judith for *People* magazine in
1988, doing myself out of an enormous fee because I thought
Kitty would do a better job. This interview turned into a disaster
even if my intentions had been good. The former *New York
Times* reporter Seymour Hersh hounded me to get him to Judith
because he also believed her stories to be true. I did and he eventually wrote a rather disappointing tome called *The Dark Side of
Camelot*. But he was only one of a host of professionals who,
after 1975, began to change their mind about Judith's rightful
place in history.

In 1996, I went to California and met Judith for the first
time. She was a slightly plump but still beautiful version of her
younger self, warm, sweet and sincere, a woman whose life had
been ruined by a forbidden romantic love and bad judgment. I
then wrote for *Vanity Fair* what I hoped was the defining be-all
and end-all on Judith Exner, including her last revelation—that
after she and JFK ended their affair, she had aborted his child in
Chicago while under the care of the Mob. Though the abortion,
or hospital stay, was on the record, there was no way to prove
that the child had been JFK's. But I instinctively felt it was true.
Most of Judith's other allegations, considered absurd at first, had
panned out.

Maybe I could encourage you to call up the *Vanity Fair*

article, January 1997. That pretty much says it all. If only future
historians would pay real attention to it. And if ever they get Judith's life story on Showtime, as planned, I hope you will keep
in mind that Judith hated everything about the script and tried
unsuccessfully to change or kill it. The producers can brag all
they like about her "cooperation." It was not true.

AND HERE'S THE MOST FASCINATING Jacqueline
Kennedy Onassis story yet. In August 1993, her last summer at
Martha's Vineyard, Jackie invited her friend the respected magazine publisher Joe Armstrong to visit. She had always trusted
him implicitly even though she knew he was a personal pal of
mine.

Joe waited until six years after Jackie's death to tell me
only this one thing about Jackie. They were walking along the
beach in the middle of a sunny afternoon, talking about books.
Jackie suddenly stopped walking, and out of the blue said, "Joe,
the Kennedys will never forgive Liz Smith."

Joe was baffled; he asked, "What for?"

Jackie said, musing, "They will never forgive her because of Judith Exner."

Joe was astonished. "She was talking as if she weren't
one of the Kennedys, which in a way, she never was! She spoke
as if distanced from them. She was completely dispassionate.
She went on to say, 'One of my children claims I am too close to
you and you are a friend of Liz's. But I just say, "Joe is true
blue. He can be loyal to me and to Liz as well." ' Jackie's next
sentence changed the subject. She brightened. 'You know when
the children were young I got them a wonderful rowboat and
named it *Beauty School Dropout*!' "

Well, it was always my personal theory that Jackie probably read the entire Judith Exner saga with great interest. She
had long before come to terms with her murdered husband's numerous infidelities and she—Jackie—was always one to relish a

bit of gossip, about herself and others. I never forgot my friend Horace Busby, the LBJ aide, who analyzed her to me like this: "Jackie was essentially a voyeur. To her, life was something like a rather revealing French film and that is how she approached everything."

MY MODERN

WOMEN

Julia

I KNOW MOVIE STARS—BIG ONES. Do I ever! But do I really know them? Probably not. VIPs are usually on their best behavior with me. There are a few I think I know pretty well: Elizabeth Taylor, Goldie Hawn, Kathleen Turner, Lauren Bacall, Barbra Streisand, Kim Basinger, Diana Ross, Loretta Young, Christine Baranski, Shirley MacLaine, Sidney Poitier, Tom Cruise, John Travolta, Tony Randall, Ron Silver, Candice Bergen, Alec Baldwin, Nicole Kidman, Lena Horne, Téa Leoni, Liza Minnelli, Harry Belafonte—but even these I wouldn't expect to trust their worst secret to me.

There is, however, one star who I feel down deep I *do* know. It started when I spent an evening with the hottest female, biggest box office draw in films, the 20-million-dollar movie star, Julia Roberts. By the time our riotous party time together ended, I had a good bead on this delightful Georgia peach—a girl who had six films in a row recently that grossed a billion dollars. (No other woman in film can make that statement.)

Julia Roberts is a nice kid from the South who dotes on

her mother, her sister, her aunts, her seven mutts from the pound. She is into growing flowers, doing needlepoint and knitting when on movie sets. These days she is a producer-entrepreneur as well as an actor and star. She'd like to spend more time at her ranch in New Mexico. As we went to press she was into a long-term relationship with the actor Benjamin Bratt and she seemed more grown-up and happier.

It's all a far cry from the first time we met in the once-trendy 150 Wooster Street café in downtown Manhattan. The night is indelibly printed on my memory because a more diverse and absurd group of people never got together before or since. Director Joel Schumacher had invited me and girl-about-NYC Suzanne Goodson to dinner. In with him trooped Julia and Kiefer Sutherland who he had directed in *Flatliners*. Now came the writer-director Nora Ephron; Hollywood's favorite big mouth Howard Rosenman; a curator of the Getty Museum, Marit Gentoff-Nilsson; the ubiquitous Professor Iris Love; photographer Bruce Weber and his lady, Nan; another lensman, Matthew Rolston; and the then Columbia movie producer Michael Nathanson. I couldn't imagine who would pay the whopping bill for this gang glut. It was a rowdy crowd, no other word for it. And we ordered everything twice, plus lots of drinks.

Julia and Kiefer were then engaged. But I saw that he was chiefly engaged in drinking a combo of scotch and Coca-Cola—a new one on me. That night Julia was all arms, legs, eyes and mouth. Her hair was a tousled mass of Rita Hayworth curls as in *Gilda*. And she seemed greedy and needy, wanting to be loved.

So we all took turns petting and kissing her and posing for Suzanne's "Brownie." Julia seldom sat down unless it was in someone's lap. She was like a puppy.

I felt like she was a girl in love with love, for I found it hard to believe she could be in love with Sutherland. In fact, I feared for the future of the human race. (Not long after, Julia figured everything out herself with no help from me. She stood Kiefer up at the altar practically.) Times weren't good then for Julia. She was termed box office poison and won bad press when she played Tinkerbell in the ill-fated *Hook*. They said she was high and mighty, hard to get along with. Personally I could hardly believe my little old "steel magnolia" was as bad as the tabloids painted her, but her then press agent kept most of us from finding out for ourselves.

The 150 Wooster evening ended in a crash. Later, I discovered that Joel had paid the entire bill and had gone back personally to be sure he left a great big tip for the waitress, who had been putting up with us. This waitress, named Julianna Margulies, later told *Premiere* magazine all about what it was like waiting on a group of crazy people who thought they were important. But the soon-to-be-a-star-herself Julianna did love her tip.*

Recently I talked to Julia Roberts for *Good Housekeeping.* I referred to a magazine story that mentioned her busted Kiefer Sutherland engagement and her divorce from Lyle Lovett as if she were some impossible man-eater. "You're only thirty years old," I said.

"Thirty-one," Julia corrected me.

I went on, "Here in the twenty-first century, you might be allowed one broken engagement, one divorce without going down in history as a scarlet woman!"

Julia sighed. "Yes, I think so."

I pressed on. "The press likes to paint you as wild, taking drugs, making trouble, picking up and discarding men like Kleenex. But I've always thought you were searching for something. I see you as true blue, a one-man-at-a-time girl."

A big tear formed in Julia's eye and spilled over. "I can't tell you what it means to me that you said that." She sniffed. I asked her if some of her movies, such as *Notting Hill*, were to make points about privacy and stardom.

"No, it never occurred to me," she said. "It didn't reflect my life. I just liked the story. Just as I liked the challenge of the *Erin Brockovich* script." But Julia went on to tell me how powerful the press can be. Remembering the press junket in *Notting Hill,* she said many reporters psychoanalyzed her during the real

---

As I write this, Julianna just turned down a $27 million offer to continue on ER.

press junket where she gave interview after interview. "At first I didn't agree with any theories they advanced. But being asked the same questions over and over by all those reporters and hoping to give each one a distinct answer, I found myself just aping them. I realized I was influenced by the suggestions they offered. I heard myself saying 'Of course, there is a similarity between real life and my art.' Yes, I was subliminally influenced by the script to do this and that. I totally lost my way. I became their creation—the creation of the press as they imagine me."

This was a really candid revelation from an actor. It reminded me that today the press influences even itself and cannibalizes itself. If one segment covers a person or event, the rest pile on. But then, Julia Roberts—the maturing star—is worth jumping on a bandwagon for.

Madonna

Madonna Louise Veronica Ciccone has caused almost as much controversy for her appearances in my column over the past two decades as she has for her own sometimes outrageous behavior. "How much is Madonna paying you?" is a frequent question.

Perhaps because Madonna was seen as being outside what should have been my interests—a sexy pop star who began her stellar life as a teen-theme sensation—reaction to her column mentions has been extreme. "Why do you write about that filthy slut all the time?" Notes like these usually come from self-described good Christians. Is it any wonder Madonna herself has issues with religion?

Actually, I wasn't paying much mind to Madonna at first. But when I questioned the validity of her being on the cover of *Time* in 1985, my then and to this day right-hand man, Denis Ferrara,* set me straight: "This girl is huge. She's going to be an

---

*I hired Denis in 1984 after he wrote me some brilliant letters about Elizabeth Taylor. I sent him to typing school. He has been invaluable to me ever since and has become a first-rate reporter and an excellent writer.

enduring star. An icon. Surely you see this?" Actually, I didn't see it. I was amazed because this guy was such a big fan of more old-fashioned stars. He was a fountain of trivia, much enamored of thirties, forties, fifties Hollywood glamour. What did Madonna, this tatty-haired sexpot, have to do with lasting stardom? Denis persisted in bringing Madonna, her remarks, her videos, her films and the inescapable world attention she was generating to the fore.

Eventually, I got it, though I continued to think of Madonna as only a so-so singer, a pretty good dancer, and a true marketing genius. Still she has a real artist's imagination and daring. She was born with an innate belief that she is special. I will never forget Rosanna Arquette talking to me after having worked with Madonna in *Desperately Seeking Susan.* She claimed Madonna said to her during filming, "Wouldn't you give just about anything in the world to be *me* for an hour??!!" This frank egocentricity spelled Madonna's faith in herself and her inevitable success.

Because of her witty "Material Girl" video, she was often unimaginatively compared to Marilyn Monroe. But I always saw her in the tradition of those great diva-egomaniacs Barbra Streisand, Diana Ross and, most especially, that immortal sexual revolutionary, the sublimely autonomous Mae West. Madonna wants to free society of its sexual inhibitions, its bigotry. She speaks out strongly on safe sex, violence against women, homophobia. It seemed to me Madonna was usually on the right side, though sometimes she took the wrong turn getting there. Her misdeeds (the *Sex* book, her expletive-peppered David Letterman appearance, etc.) were so blown out of proportion by most of the media that I felt compelled, if not to defend her, then to at least present a more balanced view. Those who loved her—and there were millions—loved me for this; those who hated her—and there were plenty of those, too, think I'm nuts and on her payroll.

I met Madonna for the first time at the premiere of her entertaining documentary, *Truth or Dare.* She was in a brunette phase, heavily made-up and encased in a glittering, revealing Versace bodysuit. Her legs were bare, and her bosom on display. She was amazingly petite and seemed oddly fragile. I thought in her garish getup she was less a sexual provocateur and more like a little girl in Mama's finery. She was nothing at all like her deliberately controversial, in-your-face image. At the time, I was the subject of a *Prime Time Live* TV segment, with Judd Rose as interviewer. ABC expected me to corral Madonna, who was in the midst of her own PR maelstrom, for a few remarks. As this was *her* night, I assumed she'd refuse to be a part of my publicity. I was wrong.

Judd Rose asked her, "What do you think of Liz?"

Madonna grinned. "I love Liz Smith because she has balls, like me!" This was a funny, raunchy remark, but of course, though ABC used it on air, they bleeped the word "balls," so the viewer probably didn't get much out of the quote.

My chief reservation about *Prime Time* was that the producers insisted I do things that weren't characteristic. I should have flatly refused, but I let them talk me into being filmed going out in the evening in a stretch limousine. Even the President of ABC News, Roone Arledge, said afterward, "We missed the entire point about you and why you are different and one of a kind."

Years later, Madonna did me the ultimate favor. From Budapest, she gave my column the exclusive on her pregnancy. I had to sit on the news for two agonizing days while the details were ironed out. But it was worth it—the biggest gossip story of the year. I was sputtering in shock when Madonna's rep, Liz Rosenberg, called. "But, she's just starting *Evita*," I said. "How can this be true?"

Madonna herself picked up the phone. "Liz, I'm pregnant," she barked. I started writing.

Denis became a close friend to the star and her press agent, the woman called "The Validator," Liz Rosenberg. This made our office privy to items Denis would insist we couldn't print. He was also the recipient of some adorable, candid and funny letters, faxes and e-mails from Madonna. I'm sure he didn't show me all, but I saw enough that my tongue hung out wanting to reprint them. But they were private. I had to pass.

Madonna, often referred to as rude and socially immature, has never failed to be gracious. She is spontaneous, unlike others for whom it's a learned response. After our first interview, she said to me, "You are not afraid of me. I like that."

Madonna once phoned my office at the height of her "unpopularity" in the wake of the *Sex* book and her *Body of Evidence* movie. "It's Madonna," she said, getting right to the point. "I just wanted to call and say thanks for the support you've given me. I know you get a lot of shit because of it."

I take perverse pride in the knowledge that the biggest star of the last years of the twentieth century—a cultural icon of her age—called me and knew what she was talking about.*

---

*My friends Diane Sawyer and Mike Nichols, knowing how much I disliked the Prime Time interview, sent me a pillow that still rests in my bedroom. One side is what Madonna said to Judd Rose. The other reads: "We love Madonna because she has balls like Liz. Love,—Mike and Diane."

THE GREATEST

STAR

IN THE LAST TEN YEARS, I have been one of the few—
perhaps the only—print journalist with access to the extremely private Katharine Hepburn. In fact, I believe I had the
last of the real interviews with this legend when she sat with me
in her Turtle Bay house in Manhattan for *Vogue* magazine, September 1991. The Great Kate wouldn't have given an interview
even then, but she was pragmatic about wanting success for her
last book. *Me* earned her a reported $4 million.

I have seen Miss Hepburn many times since she retired in
1996 to her house "Fenwick" in Old Saybrook on the Connecticut shore of Long Island Sound. Through the years I've tried to
keep my readers and her millions of fans up to date on Kate in
spite of the desperate, lurid imaginings of the supermarket
tabloids. They usually place her at death's door, or paint dire
pictures of her abandoned by friends and family, clutching piti-
fully at a photograph of Spencer Tracy. I suppose they are gambling on the odds; this fabulous woman was ninety-three as I
wrote these words in 2000.

It's been no small thing to know Miss Hepburn and especially since the American Film Institute poll in 1999 named her

the number-one female film star of all time. Humphrey Bogart was the number-one male. All Kate would say of this honor was "Why wasn't Spencer named as number one?" (Mr. Tracy, the love of Hepburn's life, came in at number eight.)

It's an odd little story, but meeting Miss Hepburn came about because of a public television program on "Ethics." Bear with me while I explain. The late Fred W. Friendly—producer for the legend Edward R. Murrow and former president of CBS News—was then at the Columbia Graduate School of Journalism. Mr. Friendly brought forth roundtable discussions on various important issues of the day. These Socratic dialogues were among the most popular programs ever seen on PBS. Everybody who was anybody (or so it seemed) had been invited to appear. It was an honor to be asked and few declined.

In 1987, Friendly produced a twelve-part series on Ethics and the Professions—medical, legal, government, the military, journalism, etc. He selected Mike Wallace, Peter Jennings, Katharine Graham of *The Washington Post*, Katherine Fanning of the *Christian Science Monitor*, R. W. Apple, Jr., of *The New York Times*, former vice-presidential candidate Geraldine Ferraro, Congressman Barney Frank, General William Westmoreland, Senator Alan Simpson, Lyle Denniston of the *Baltimore Sun*, Jeff Greenfield and others for the journalism ethics portion.

A dynamic young woman named Cynthia McFadden was Friendly's executive producer. She suggested he add me to the mix. Friendly reacted with fury and disdain, refusing. Cynthia kept arguing: "You intend to have a high-level panel about Ethics in Journalism and not have the premier gossip columnist in America participate?"

Finally, Friendly shook his famous crooked finger in her face and answered: "All right. Ask her. But if it doesn't work, it's your job!"

Soon the bright and brilliant Miss McFadden was at my door to pre-interview me. I was flattered, taken with what seemed to be her obvious admiration. "You actually make corrections in your columns when you are wrong," she said. "Almost no columnist does that except under threat of death or libel."

Whether or not I was all that admirable to Miss McFadden, she was determined to get me into the best possible state of mind and to prove her boss wrong.

At the seminar taping in Boston I was seated between Mike Wallace and Peter Jennings in a horseshoe circle. I realized I was in the upper reaches of Fourth Estate heaven. The interrogator, Charlie Nesson, a Harvard law professor, offered us a number of hypothetical "situations" and each of us responded as to what we'd do or say. Those defending the right of the press to know and print or show were opposed to those who felt they'd unfairly had their own privacy invaded.

At one point Professor Nesson wanted to know who were my best sources? I said, "Other journalists who are frustrated by what they know but have no venue to get it into print." He asked if I'd name my sources and I said no, but some of them were sitting on the panel and were my friends.

Peter Jennings piped up: "Used to be, Liz, we used to be your friends." It was a merry set-to and I tried to hold my own.

Eventually I remarked that I supposed I was "just the garbage pail of journalism," a remark that so tickled Friendly, it made his "favorite moments" composite of the program. I have seen the rerun of this now somewhat "classic" show several times without having to slit my wrists.

The best result was the glee Fred Friendly took in what became "his" inspiration to have had me be a part of it. This most dynamic and tempestuous critic of media, a man who carried the Constitution around in his pocket, was frightening to most people. But through Cynthia, I became friendly with Fred and his wife, Ruth. And I always found he was a big pussycat.*

Cynthia was vastly amused by Fred's claim to have wanted me all along. One smart cookie, she was a Phi Beta

*Friendly died in 1999. He left me one of my all-time favorite quotes: "Nobody ever got rich undertipping waiters and stiffing cabdrivers."

Kappa from Bowdoin College in Maine, and had gone on to graduate from the Law School at Columbia University. She became Fred's teaching assistant and then his producer on PBS, hoping for a career in journalism covering the law. I did not see Cynthia for sometime after this PBS show. She had married the Pulitzer prize-winning editor-publisher Michael Davies, who was running, first, the *Hartford Courant* and then the *Baltimore Sun*.

A year or so later, I heard Cynthia had left Friendly's operation and I wrote a brief column item about a TV show on abortion that Cynthia ended up hosting for Lifetime TV. She was very good in this taped outing—the very first time she had ever appeared on television and the item caused Steve Brill to call. He said, "Unaccustomed as I am to hiring people out of the Liz Smith column, I'd like to talk to you about an idea." She went to see him and helped him found the astonishing *Court TV*. This catapulted her to a fame of her own, covering hundreds of trials for *Court TV* before vaulting to ABC News, where she became a star covering the O.J. Simpson trials.

About the same time in 1990, my pal Iris Love and I had gone down to cruise through Florida's Inland Waterway with her sister, Noel, and brother-in-law, Nelson Gross. We left the boat at Fort Myers and got on a plane for NYC. Passing awkwardly through first class (I seemed always to be passing awkwardly through first class), who should we see but Cynthia sitting in the bulkhead seat with—good grief—Katharine Hepburn. I knew vaguely that Hepburn was a sort of "fairy godmother" to Cynthia. She and Michael had been married in Kate's house in Fenwick. Cynthia had known the great star since visiting Fenwick as a college student. Cynthia often joined Kate in a winter outing to Boca Grande, where the star liked to play tennis and socialize with the likes of her cousin Arthur Houghton or with Brooke Astor and Jane Engelhard.

On the plane, Cynthia introduced us. Iris and I tried to be glib and not behave like awkward fans. As passengers jammed up behind us, we had to lumber on to economy class. It was raining when we landed in NYC and Hepburn insisted on giving us a ride into town. Iris and I put on one of our best acts and entertainments for this great star, who seemed to be mildly amused. Soon after, Hepburn began inviting us to dinner at her town house.

We couldn't believe our luck. Our friends were beside themselves with jealousy. They begged us to get them invited. Barbara Walters, who had known Hepburn for years and simply worshipped her, insisted we take her with us so she could see Hepburn again and we did. Soon it became a monthly ritual. We'd arrive at the front door gate promptly at 6:00 P.M. We did not dare be late.

In the beginning, Kate would bound down the stairs to bring us up. "Do you drink?" she'd say. (Cynthia had warned us to say yes.) Hepburn liked to jump up and refill your glass. Soon you'd be quite happy and looking for a potted plant. Hepburn turned out to be more of a director than an actor in private. She'd leap up to poke the fire, or arrange exactly where you should sit. "No, not there; here!" She'd object if you brought anything into the room—a briefcase, an umbrella, an unworn jacket or sweater. It would be banished from sight. The star had a few stock phrases like, "Thank God I don't have to go" when we'd talk of occasions. Or if we spoke of people in the news, she'd usually say, "Who? Don't know them!" If we discussed our own careers, she'd snort: "I could never do that."

By the time Nora, her cook and housekeeper, came up with the dinner trays, Kate was well seated in her particular easy chair. Trencherman meals would follow, from soup to nuts. When Hepburn put her spoon down beside her empty ice-cream bowl, the evening had ended. We'd say quick good-byes and hit the streets at 8:30 P.M.

One night, Kate and Iris were discussing fame. Both insisted that they could never settle for second best. It was the top or nothing. Cynthia and I said we were happy just "to be along for the limousine ride" of others who were famous. Hepburn looked at us with contempt.

We would now and then get Kate to discuss her career or famous actors and directors she had known. Usually she'd say she had forgotten them. But she didn't mind talking about "The

Creature"—the public person she created that people made her out to be—her legendary movie star or Broadway actor self. "They expect The Creature and then I turn up in these old clothes; I expect they're disappointed." But nobody was disappointed to see the Great Kate and one way to see her in those days was to go to the theater.

She fed us early and bundled us off regularly to plays and musicals for which she had gotten the tickets, providing also the car and driver. "My car is white so we can easily find it in the dark and make a quick getaway." But Hepburn never really made a quick getaway. She felt compelled to go backstage and offer the actors her support and congratulations. They would stand stunned into reverence, which amazed Hepburn. And before her retirement she even endorsed certain shows—notably *A Few Good Men*—to help them go on running.

At home Hepburn was fascinating, enigmatic, shy, generous and intelligent. She was opinionated but somewhat taciturn and would say to us now and then, "You know, you talk too much!" To me she'd say, "How can you stand to do what you do—write that drivel for the newspapers?" Many of our discussions formed around controversies about marriage, men, love, sex, child rearing or divorce. Now and then I would feel as if trapped in a *New Yorker* cartoon by James Thurber: "The War Between Men and Women." Hepburn was already famous for saying, "Men and women should never live together, but next-door to one another where they could visit."

She could be critical. One night I wore red cowboy boots. Kate declared them "the ugliest things I've ever seen." She had worn beautiful clothes herself in films but in private life she was in well-pressed if threadbare pants, a ragged clean white shirt or black turtleneck and a raveling red cashmere sweater. She had once lamented to Cynthia the underdressed crowds on Madison Avenue coming out of The Gap: "And to think, this is all *my* fault!"

When I got home I threw my boots to the back of my closet and have never worn them again. The star was a powerful influence on me, too powerful to resist. But it makes me happy to think I had a tiny bit to do with her making a final movie, *Love Affair*.

Warren Beatty desperately wanted Hepburn for this film he was remaking with Annette Bening. He couldn't get to first base. Finally I said to him, "You need to call Cynthia McFadden and make your pitch to her. If she believes Kate is up to it, she may try to talk her into it." This he did and Cynthia advised him simply to woo Kate. "I hear you're quite good at romancing ladies; it's just exactly like any romance—candy, flowers, caviar, private jets, you know." Warren did all this with style and Hepburn relented. She couldn't resist Warren either. The movie was a flop, but she was very good in it.

Soon after, Hepburn retired to her country home, which looks across the Sound to Long Island in the distance and back onto the Fenwick golf course. As Cynthia rose in the ABC hierarchy to be a correspondent on *Prime Time Live* and then on *20/20,* we became good friends. She nominated herself as the ethics monitor of my career, constantly nagging me to do better, check further, get proof, dig deeper. Her nuisance value as a brake on my own brand of impetuous, freewheeling reportage could be irritating, but important. I have no doubt that she improved me.

At one point, other gossip columnists decided to investigate Cynthia's tie to Kate. Page Six of the *Post* offered this thesis: Cynthia is Kate's and Spencer Tracy's own love child, offered up for adoption in Maine in a year when it is on the record that Hepburn had been to that state. And in a fanciful spin and with photos to match, the tabloids showed how much they thought Cynthia resembled both stars.

Hepburn absolutely relished this incredible rumor and added fuel to the fire by vigorously nodding her head if anyone brought it up, exclaiming: "Of course, but of course! Can't you see she has all my worst qualities?"

These days, the great star has terrific people caring for her, as she lives in Fenwick with her brother Dick. Their sister Peg and brother Robert and various other Hepburns often visit. Kate receives on weekends. She sees Cynthia, the producer

Robert Whitehead and his wife, Zoe Caldwell, her *Lion in Winter* director Tony Harvey, her friend Lauren Bacall, etc. Kate loves candy, flowers, good substantial food, white linens and a fire burning brightly on the hearth every single day. She likes being driven around the shoreline. She still embodies the true Yankee New England spirit that helped make America great: hard work, ethical behavior to others, true to oneself, independence. I am always amazed by her indomitable spirit and grateful to have known this legend even ever so slightly.

I THINK . . .

I BELIEVE

AFTER THE POPULAR JESSE VENTURA suffered a ratings drop from attacking "organized religion," I began to worry about the rather cavalier approach to spirituality in this book. Since I often feel uncertain myself, I think I should try to clear up my ideas on religion, spirituality and "morals." But usually I can't. I often pray the prayer of St. Mark: "Lord, I believe. Help thou mine unbelief!" Or, if I am terribly afraid, say in airplanes, I'll offer the prayer of the Bene Gesserit from the sci-fi novel *Dune*. (It goes, "I must not fear. Fear is the mind-killer. Fear is the little death that brings total obliteration. I will face my fear. I will permit it to pass over me and through me. And when it has gone past, I will turn the inner eye to see its path. Where the fear has gone there will be nothing. Only I will remain.")

I do believe there is a God. But whatever we call Him, surely He is so great that He isn't sitting around micromanaging the universe. And He just can't be the avenging, jealous, hurtful God of much of the Old Testament and some of the New. The natural laws of physics, nature and human nature pretty much explain some of the bad things that happen to good and bad people alike. Like anyone who tries to concentrate on religious theory I am appalled by the problems of theodicy, which the writer Ron Rosenbaum explains thusly. ("Reconciling the frequent triumphs of catastrophic evil in human history—massacres of the innocents, mass murders, the Holocaust, etc.—with the assertion that God is all-powerful and just." How can that be?) We also might refer to the paradox of mortals who thank the Lord for saving them when others perish. Are "the others" less worthy? As Ron points out, saying that God moves in mysterious ways doesn't really satisfy us.

But even if I can't resolve these larger more pressing questions, some types of so-called moral and immoral behavior seem to fall pretty far down on the scale of importance. I can't honestly believe that God cares how we conduct something as idiotic as our sex lives. Moral rules about things like that were made up by shamans, medicine men, priests and other control freaks on earth. (Much of it was about protecting property and being sure children were born of the proper father's line.) Hurting, torturing, cheating, defrauding, misleading other people is probably a different matter. And hell may very well be a concept of conditions that exist here on earth. Recently the Pope said that hell is overimagined, overdescribed, overpainted and not as we may believe. When Sartre said, "Hell is other people," he had something there.

I took this list off the Internet and hope it won't offend too many people. I have examined it carefully and find it contains certain truths even in its sacrilegious, profane jocularity.

The Religions

TAOISM: Shit happens.
HINDUISM: This shit happened before.
CONFUCIANISM: Confucius say: Shit happens.
BUDDHISM: It is only an illusion of shit happening.
ZEN: What is the sound of shit happening?
ISLAM: If shit happens, it is the will of Allah.

JEHOVAH'S WITNESSES: Knock, knock: "Shit happens."
ATHEISM: There is no such thing as shit.
AGNOSTICISM: Maybe shit happens, and maybe it doesn't.
PROTESTANTISM: Shit won't happen if I work harder.
CATHOLICISM: If shit happens, I deserve it.
JUDAISM: Why does shit always happen to me?
TELEVANGELISM: Send money or shit will happen to you.

When I told *Vanity Fair* that the historical person I most identified with was Voltaire, I wasn't equating myself with his brilliance but with the fact that he is the number-one deathbed convert. It seemed pragmatic for Voltaire to live pretty much as he pleased in dangerous times, but then to re-embrace his Catholic religion as he lay dying. I understand this perfectly.

The only problem with such a naughty approach to salvation is that you might not get the chance for a deathbed confession and then where would you be? I was raised a Southern Baptist and I am glad of it. Even if I fall short of the glory, I did learn the difference between right and wrong. The Golden Rule has always haunted me and I have tried—and often failed—to keep to it. I had the requisite guilt for the times. And I confess I love the Christian ideal, the image of a risen Savior, the idea of faith moving mountains, the concept of forgiveness, the divinity of the Trinity. I can never forsake that even if I have to end up calling myself a very poor Christian.

I am interested in the rituals, the music and the artifacts of almost all religions. I know history might be less bloody and tortured and unfair without some religions, but on the other hand, life on earth would probably be totally brutal and uncivilized if no religions had existed. For instance, Renaissance art and Western civilization owe much to Christianity. Yet, was it a "fair" trade-off for the horrors of the Inquisition? Like almost everything else in life, religion is a catch-22. (My friend, the brilliant Joseph Heller, was into a philosophy greater than even he knew when he dreamed that up for a book about World War II.)

So what am I? I see myself as a Christian humanist. The fundamentalist preachers would say this is an oxymoron and a contradiction in terms. But I don't have much use for most fundamentalist preachers and fear I lump them with those other three detested classes: most politicians, most lawyers and most journalists. (There are, of course, brilliant exceptions in every class.)

A HAPPY

ENDING?

WRITING WHAT ONE REMEMBERS OF a life is a bit like preparing to meet one's Maker. You have handled the beginning, the middle and the omnipresent present. It's impossible not to think at least winkingly of "The End."

Will it be sudden, you wonder? Will it drag itself out? Will you meet it with fortitude and courage? Will you chicken out and be a pain in the ass? Will it be with a bang or a whimper? I'm not really the type to dwell on it.

I say this in spite of the fact that I have in the works what I hope is a comic novel about life after death. It's full of angels, devils, Jesus, Satan, Mohammed, Buddha, Allah, Zeus, Ahura Mazda, the "Wise Lord" of Zoroastrianism, the Virgin Mary, the misunderstood Mary Magdalene and Jehovah himself. All of these characters wear the guises of movie stars in order to make them less intimidating for the newly dead and fearful. (Even my intimations of immortality depend on the movies. And I still go to a lot of movies for I have a superstition that when one gives up going to the flicks, one grows old—and out of it.)

Do I believe there is life after death? Well, why should I be different? It seems about eighty-five percent of the world's people do believe. I take the view of a jazz guy I once dated. He'd say: "I don't know if there is a God, but if there is—gee, that's keen!"

So, fatalistically and optimistically, I come to the close of this. Lucky me, born twenty-three years after 1900; living into the amazing twenty-first century. (Will 20th Century Fox ever change its name?) As the century turned, I was working for the healthy and wealthy *Newsday* of Long Island. This solid citizen's newspaper with its elegant makeup, its fantastic Japanese color presses and big advertising, remained a bulwark of middle American journalism: solid and successful and very good to me for the last ten years plus. Add to this, for five years I have also been appearing in and working for New York's liveliest and most controversial newspaper, the *New York Post*. The *Post* has run the gamut from being created in 1801 by Alexander Hamilton, to being a bastion of liberal Jewish readers under Dolly Schiff in the fifties, and then being taken over by the international press baron Rupert Murdoch. The *Post* is now the tabloid antidote to every newspaper of record. I may not fit the *Post*'s conservative political mode, but by the time I began appearing there, I was my own established self and I like to think my column offers some comic—or other—relief. Recently I signed contracts with both of these newspapers for the future.

My pet charity, Literacy Partners, advises that we have raised almost $5 million for The Liz Smith Fund and over $15 million in our long fight against illiteracy. The spiffy editor Ellen Levine of *Good Housekeeping* assures me they couldn't live without my occasional cover stories with film stars. Channel Five recently invited me back to *Good Day New York*. (Like Jack Benny, "I'm thinking, I'm thinking...")

My astrologer Maxine Fiel has predicted seven years of good fortune for us Aquarians. We'll see if she is right. My good friends Joan Ganz Cooney and Pete Peterson have more or less adopted me (although I am older than both of them), so I am no longer an orphan. I like their luxurious houses, their big family, their helicopter, their jet plane and their hospitality. They know all the greatest doctors in America. I needed a "family" like that.

My brother Bobby stopped smoking and drinking five years ago and rejoined the human race. What's lost has been refound. So I am tempted to echo the Kander and Ebb song from *Chicago*. "It's good, isn't it—grand? Isn't it—great? Isn't it—swell?"

Well, something really swell happened to me as I was winding up this memoir…One night I dressed to go out, calling for a car to pick me up at the end of the drive-through that connects my building from 37th to 38th Streets. I'd had my hair done that day by Vincent, the old "natural blonde" himself. I had makeup on from doing TV. I was dressed up and contemplated with delight meeting Barbara Walters, Joel Schumacher and Cynthia McFadden for dinner at Orso for absolutely no good reason. I knew it would be a night of fun, jokes and gossip and that several times in the course of the night each of these three stars would say to me, "But don't print it!"

A soft dusk descended and a few lights came on. The restaurant on the ground floor of my building began the margarita hum of its nightly "make-out" ritual. I always take pleasure in watching young Manhattanites congregate here.

A nice-looking guy who appeared to be about thirty-five or forty stopped in front of me to ask, "Do you know where the El Rio Grande is?"

I pointed. "It's right there. But if you are meeting someone, the café is divided in two parts—the Mexican and the Texas sides. So look in both."

He thanked me and stepped away. I looked up toward Lexington Avenue for my car. Suddenly the guy came back. "Say"—he paused— "would you like to go in and have a drink with me?"

I looked at him. He was very attractive. But it was now pretty dark. Maybe if I had been fifty years old—or even sixty—or heck, even only seventy, I'd have been tempted to say yes. But I had a vision of ordering drinks and having him realize that he had picked up a woman who is—in the words of my pal Pete Peterson— "no spring chicken." "Thanks," I said, "but I'm waiting for my ride. Maybe some other time."

Listen, folks, as Mehitabel the cat said to Archie the cockroach: "Maybe there's a dance in the old dame yet!"

WHAT IN THE WORLD HAD I expected of life? Looking back, I see I wanted to be in show business. It came to pass. I wanted to win friends and influence people. It happened. I wanted a voice. I got one six days a week and in syndication for almost thirty years. I dreamed of the "bright lights, big city" but desired to keep my Texas roots. Okay. I wanted to meet famous people and for them to meet me. So be it. I longed to know intellectuals, thinkers, great writers and philosophers. I do. I wanted the silly, campy side of life as well. My wish was granted. I yearned to find myself on world stages. There I was— singing, dancing, kidding around at Carnegie Hall, the Metropolitan Opera, Town Hall, the Shubert Theatre, Radio City Music Hall and other grand venues beyond my wildest dreams. I lusted after respectable honors and a few rolled my way. I wanted to meet my idols of the silver screen, the media, of publishing and government. I won access to hundreds of them. I wanted to make money so the Depression era would recede and I could care for myself and the people I loved. Eventually, finances came up a green light. I had ambitions to conquer TV and found myself before the cameras for years, usually live and living dangerously. I dreamed of my name in lights and won a long-playing byline. I wanted to translate Mary Elizabeth into something snappier. Liz Smith appeared (and now sometimes I'm nostalgic for Mary E. again). I longed to make a newspaper column into a positive instrument—and through the banal mediums of gossip and entertainment I hope I succeeded. I wanted to work hard and be so absorbed that sleep would fall on me nightly like a blessing. It does. I loved children but knew I'd be a terrible, permissive parent. I was rewarded anyway with six nieces and nephews, eight great ones, and several stunningly adorable godchildren. I craved laughter, excitement, intimacy and intricacy. It came to me in abundance. I wanted to remain, not sentimental, but full of sentiment. So I still cry at the 23rd Psalm, "The Star Spangled Banner" and at the movies. I romanticized having one true love but fate served up a fuller, more complex menu. I hoped to live in interesting times. I did and I do. I hated being bored and seldom have been. I felt crushed by fundamentalism and sought refuge also in meditation, Judaism, the rituals of the Church of England, Zen, reading history, biography, philosophy, astrology, massage, exercise, superstition and worshipping in the Temple of the Unknown God.

I never imagined I could translate my life into the pages of a book, but here it is. Often, I have failed others, and myself. But I have dared hope for forgiveness and absolution. As I have, quite incredibly, always enjoyed excellent health and seldom been sick a day in my life, I feared putting a curse on myself or having the gods notice my hubris, so I utter a *kinehura* against evil. My conclusion?

When the Fates ladled out their stuff, they said: "We'll make this one insecure and give her an inferiority complex. She'll end up behaving as if she has a massive ego, so no one will know the difference. Let's also give her lots and lots of luck."

They did; so far.

INDEX